I bito ·空·

UUKI IINUMA

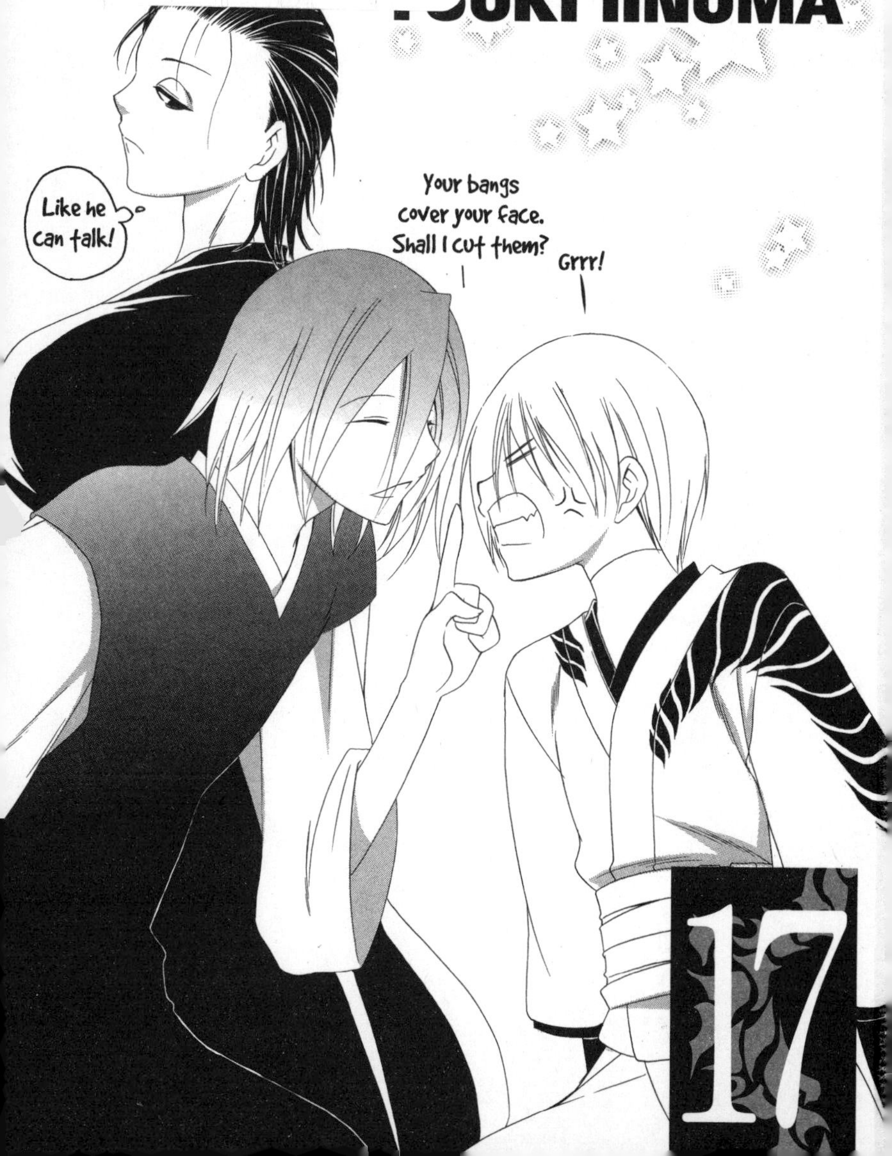
Like he can talk!
Your bangs cover your face. Shall I cut them?
Grrr!

17

Contents

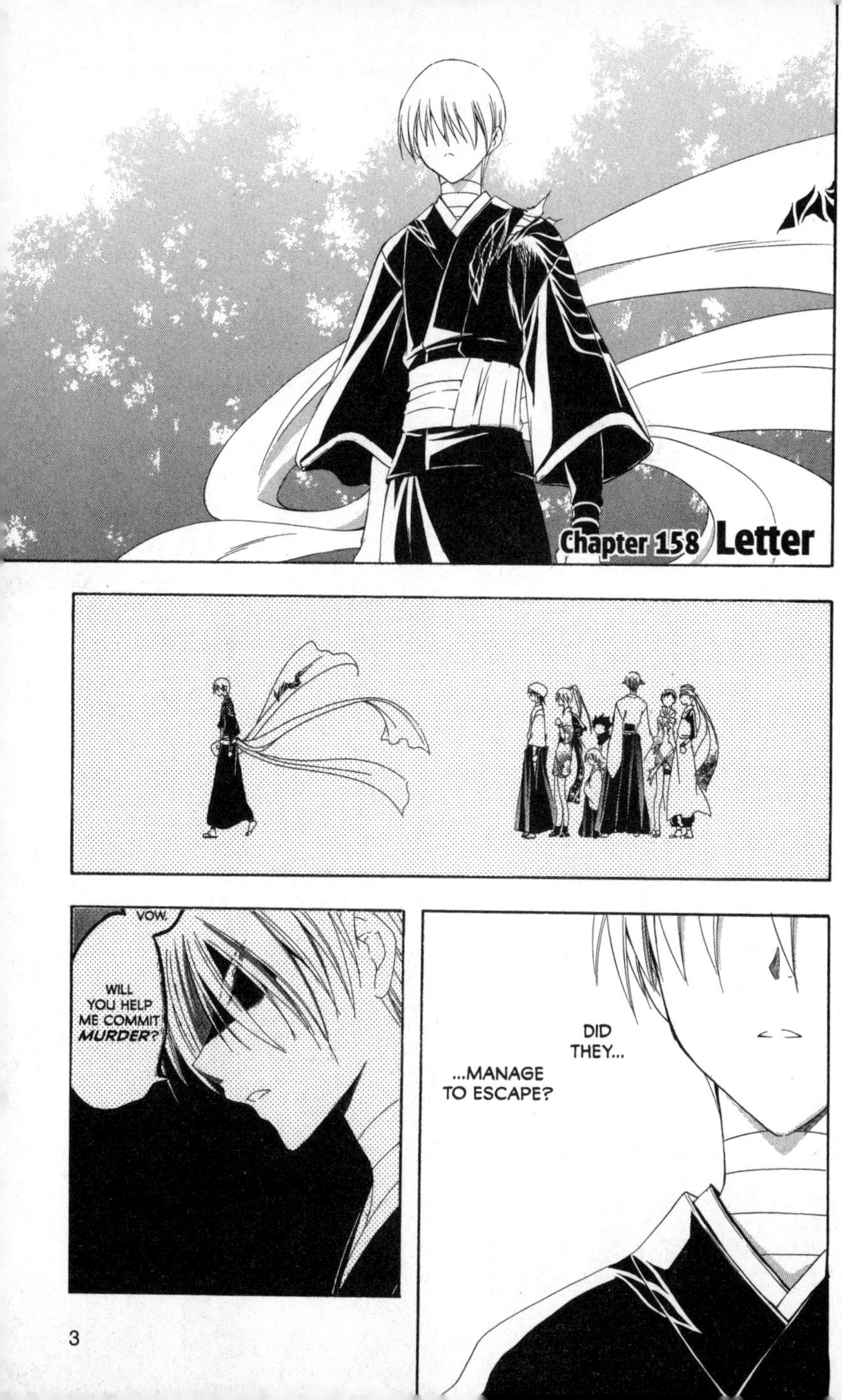
Chapter 158 Letter
DID THEY...
...MANAGE TO ESCAPE?
VOW.
WILL YOU HELP ME COMMIT *MURDER*?

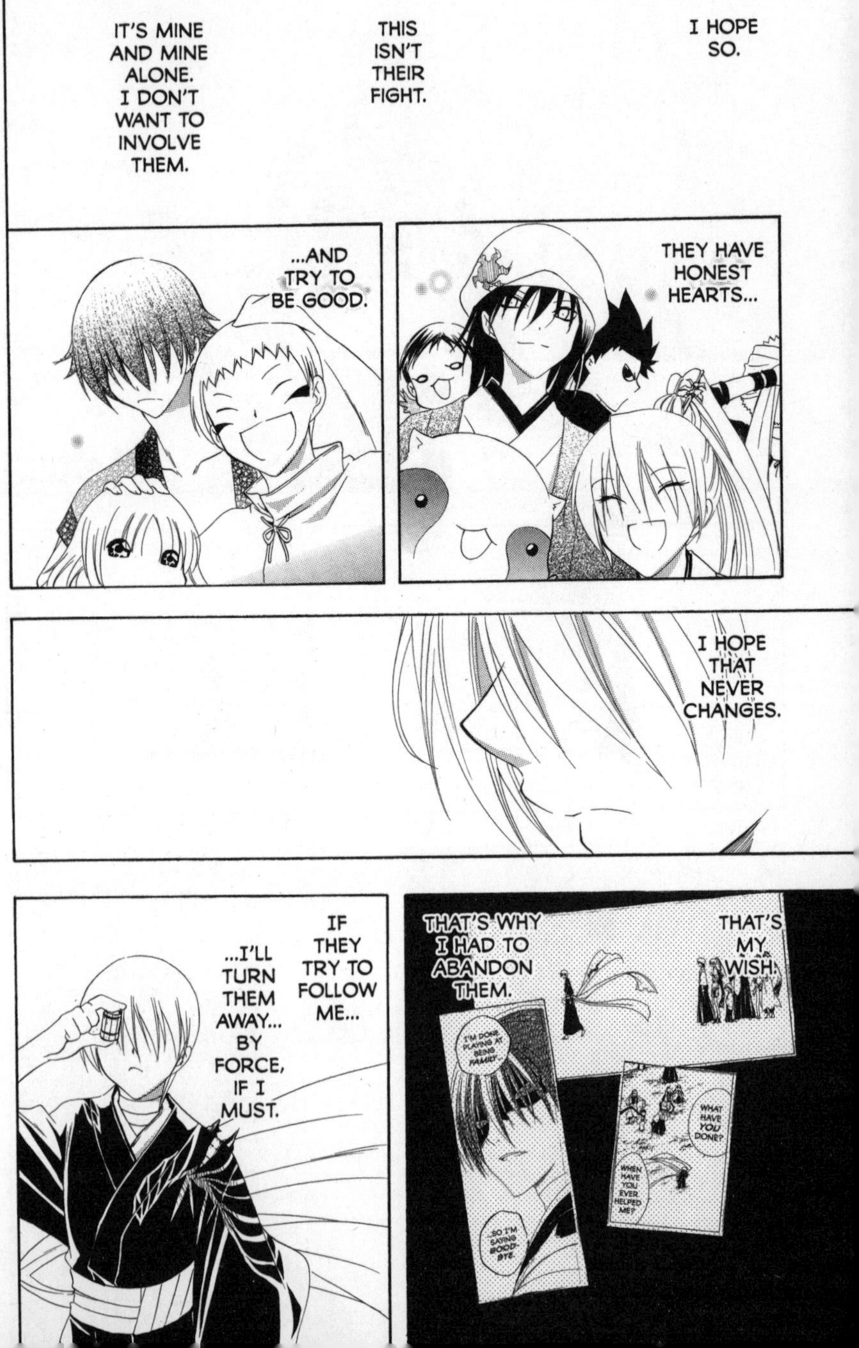
I HOPE SO.
THIS ISN'T THEIR FIGHT.
IT'S MINE AND MINE ALONE. I DON'T WANT TO INVOLVE THEM.
THEY HAVE HONEST HEARTS...
...AND TRY TO BE GOOD.
I HOPE THAT NEVER CHANGES.
THAT'S MY WISH.
THAT'S WHY I HAD TO ABANDON THEM.
I'M DONE PLAYING AT BEING FAMILY.
SO I'M SAYING GOOD-BYE.
WHAT HAVE YOU DONE?
WHEN HAVE YOU EVER HELPED ME?
IF THEY TRY TO FOLLOW ME...
...I'LL TURN THEM AWAY... BY FORCE, IF I MUST.

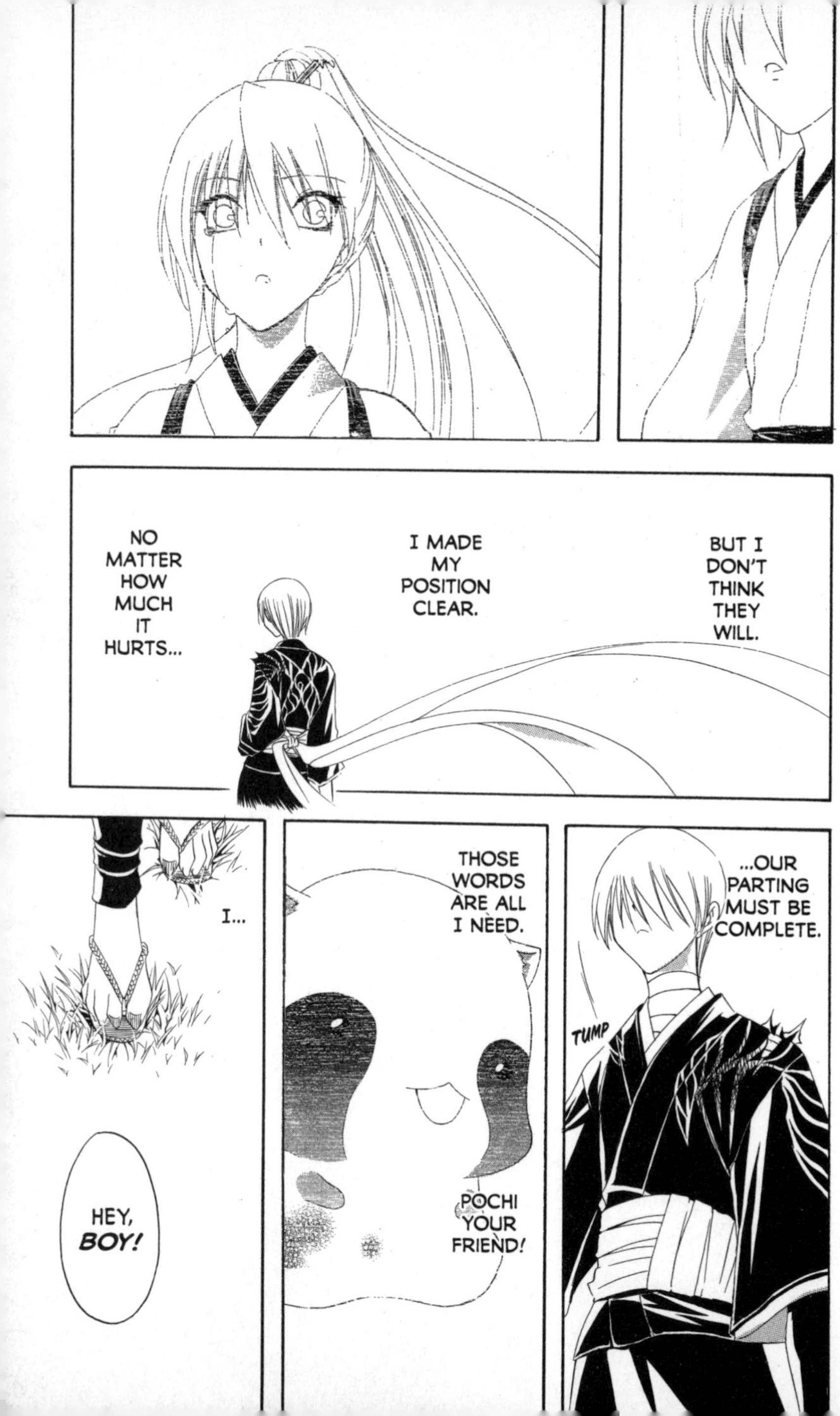
BUT I DON'T THINK THEY WILL.
I MADE MY POSITION CLEAR.
NO MATTER HOW MUCH IT HURTS...
...OUR PARTING MUST BE COMPLETE.
TUMP
THOSE WORDS ARE ALL I NEED.
POCHI YOUR FRIEND!
I...
HEY, BOY!

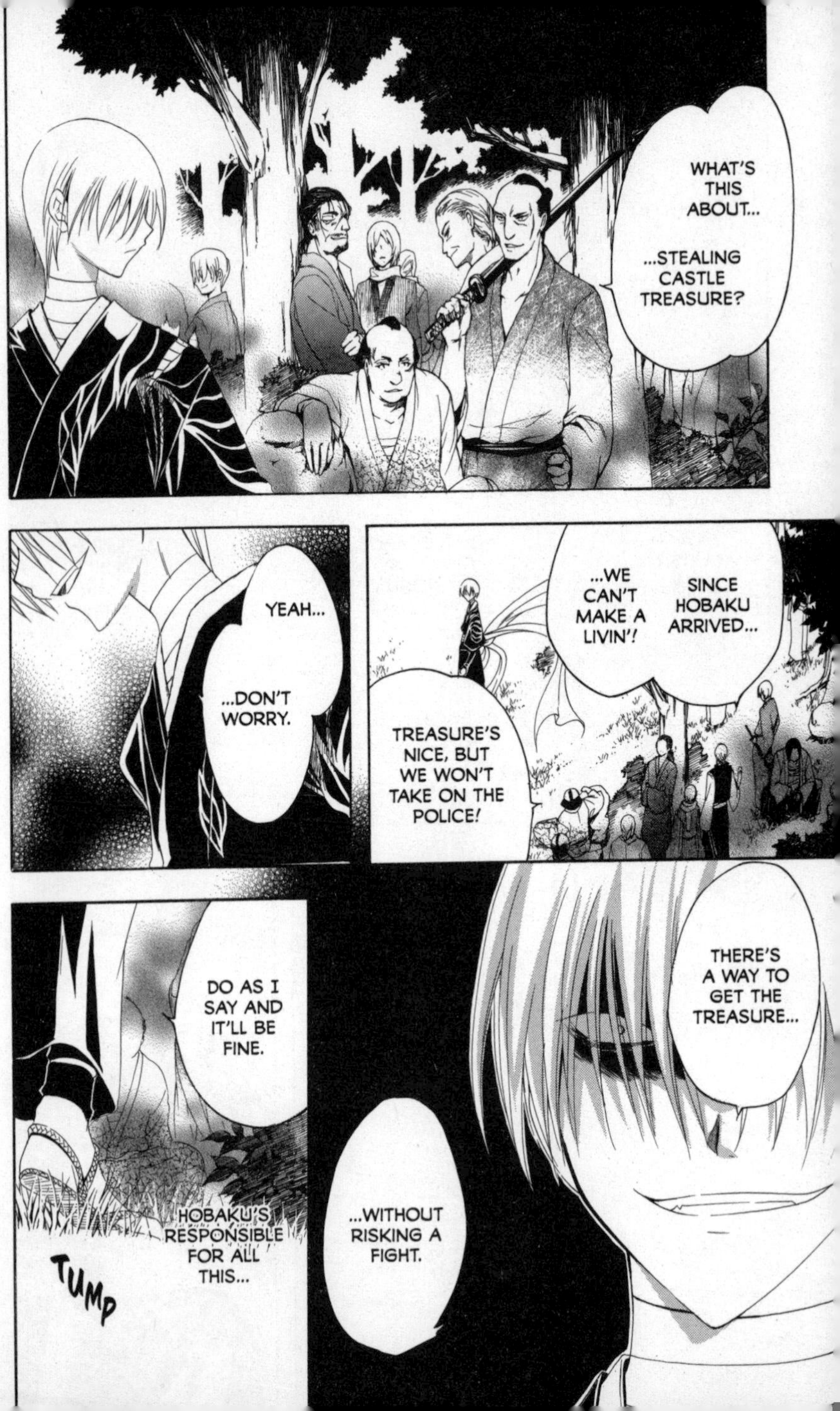
WHAT'S THIS ABOUT...
...STEALING CASTLE TREASURE?
SINCE HOBAKU ARRIVED...
...WE CAN'T MAKE A LIVIN'!
TREASURE'S NICE, BUT WE WON'T TAKE ON THE POLICE!
YEAH...
...DON'T WORRY.
THERE'S A WAY TO GET THE TREASURE...
...WITHOUT RISKING A FIGHT.
DO AS I SAY AND IT'LL BE FINE.
HOBAKU'S RESPONSIBLE FOR ALL THIS...
TUMP

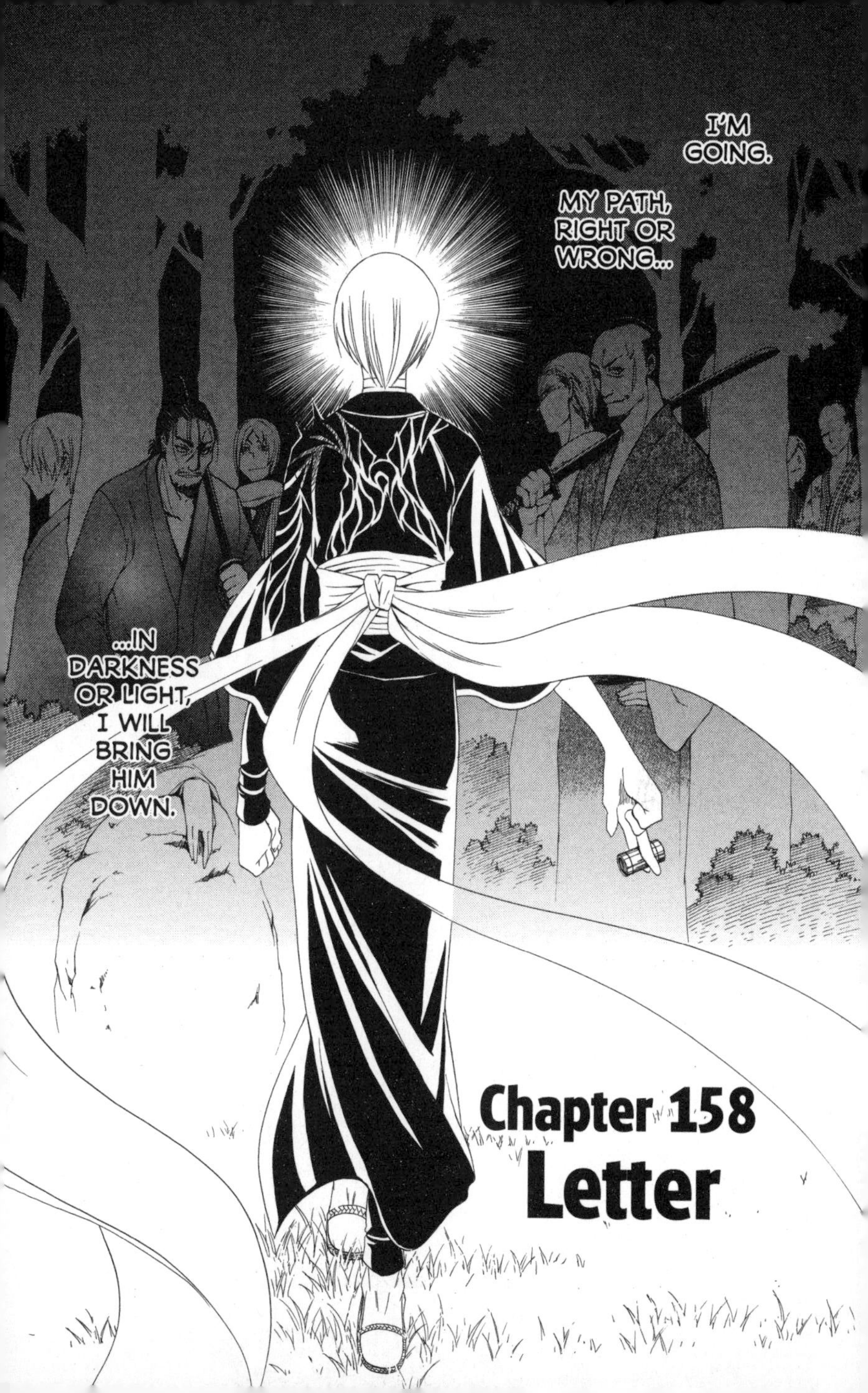
I'M GOING.
MY PATH, RIGHT OR WRONG...
...IN DARKNESS OR LIGHT, I WILL BRING HIM DOWN.
Chapter 158
Letter

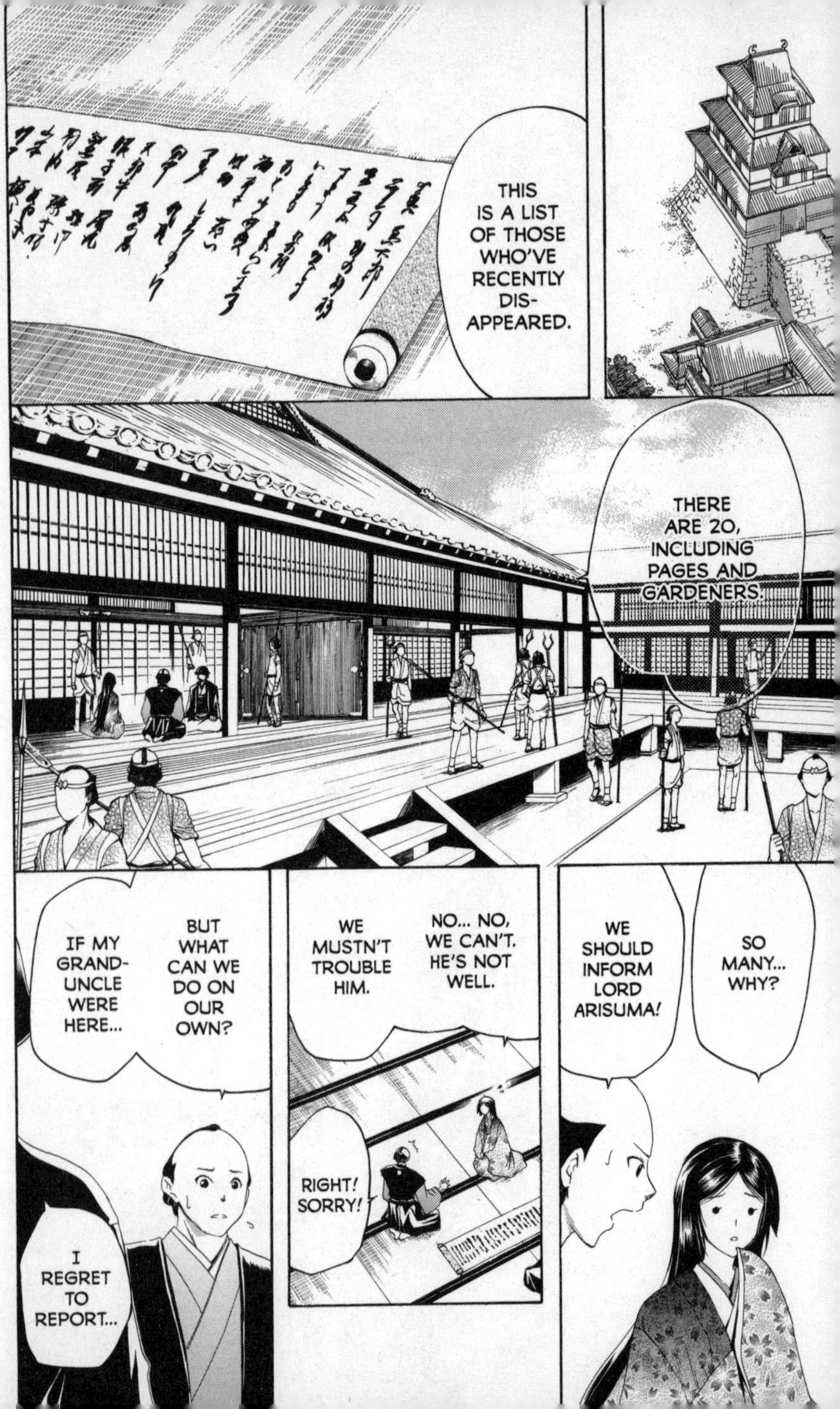
THIS IS A LIST OF THOSE WHO'VE RECENTLY DIS-APPEARED.
THERE ARE 20, INCLUDING PAGES AND GARDENERS.
SO MANY... WHY?
WE SHOULD INFORM LORD ARISUMA!
NO... NO, WE CAN'T. HE'S NOT WELL.
WE MUSTN'T TROUBLE HIM.
RIGHT! SORRY!
BUT WHAT CAN WE DO ON OUR OWN?
IF MY GRAND-UNCLE WERE HERE...
I REGRET TO REPORT...

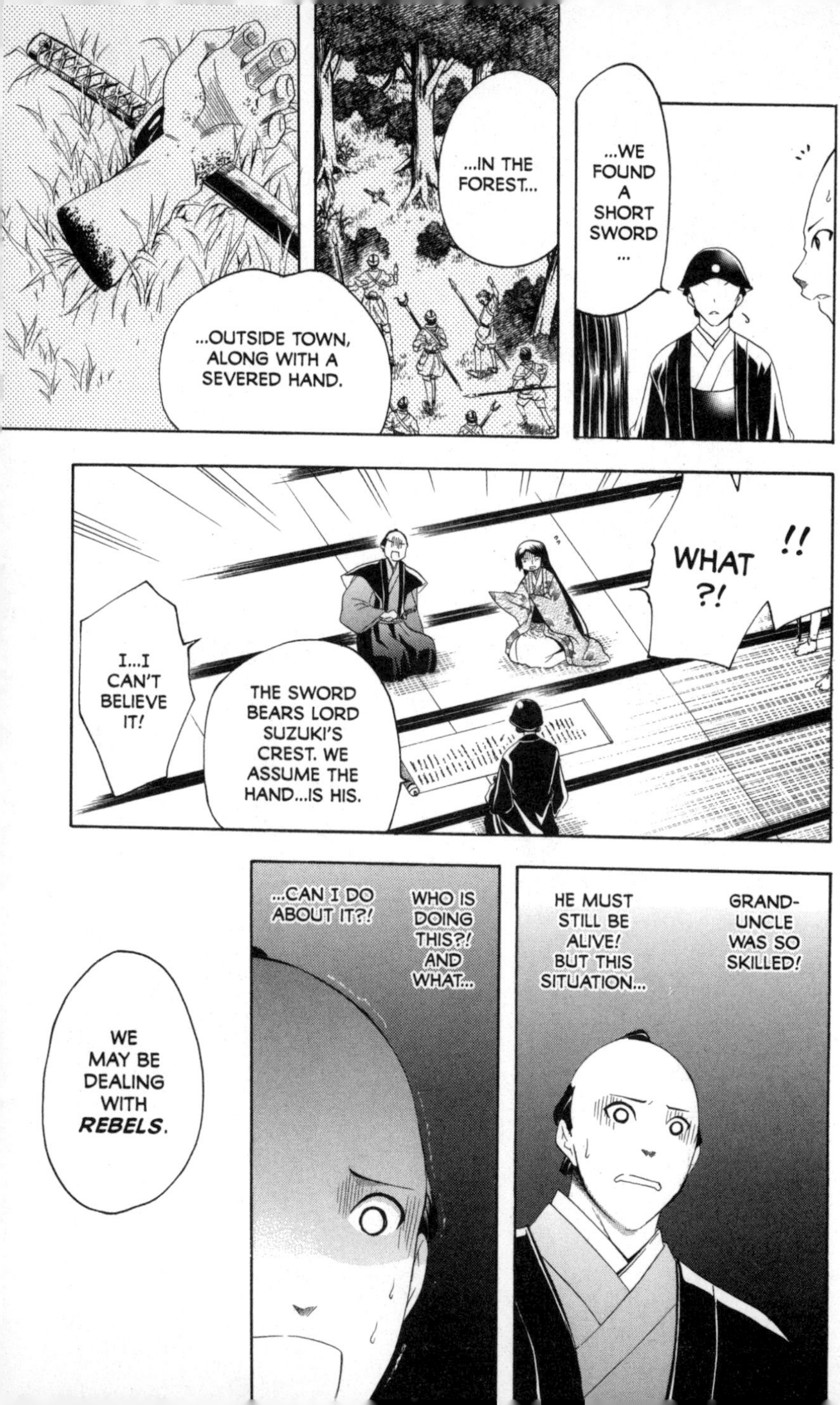
...WE FOUND A SHORT SWORD ...
...IN THE FOREST...
...OUTSIDE TOWN, ALONG WITH A SEVERED HAND.
WHAT ?!
!!
I...I CAN'T BELIEVE IT!
THE SWORD BEARS LORD SUZUKI'S CREST. WE ASSUME THE HAND...IS HIS.
GRAND-UNCLE WAS SO SKILLED!
HE MUST STILL BE ALIVE! BUT THIS SITUATION...
WHO IS DOING THIS?! AND WHAT...
...CAN I DO ABOUT IT?!
WE MAY BE DEALING WITH *REBELS*.

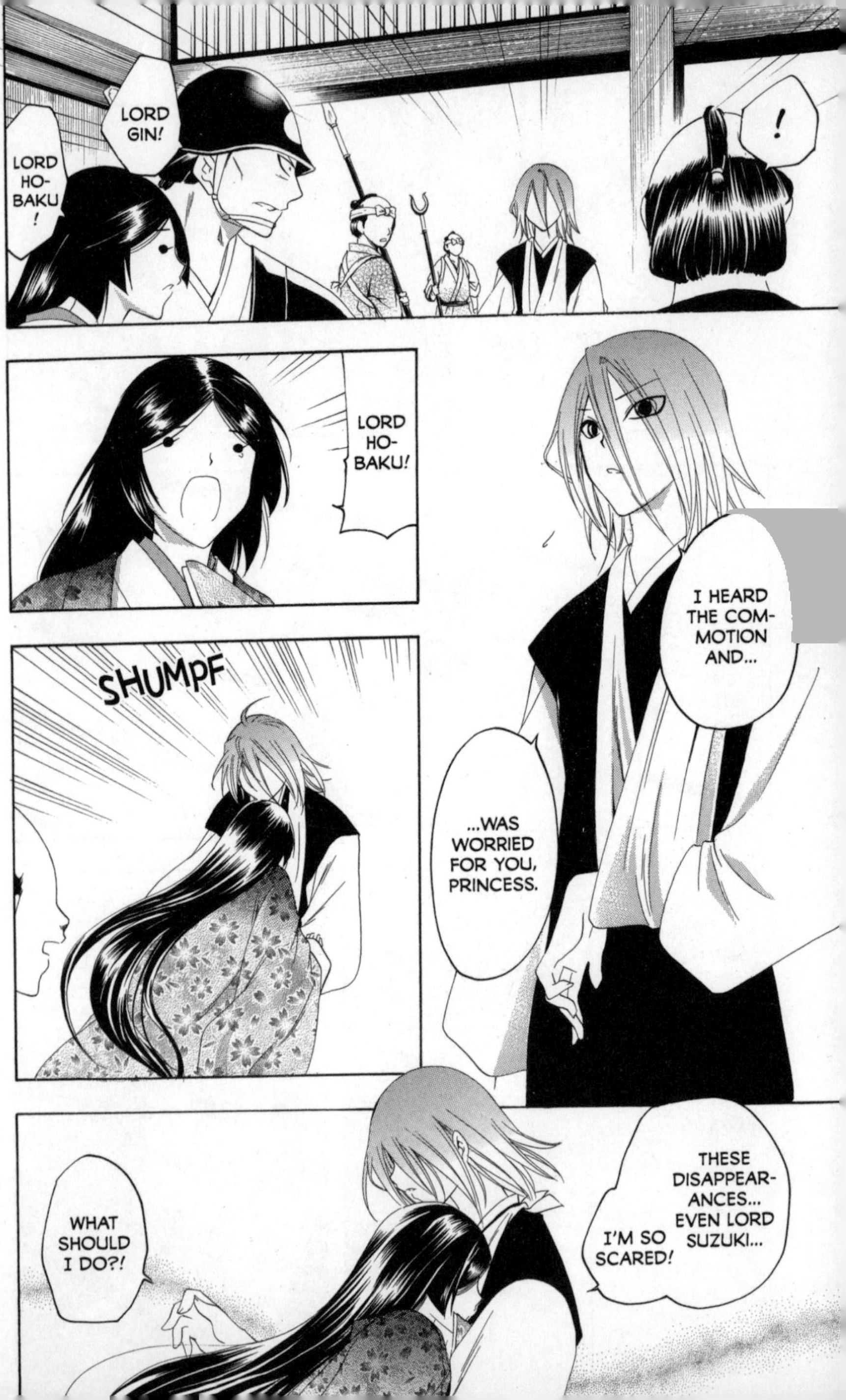
!
LORD GIN!
LORD HO-BAKU!
I HEARD THE COM-MOTION AND...
...WAS WORRIED FOR YOU, PRINCESS.
LORD HO-BAKU!
SHUMPF
THESE DISAPPEAR-ANCES... EVEN LORD SUZUKI...
I'M SO SCARED!
WHAT SHOULD I DO?!

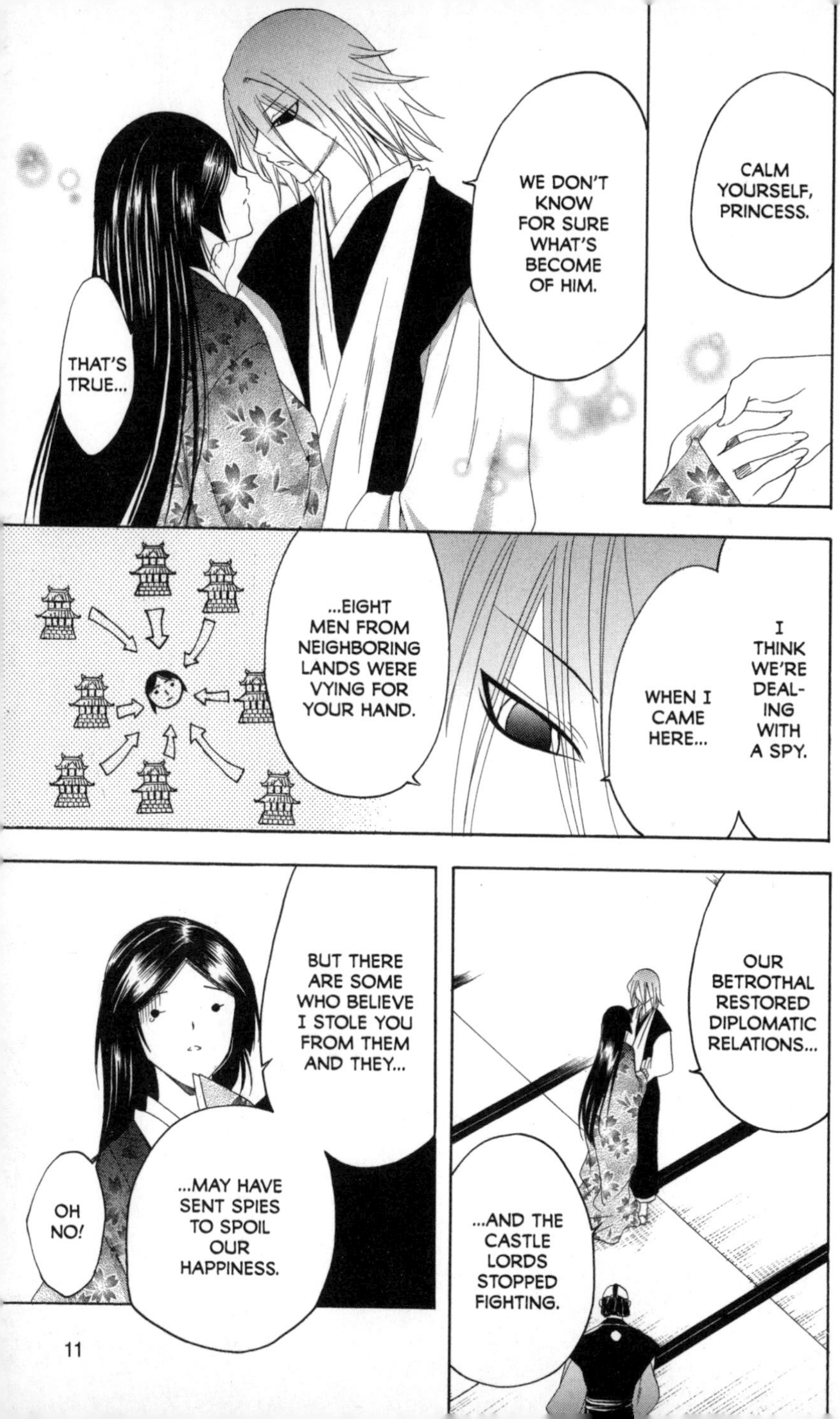

CALM YOURSELF, PRINCESS.
WE DON'T KNOW FOR SURE WHAT'S BECOME OF HIM.
THAT'S TRUE...
I THINK WE'RE DEAL-ING WITH A SPY.
WHEN I CAME HERE...
...EIGHT MEN FROM NEIGHBORING LANDS WERE VYING FOR YOUR HAND.
OUR BETROTHAL RESTORED DIPLOMATIC RELATIONS...
...AND THE CASTLE LORDS STOPPED FIGHTING.
BUT THERE ARE SOME WHO BELIEVE I STOLE YOU FROM THEM AND THEY...
...MAY HAVE SENT SPIES TO SPOIL OUR HAPPINESS.
OH NO!

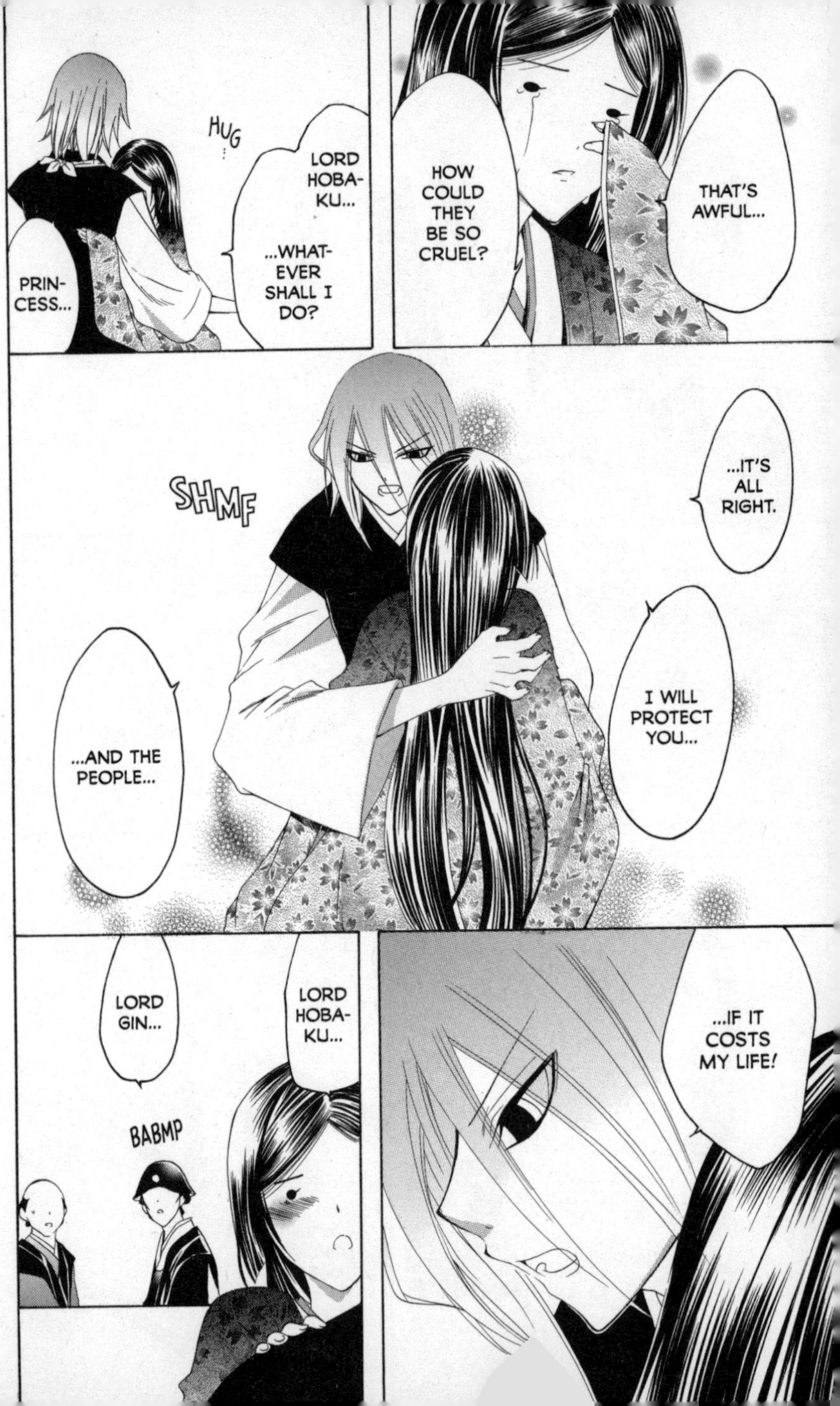
THAT'S AWFUL...
HOW COULD THEY BE SO CRUEL?
HUG
LORD HOBAKU...
...WHATEVER SHALL I DO?
PRINCESS...
...IT'S ALL RIGHT.
SHMF
I WILL PROTECT YOU...
...AND THE PEOPLE...
...IF IT COSTS MY LIFE!
LORD HOBAKU...
LORD GIN...
BABMP

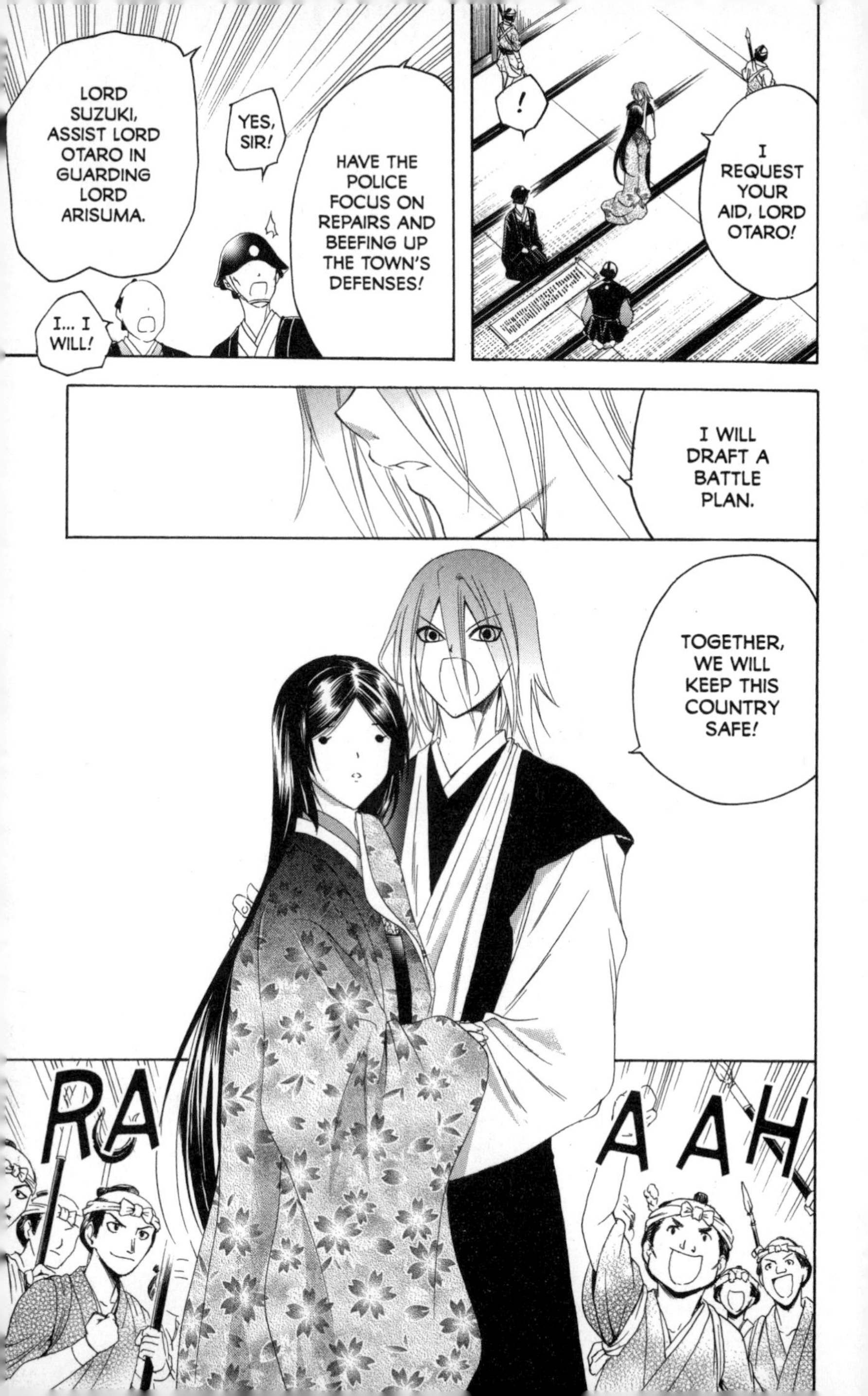
I REQUEST YOUR AID, LORD OTARO!
!
HAVE THE POLICE FOCUS ON REPAIRS AND BEEFING UP THE TOWN'S DEFENSES!
YES, SIR!
LORD SUZUKI, ASSIST LORD OTARO IN GUARDING LORD ARISUMA.
I... I WILL!
I WILL DRAFT A BATTLE PLAN.
TOGETHER, WE WILL KEEP THIS COUNTRY SAFE!
RA
AAH

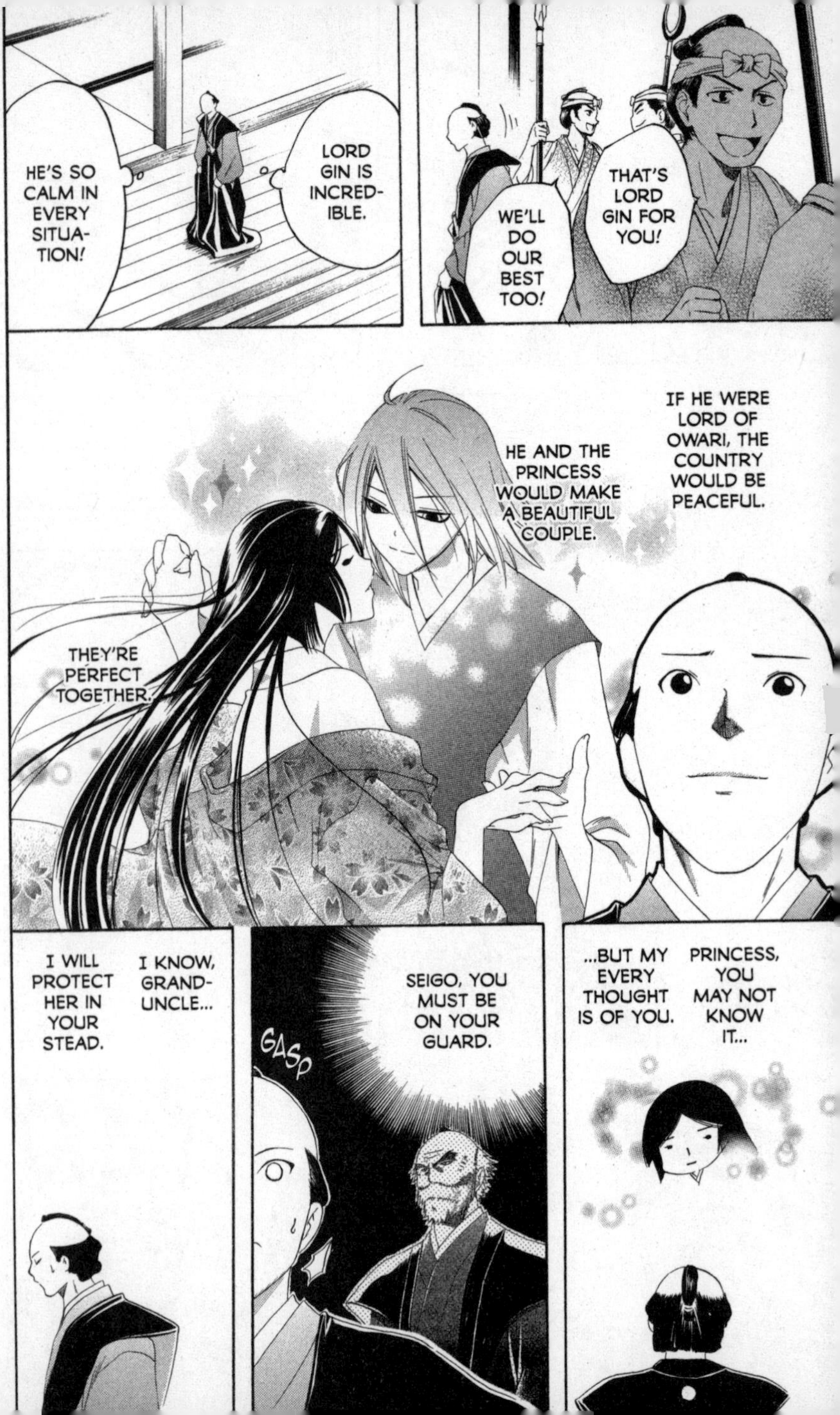
THAT'S LORD GIN FOR YOU!
WE'LL DO OUR BEST TOO!
LORD GIN IS INCREDIBLE.
HE'S SO CALM IN EVERY SITUATION!
IF HE WERE LORD OF OWARI, THE COUNTRY WOULD BE PEACEFUL.
HE AND THE PRINCESS WOULD MAKE A BEAUTIFUL COUPLE.
THEY'RE PERFECT TOGETHER.
PRINCESS, YOU MAY NOT KNOW IT...
...BUT MY EVERY THOUGHT IS OF YOU.
SEIGO, YOU MUST BE ON YOUR GUARD.
GASP
I KNOW, GRANDUNCLE...
I WILL PROTECT HER IN YOUR STEAD.

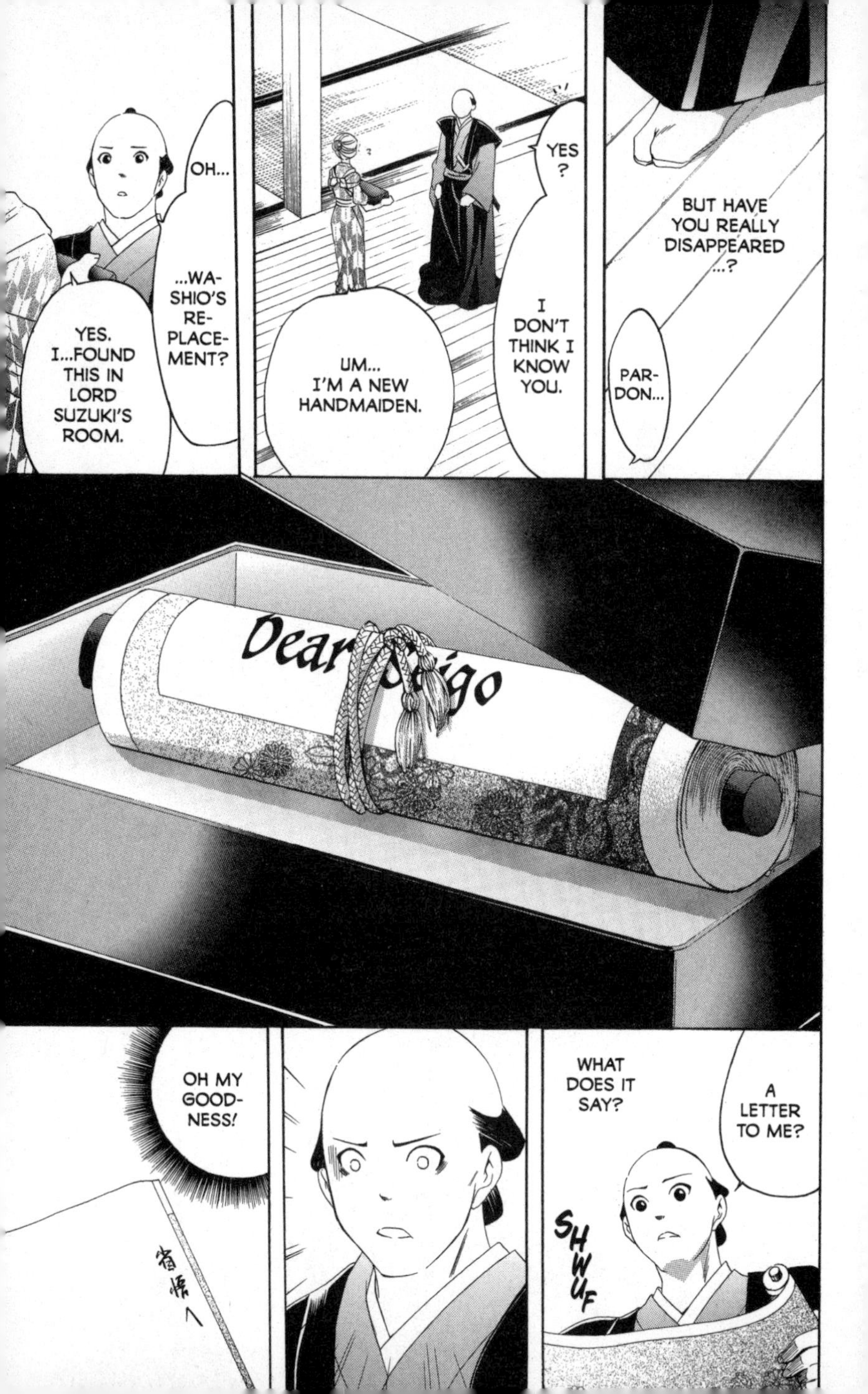
BUT HAVE YOU REALLY DISAPPEARED ...?
PAR-DON...
YES ?
I DON'T THINK I KNOW YOU.
UM... I'M A NEW HANDMAIDEN.
OH...
...WA-SHIO'S RE-PLACE-MENT?
YES. I...FOUND THIS IN LORD SUZUKI'S ROOM.
Dear
A LETTER TO ME?
WHAT DOES IT SAY?
SHWUF
OH MY GOOD-NESS!

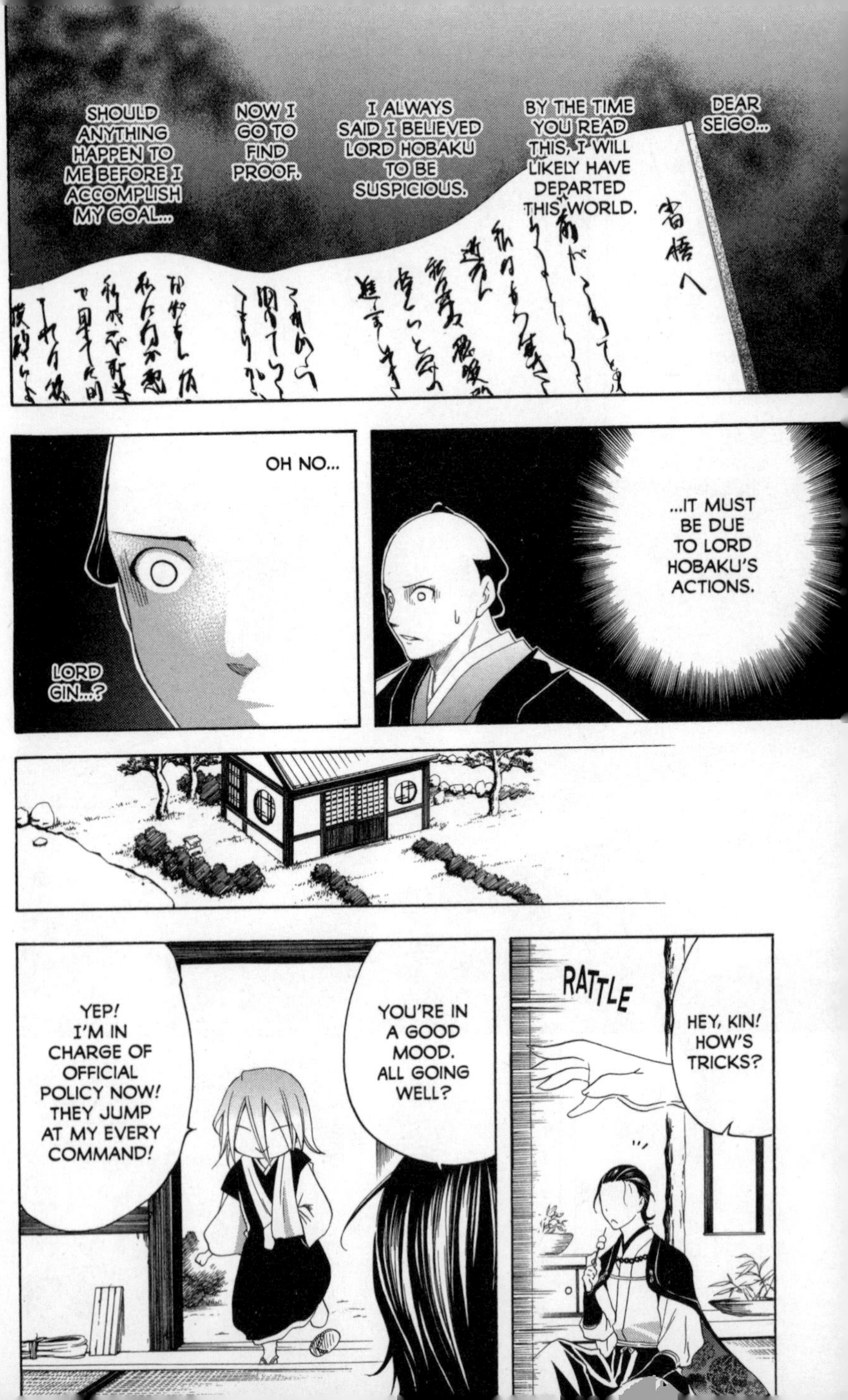
DEAR SEIGO...
BY THE TIME YOU READ THIS, I WILL LIKELY HAVE DEPARTED THIS WORLD.
I ALWAYS SAID I BELIEVED LORD HOBAKU TO BE SUSPICIOUS.
NOW I GO TO FIND PROOF.
SHOULD ANYTHING HAPPEN TO ME BEFORE I ACCOMPLISH MY GOAL...
...IT MUST BE DUE TO LORD HOBAKU'S ACTIONS.
OH NO...
LORD GIN...?
RATTLE
HEY, KIN! HOW'S TRICKS?
YOU'RE IN A GOOD MOOD. ALL GOING WELL?
YEP! I'M IN CHARGE OF OFFICIAL POLICY NOW! THEY JUMP AT MY EVERY COMMAND!

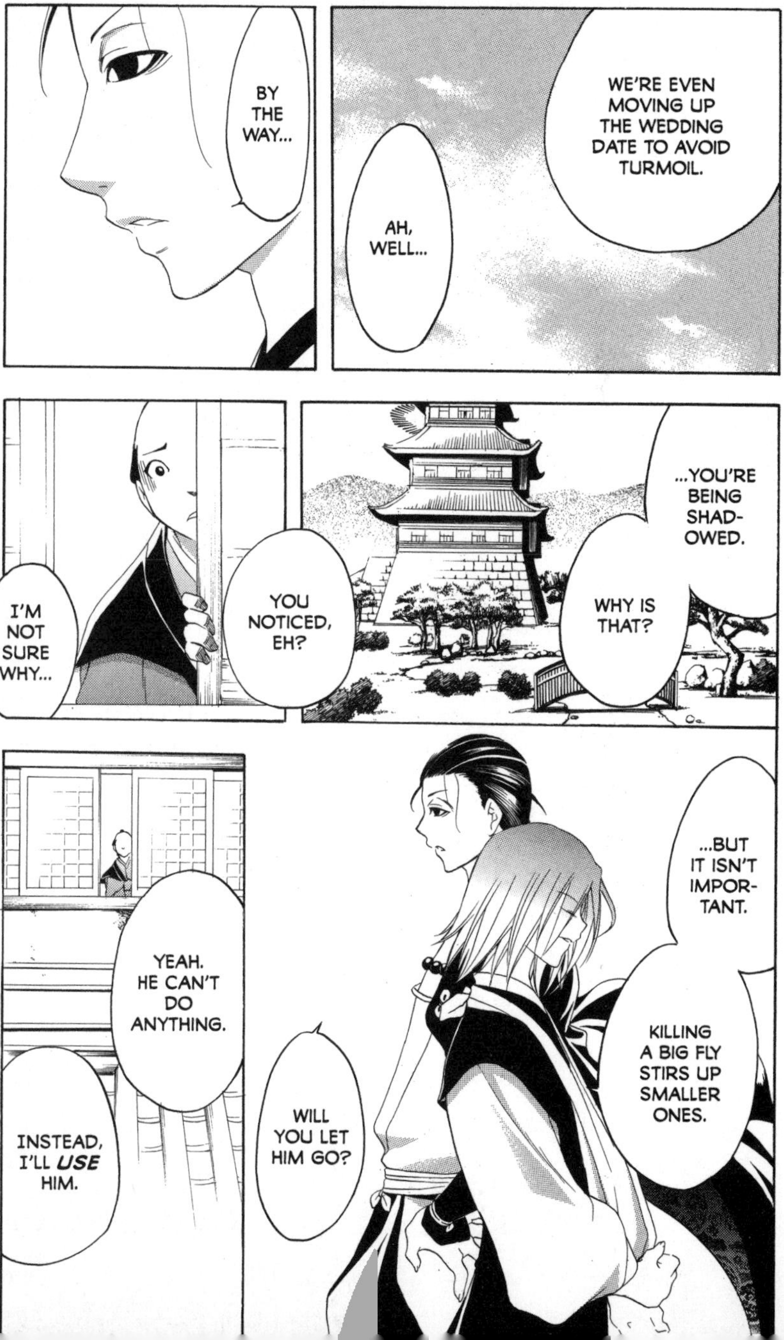

WE'RE EVEN MOVING UP THE WEDDING DATE TO AVOID TURMOIL.
AH, WELL...
BY THE WAY...
...YOU'RE BEING SHADOWED.
WHY IS THAT?
YOU NOTICED, EH?
I'M NOT SURE WHY...
...BUT IT ISN'T IMPORTANT.
KILLING A BIG FLY STIRS UP SMALLER ONES.
WILL YOU LET HIM GO?
YEAH. HE CAN'T DO ANYTHING.
INSTEAD, I'LL *USE* HIM.

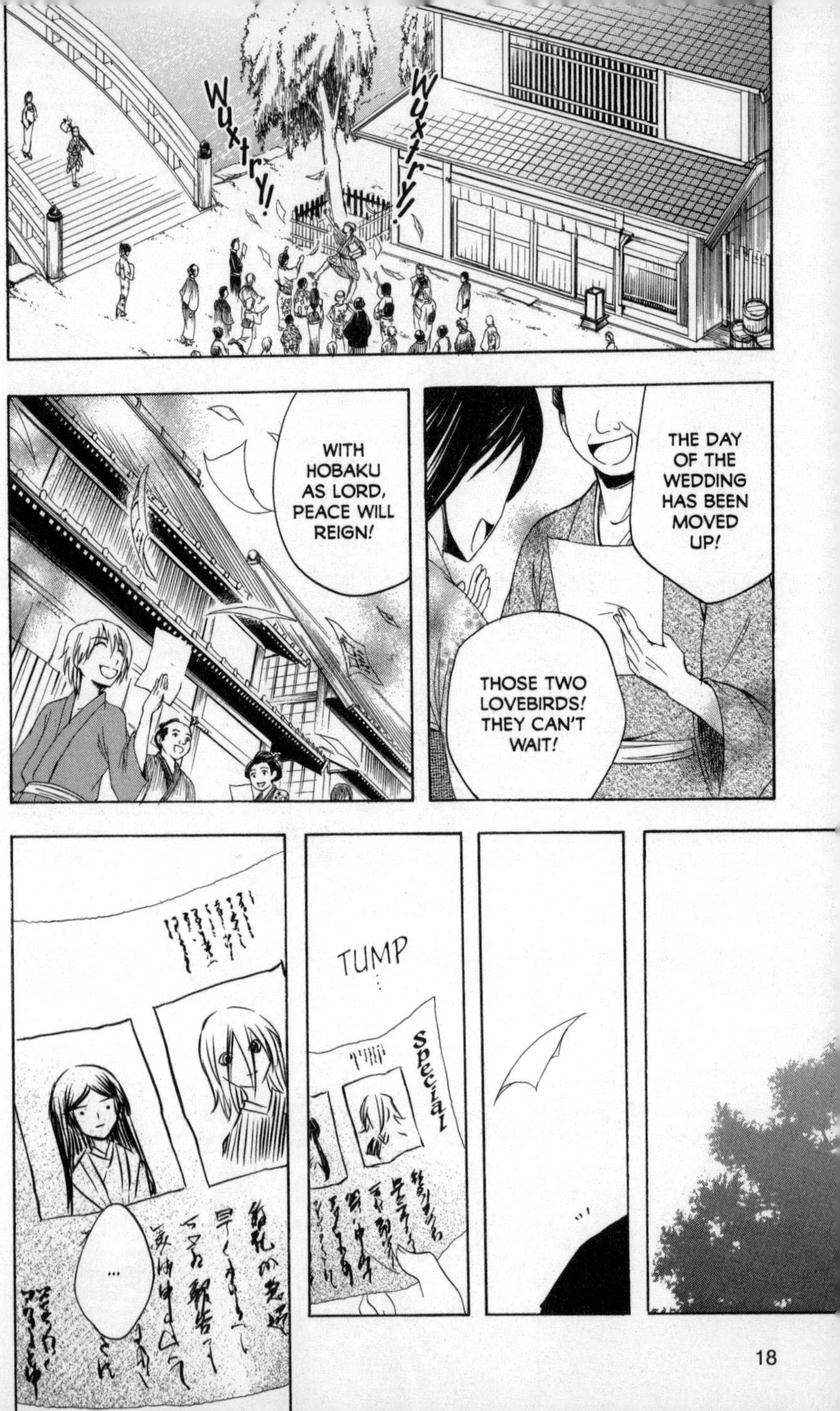
Wuxtry!
Wuxtry!
THE DAY OF THE WEDDING HAS BEEN MOVED UP!
THOSE TWO LOVEBIRDS! THEY CAN'T WAIT!
WITH HOBAKU AS LORD, PEACE WILL REIGN!
TUMP
Special
...

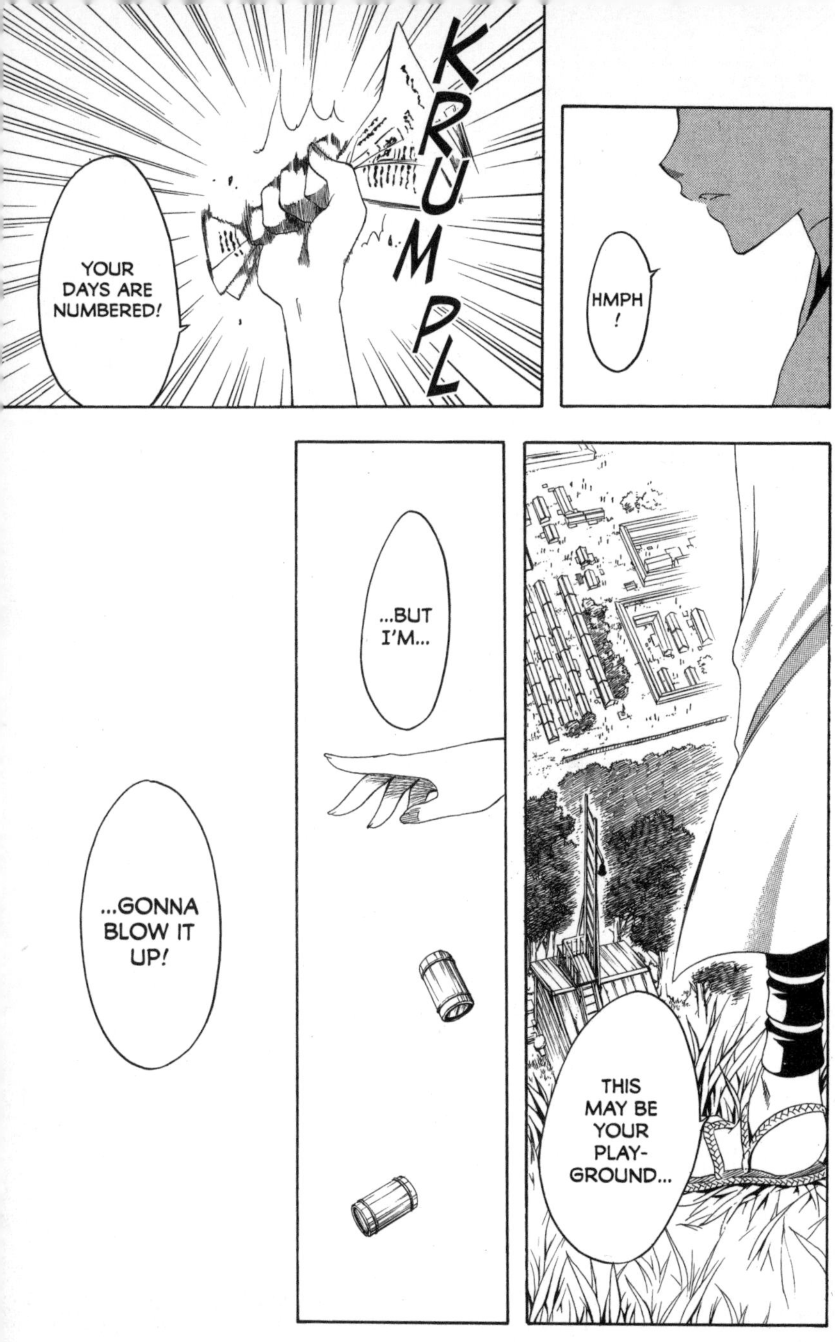
HMPH!
KRUMPL
YOUR DAYS ARE NUMBERED!
THIS MAY BE YOUR PLAY-GROUND...
...BUT I'M...
...GONNA BLOW IT UP!

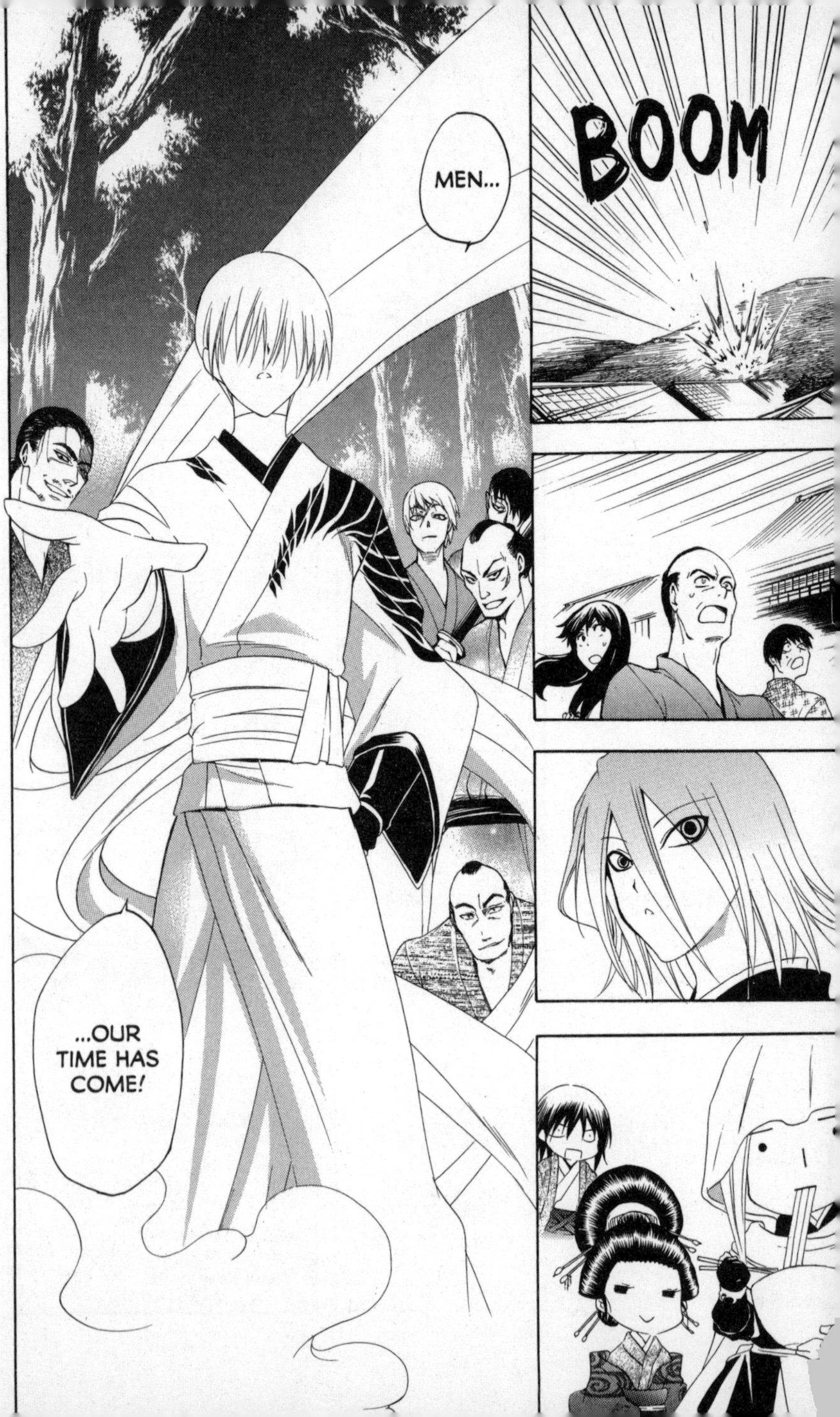
BOOM
MEN...
...OUR TIME HAS COME!

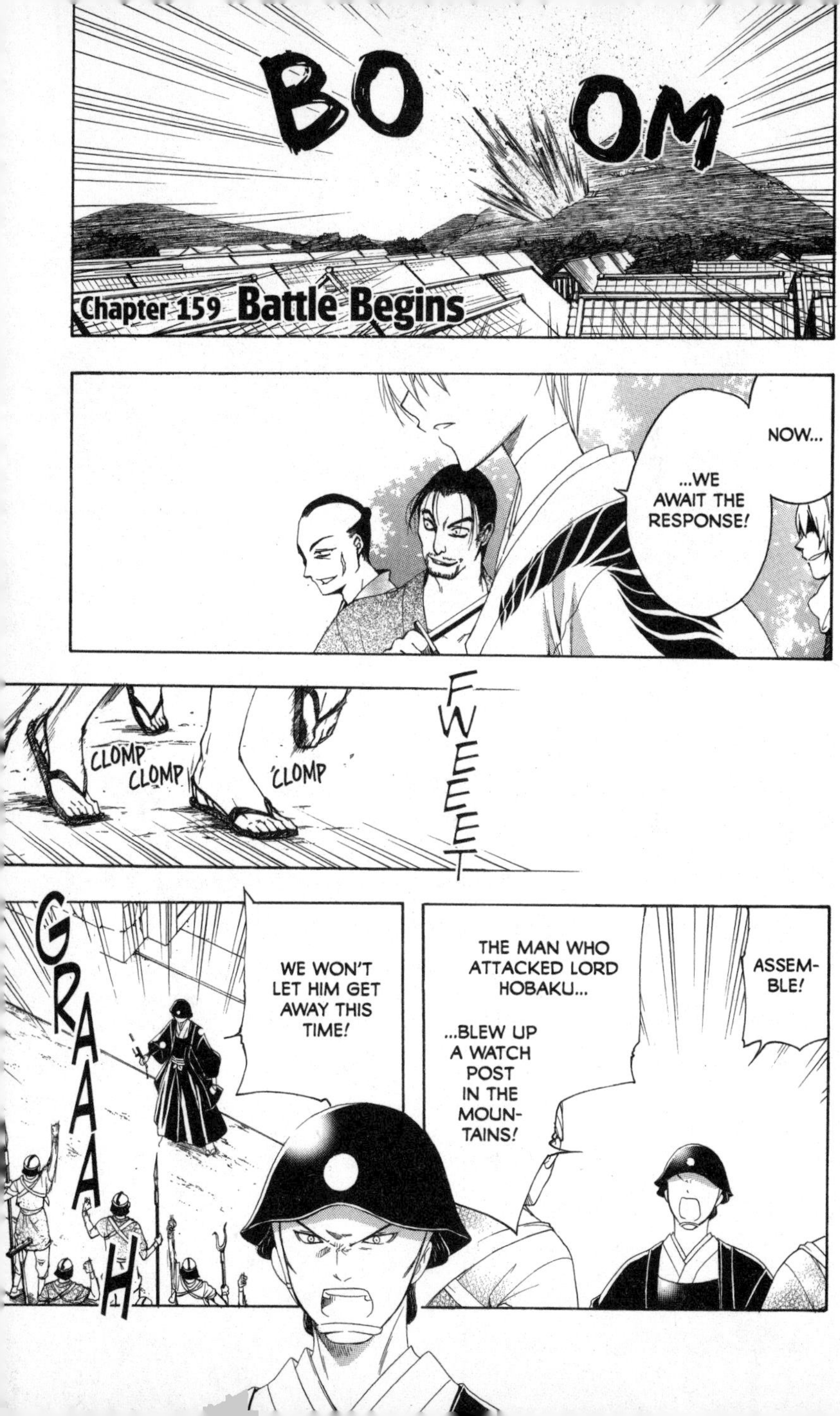
BOOM
Chapter 159 Battle Begins
NOW...
...WE AWAIT THE RESPONSE!
FWEEET
CLOMP
CLOMP CLOMP
ASSEM-BLE!
THE MAN WHO ATTACKED LORD HOBAKU...
...BLEW UP A WATCH POST IN THE MOUN-TAINS!
WE WON'T LET HIM GET AWAY THIS TIME!
GRAAAAH

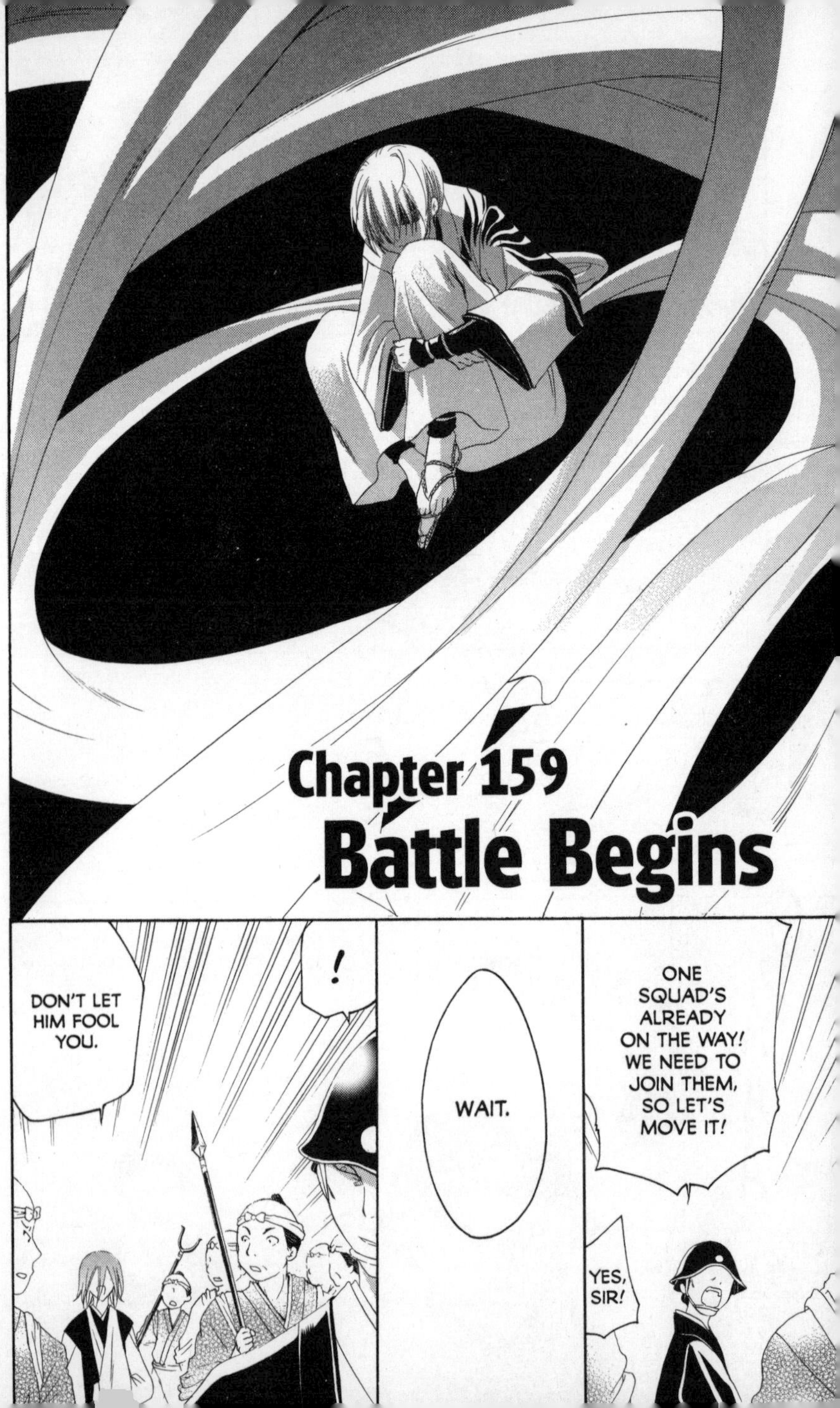
Chapter 159
Battle Begins
ONE SQUAD'S ALREADY ON THE WAY! WE NEED TO JOIN THEM, SO LET'S MOVE IT!
YES, SIR!
WAIT.
!
DON'T LET HIM FOOL YOU.

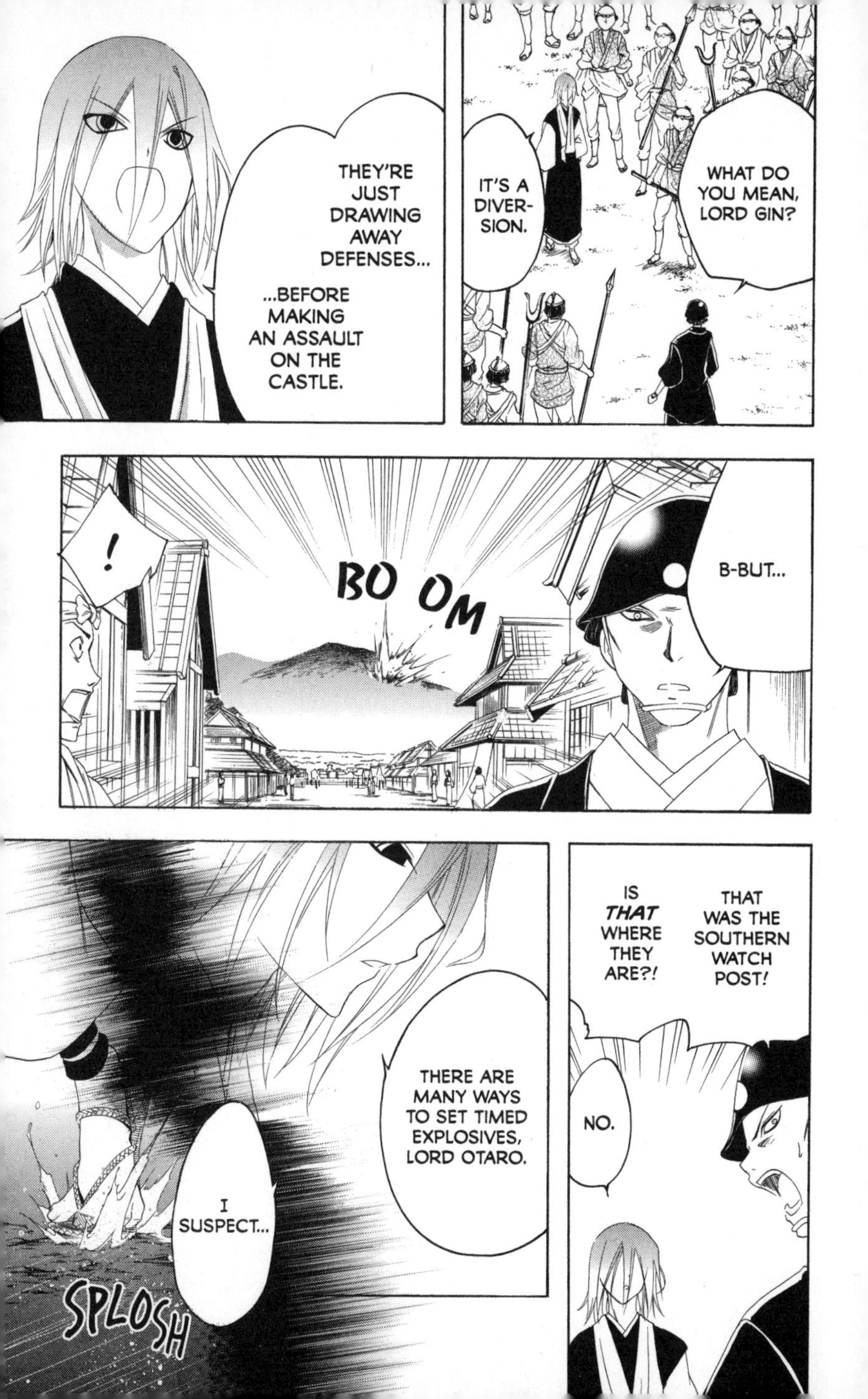
WHAT DO YOU MEAN, LORD GIN?
IT'S A DIVERSION.
THEY'RE JUST DRAWING AWAY DEFENSES...
...BEFORE MAKING AN ASSAULT ON THE CASTLE.
B-BUT...
BOOM
!
THAT WAS THE SOUTHERN WATCH POST!
IS *THAT* WHERE THEY ARE?!
NO.
THERE ARE MANY WAYS TO SET TIMED EXPLOSIVES, LORD OTARO.
I SUSPECT...
SPLOSH

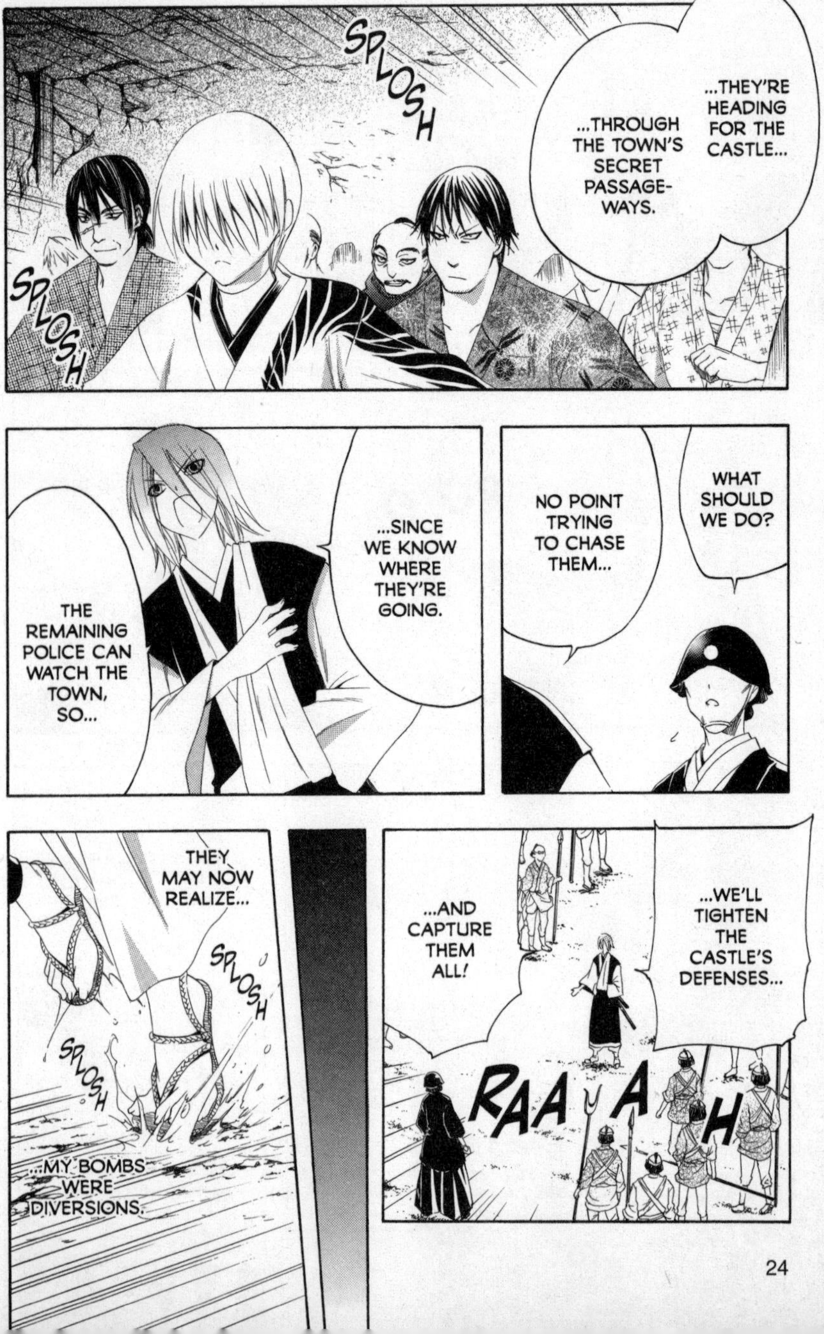
...THEY'RE HEADING FOR THE CASTLE...
...THROUGH THE TOWN'S SECRET PASSAGE-WAYS.
SPLOSH
SPLOSH
WHAT SHOULD WE DO?
NO POINT TRYING TO CHASE THEM...
...SINCE WE KNOW WHERE THEY'RE GOING.
THE REMAINING POLICE CAN WATCH THE TOWN, SO...
...WE'LL TIGHTEN THE CASTLE'S DEFENSES...
...AND CAPTURE THEM ALL!
RAAAH
THEY MAY NOW REALIZE...
SPLOSH
SPLOSH
...MY BOMBS WERE DIVERSIONS.

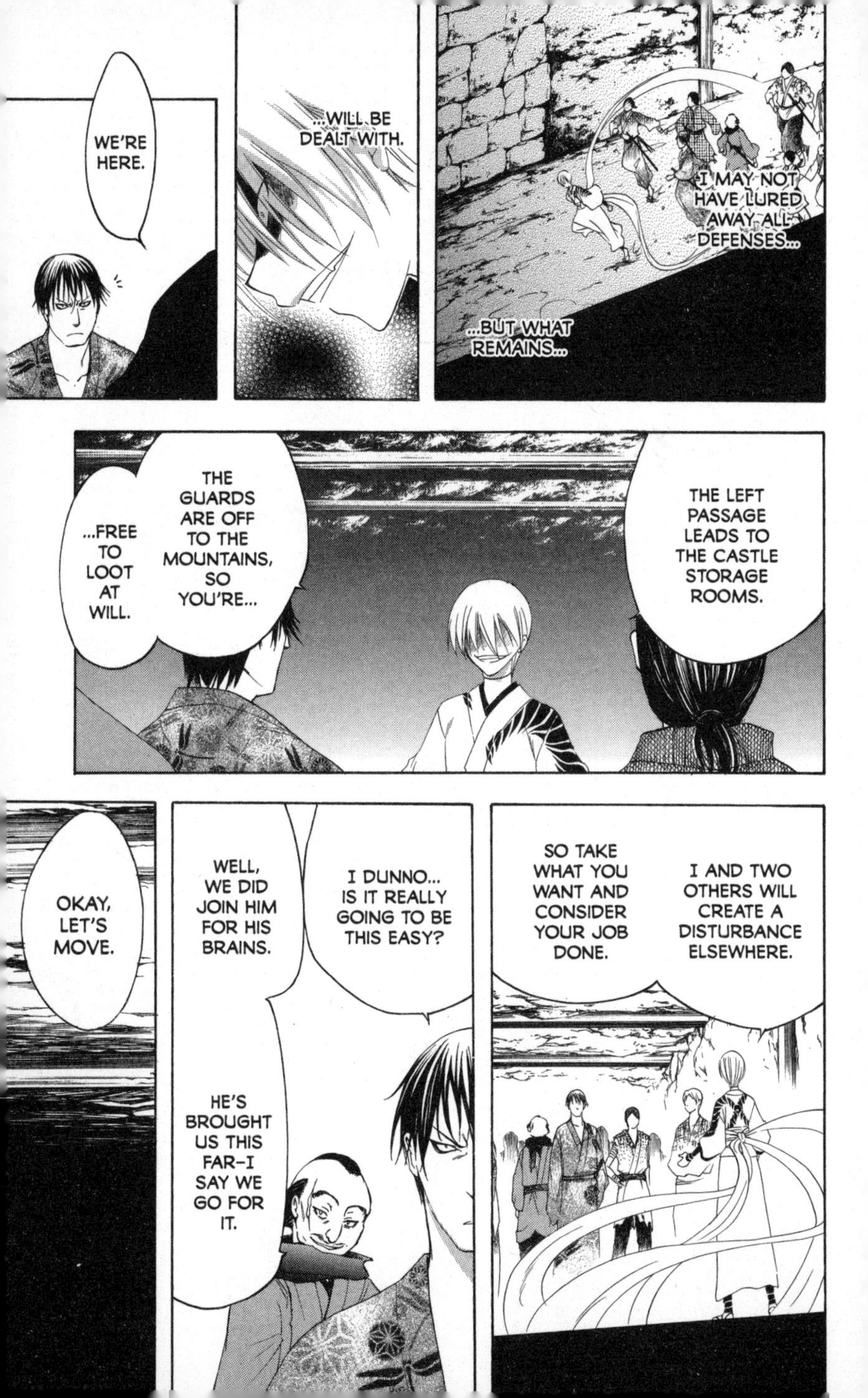
I MAY NOT HAVE LURED AWAY ALL DEFENSES...
...BUT WHAT REMAINS...
...WILL BE DEALT WITH.
WE'RE HERE.
THE LEFT PASSAGE LEADS TO THE CASTLE STORAGE ROOMS.
THE GUARDS ARE OFF TO THE MOUNTAINS, SO YOU'RE...
...FREE TO LOOT AT WILL.
I AND TWO OTHERS WILL CREATE A DISTURBANCE ELSEWHERE.
SO TAKE WHAT YOU WANT AND CONSIDER YOUR JOB DONE.
I DUNNO... IS IT REALLY GOING TO BE THIS EASY?
WELL, WE DID JOIN HIM FOR HIS BRAINS.
HE'S BROUGHT US THIS FAR—I SAY WE GO FOR IT.
OKAY, LET'S MOVE.

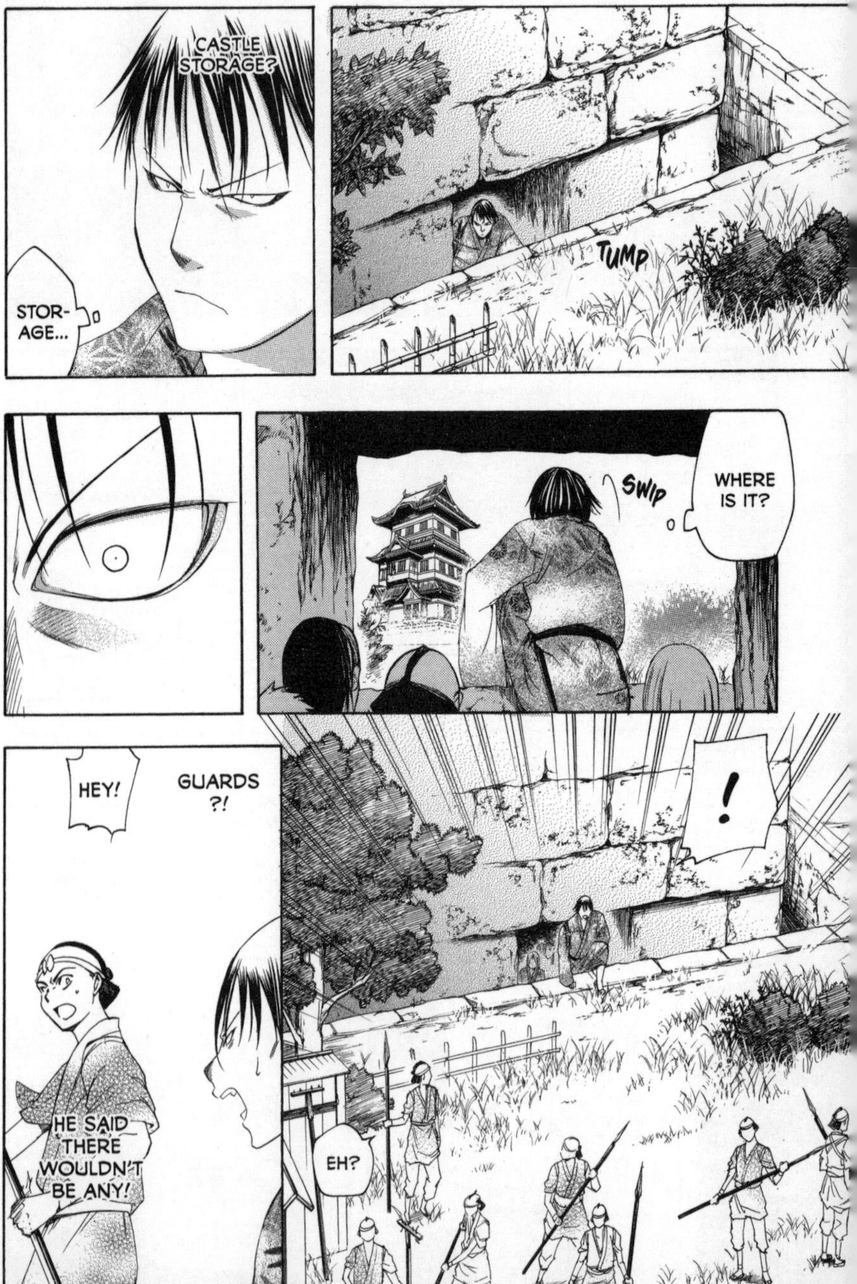
TUMP
CASTLE STORAGE?
STORAGE...
SWIP
WHERE IS IT?
!
EH?
GUARDS?!
HEY!
HE SAID THERE WOULDN'T BE ANY!

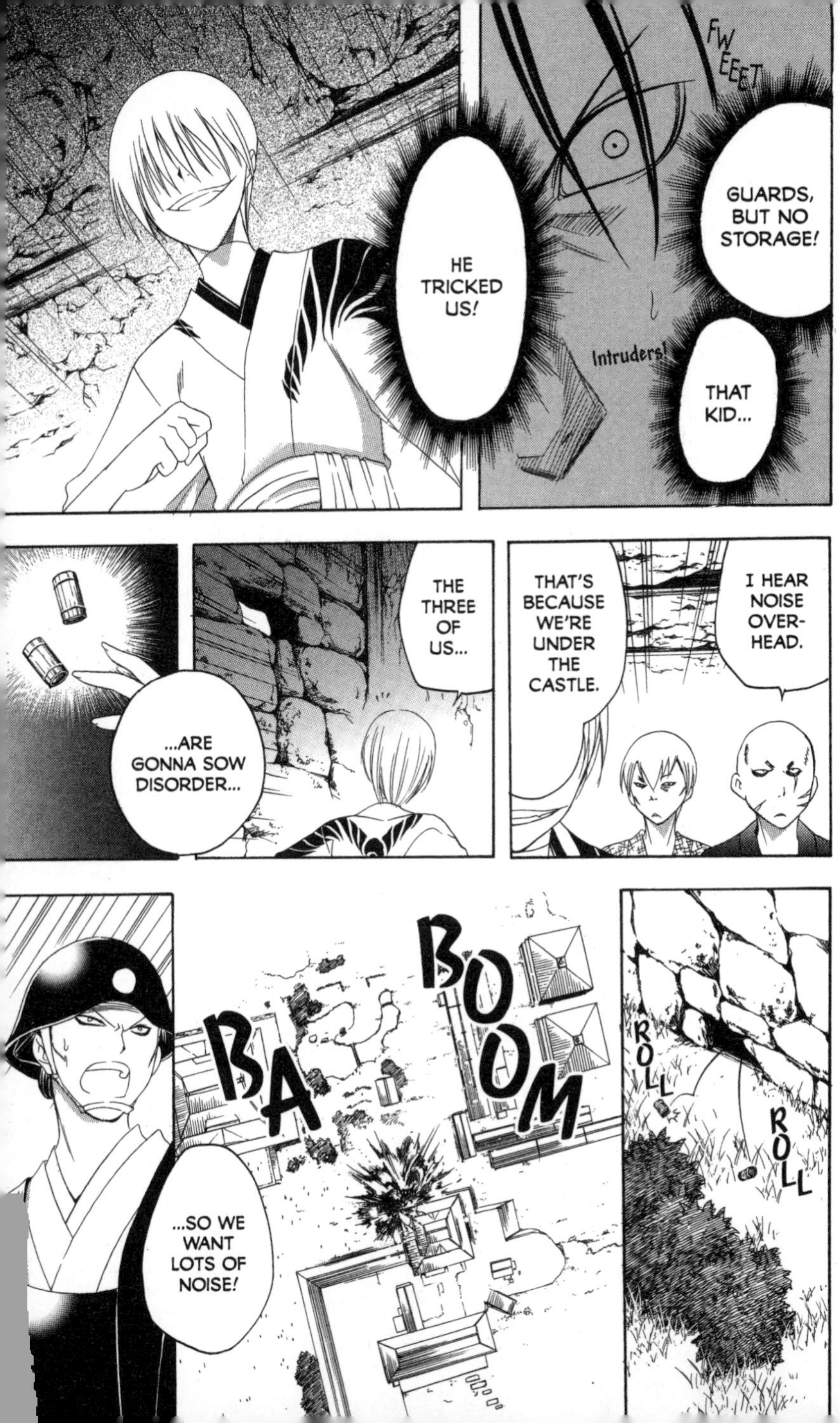
FWEEET
GUARDS, BUT NO STORAGE!
THAT KID...
Intruders!
HE TRICKED US!
I HEAR NOISE OVER-HEAD.
THAT'S BECAUSE WE'RE UNDER THE CASTLE.
THE THREE OF US...
...ARE GONNA SOW DISORDER...
ROLL
ROLL
BA BOOM
...SO WE WANT LOTS OF NOISE!

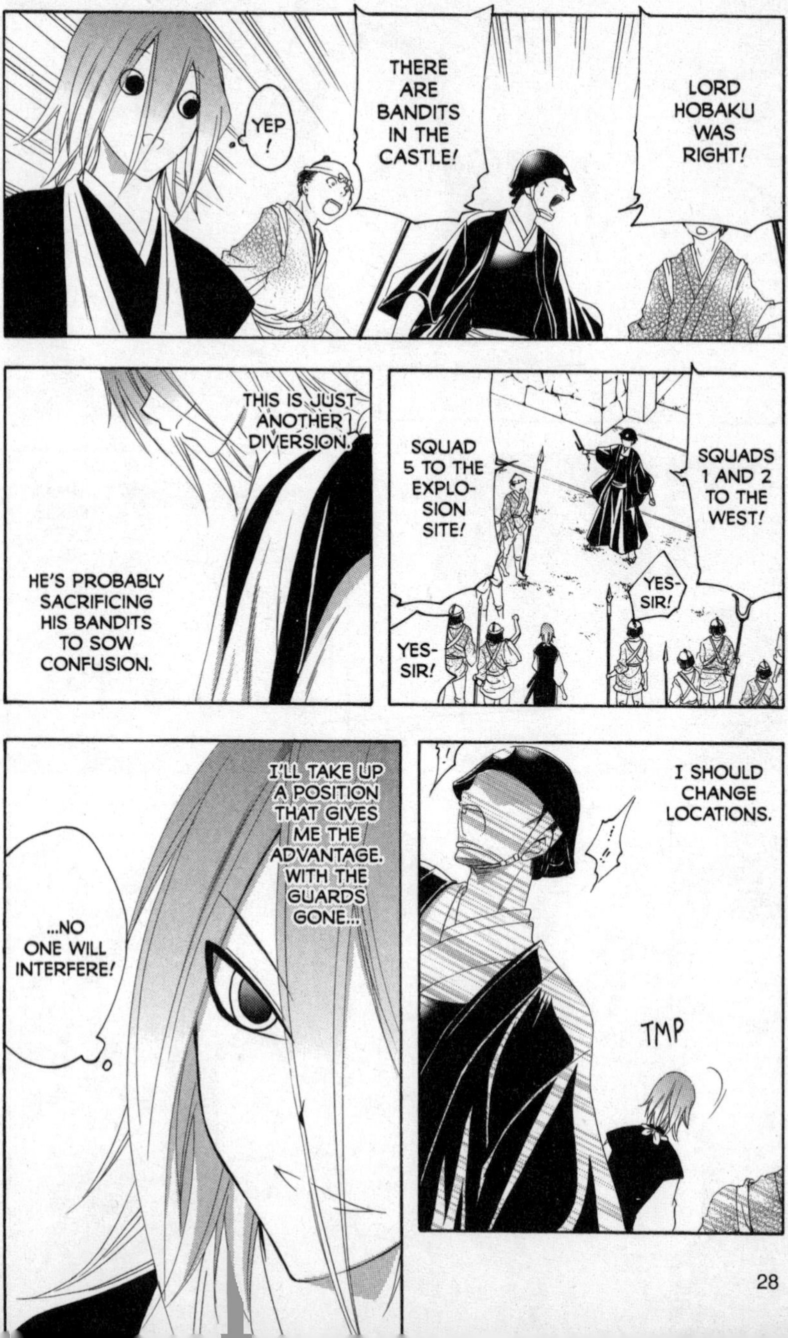
LORD HOBAKU WAS RIGHT!
THERE ARE BANDITS IN THE CASTLE!
YEP!
SQUADS 1 AND 2 TO THE WEST!
SQUAD 5 TO THE EXPLOSION SITE!
YES-SIR!
YES-SIR!
THIS IS JUST ANOTHER DIVERSION.
HE'S PROBABLY SACRIFICING HIS BANDITS TO SOW CONFUSION.
!
I SHOULD CHANGE LOCATIONS.
!!
TMP
I'LL TAKE UP A POSITION THAT GIVES ME THE ADVANTAGE. WITH THE GUARDS GONE...
...NO ONE WILL INTERFERE!

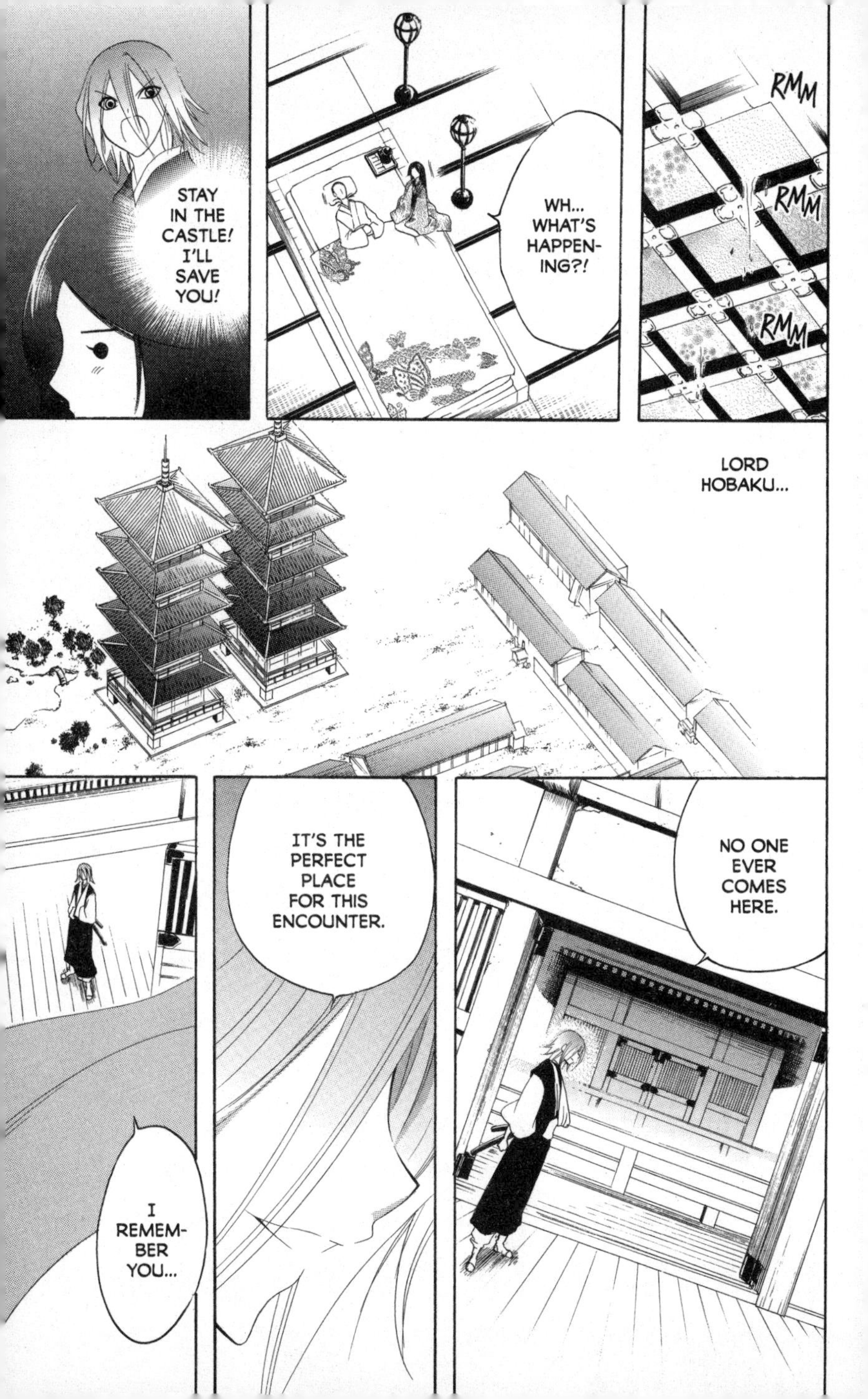
RMM
RMM
RMM
WH... WHAT'S HAPPEN-ING?!
STAY IN THE CASTLE! I'LL SAVE YOU!
LORD HOBAKU...
NO ONE EVER COMES HERE.
IT'S THE PERFECT PLACE FOR THIS ENCOUNTER.
I REMEM-BER YOU...

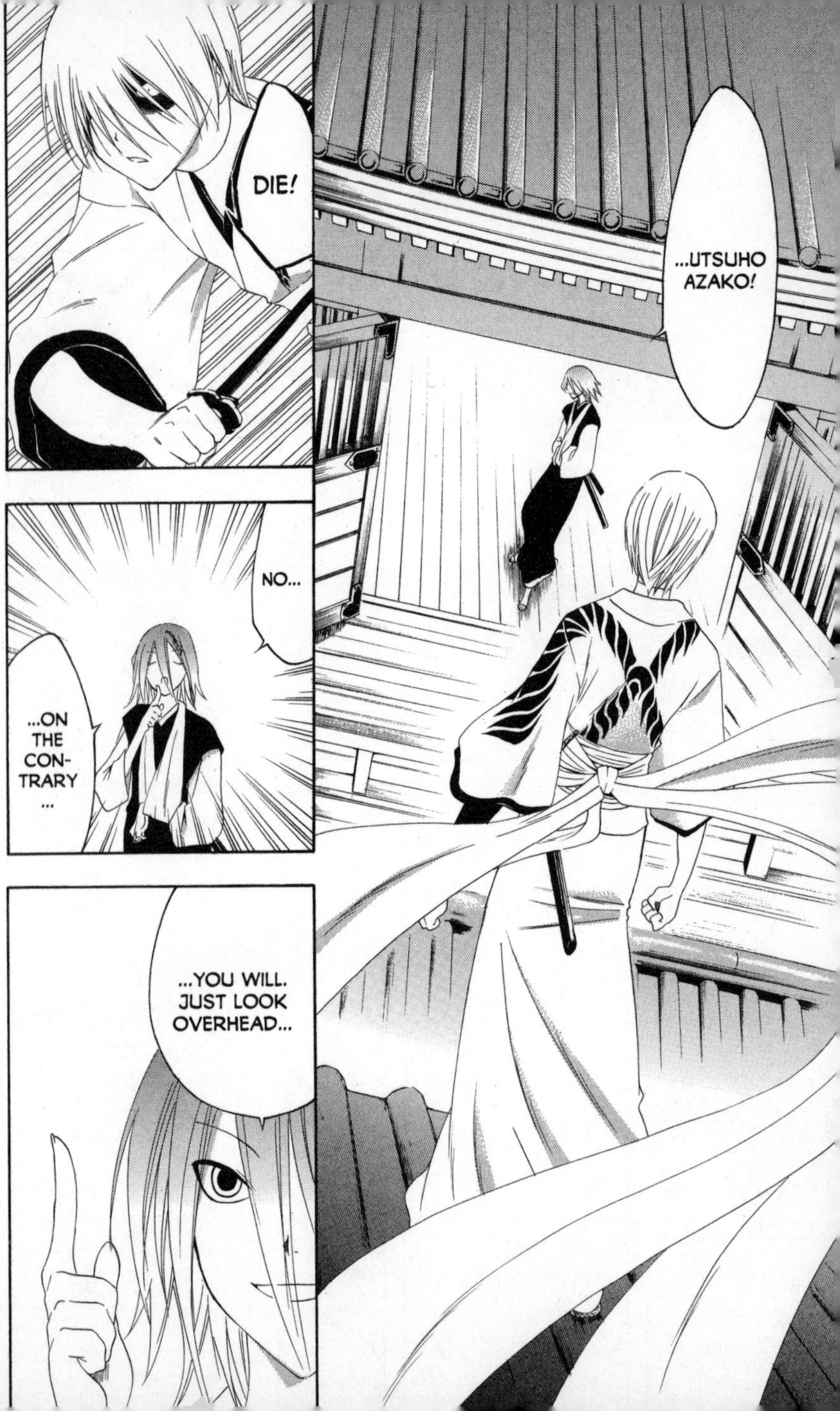
...UTSUHO AZAKO!
DIE!
NO...
...ON THE CON- TRARY ...
...YOU WILL. JUST LOOK OVERHEAD...

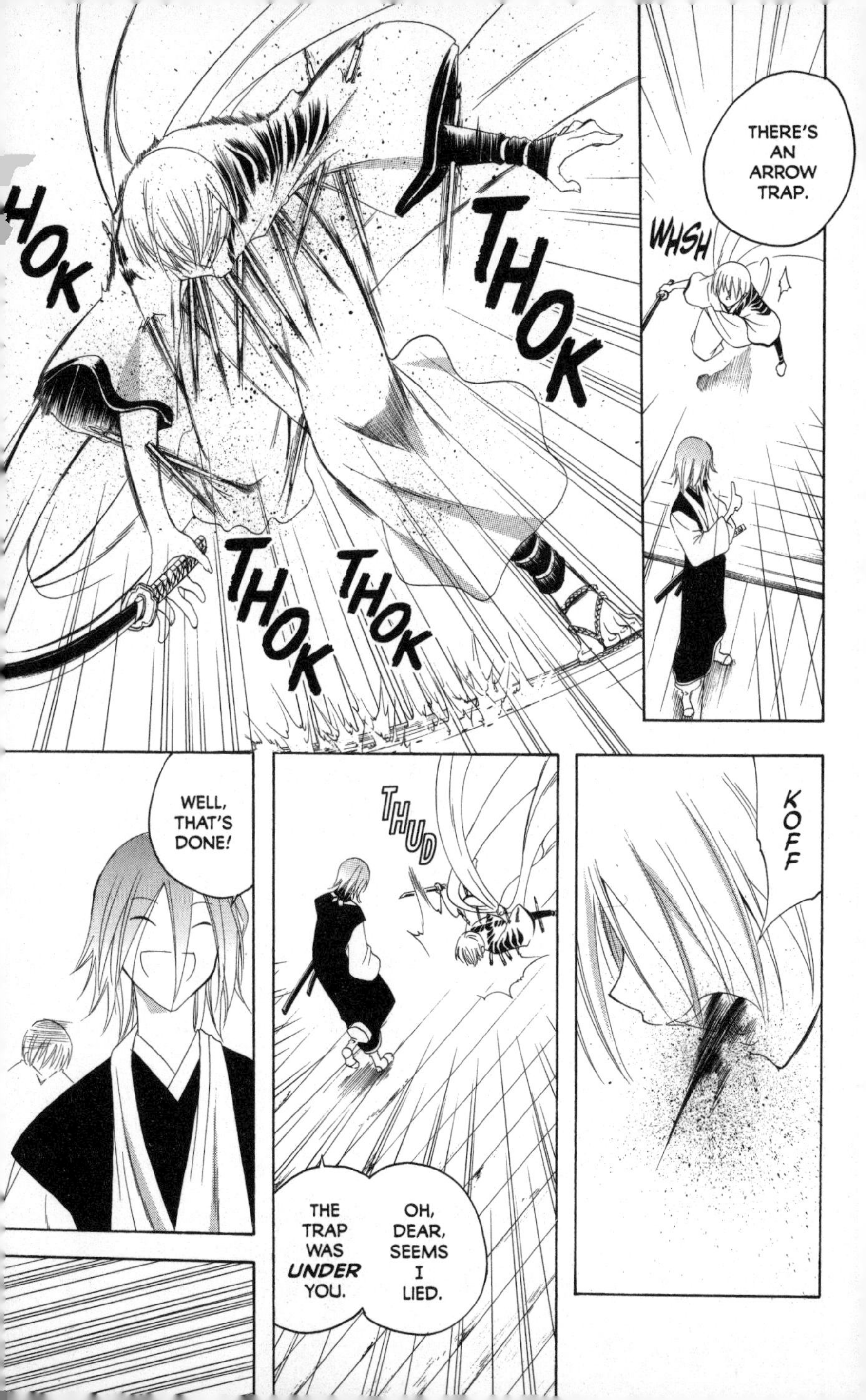
THERE'S AN ARROW TRAP.
WHSH
THOK
THOK
THOK
THOK
KOFF
THUD
OH, DEAR, SEEMS I LIED.
THE TRAP WAS *UNDER* YOU.
WELL, THAT'S DONE!

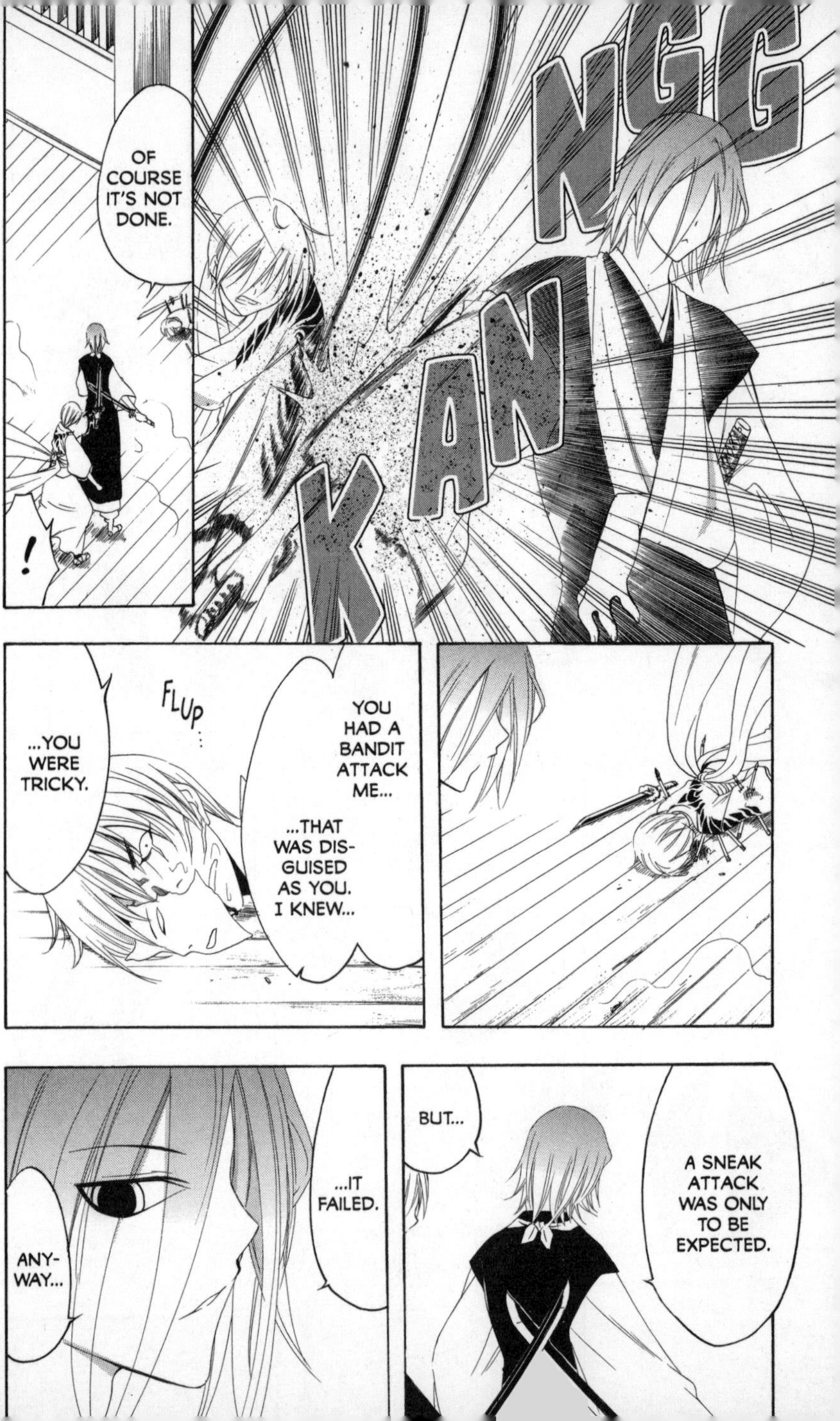
KANNGG
OF COURSE IT'S NOT DONE.
!
YOU HAD A BANDIT ATTACK ME...
...THAT WAS DISGUISED AS YOU. I KNEW...
FLUP...
...YOU WERE TRICKY.
A SNEAK ATTACK WAS ONLY TO BE EXPECTED.
BUT...
...IT FAILED.
ANYWAY...

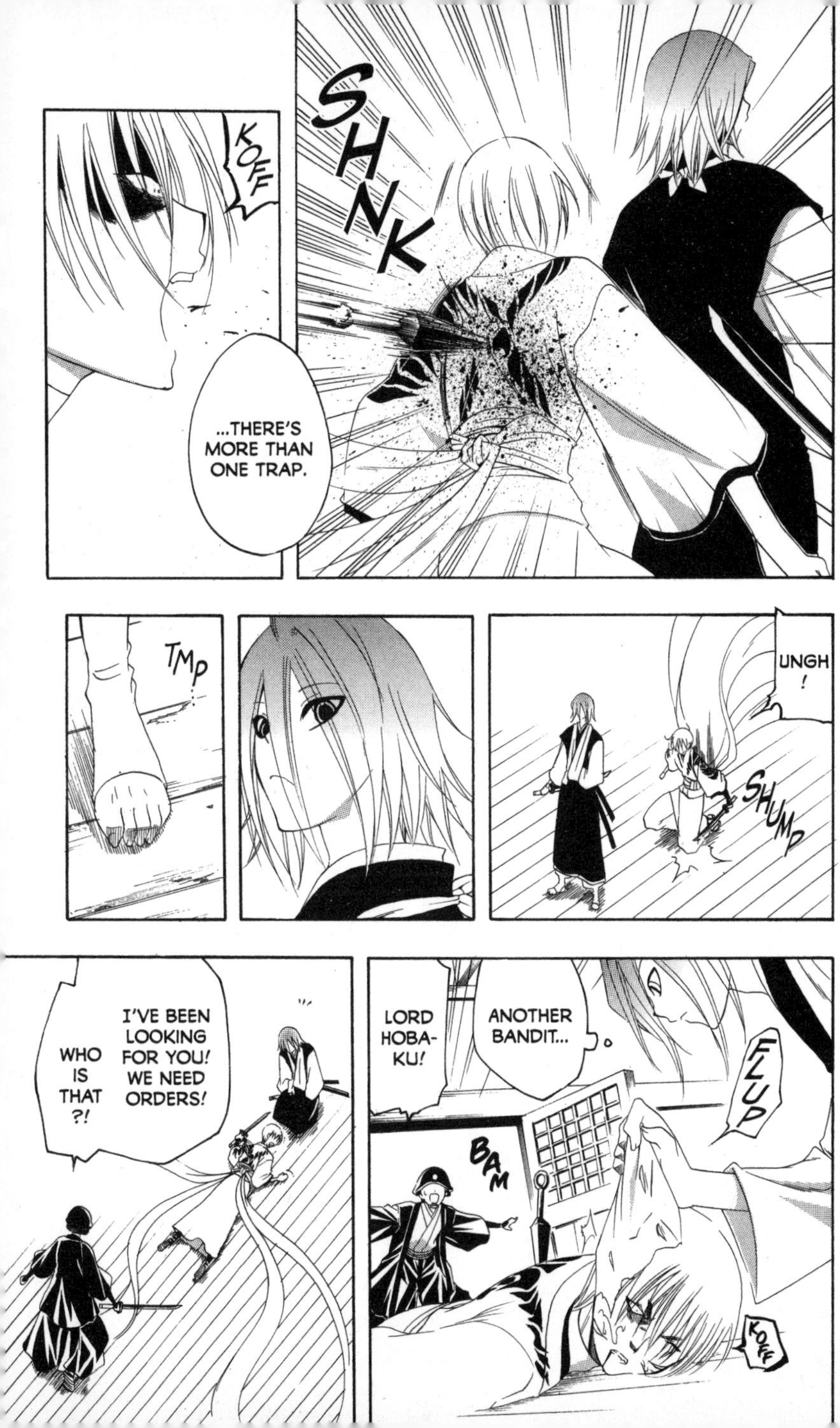
SHNK
KOFF
...THERE'S MORE THAN ONE TRAP.
UNGH!
SHUMP
TMP
ANOTHER BANDIT...
LORD HOBA-KU!
FLUP
BAM
KOFF
I'VE BEEN LOOKING FOR YOU! WE NEED ORDERS!
WHO IS THAT?!

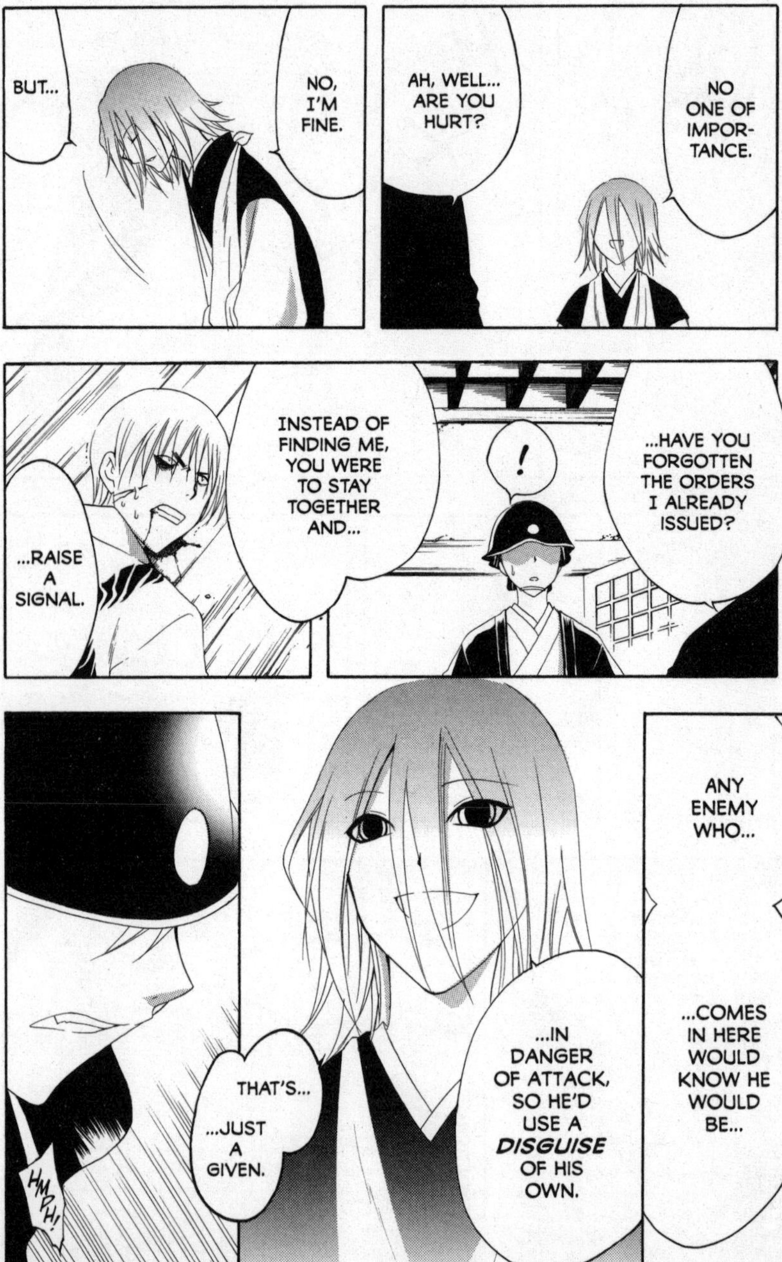
NO ONE OF IMPORTANCE.
AH, WELL... ARE YOU HURT?
NO, I'M FINE.
BUT...
!
...HAVE YOU FORGOTTEN THE ORDERS I ALREADY ISSUED?
INSTEAD OF FINDING ME, YOU WERE TO STAY TOGETHER AND...
...RAISE A SIGNAL.
ANY ENEMY WHO...
...COMES IN HERE WOULD KNOW HE WOULD BE...
...IN DANGER OF ATTACK, SO HE'D USE A *DISGUISE* OF HIS OWN.
THAT'S...
...JUST A GIVEN.
HMPH!

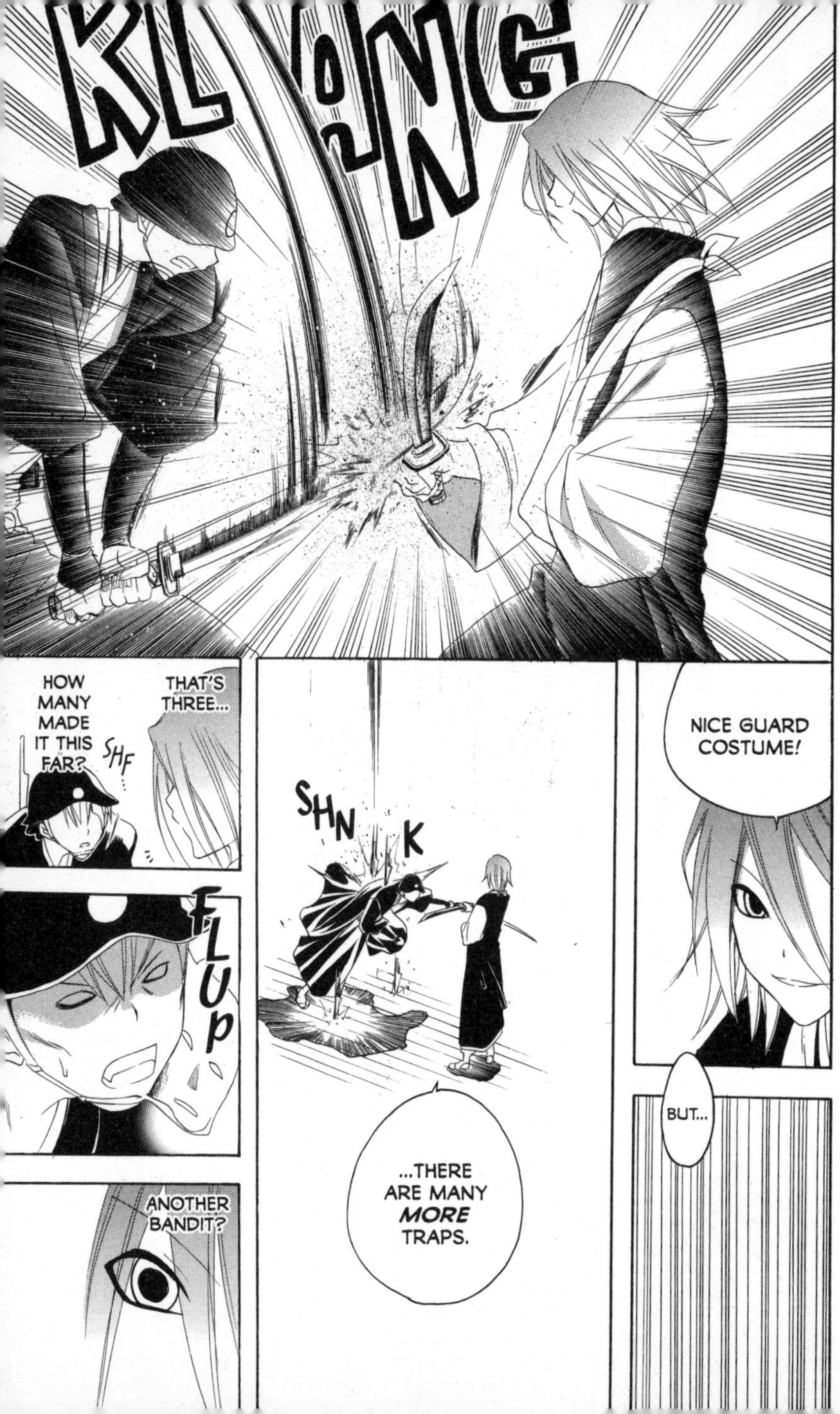
NICE GUARD COSTUME!
BUT...
SHNK
...THERE ARE MANY *MORE* TRAPS.
THAT'S THREE...
SHF
HOW MANY MADE IT THIS FAR?
FLUP
ANOTHER BANDIT?

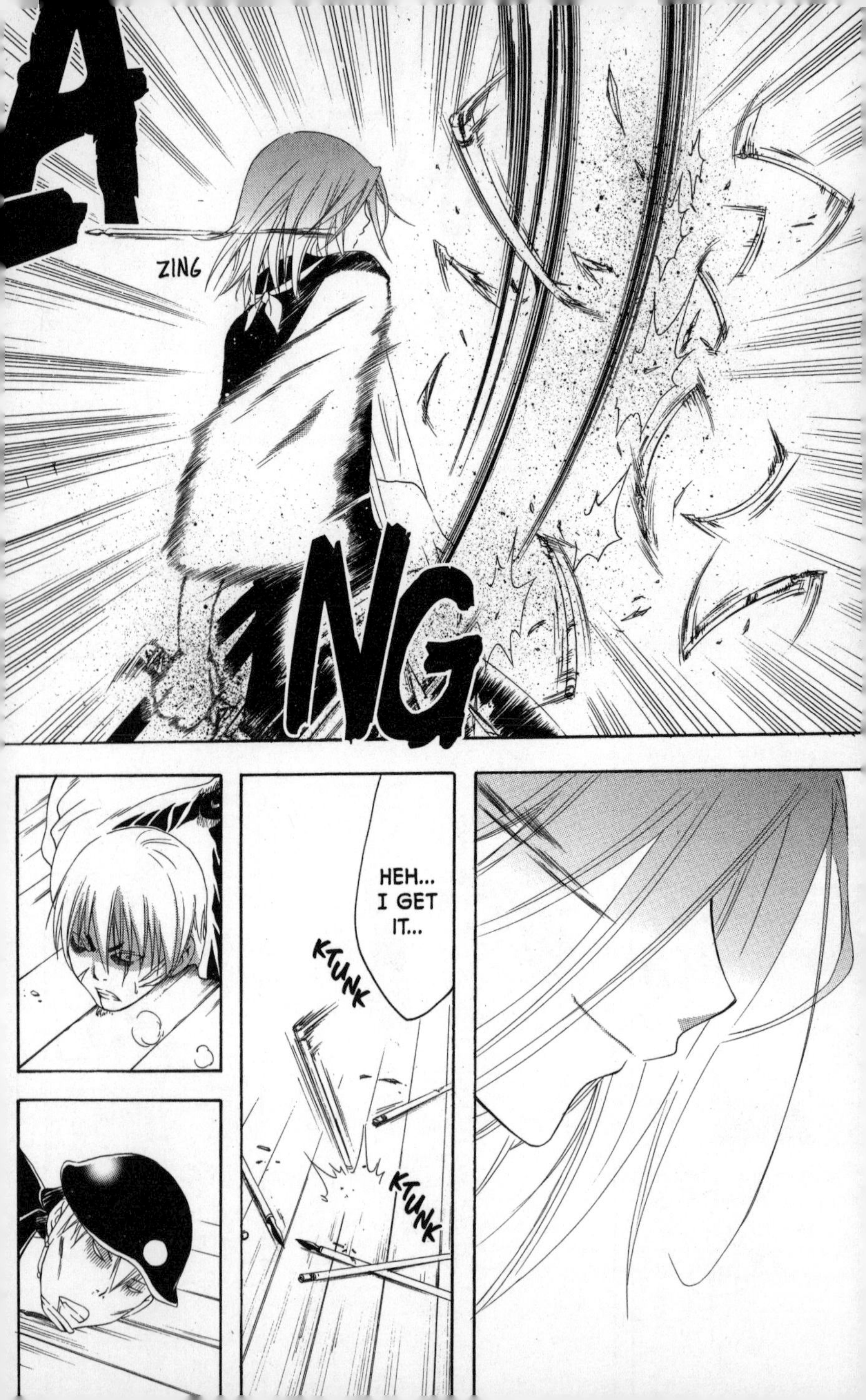
ZING
HEH... I GET IT...
KTUNK
KTUNK

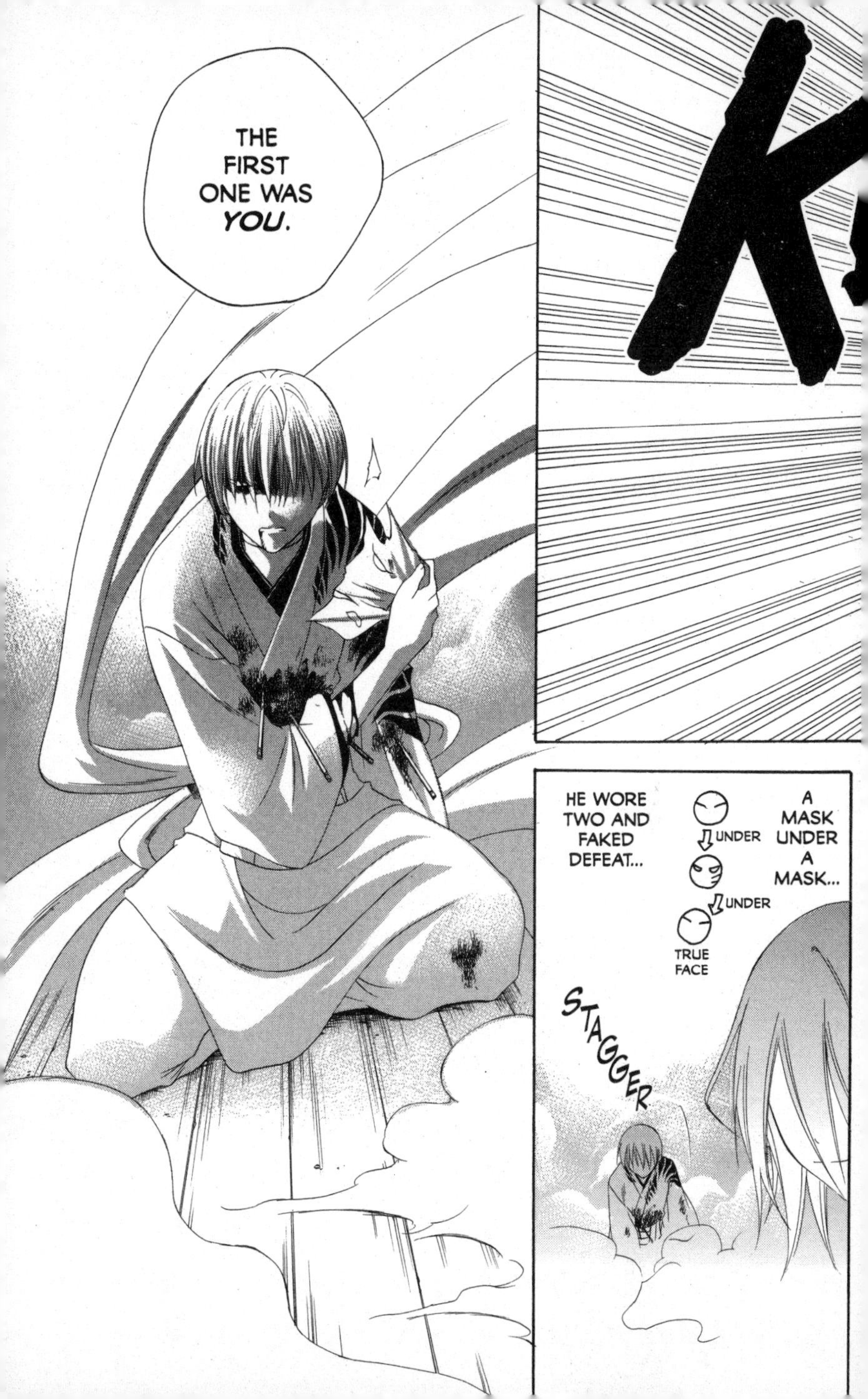
K
A MASK UNDER A MASK...
UNDER
UNDER
TRUE FACE
HE WORE TWO AND FAKED DEFEAT...
STAGGER
THE FIRST ONE WAS *YOU*.

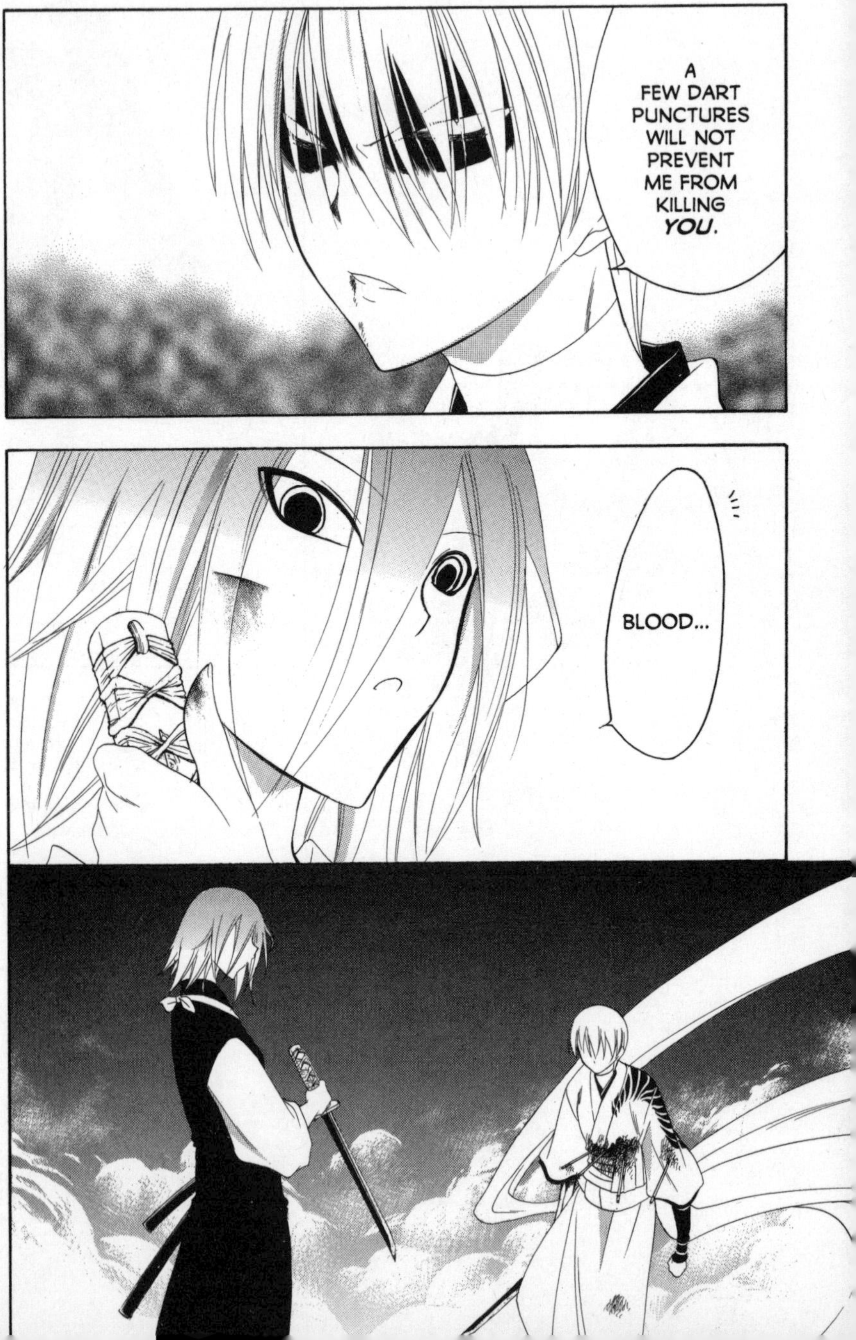
A FEW DART PUNCTURES WILL NOT PREVENT ME FROM KILLING *YOU*.
BLOOD...

Chapter 160 What's Important

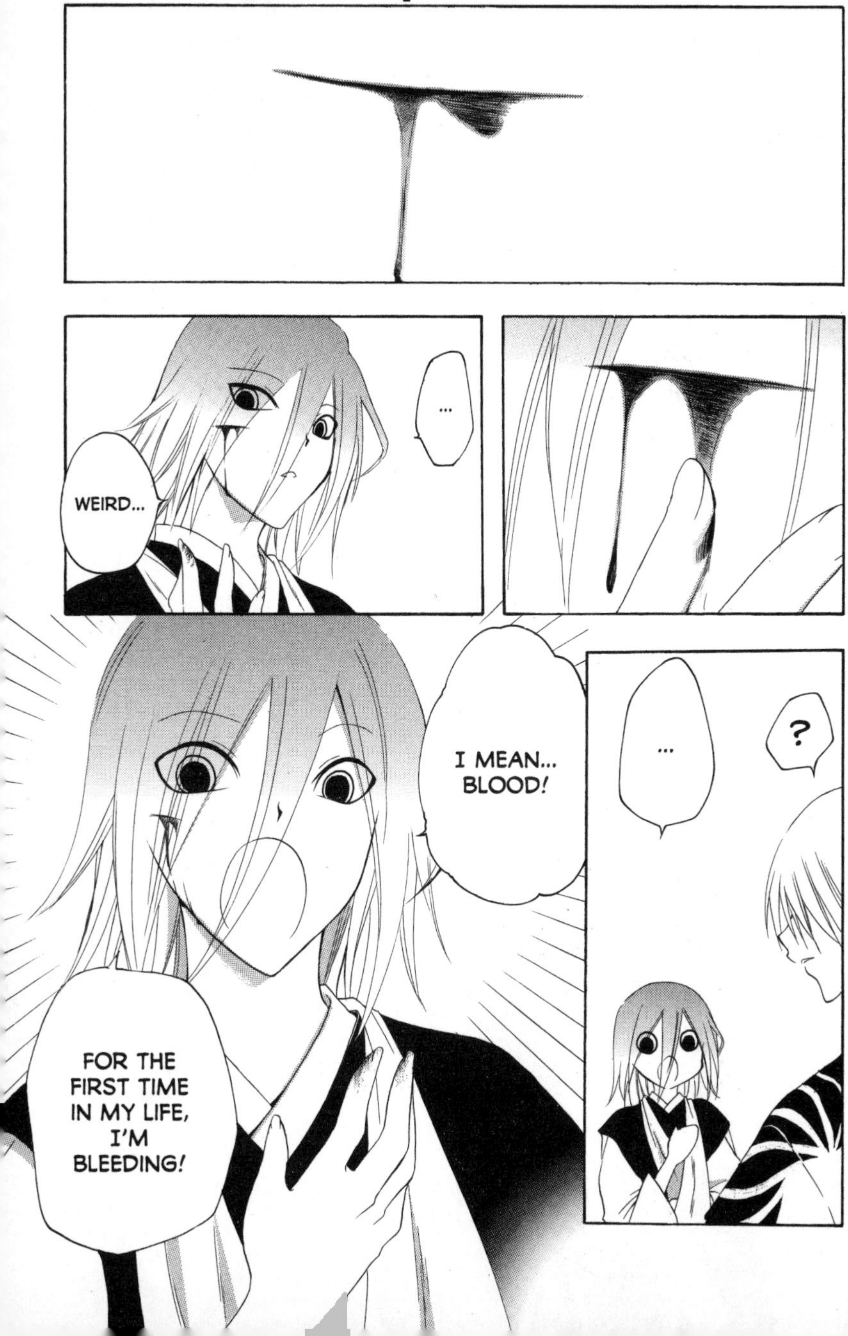
...
WEIRD...
?
...
I MEAN... BLOOD!
FOR THE FIRST TIME IN MY LIFE, I'M BLEEDING!

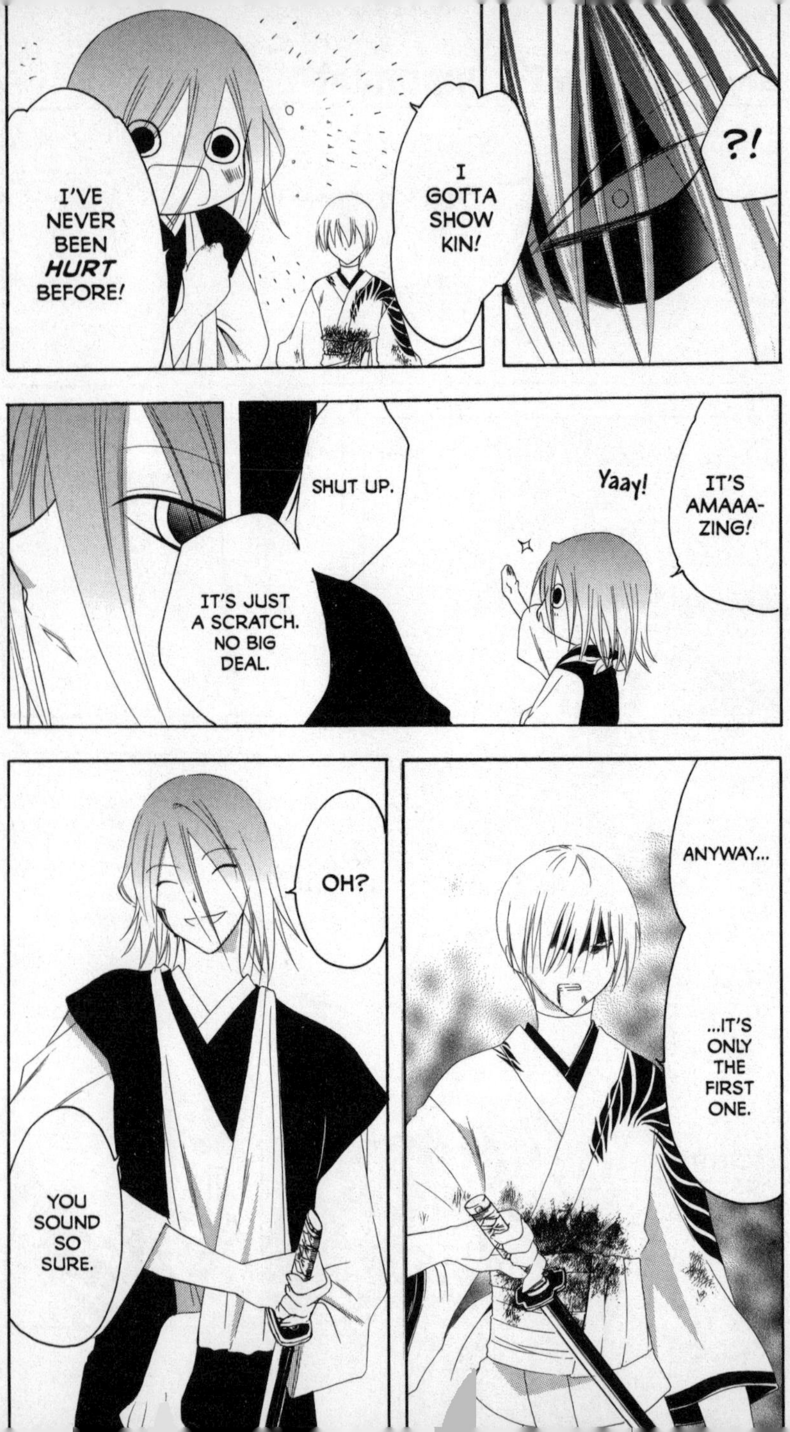
?!
I GOTTA SHOW KIN!
I'VE NEVER BEEN *HURT* BEFORE!
IT'S AMAAA-ZING!
Yaay!
SHUT UP.
IT'S JUST A SCRATCH. NO BIG DEAL.
ANYWAY...
...IT'S ONLY THE FIRST ONE.
OH?
YOU SOUND SO SURE.

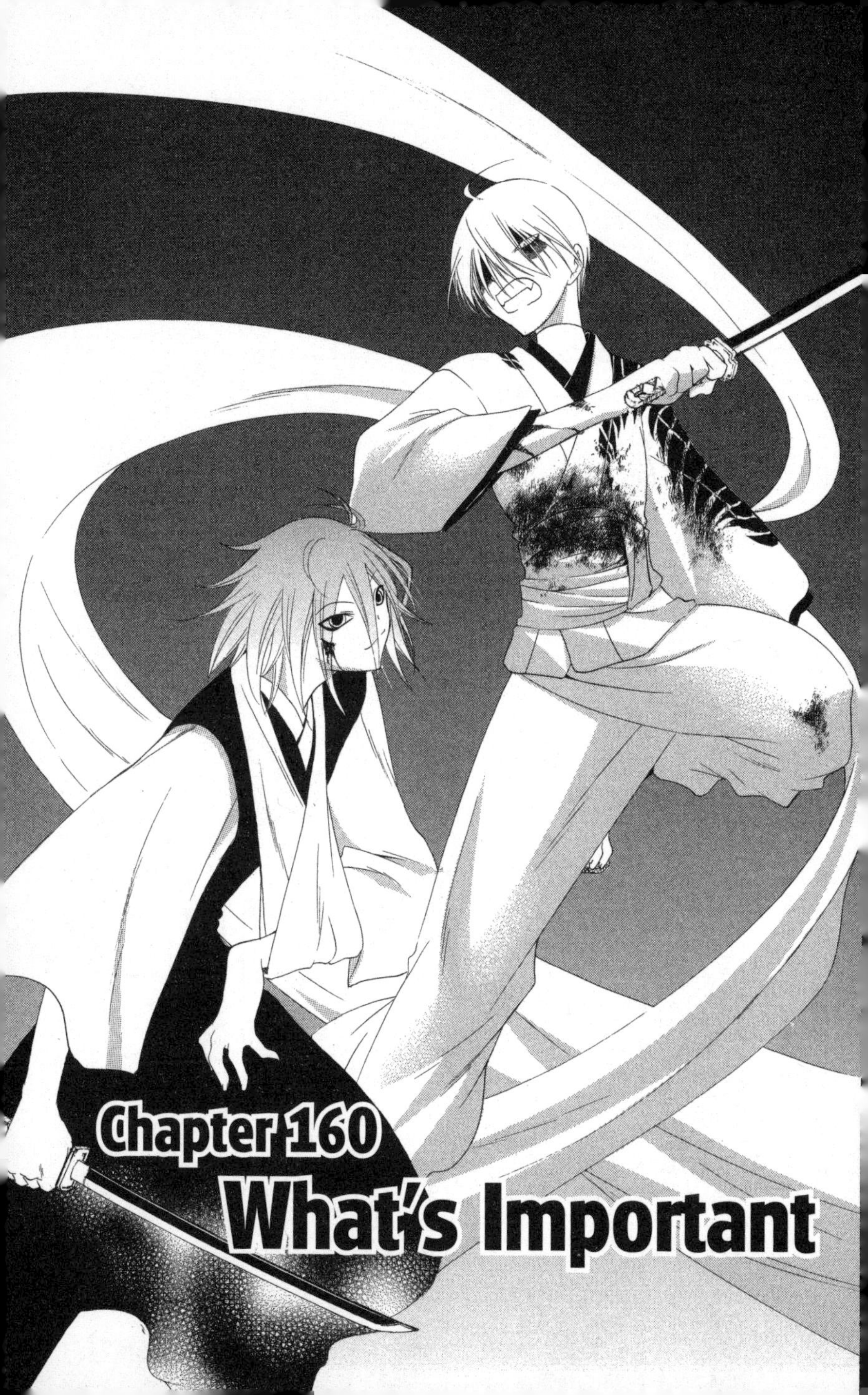
Chapter 160
What's Important

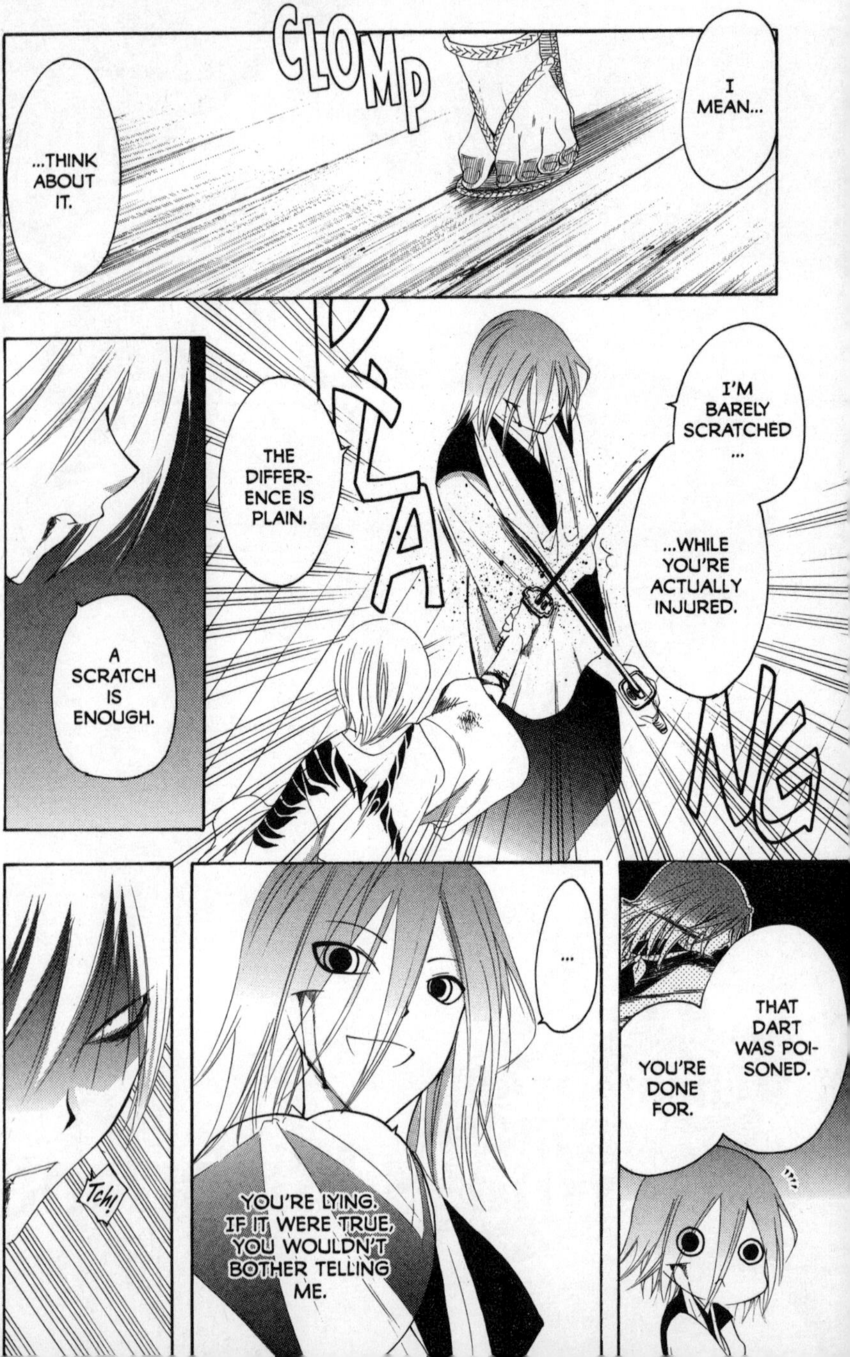
CLOMP
I MEAN...
...THINK ABOUT IT.
I'M BARELY SCRATCHED ...
...WHILE YOU'RE ACTUALLY INJURED.
THE DIFFER-ENCE IS PLAIN.
KLANG
A SCRATCH IS ENOUGH.
THAT DART WAS POI-SONED.
YOU'RE DONE FOR.
...
YOU'RE LYING. IF IT WERE TRUE, YOU WOULDN'T BOTHER TELLING ME.
Tch!

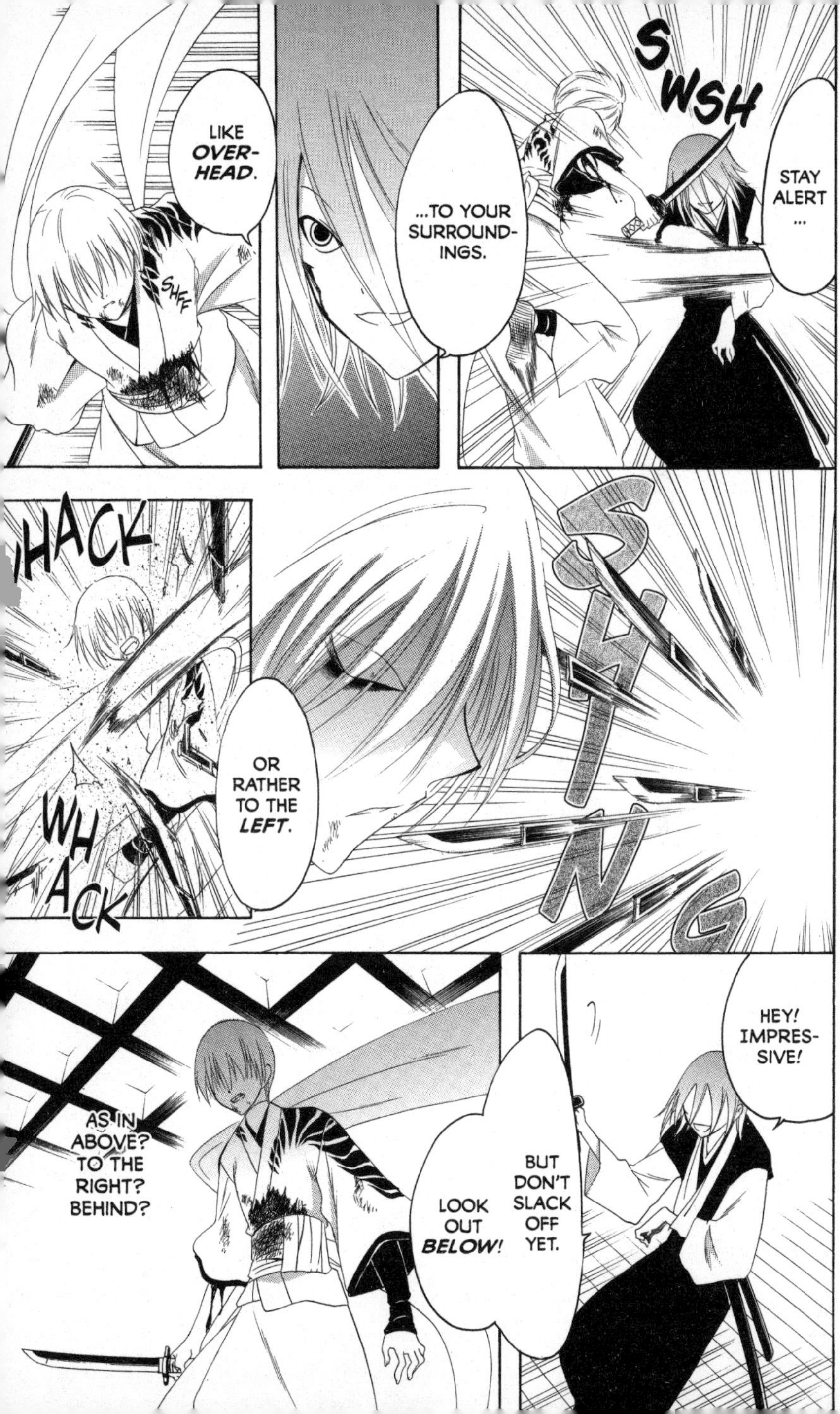
SWSH
STAY ALERT ...
...TO YOUR SURROUND-INGS.
LIKE OVER-HEAD.
SHFF
SHING
OR RATHER TO THE LEFT.
HACK
WHACK
HEY! IMPRES-SIVE!
BUT DON'T SLACK OFF YET.
LOOK OUT BELOW!
AS IN ABOVE? TO THE RIGHT? BEHIND?

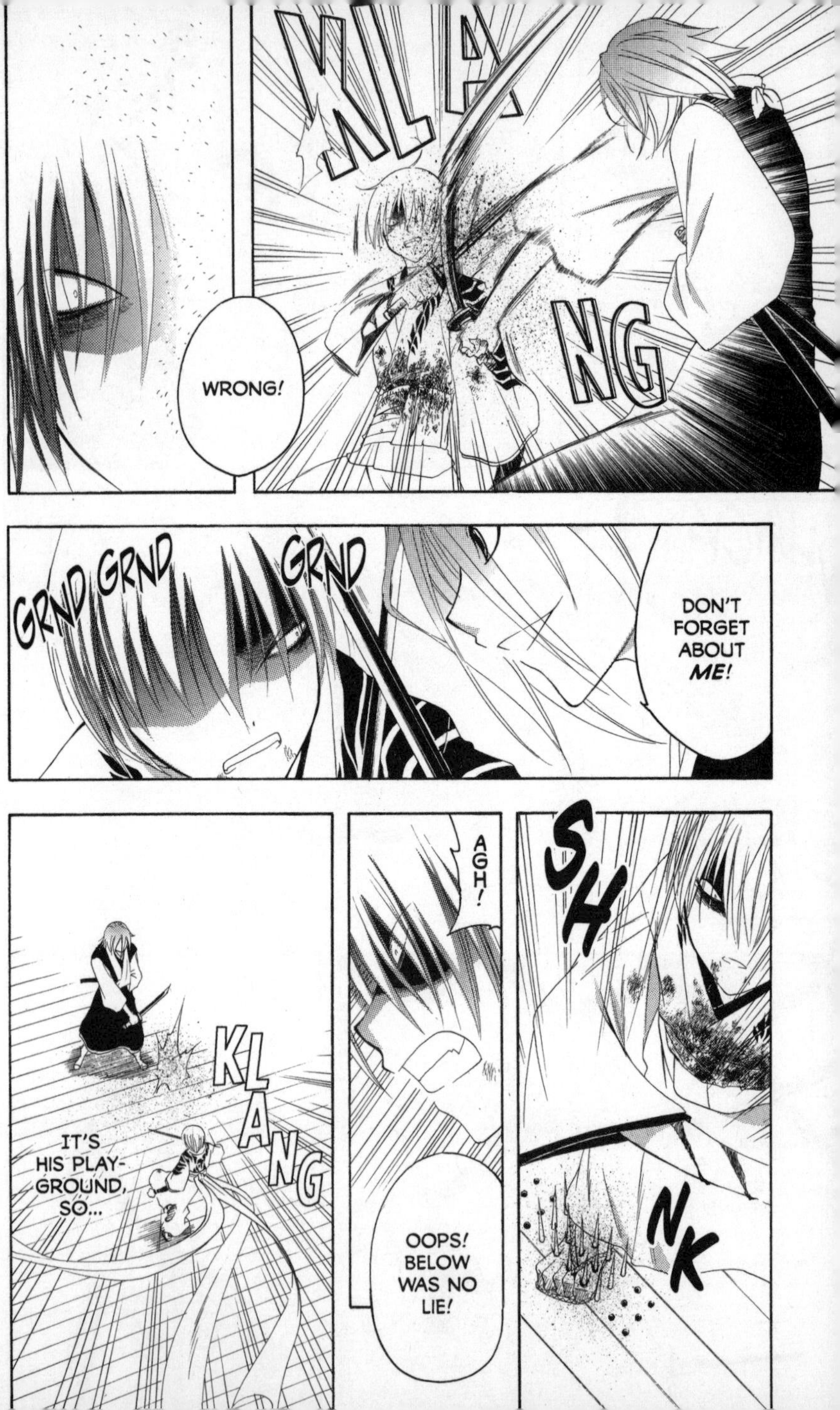

KLANG
WRONG!
DON'T FORGET ABOUT *ME!*
GRND
GRND GRND
SHNK
AGH!
OOPS! BELOW WAS NO LIE!
KLANG
IT'S HIS PLAY-GROUND, SO...

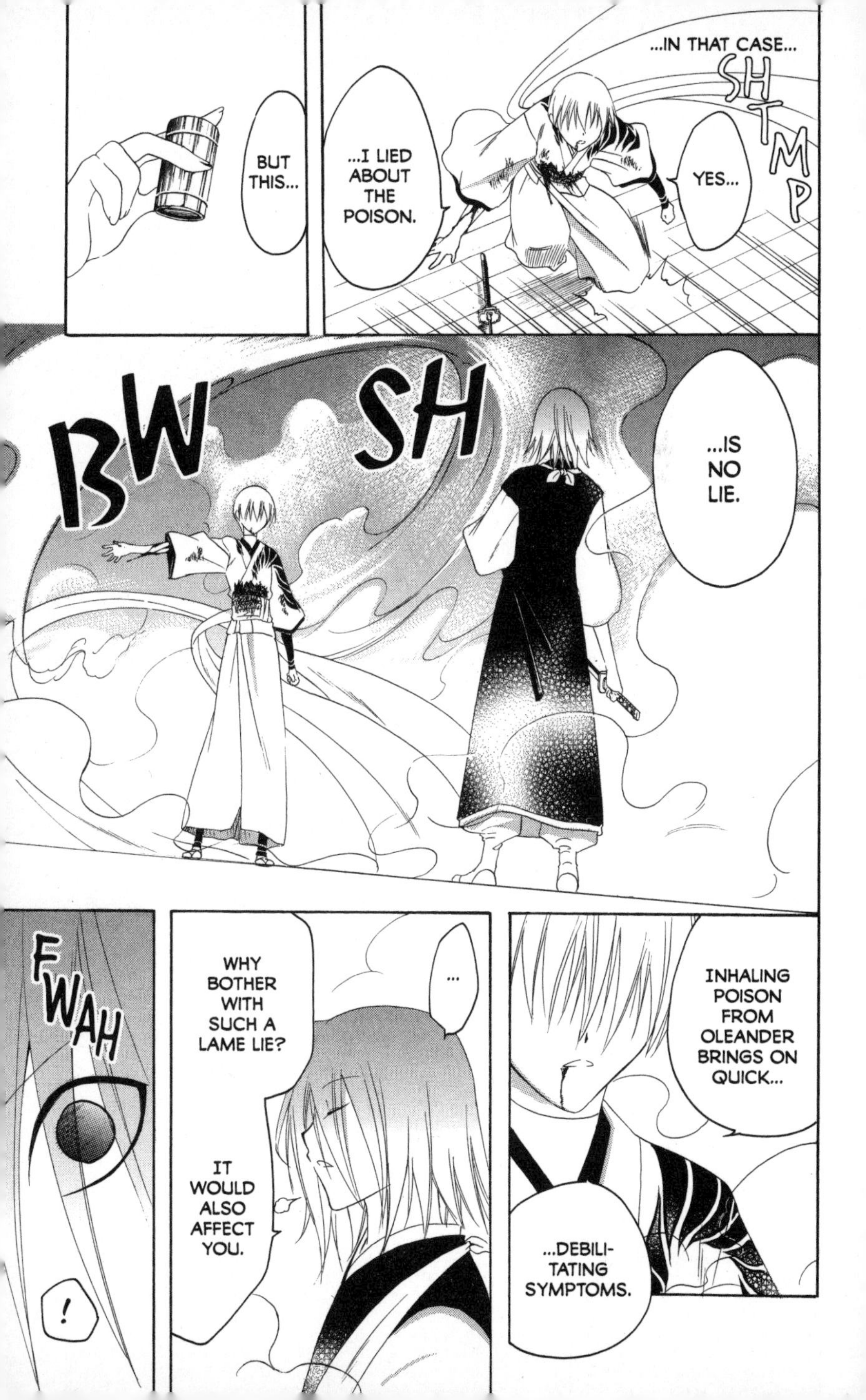
...IN THAT CASE...
SHTMP
YES...
...I LIED ABOUT THE POISON.
BUT THIS...
...IS NO LIE.
BWSH
INHALING POISON FROM OLEANDER BRINGS ON QUICK...
...DEBILI-TATING SYMPTOMS.
...
WHY BOTHER WITH SUCH A LAME LIE?
IT WOULD ALSO AFFECT YOU.
FWAH
!

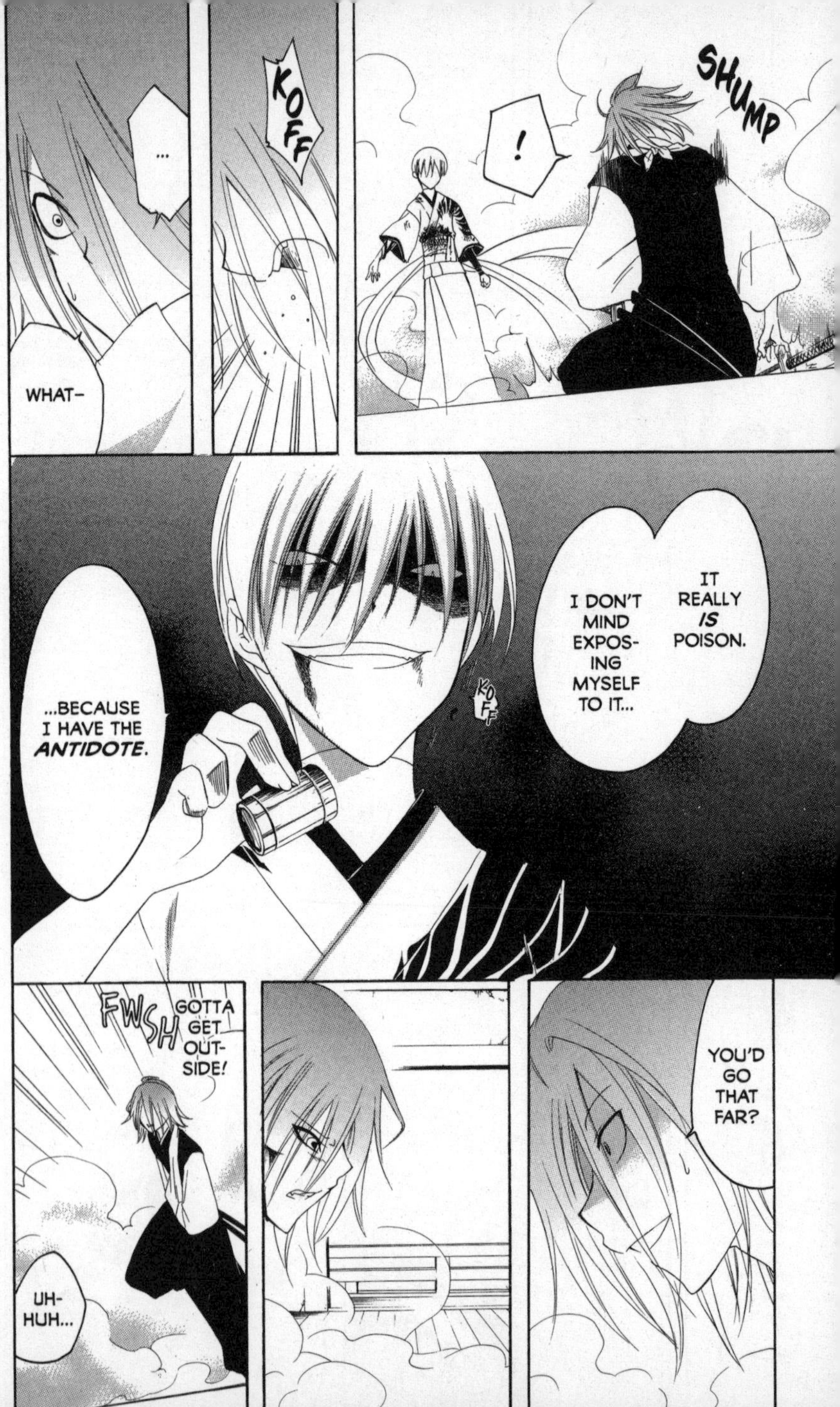
SHUMP
!
KOFF
...
WHAT–
IT REALLY *IS* POISON.
I DON'T MIND EXPOSING MYSELF TO IT...
KOFF
...BECAUSE I HAVE THE *ANTIDOTE*.
YOU'D GO THAT FAR?
FWSH
GOTTA GET OUTSIDE!
UH-HUH...

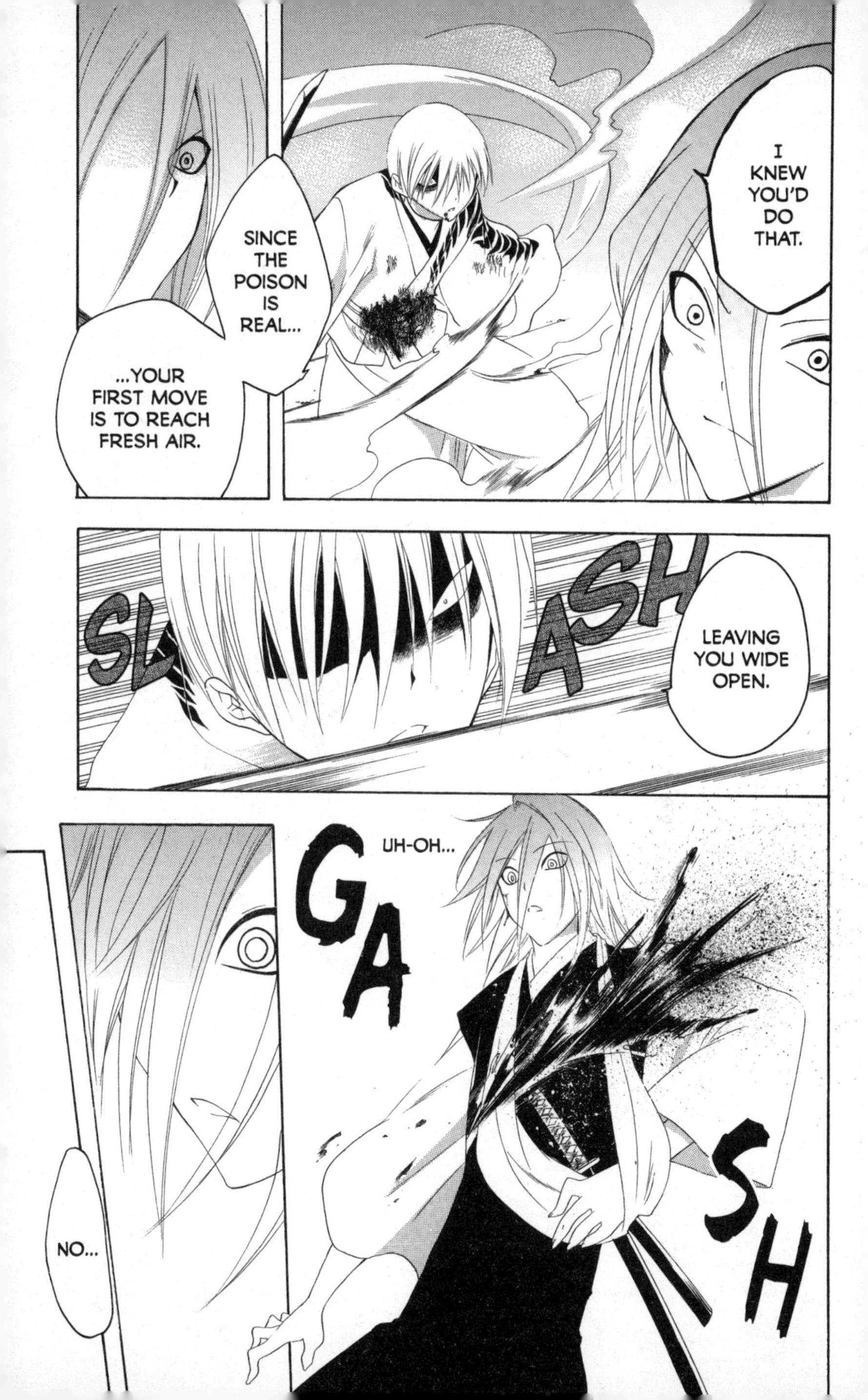
I KNEW YOU'D DO THAT.
SINCE THE POISON IS REAL...
...YOUR FIRST MOVE IS TO REACH FRESH AIR.
LEAVING YOU WIDE OPEN.
SLASH
UH-OH...
GASH
NO...

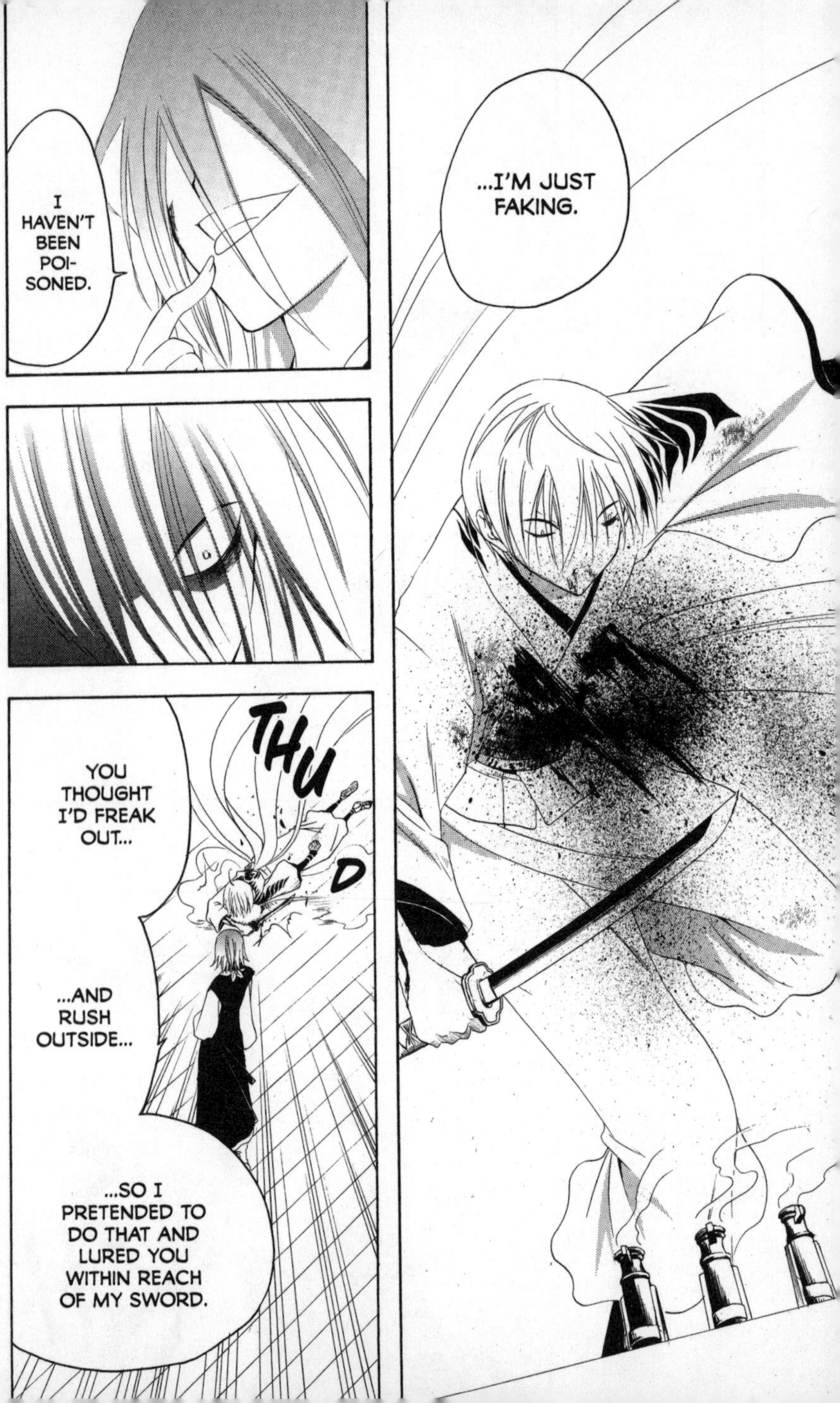
I HAVEN'T BEEN POI-SONED.
...I'M JUST FAKING.
YOU THOUGHT I'D FREAK OUT...
THUD
...AND RUSH OUTSIDE...
...SO I PRETENDED TO DO THAT AND LURED YOU WITHIN REACH OF MY SWORD.

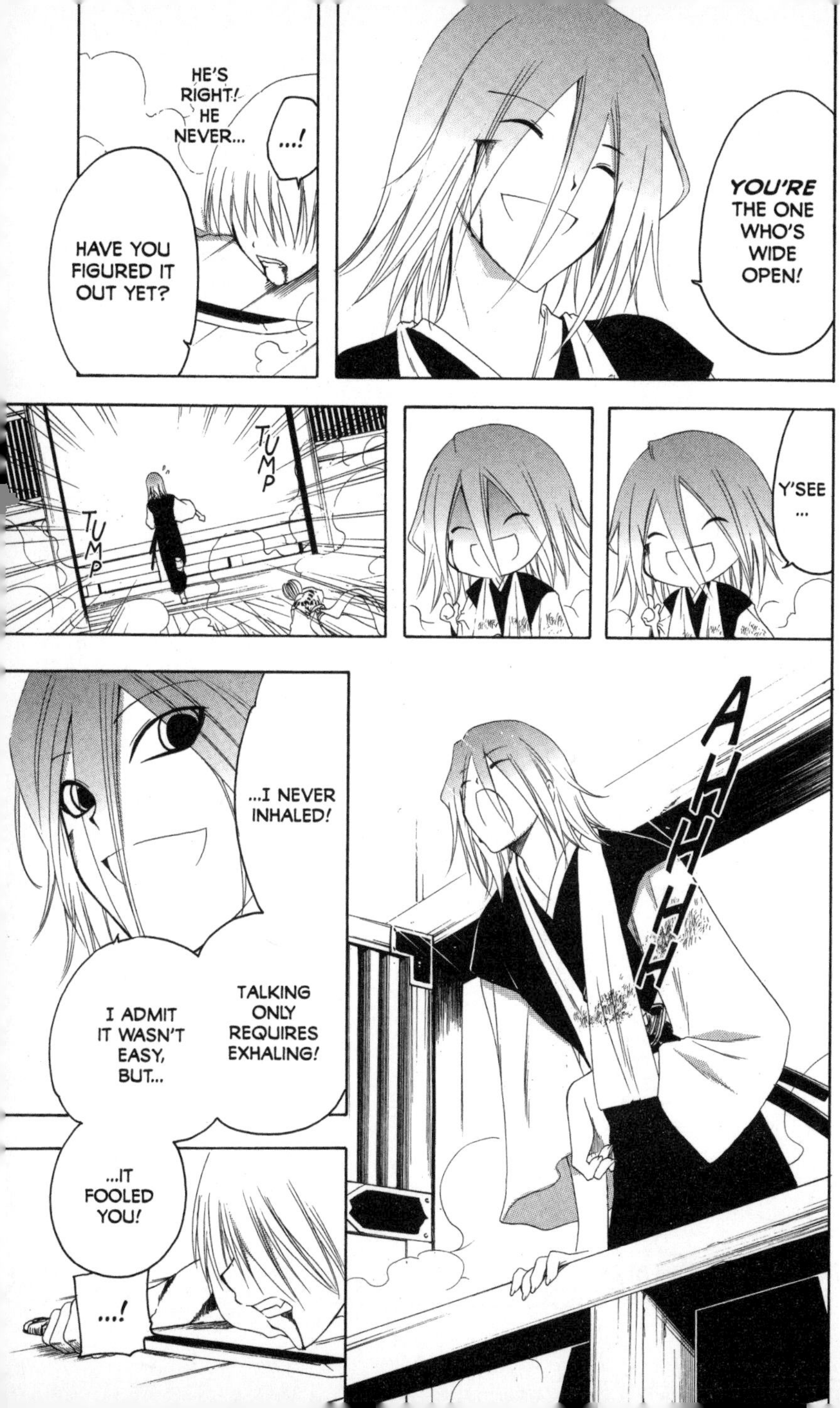
YOU'RE THE ONE WHO'S WIDE OPEN!
...!
HE'S RIGHT! HE NEVER...
HAVE YOU FIGURED IT OUT YET?
Y'SEE ...
TUMP
TUMP
AHHHHHH
...I NEVER INHALED!
TALKING ONLY REQUIRES EXHALING!
I ADMIT IT WASN'T EASY, BUT...
...IT FOOLED YOU!
...!

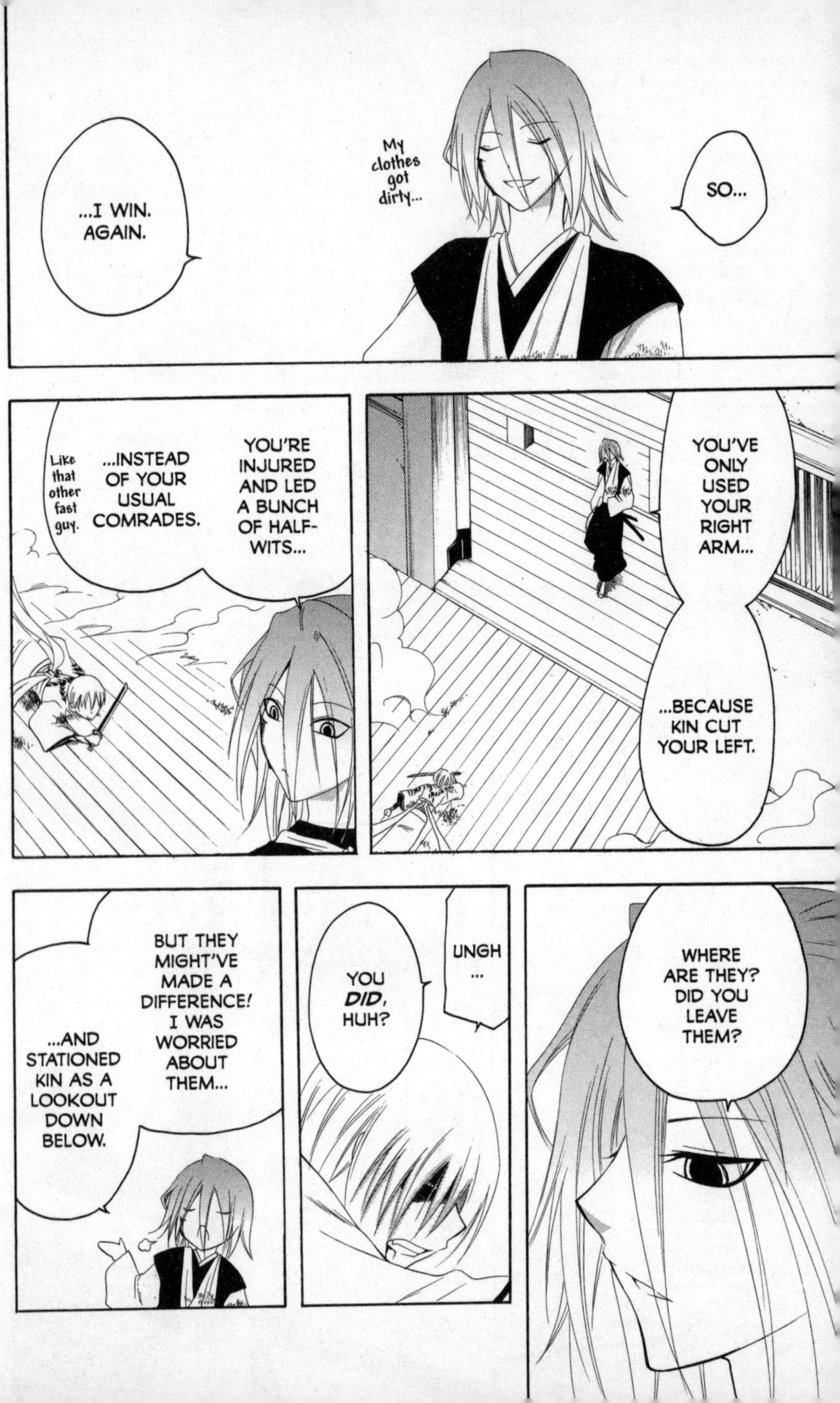
SO...
My clothes got dirty...
...I WIN. AGAIN.
YOU'VE ONLY USED YOUR RIGHT ARM...
...BECAUSE KIN CUT YOUR LEFT.
YOU'RE INJURED AND LED A BUNCH OF HALF-WITS...
...INSTEAD OF YOUR USUAL COMRADES.
Like that other fast guy.
WHERE ARE THEY? DID YOU LEAVE THEM?
UNGH ...
YOU *DID*, HUH?
BUT THEY MIGHT'VE MADE A DIFFERENCE! I WAS WORRIED ABOUT THEM...
...AND STATIONED KIN AS A LOOKOUT DOWN BELOW.

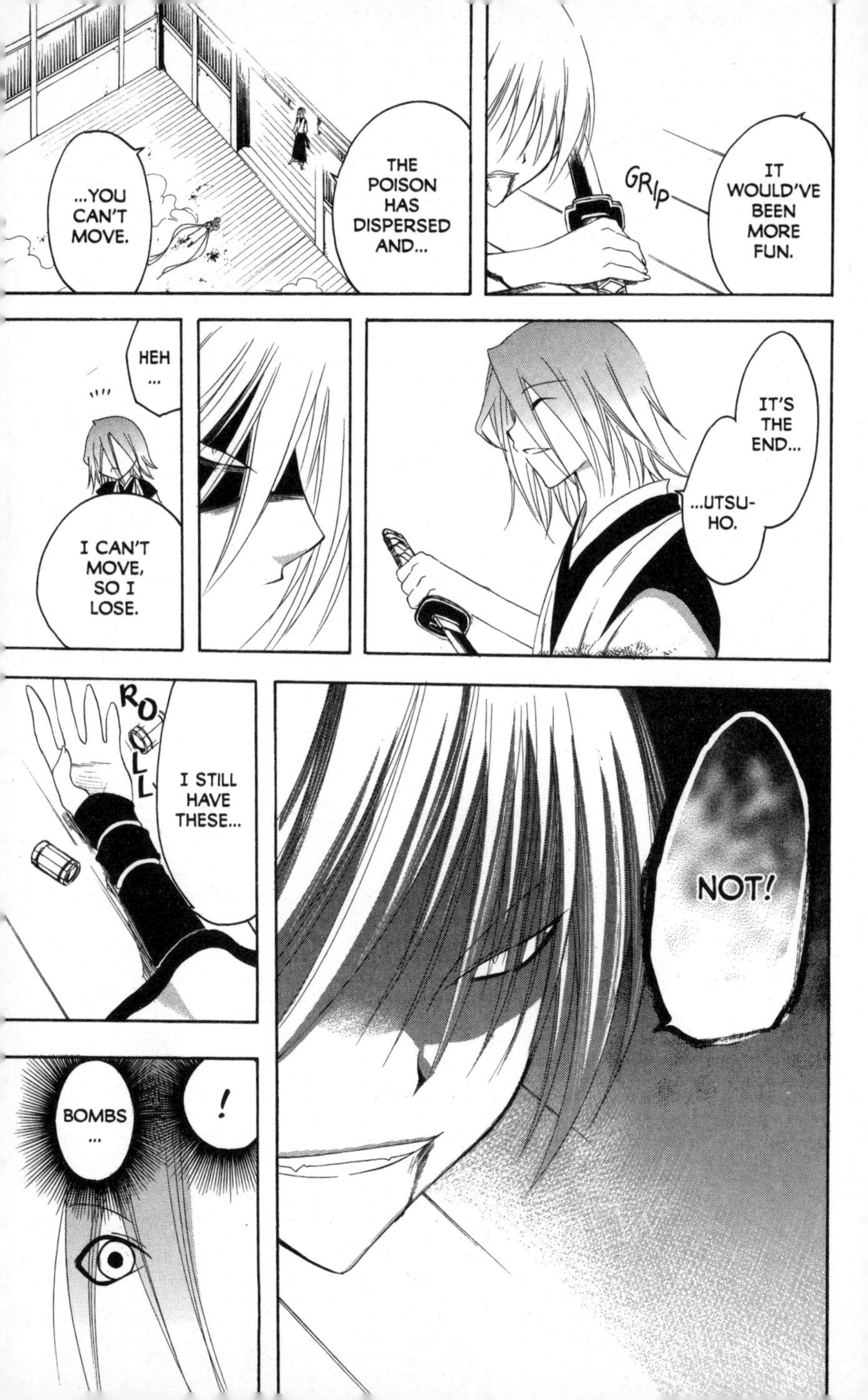
GRIP
IT WOULD'VE BEEN MORE FUN.
THE POISON HAS DISPERSED AND...
...YOU CAN'T MOVE.
IT'S THE END...
...UTSU-HO.
HEH...
I CAN'T MOVE, SO I LOSE.
NOT!
ROLL
I STILL HAVE THESE...
!
BOMBS...

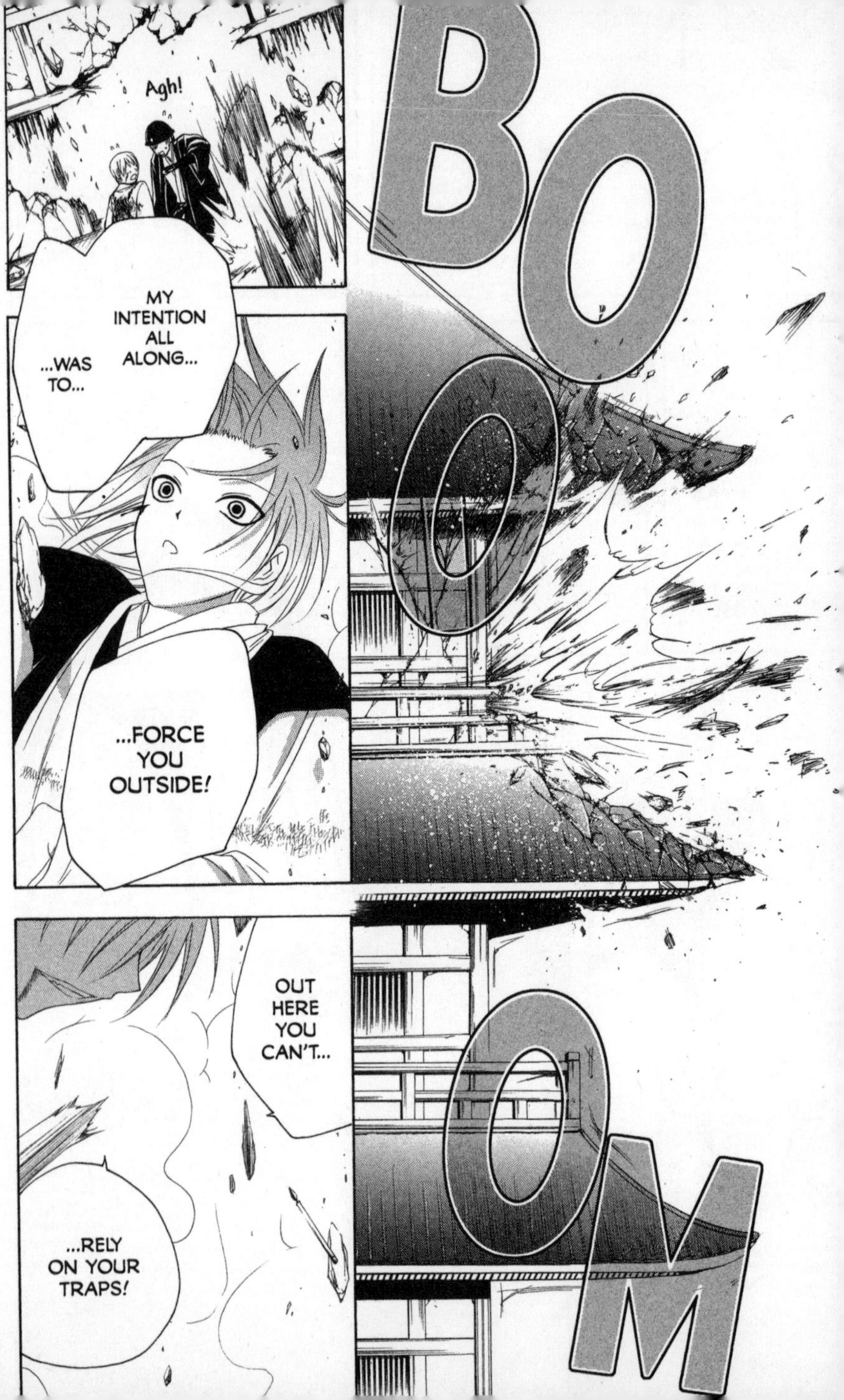
BOOOM
Agh!
MY INTENTION ALL ALONG...
...WAS TO...
...FORCE YOU OUTSIDE!
OUT HERE YOU CAN'T...
...RELY ON YOUR TRAPS!

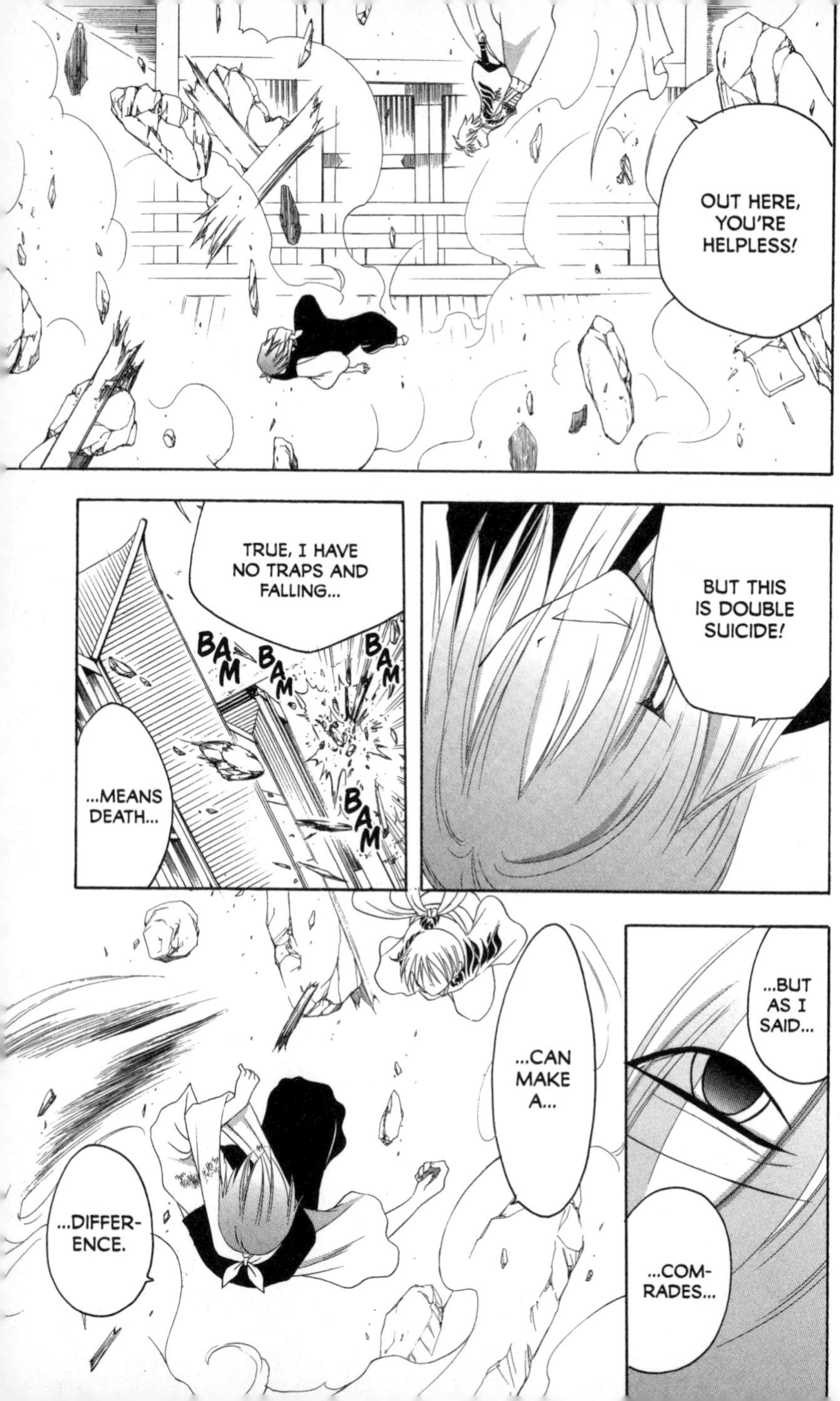

OUT HERE, YOU'RE HELPLESS!
BUT THIS IS DOUBLE SUICIDE!
TRUE, I HAVE NO TRAPS AND FALLING...
BAM BAM BAM BAM
...MEANS DEATH...
...BUT AS I SAID...
...COMRADES...
...CAN MAKE A...
...DIFFER-ENCE.

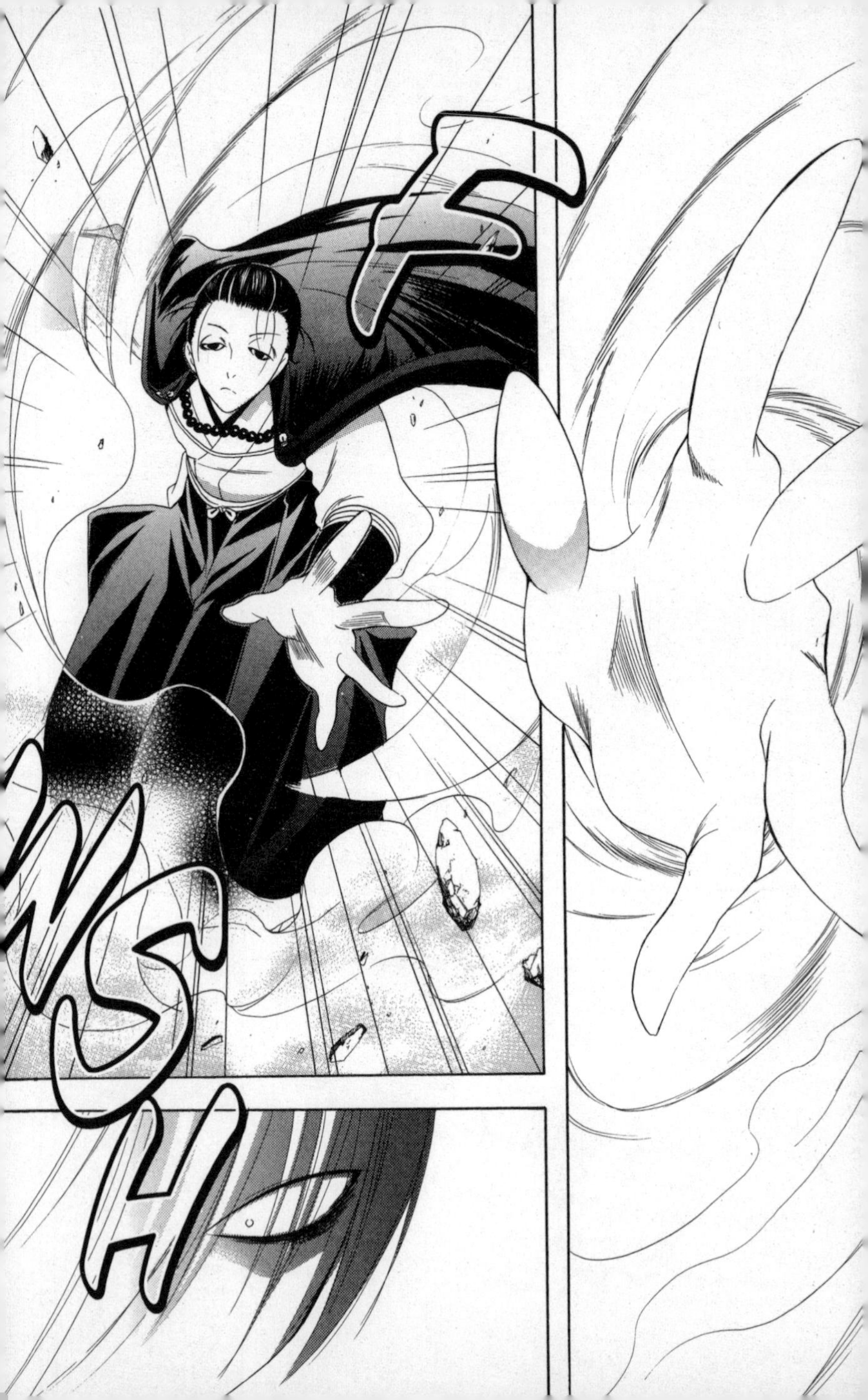
F
WSH

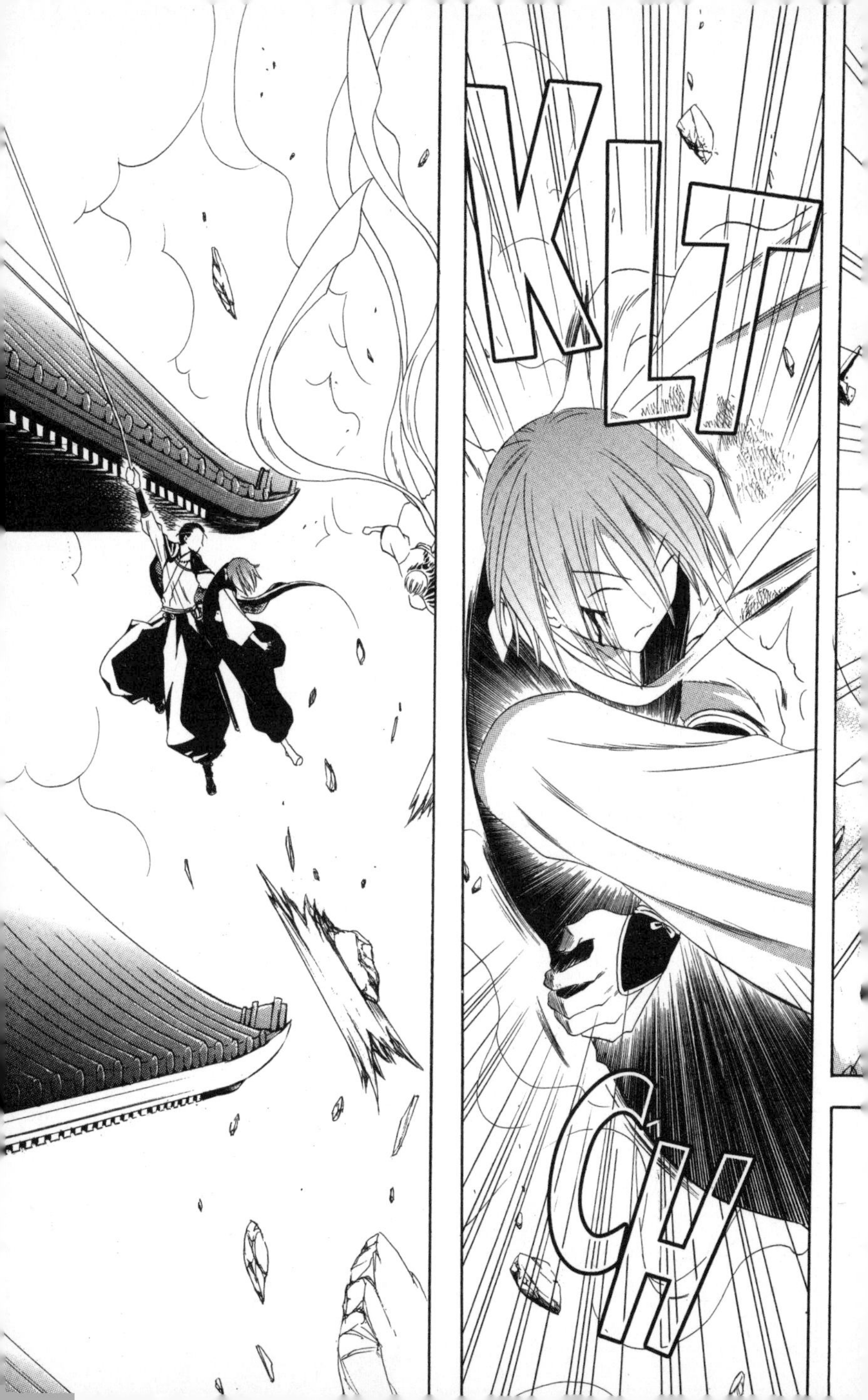
KLIT
CH

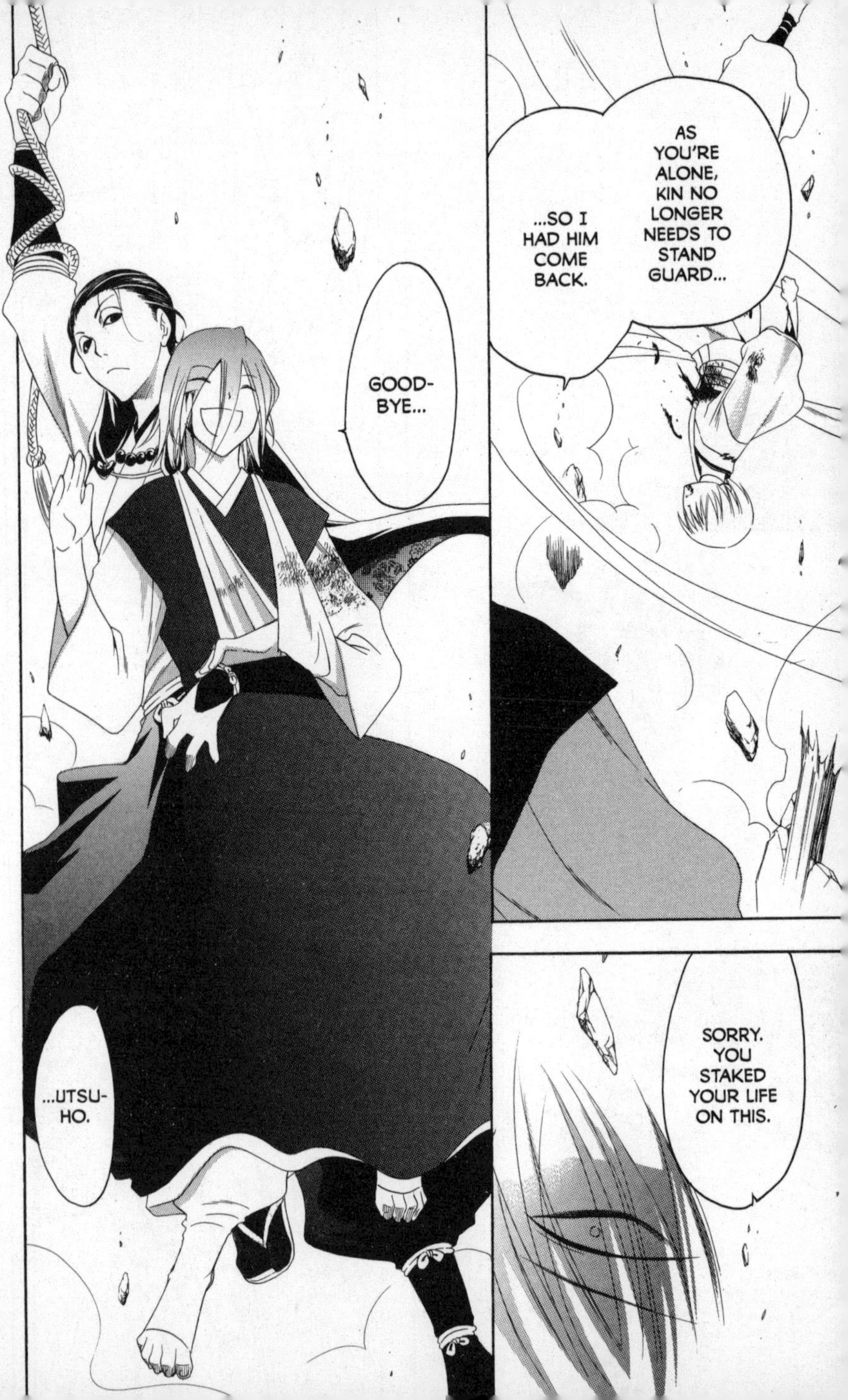
AS YOU'RE ALONE, KIN NO LONGER NEEDS TO STAND GUARD...
...SO I HAD HIM COME BACK.
SORRY. YOU STAKED YOUR LIFE ON THIS.
GOOD-BYE...
...UTSU-HO.

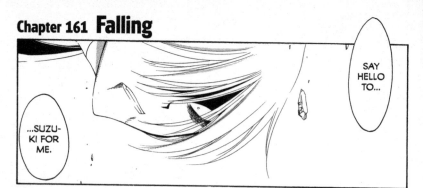

SAY HELLO TO...

...SUZU-KI FOR ME.

IS IT OVER NOW?

YEP.

HE WON'T SURVIVE THAT FALL.

AND IT WAS OKAY TO LEAVE MY POST?

....!

...

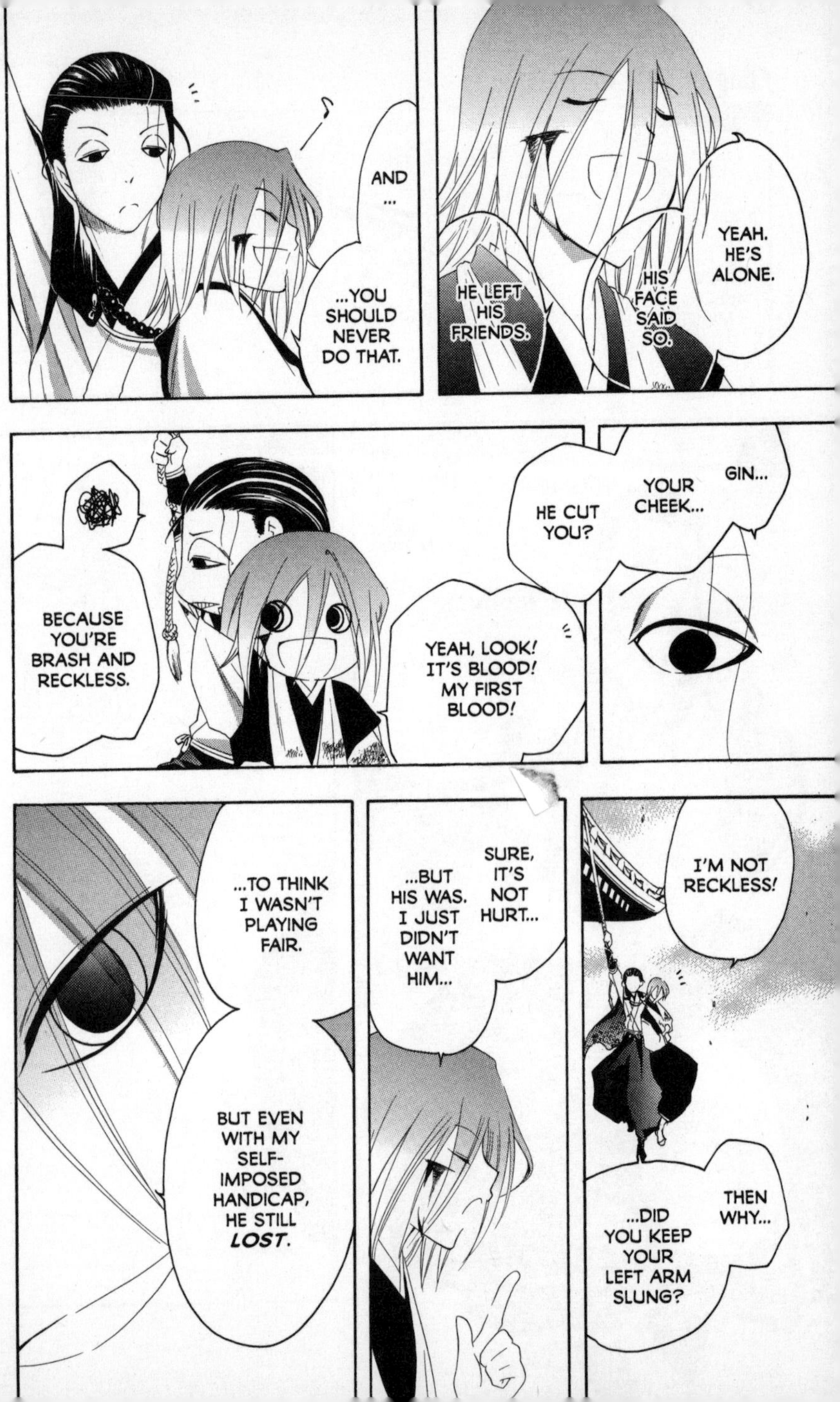
YEAH. HE'S ALONE.
HIS FACE SAID SO.
HE LEFT HIS FRIENDS.
AND ...
...YOU SHOULD NEVER DO THAT.
GIN...
YOUR CHEEK...
HE CUT YOU?
YEAH, LOOK! IT'S BLOOD! MY FIRST BLOOD!
BECAUSE YOU'RE BRASH AND RECKLESS.
I'M NOT RECKLESS!
THEN WHY...
...DID YOU KEEP YOUR LEFT ARM SLUNG?
SURE, IT'S NOT HURT...
...BUT HIS WAS. I JUST DIDN'T WANT HIM...
...TO THINK I WASN'T PLAYING FAIR.
BUT EVEN WITH MY SELF-IMPOSED HANDICAP, HE STILL *LOST*.

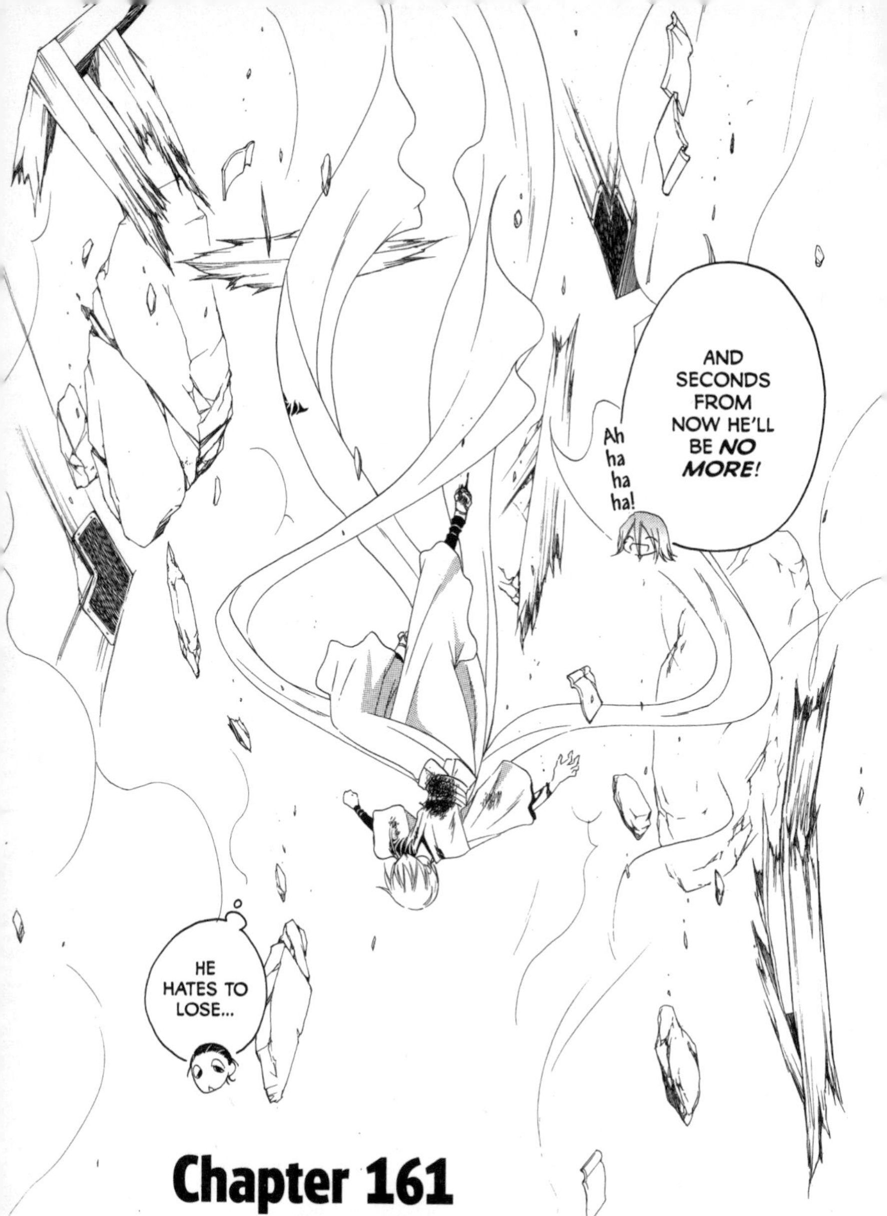
AND SECONDS FROM NOW HE'LL BE ***NO MORE!***
Ah ha ha ha!
HE HATES TO LOSE...

Chapter 161
Falling

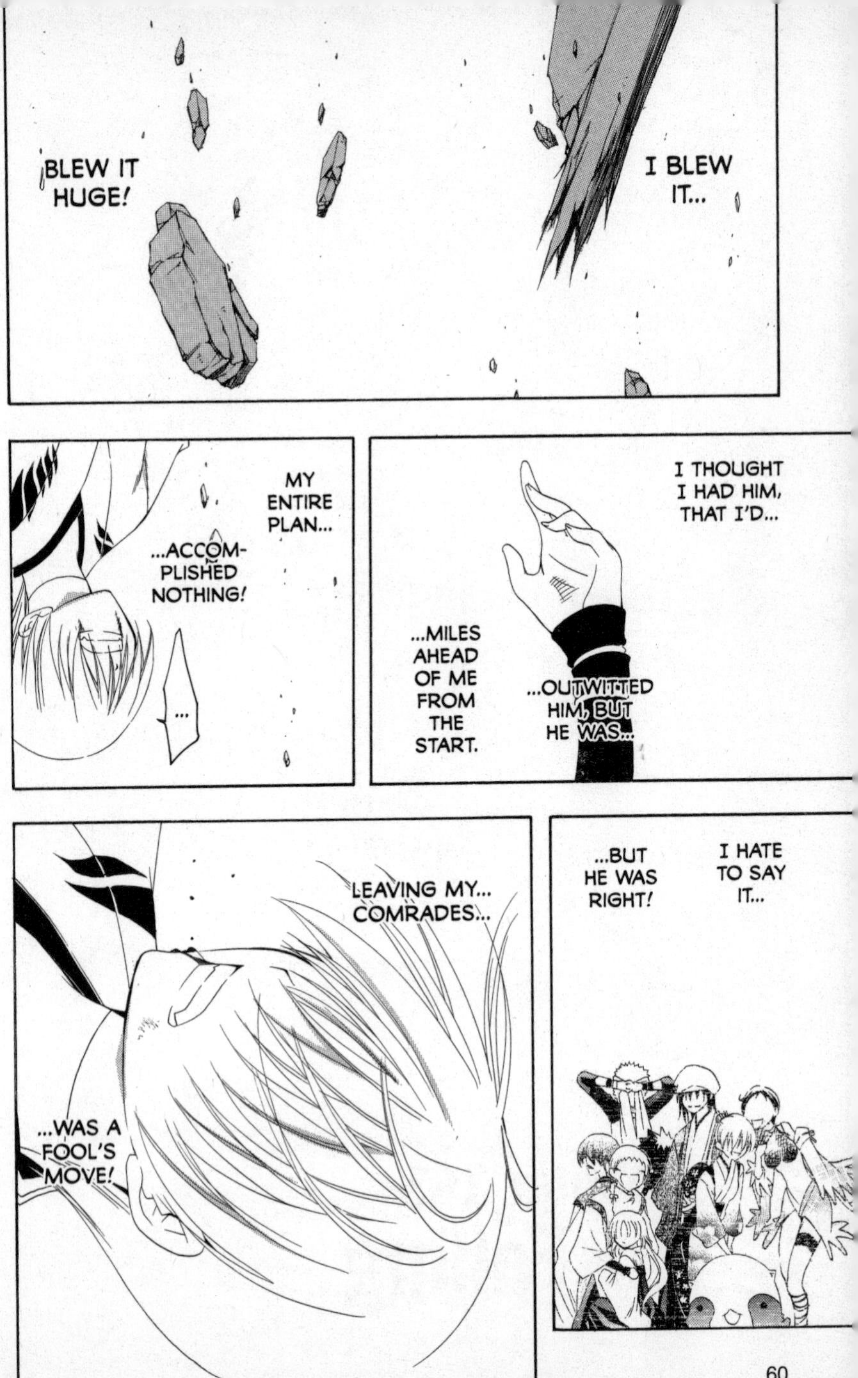
I BLEW IT...
BLEW IT HUGE!
I THOUGHT I HAD HIM, THAT I'D...
...OUTWITTED HIM, BUT HE WAS...
...MILES AHEAD OF ME FROM THE START.
MY ENTIRE PLAN...
...ACCOM-PLISHED NOTHING!
...
I HATE TO SAY IT...
...BUT HE WAS RIGHT!
LEAVING MY... COMRADES...
...WAS A FOOL'S MOVE!

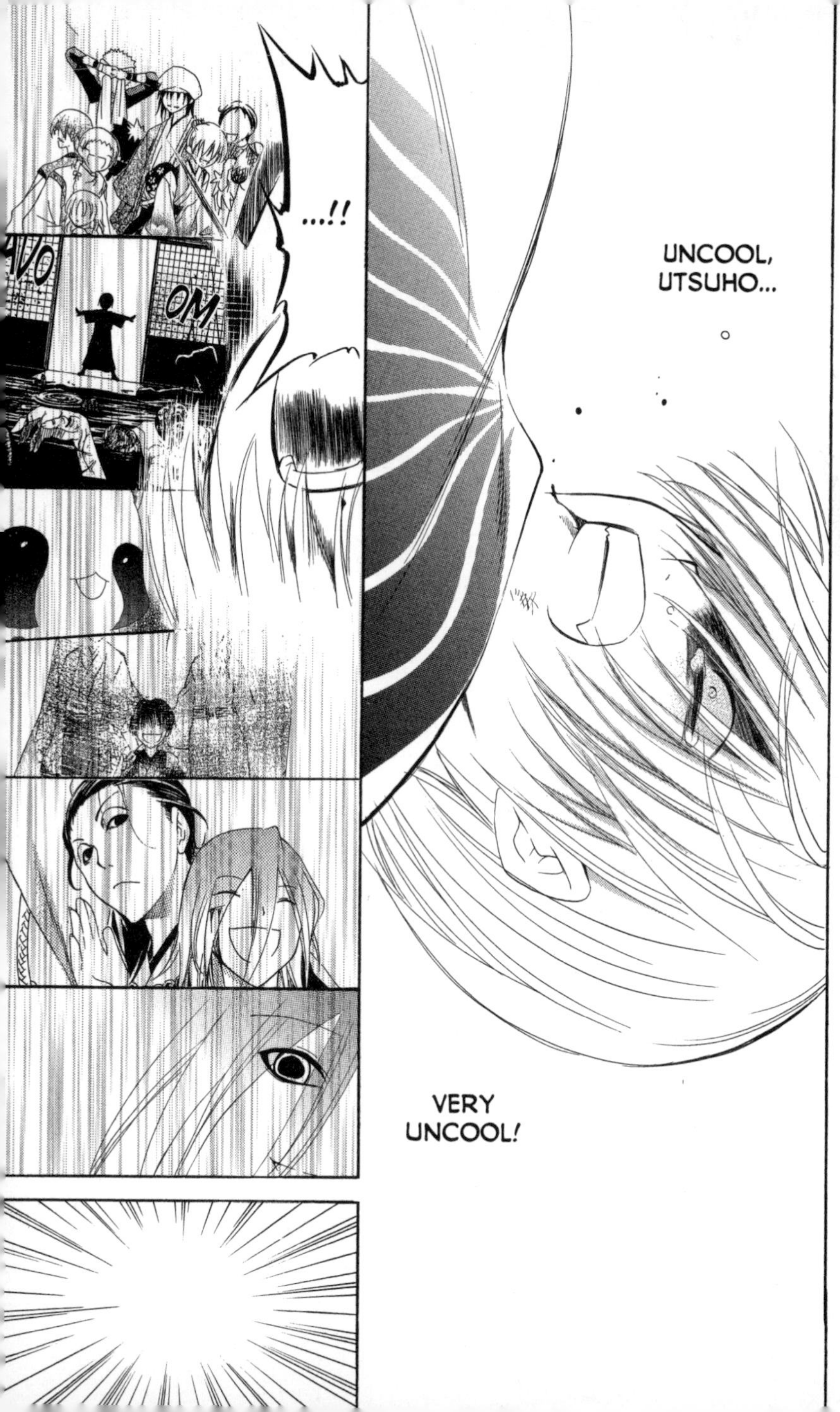
UNCOOL, UTSUHO...
VERY UNCOOL!
...!!
VO
OM

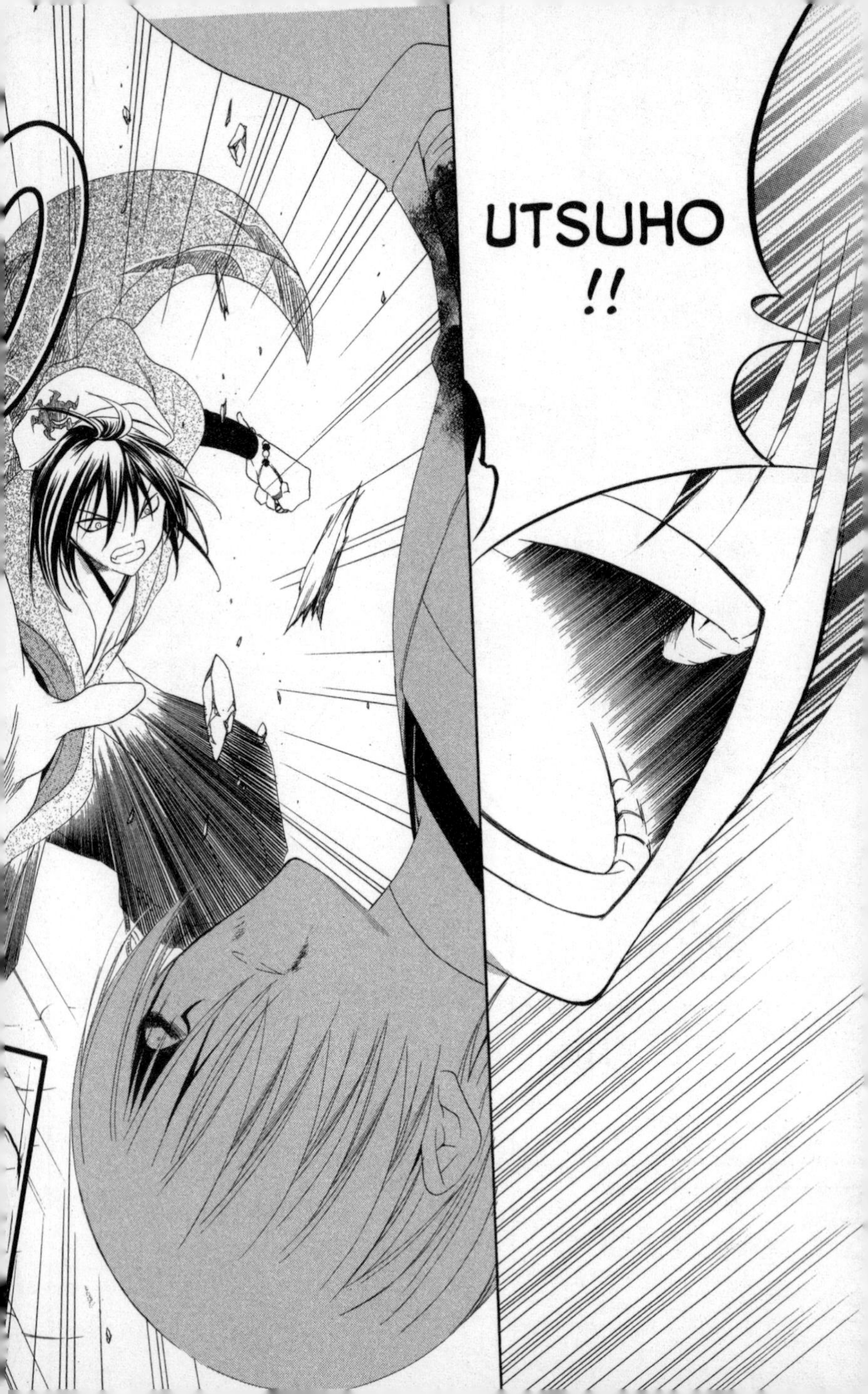
UTSUHO
!!

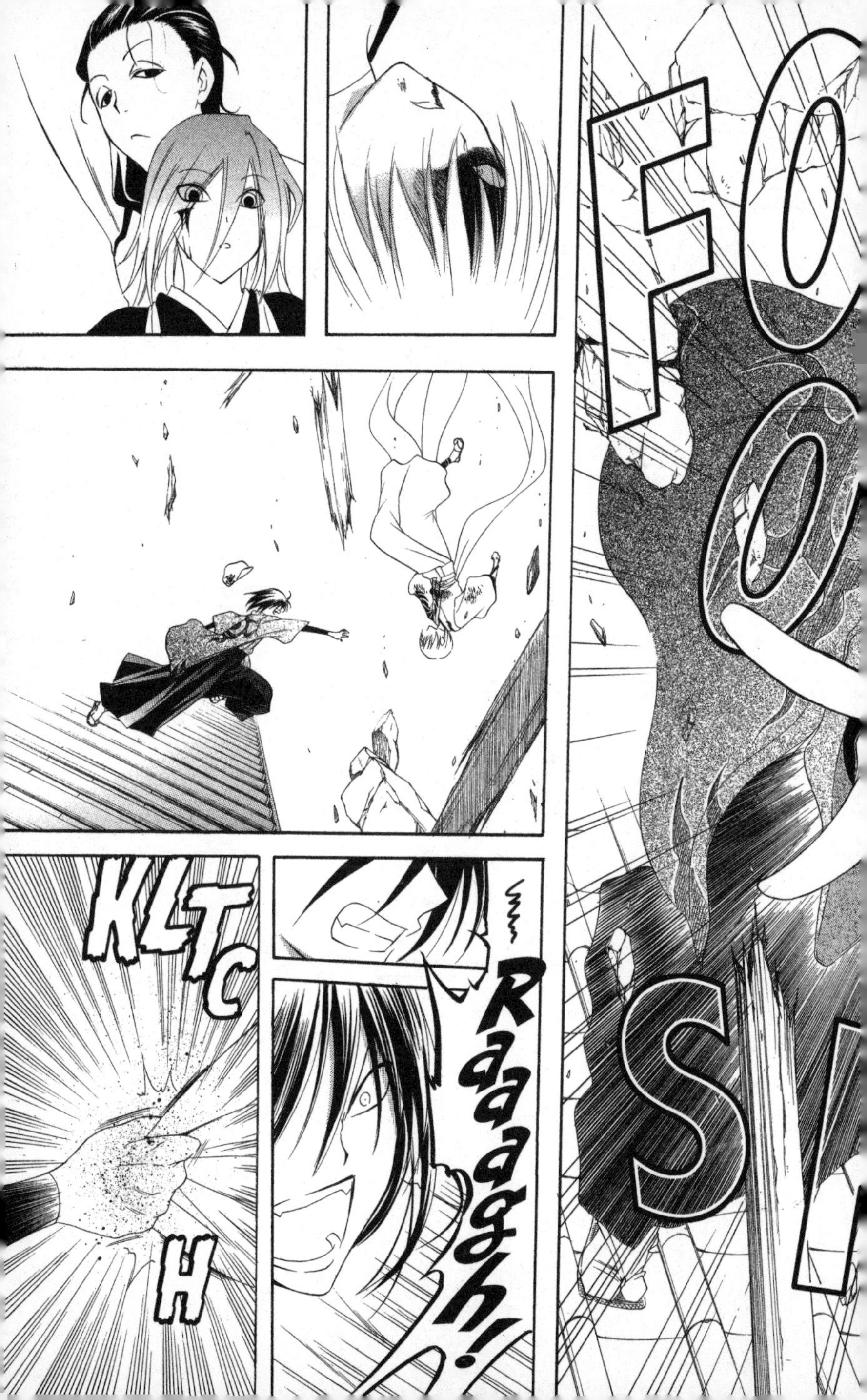
FOOS
Raaaagh!!
KLTCH

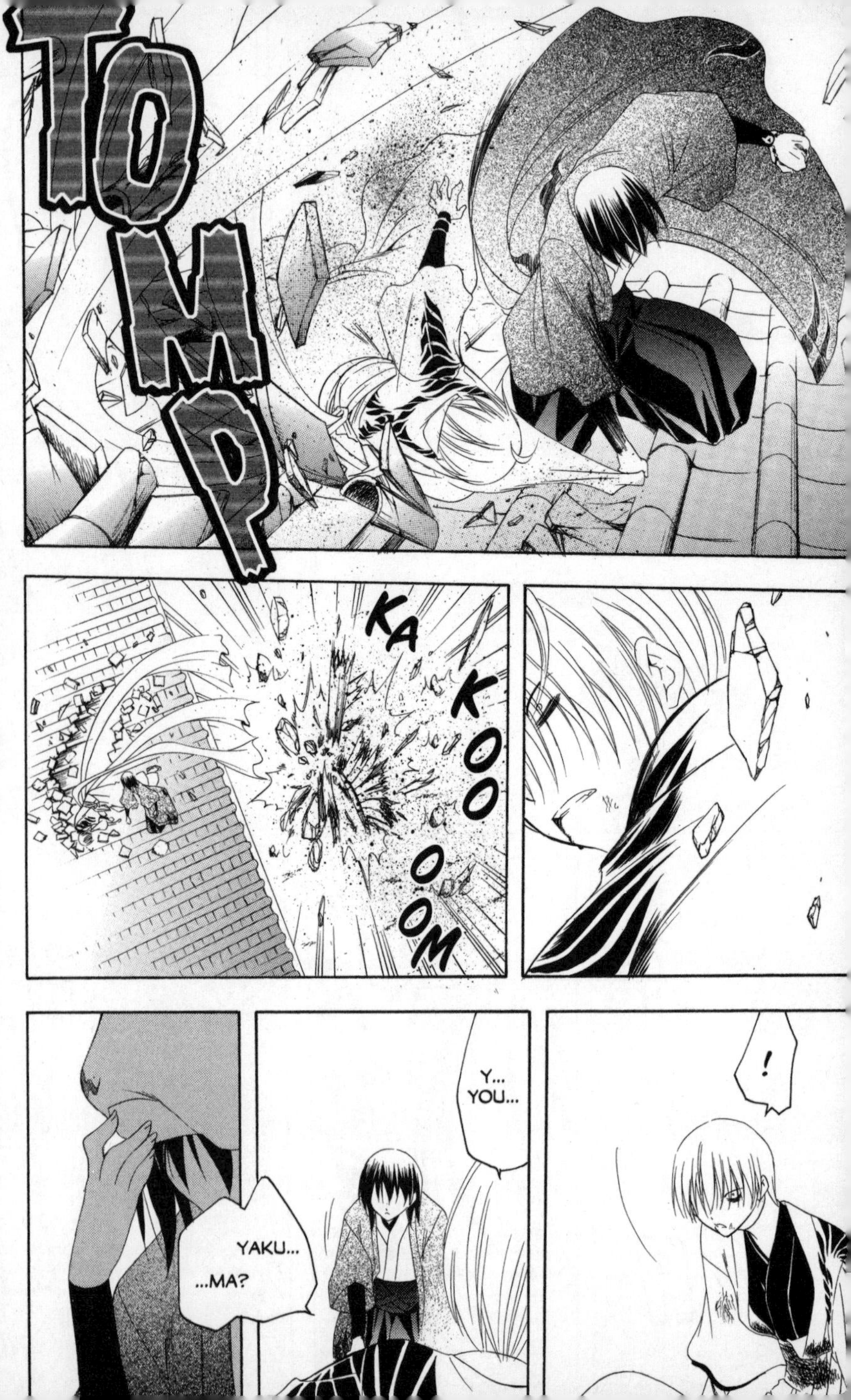
TOMP
KAKOOOOM
!
Y... YOU...
YAKU... ...MA?

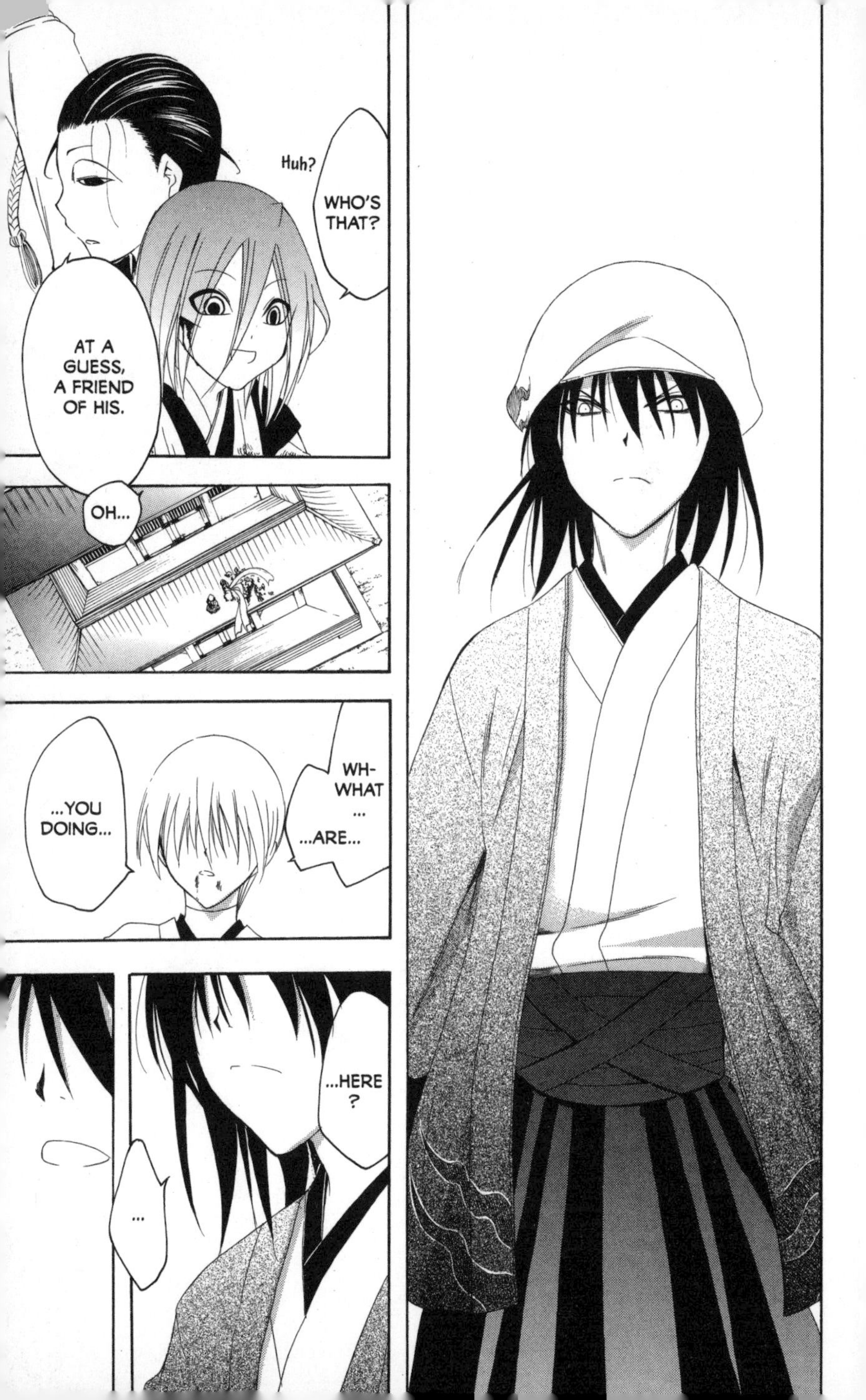
Huh?
WHO'S THAT?
AT A GUESS, A FRIEND OF HIS.
OH...
WH- WHAT ... ...ARE...
...YOU DOING...
...HERE ?
...

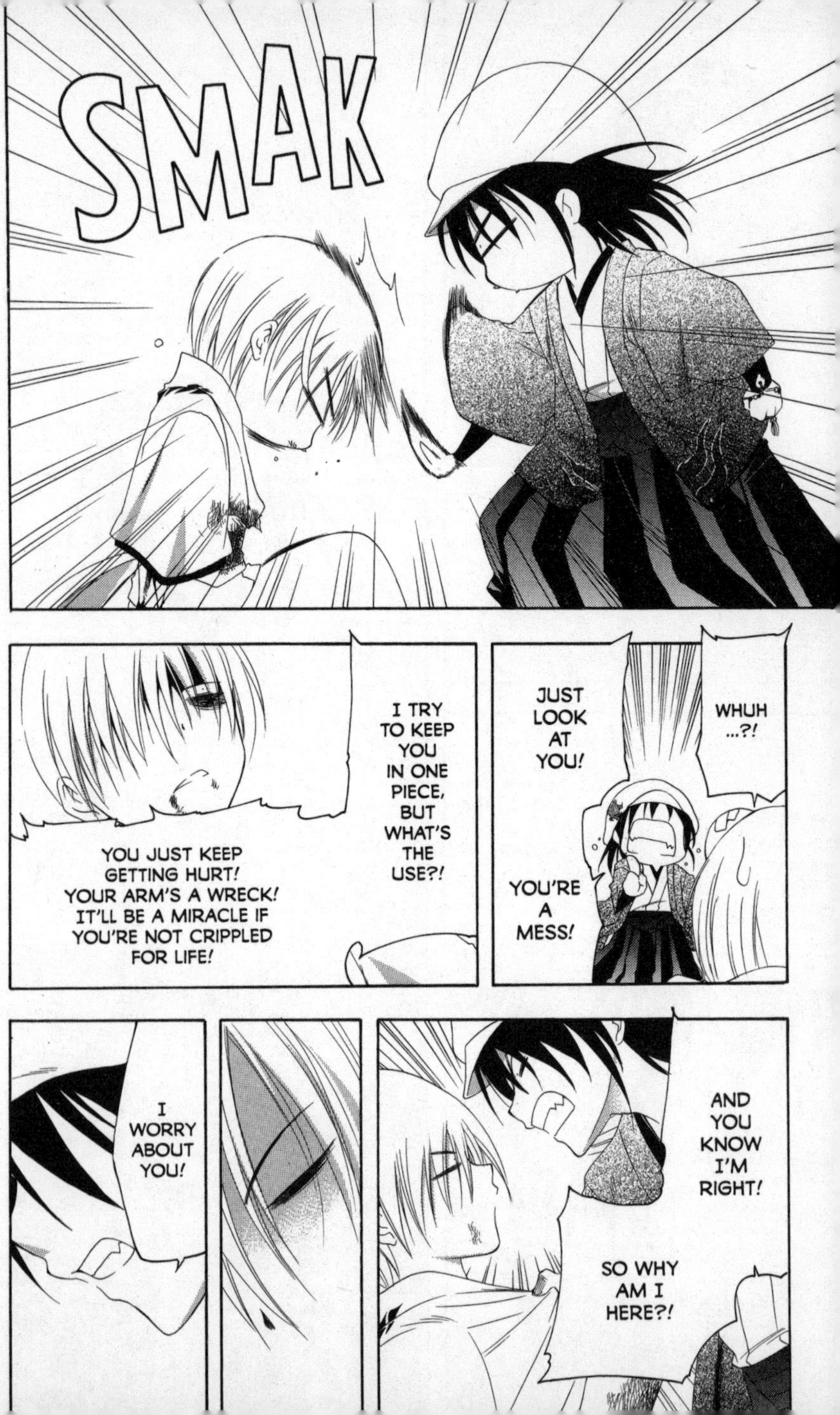
SMAK
WHUH ...?!
JUST LOOK AT YOU!
YOU'RE A MESS!
I TRY TO KEEP YOU IN ONE PIECE, BUT WHAT'S THE USE?!
YOU JUST KEEP GETTING HURT! YOUR ARM'S A WRECK! IT'LL BE A MIRACLE IF YOU'RE NOT CRIPPLED FOR LIFE!
AND YOU KNOW I'M RIGHT!
SO WHY AM I HERE?!
I WORRY ABOUT YOU!

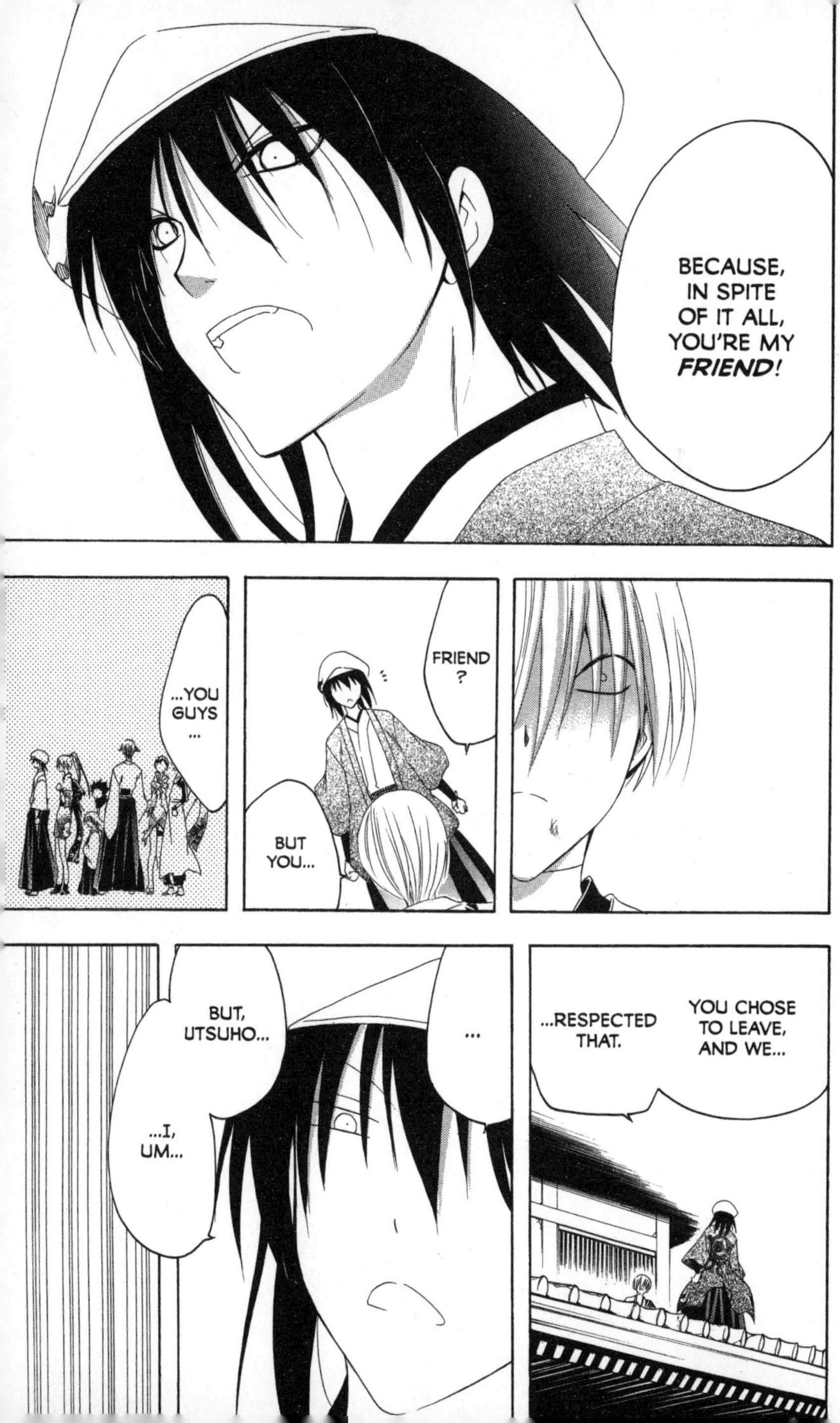
BECAUSE, IN SPITE OF IT ALL, YOU'RE MY *FRIEND*!
FRIEND?
BUT YOU...
...YOU GUYS ...
YOU CHOSE TO LEAVE, AND WE...
...RESPECTED THAT.
...
BUT, UTSUHO...
...I, UM...

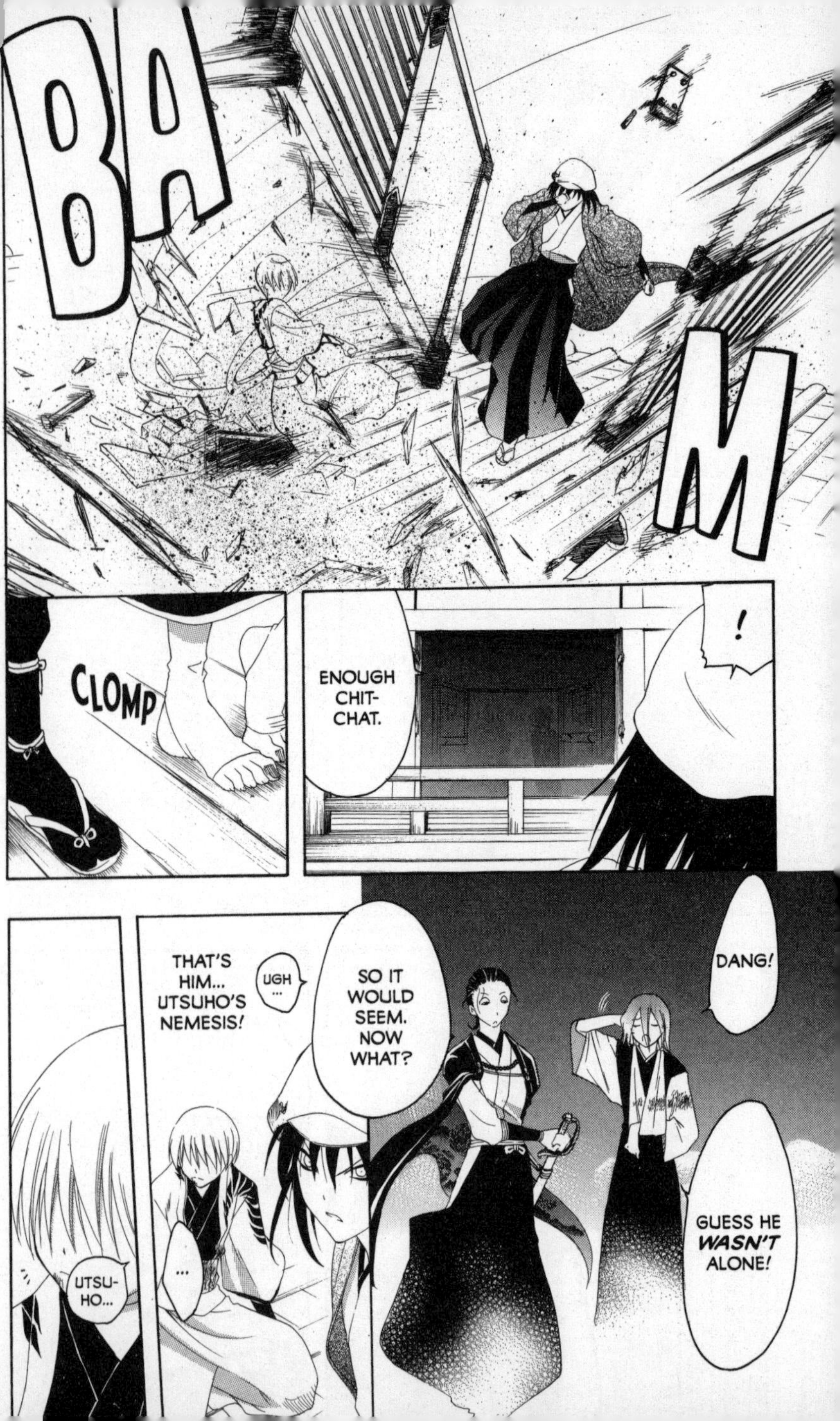
BAM
!
ENOUGH CHIT-CHAT.
CLOMP
DANG!
GUESS HE *WASN'T* ALONE!
SO IT WOULD SEEM. NOW WHAT?
UGH...
THAT'S HIM... UTSUHO'S NEMESIS!
...
UTSU-HO...

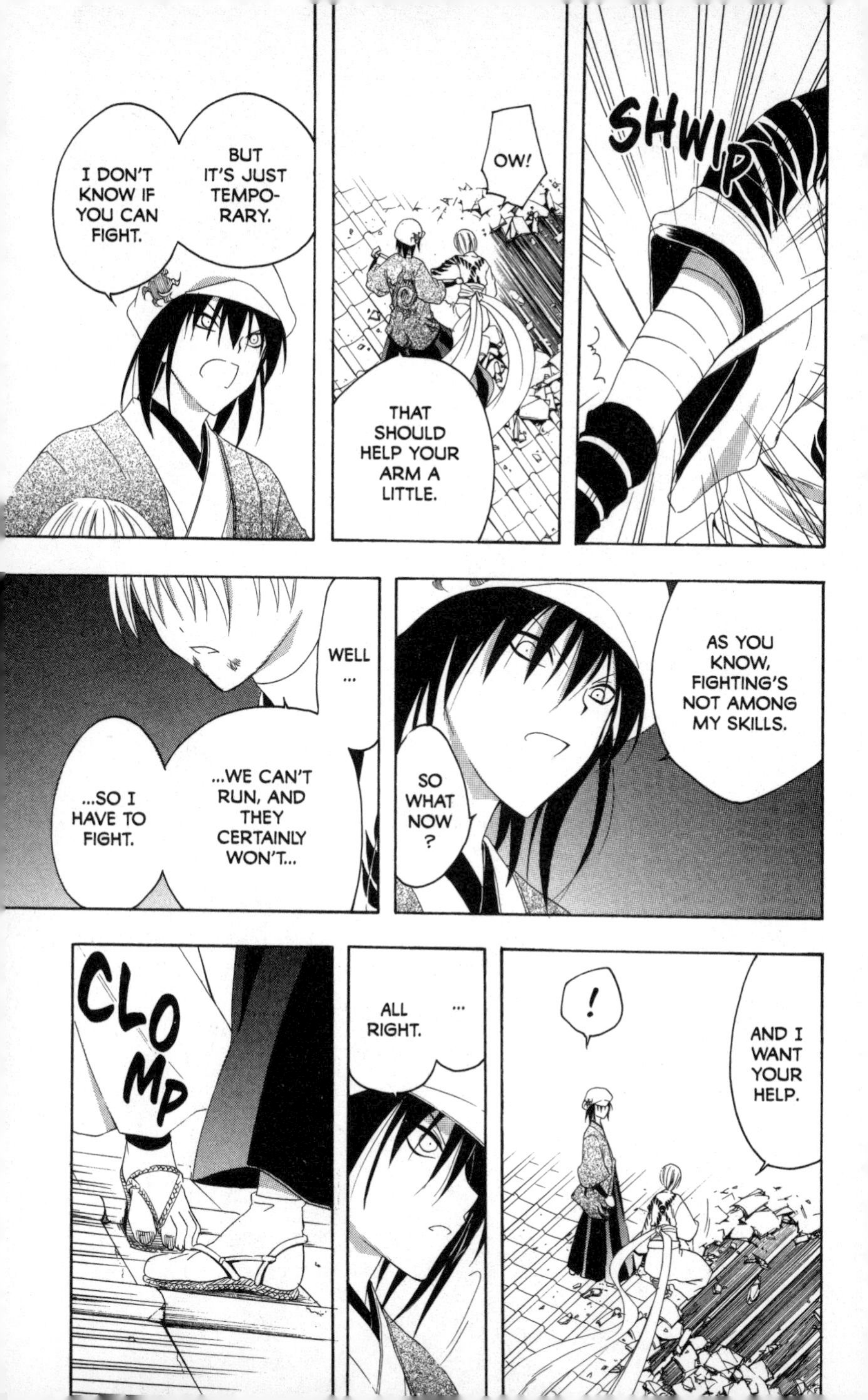
SHWIP
OW!
THAT SHOULD HELP YOUR ARM A LITTLE.
BUT IT'S JUST TEMPO-RARY.
I DON'T KNOW IF YOU CAN FIGHT.
AS YOU KNOW, FIGHTING'S NOT AMONG MY SKILLS.
SO WHAT NOW?
WELL...
...WE CAN'T RUN, AND THEY CERTAINLY WON'T...
...SO I HAVE TO FIGHT.
AND I WANT YOUR HELP.
!
... ALL RIGHT.
CLOMP

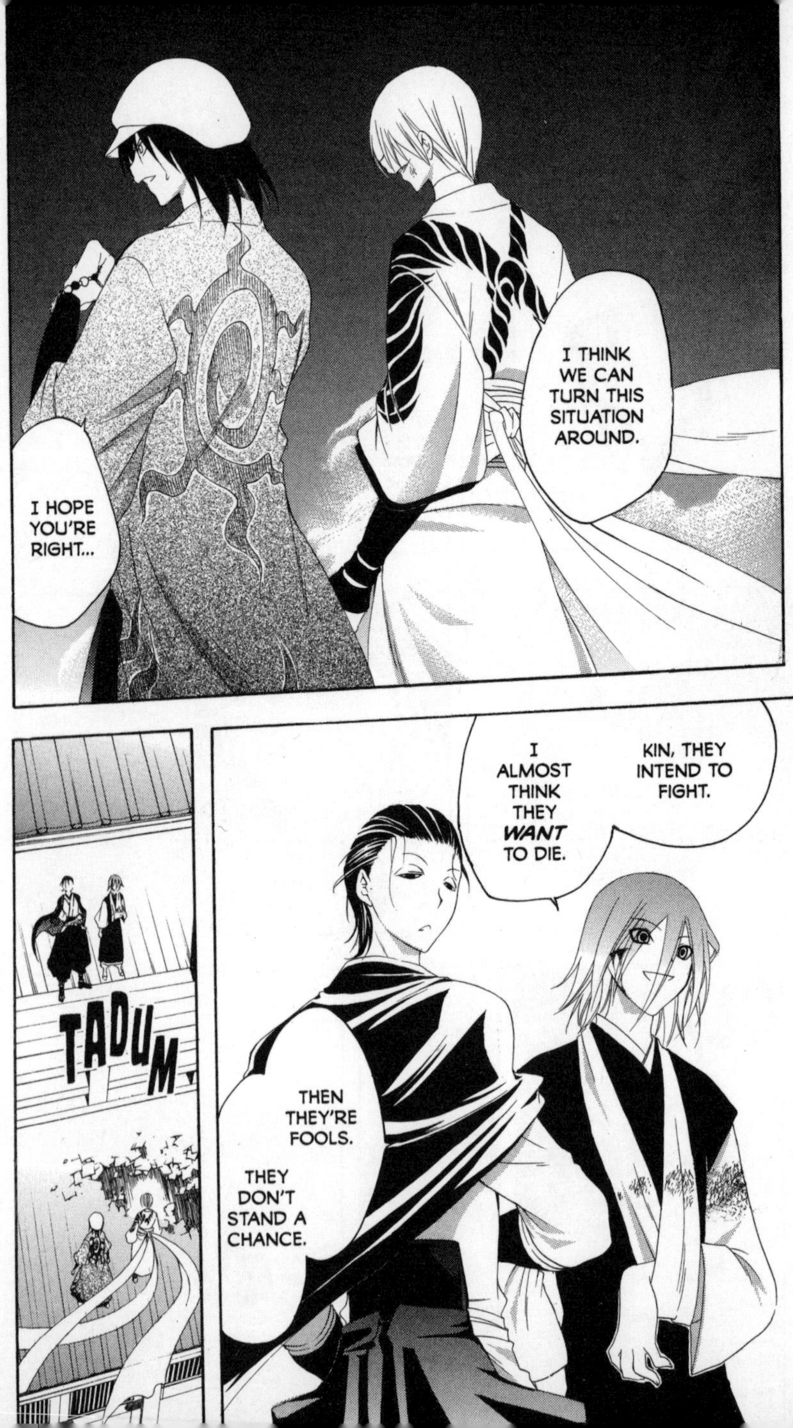
I THINK WE CAN TURN THIS SITUATION AROUND.
I HOPE YOU'RE RIGHT...
KIN, THEY INTEND TO FIGHT.
I ALMOST THINK THEY *WANT* TO DIE.
THEN THEY'RE FOOLS.
THEY DON'T STAND A CHANCE.
TADUM

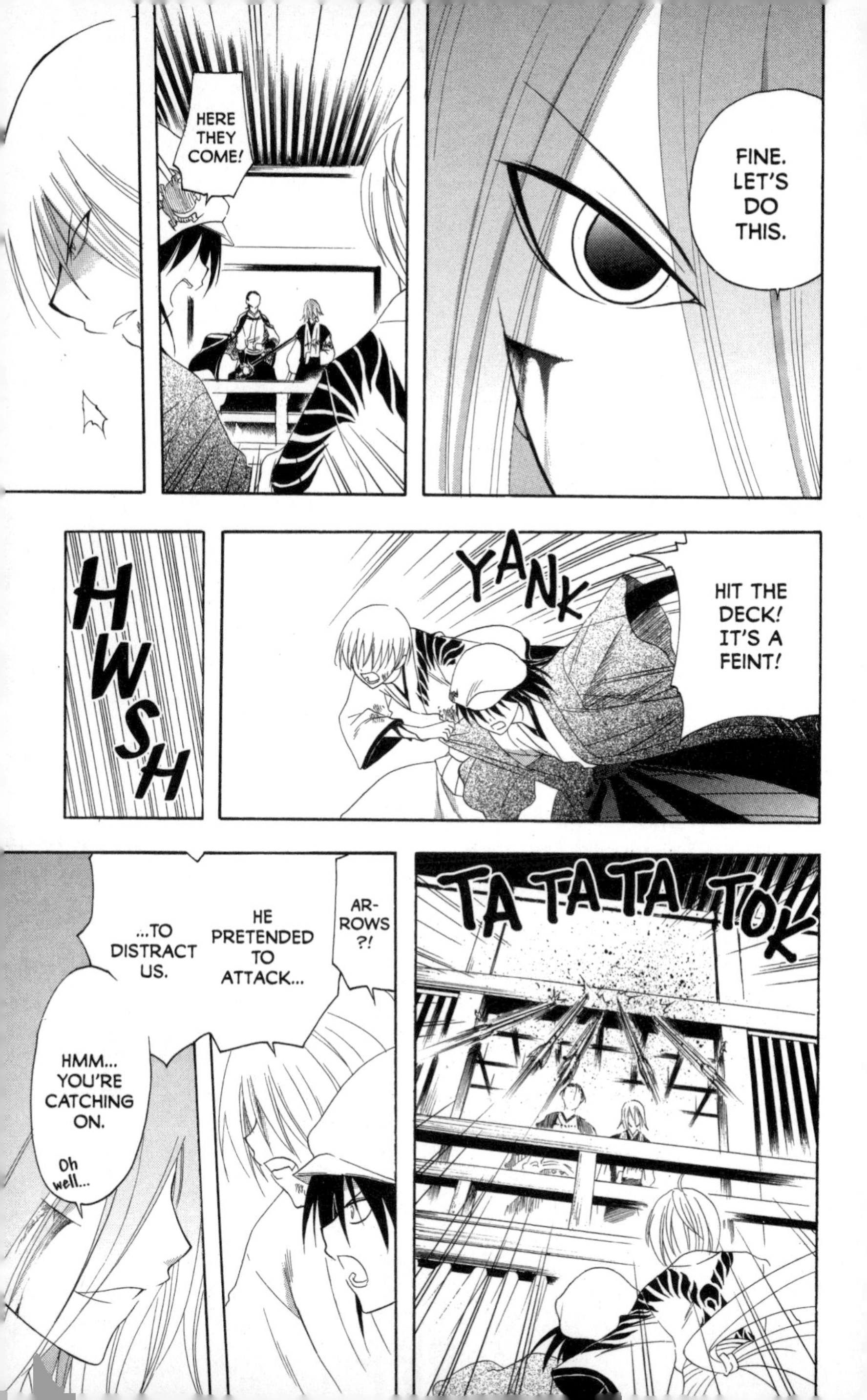
FINE. LET'S DO THIS.
HERE THEY COME!
HIT THE DECK! IT'S A FEINT!
YANK
HWSH
TA TA TA TOK
AR-ROWS?!
HE PRETENDED TO ATTACK...
...TO DISTRACT US.
HMM... YOU'RE CATCHING ON.
Oh well...

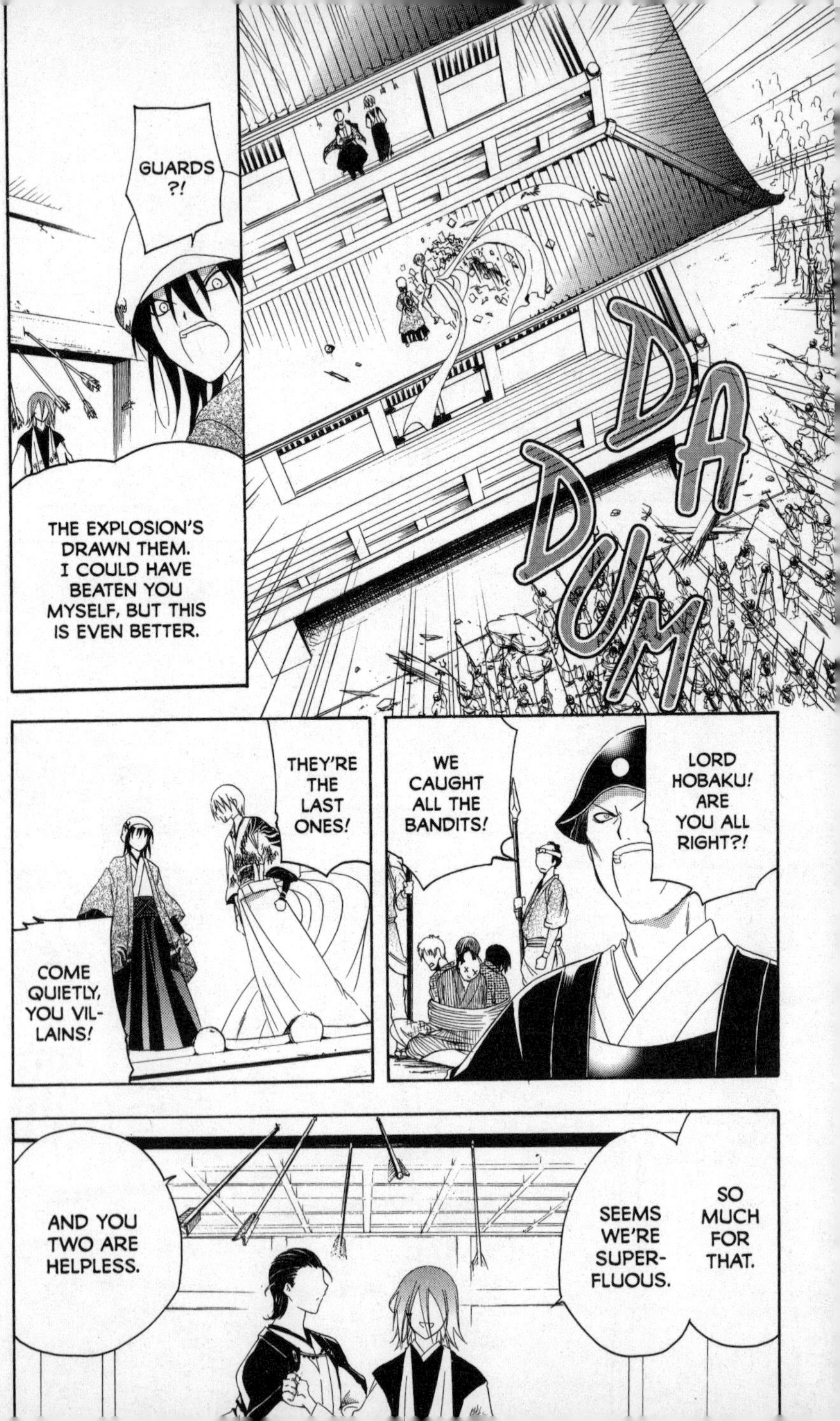
DA DUM
GUARDS?!
THE EXPLOSION'S DRAWN THEM. I COULD HAVE BEATEN YOU MYSELF, BUT THIS IS EVEN BETTER.
LORD HOBAKU! ARE YOU ALL RIGHT?!
WE CAUGHT ALL THE BANDITS!
THEY'RE THE LAST ONES!
COME QUIETLY, YOU VILLAINS!
SO MUCH FOR THAT.
SEEMS WE'RE SUPERFLUOUS.
AND YOU TWO ARE HELPLESS.

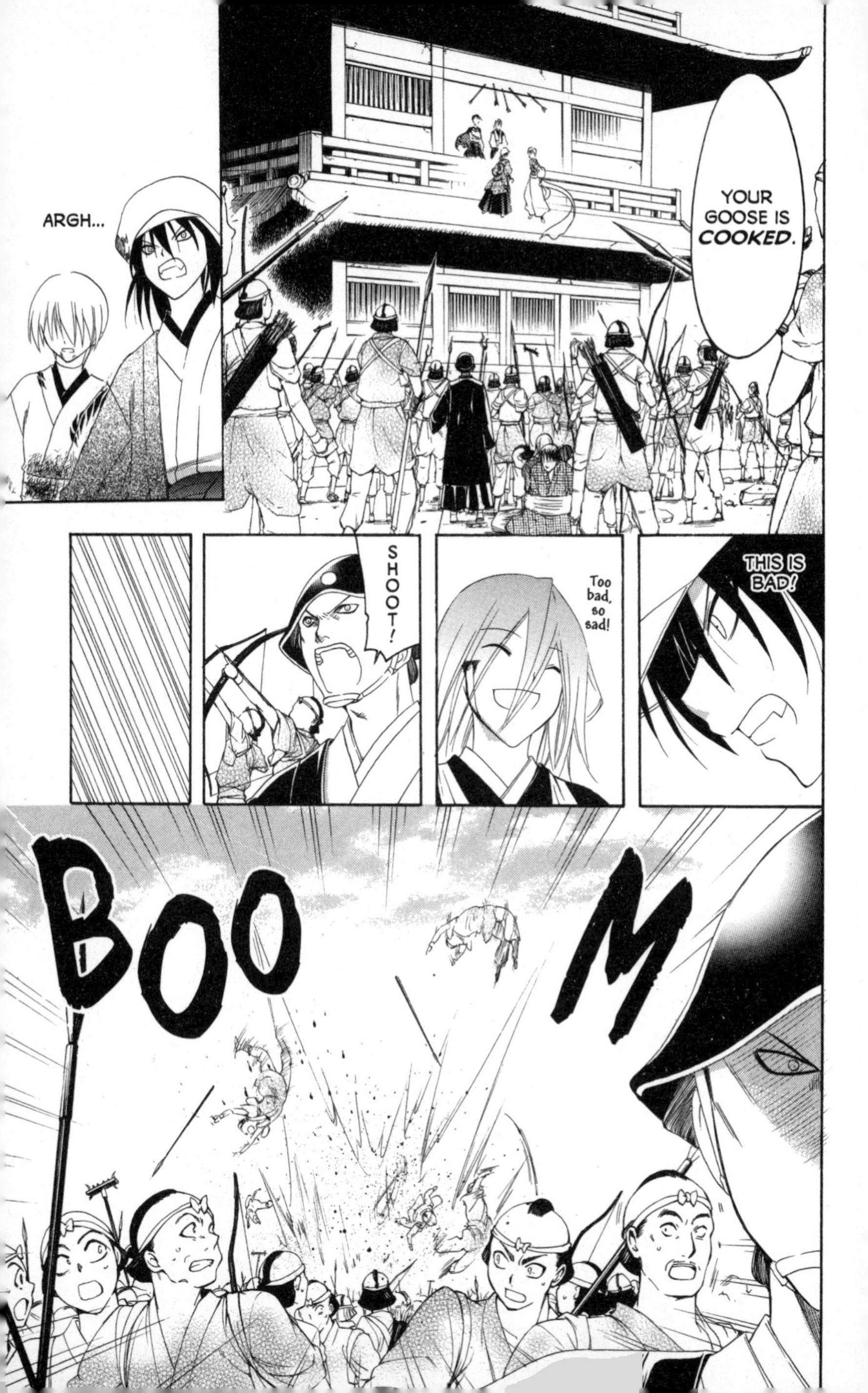
YOUR GOOSE IS *COOKED*.
ARGH...
THIS IS BAD!
Too bad, so sad!
SHOOT!
BOOM

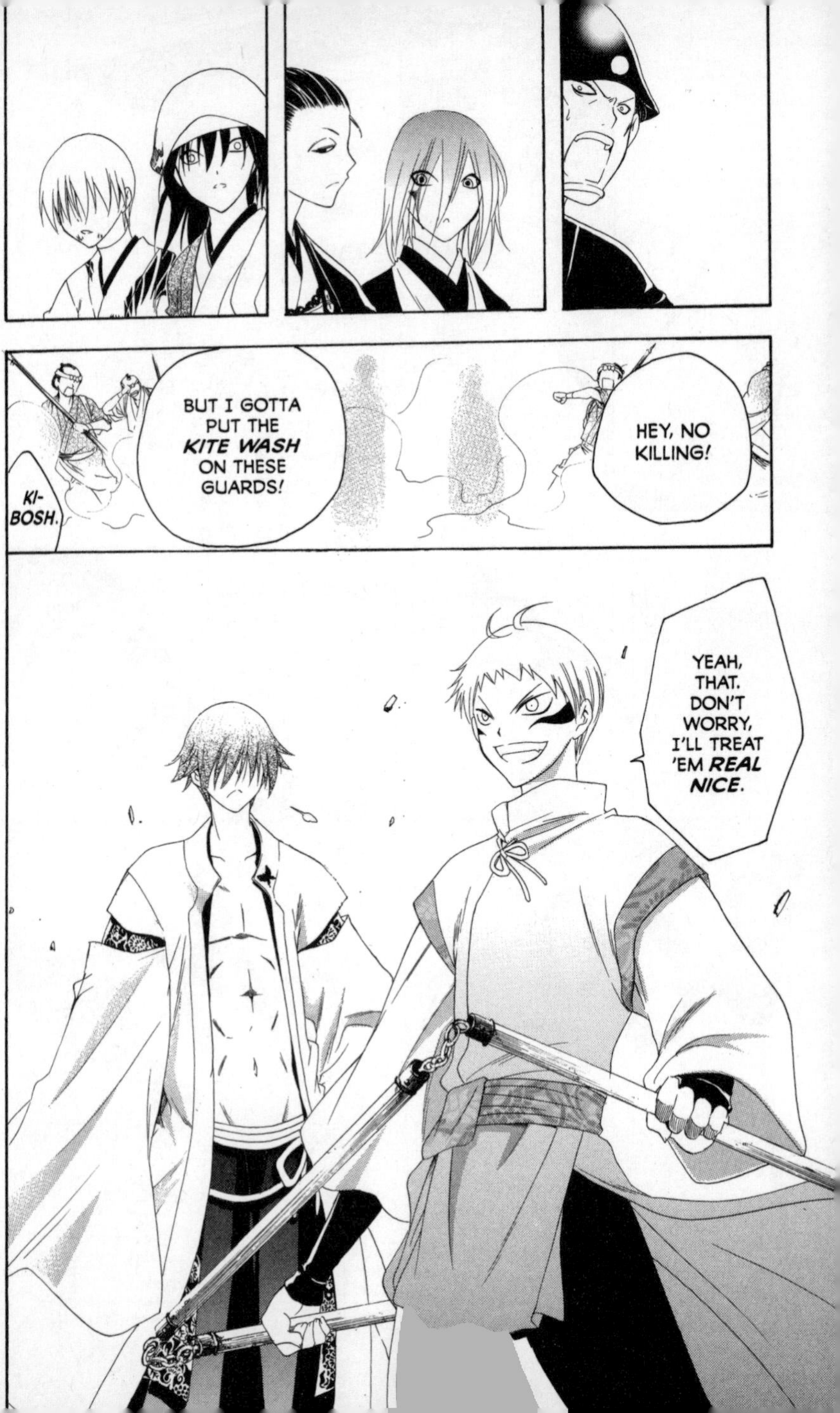
HEY, NO KILLING!
BUT I GOTTA PUT THE KITE WASH ON THESE GUARDS!
KI-BOSH.
YEAH, THAT. DON'T WORRY, I'LL TREAT 'EM REAL NICE.

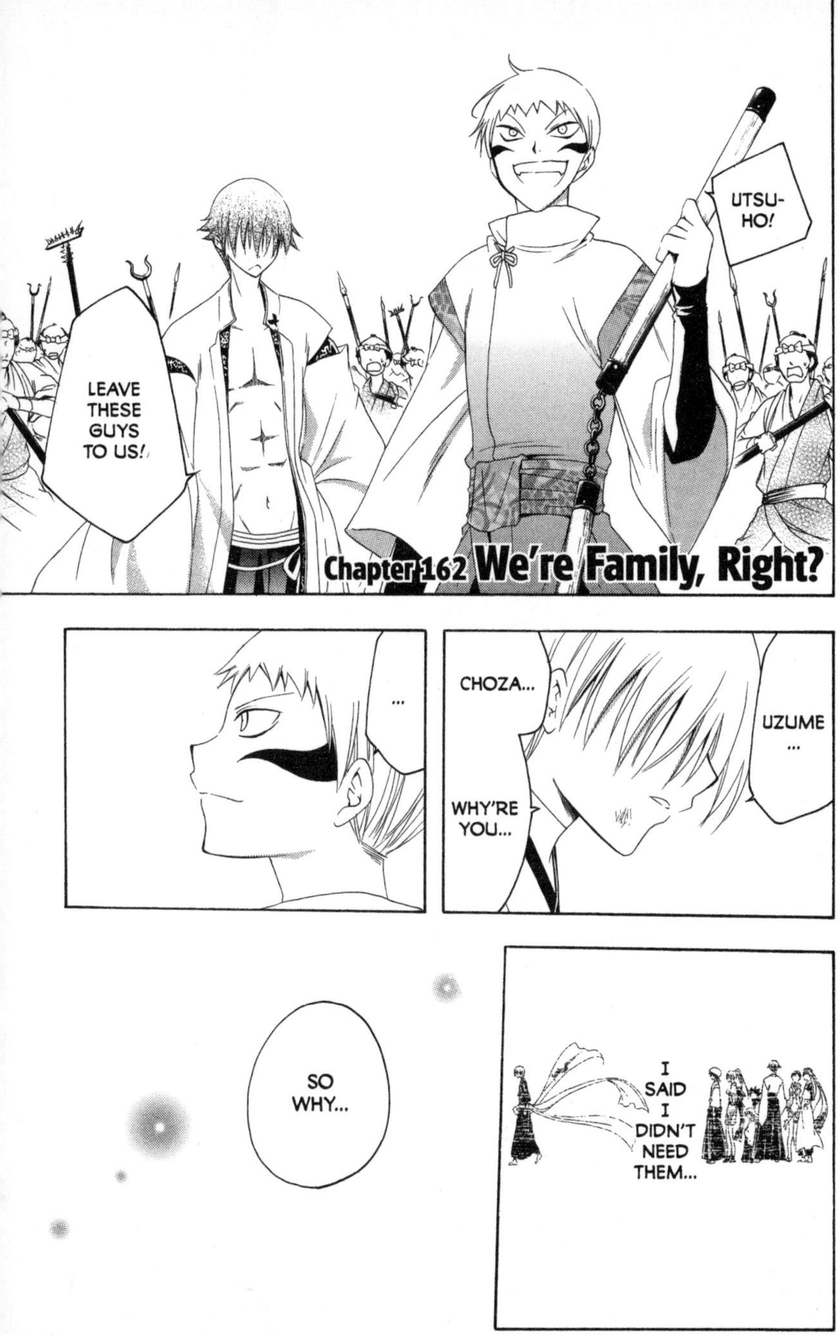
UTSU-HO!
LEAVE THESE GUYS TO US!
Chapter 162 We're Family, Right?
UZUME...
CHOZA...
WHY'RE YOU...
...
I SAID I DIDN'T NEED THEM...
SO WHY...

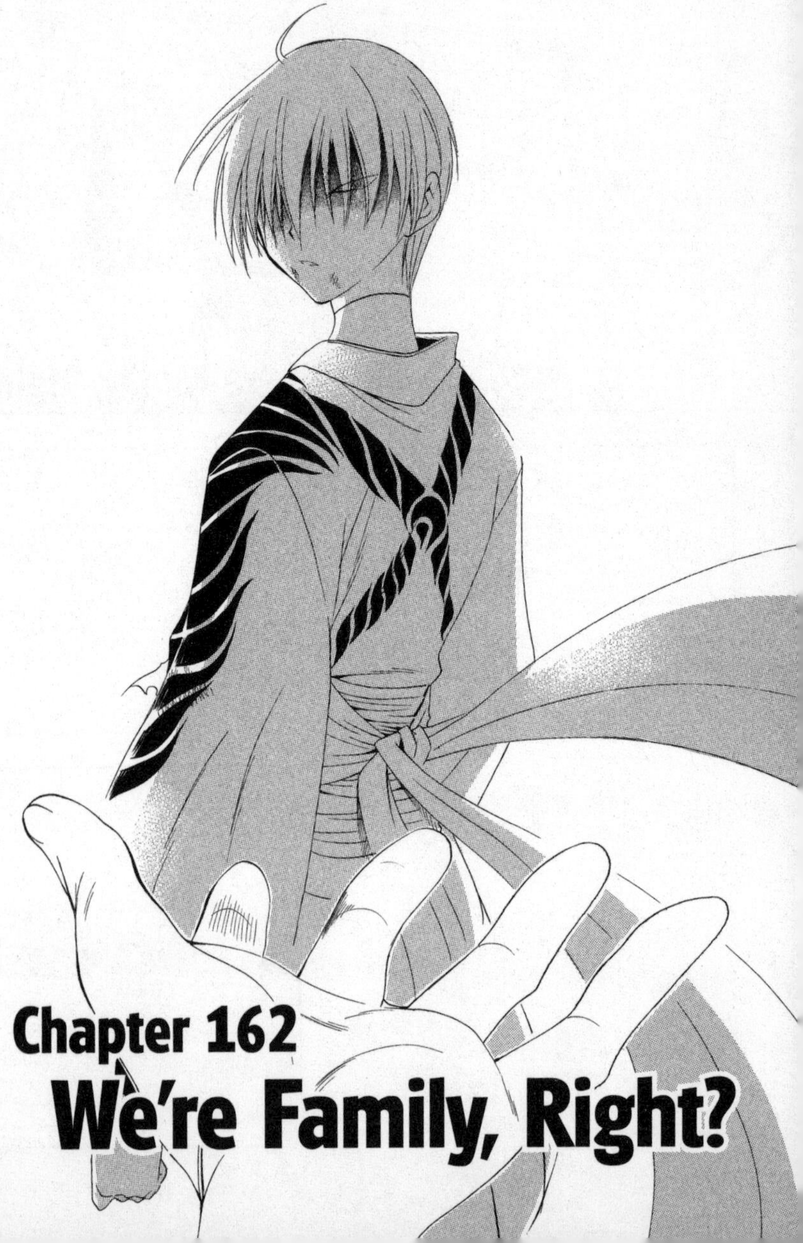
Chapter 162
We're Family, Right?

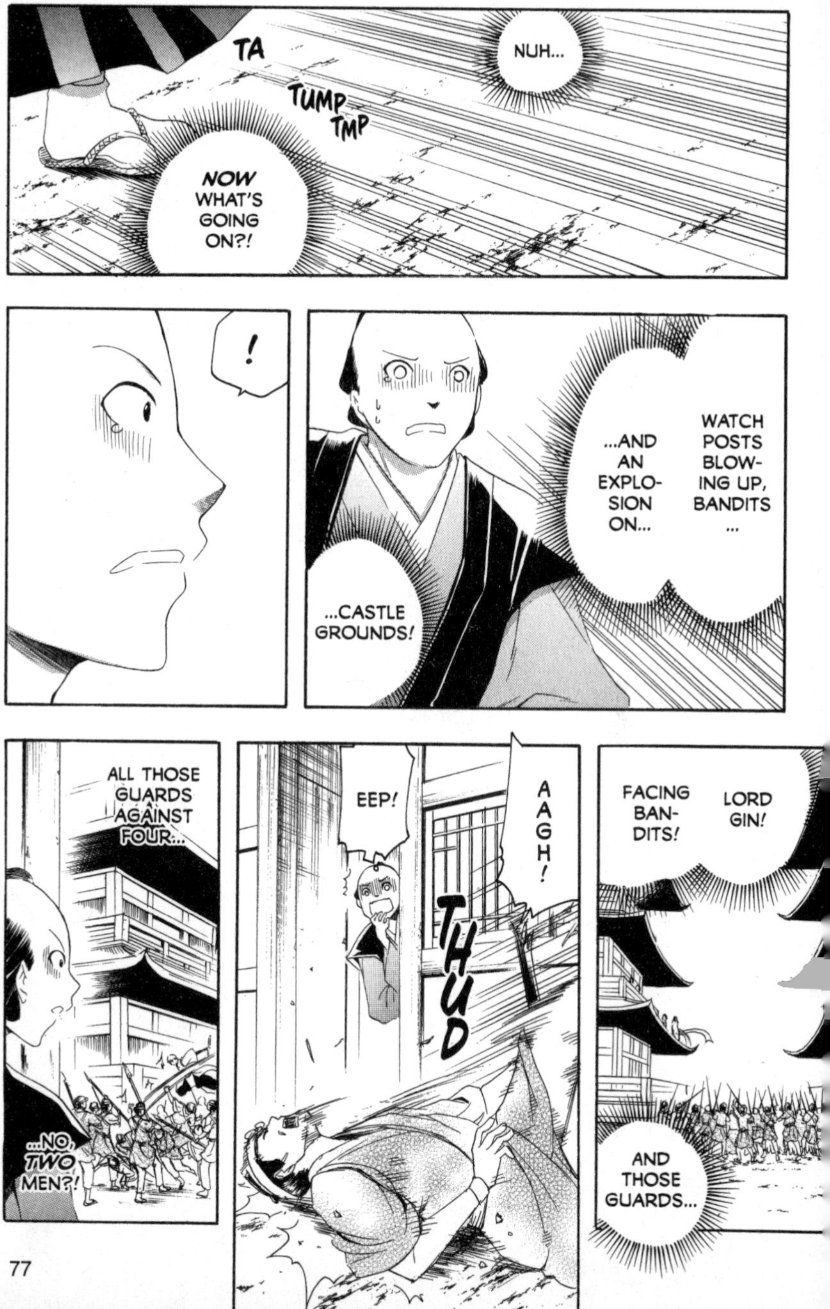
NUH...
TA
TUMP TMP
NOW WHAT'S GOING ON?!
WATCH POSTS BLOW-ING UP, BANDITS ...
...AND AN EXPLO-SION ON...
...CASTLE GROUNDS!
!
LORD GIN!
FACING BAN-DITS!
AND THOSE GUARDS...
AAGH!
EEP!
THUD
ALL THOSE GUARDS AGAINST FOUR...
...NO, TWO MEN?!

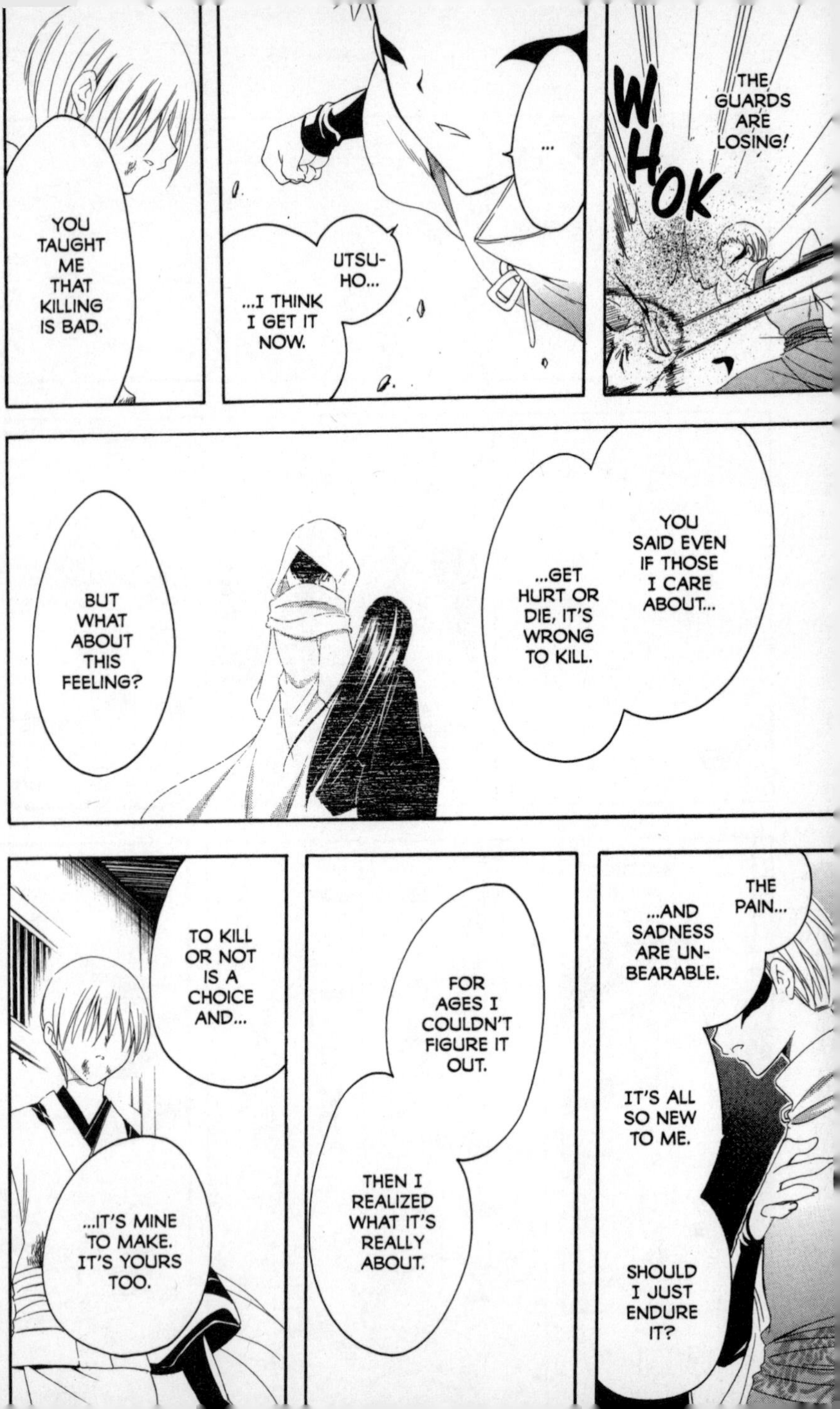
THE GUARDS ARE LOSING!
WHOK
...
UTSU-HO...
...I THINK I GET IT NOW.
YOU TAUGHT ME THAT KILLING IS BAD.
YOU SAID EVEN IF THOSE I CARE ABOUT...
...GET HURT OR DIE, IT'S WRONG TO KILL.
BUT WHAT ABOUT THIS FEELING?
THE PAIN...
...AND SADNESS ARE UN-BEARABLE.
IT'S ALL SO NEW TO ME.
SHOULD I JUST ENDURE IT?
FOR AGES I COULDN'T FIGURE IT OUT.
THEN I REALIZED WHAT IT'S REALLY ABOUT.
TO KILL OR NOT IS A CHOICE AND...
...IT'S MINE TO MAKE. IT'S YOURS TOO.

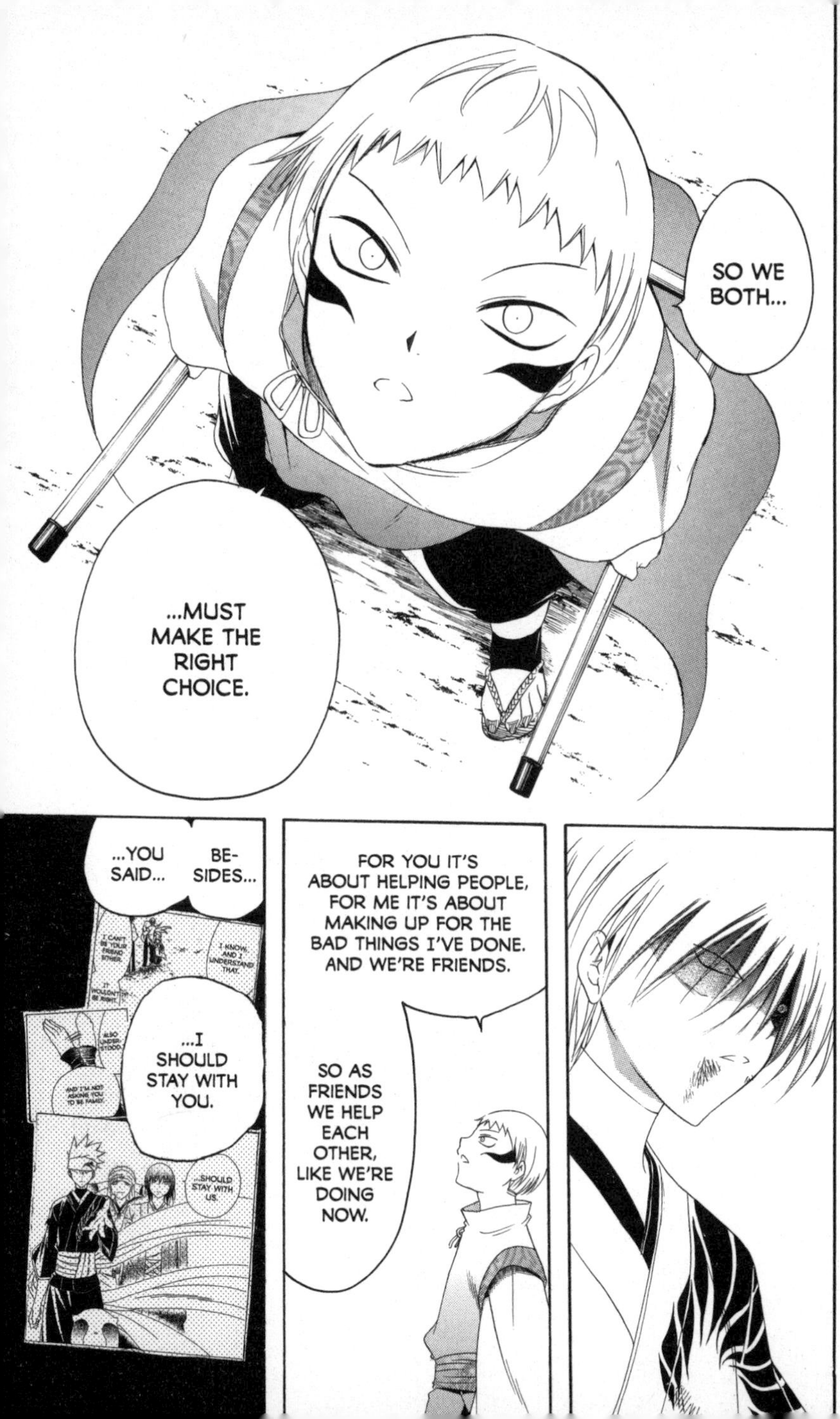
SO WE BOTH...
...MUST MAKE THE RIGHT CHOICE.
FOR YOU IT'S ABOUT HELPING PEOPLE, FOR ME IT'S ABOUT MAKING UP FOR THE BAD THINGS I'VE DONE. AND WE'RE FRIENDS.
SO AS FRIENDS WE HELP EACH OTHER, LIKE WE'RE DOING NOW.
BE-SIDES...
...YOU SAID...
I KNOW. AND I UNDERSTAND THAT.
I CAN'T BE YOUR FRIEND EITHER.
IT WOULDN'T BE RIGHT.
ALSO UNDER-STOOD.
AND I'M NOT ASKING YOU TO BE FAMILY.
...I SHOULD STAY WITH YOU.
...SHOULD STAY WITH US.

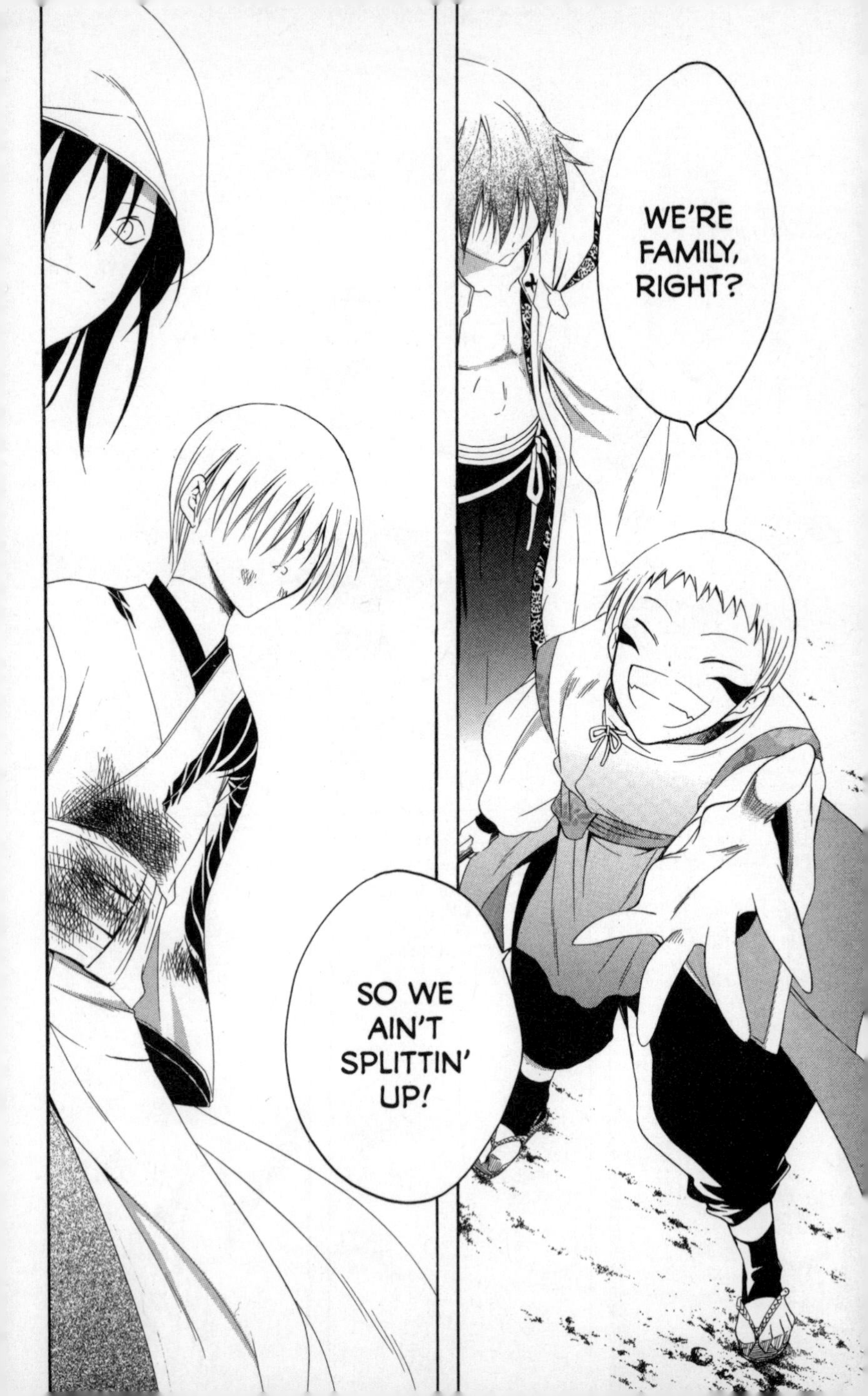
WE'RE FAMILY, RIGHT?
SO WE AIN'T SPLITTIN' UP!

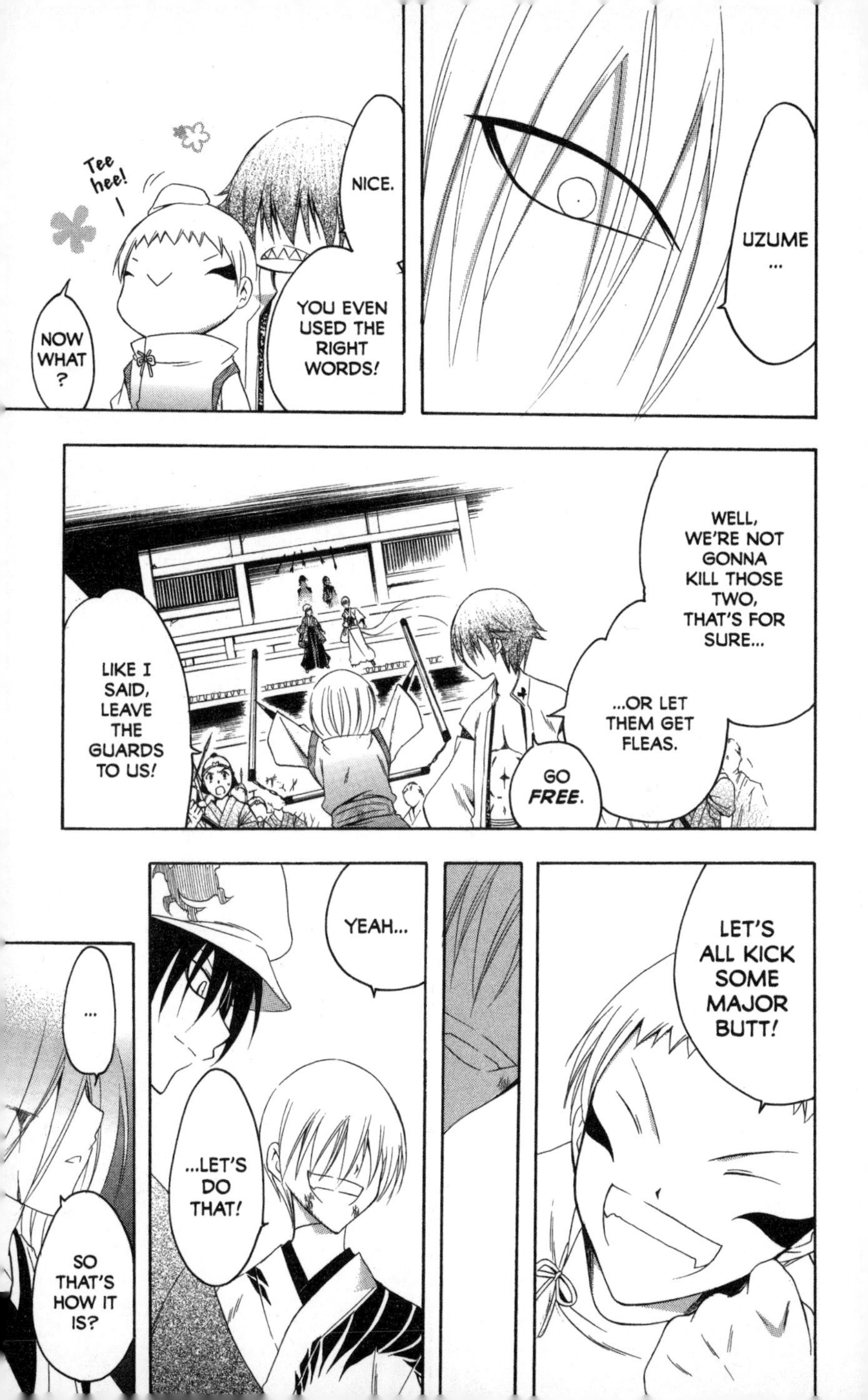
UZUME ...
NICE.
YOU EVEN USED THE RIGHT WORDS!
Tee hee!
NOW WHAT?
WELL, WE'RE NOT GONNA KILL THOSE TWO, THAT'S FOR SURE...
...OR LET THEM GET FLEAS.
GO *FREE*.
LIKE I SAID, LEAVE THE GUARDS TO US!
LET'S ALL KICK SOME MAJOR BUTT!
YEAH...
...LET'S DO THAT!
...
SO THAT'S HOW IT IS?

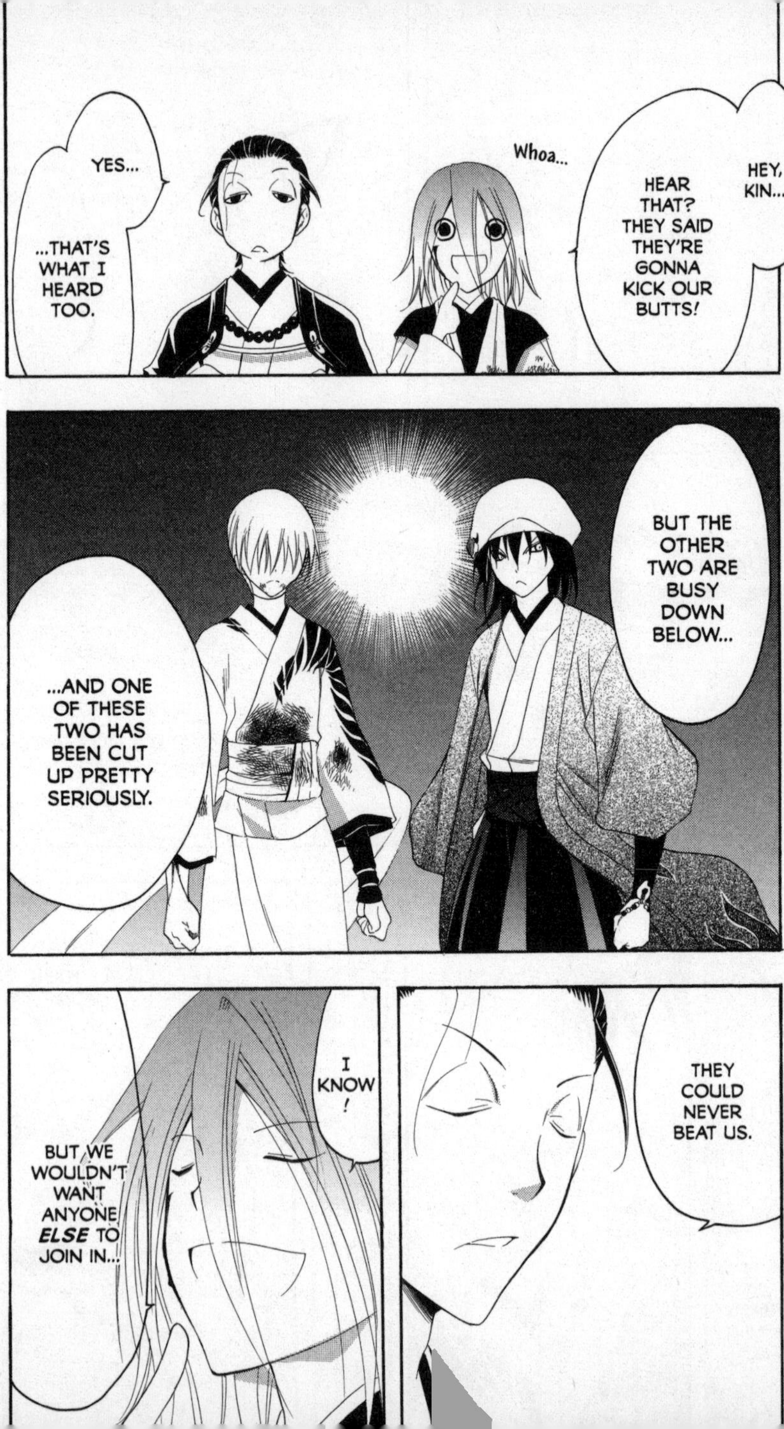
HEY, KIN... HEAR THAT? THEY SAID THEY'RE GONNA KICK OUR BUTTS!
Whoa...
YES... ...THAT'S WHAT I HEARD TOO.
BUT THE OTHER TWO ARE BUSY DOWN BELOW...
...AND ONE OF THESE TWO HAS BEEN CUT UP PRETTY SERIOUSLY.
THEY COULD NEVER BEAT US.
I KNOW!
BUT WE WOULDN'T WANT ANYONE *ELSE* TO JOIN IN...

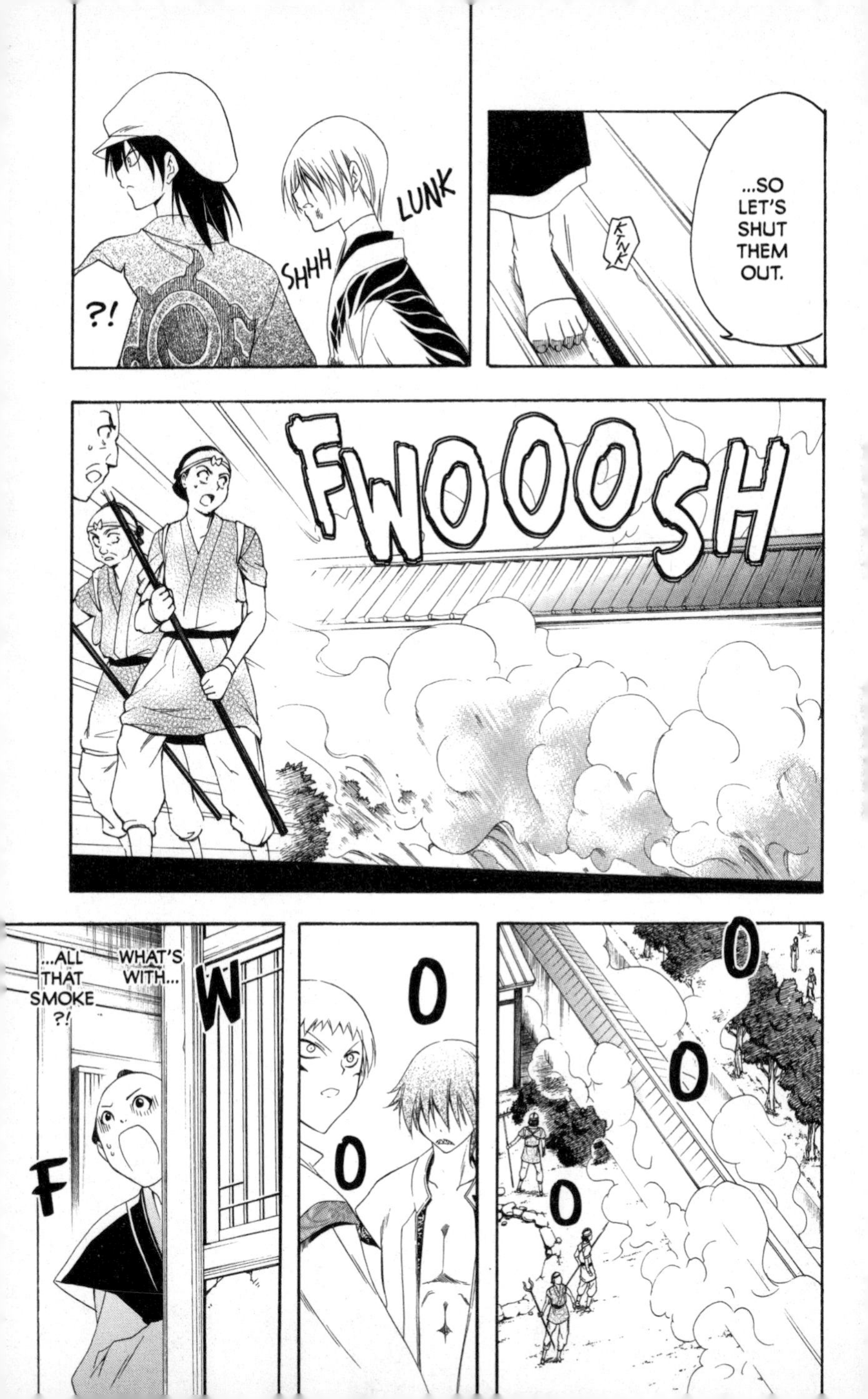

...SO LET'S SHUT THEM OUT.
KTNK
LUNK
SHHH
?!
FWOOOSH
WHAT'S WITH...
...ALL THAT SMOKE?!
FWOOOOO

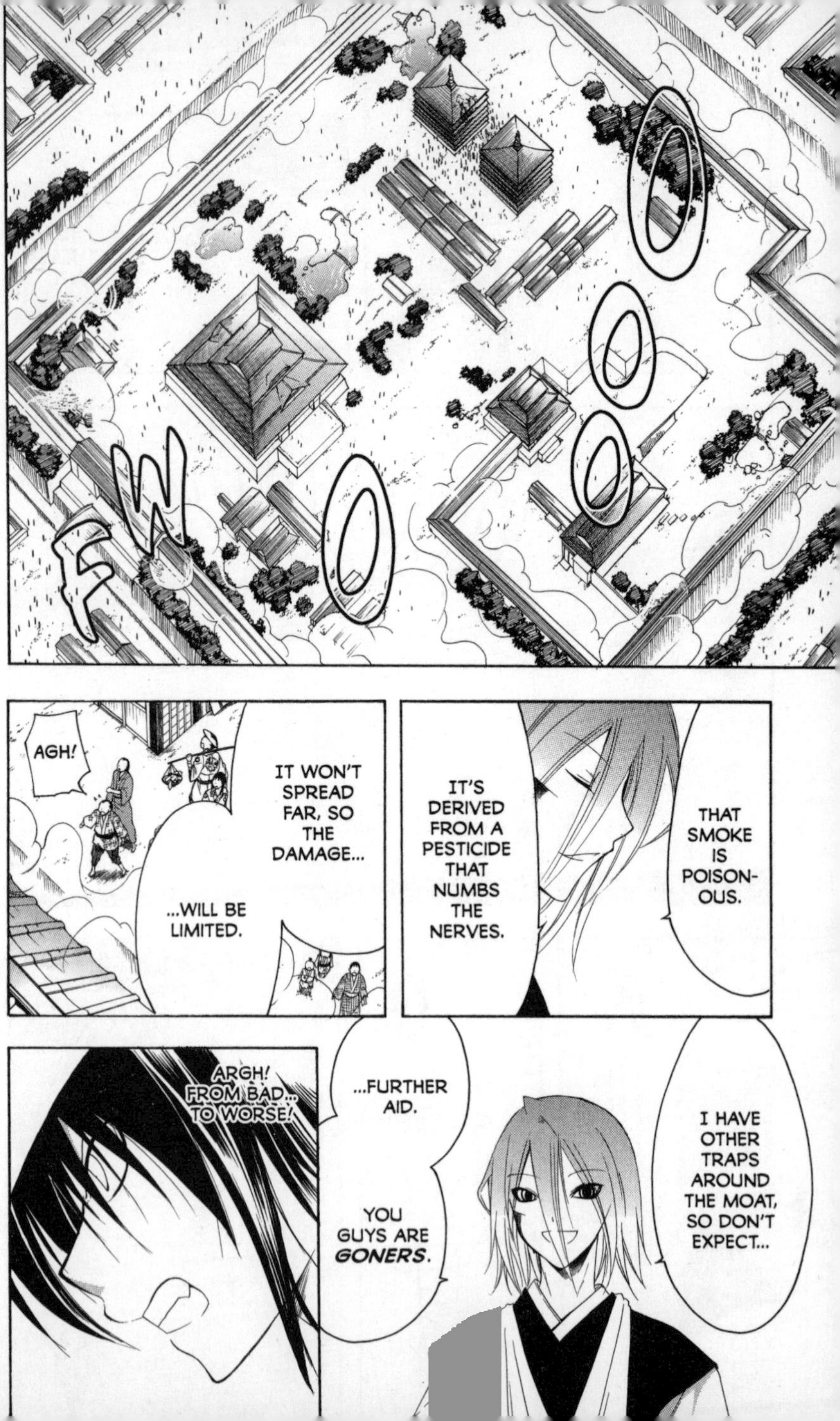
FWOOOO
THAT SMOKE IS POISON-OUS.
IT'S DERIVED FROM A PESTICIDE THAT NUMBS THE NERVES.
IT WON'T SPREAD FAR, SO THE DAMAGE...
AGH!
...WILL BE LIMITED.
I HAVE OTHER TRAPS AROUND THE MOAT, SO DON'T EXPECT...
...FURTHER AID.
YOU GUYS ARE *GONERS*.
ARGH! FROM BAD... TO WORSE!

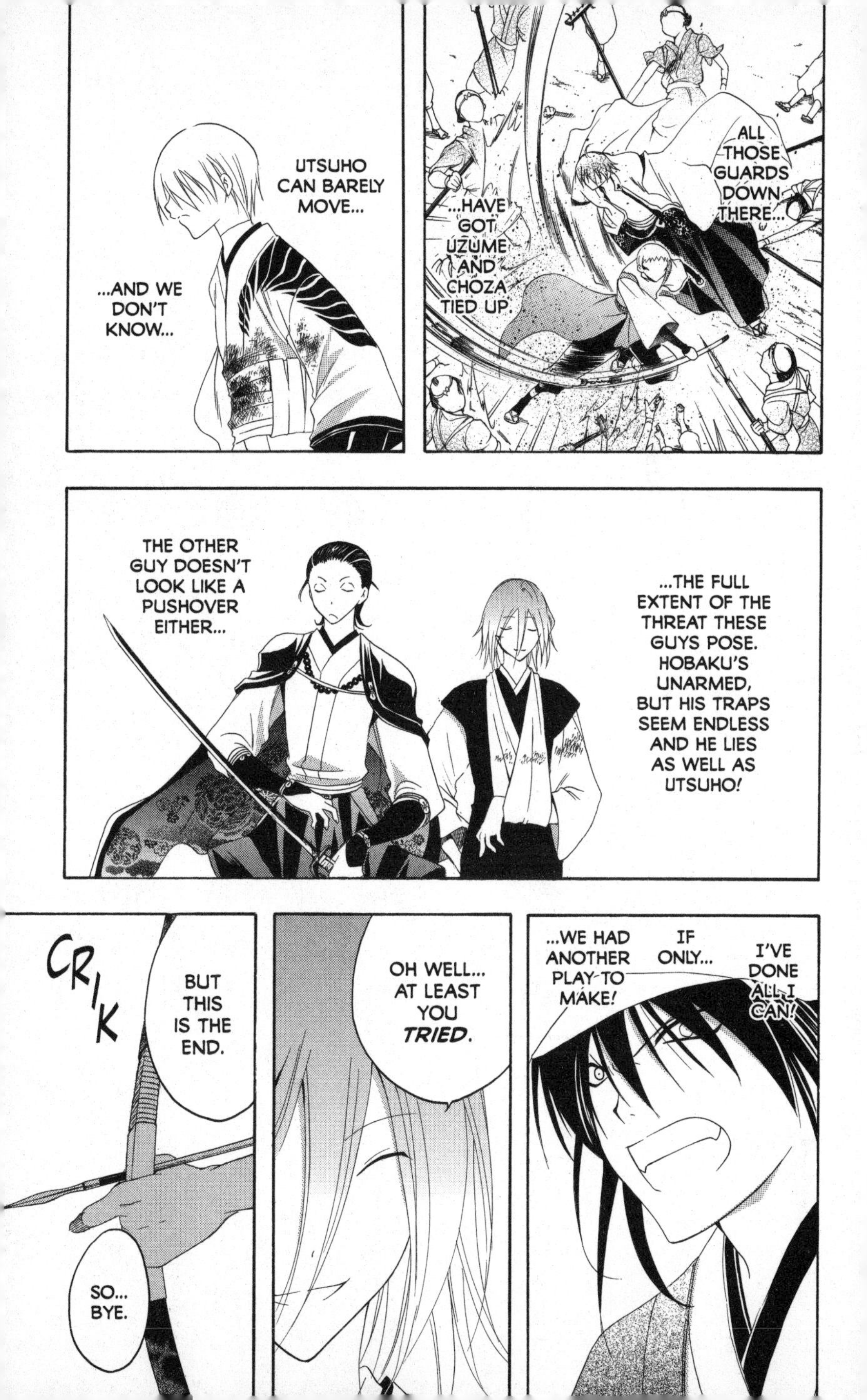
ALL THOSE GUARDS DOWN THERE...
...HAVE GOT UZUME AND CHOZA TIED UP.
UTSUHO CAN BARELY MOVE...
...AND WE DON'T KNOW...
...THE FULL EXTENT OF THE THREAT THESE GUYS POSE. HOBAKU'S UNARMED, BUT HIS TRAPS SEEM ENDLESS AND HE LIES AS WELL AS UTSUHO!
THE OTHER GUY DOESN'T LOOK LIKE A PUSHOVER EITHER...
I'VE DONE ALL I CAN!
IF ONLY...
...WE HAD ANOTHER PLAY TO MAKE!
OH WELL... AT LEAST YOU *TRIED*.
CRIK
BUT THIS IS THE END.
SO... BYE.

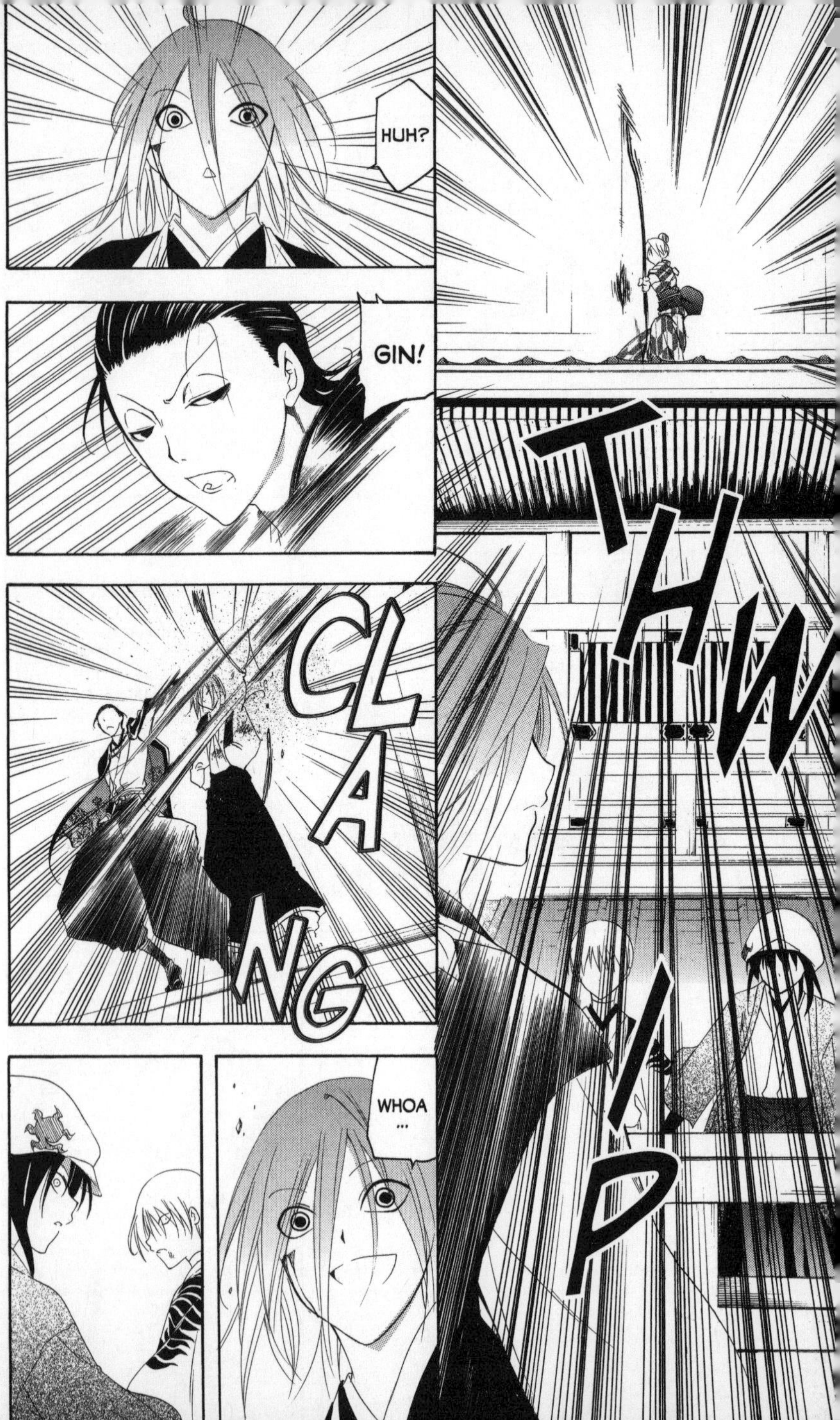
THWIP
HUH?
GIN!
CLANG
WHOA ...

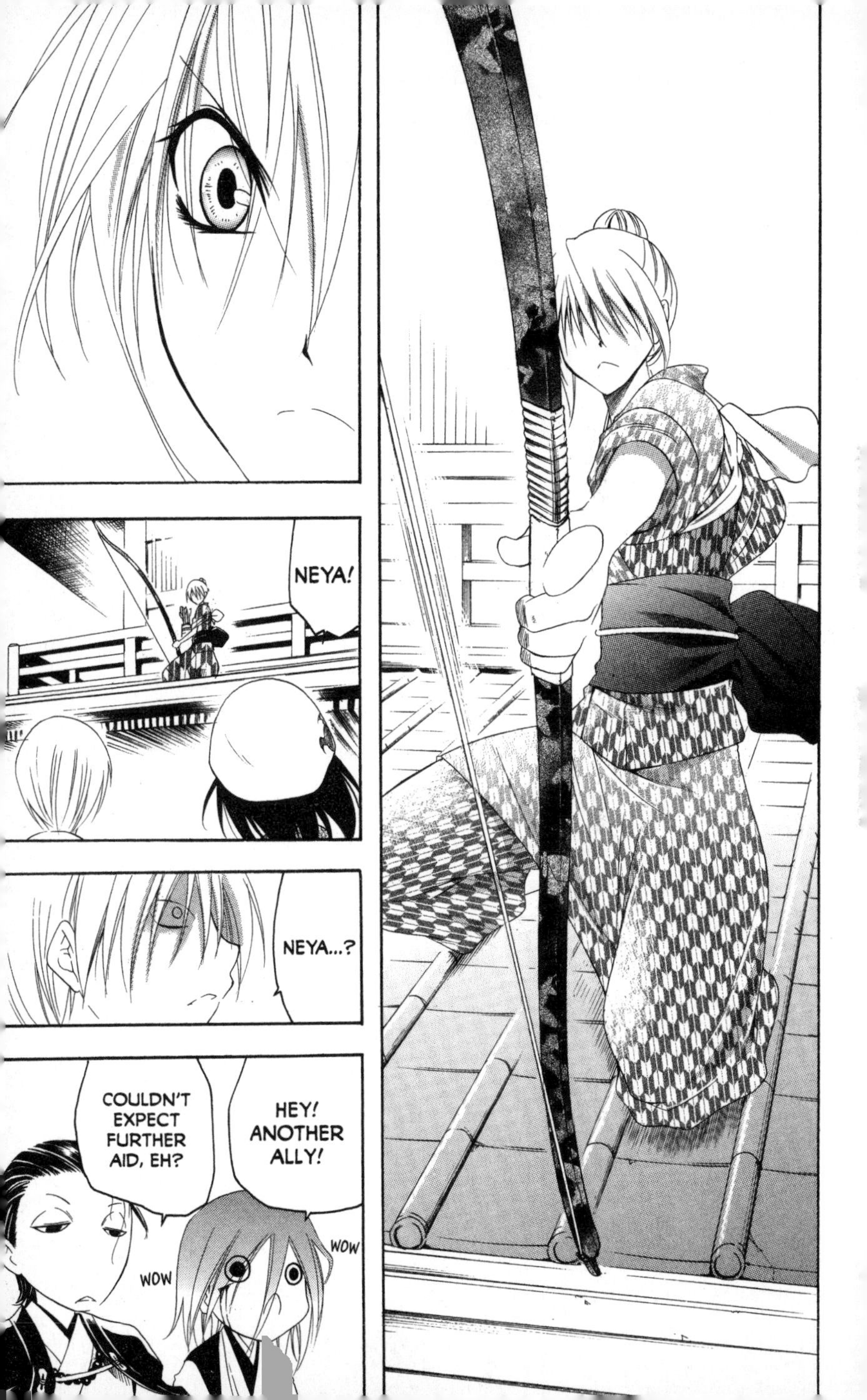
NEYA!
NEYA...?
HEY! ANOTHER ALLY!
COULDN'T EXPECT FURTHER AID, EH?
WOW
WOW

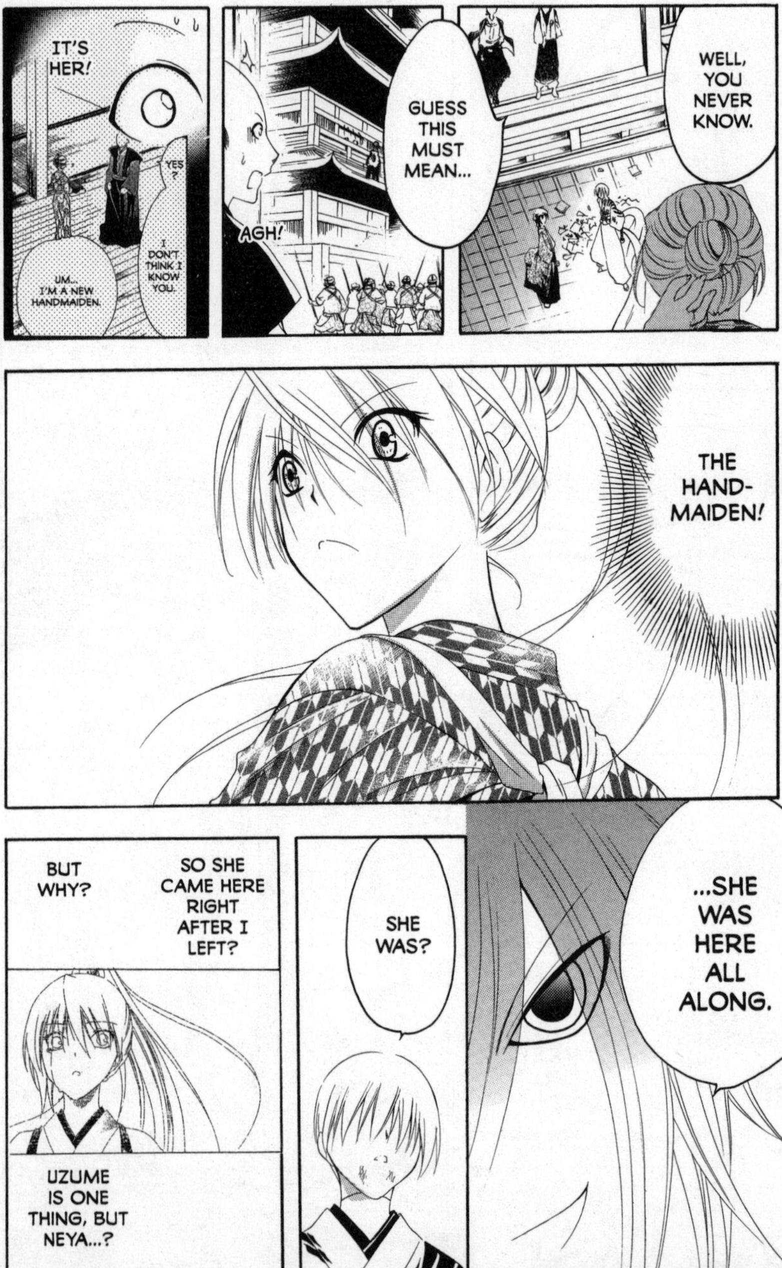
WELL, YOU NEVER KNOW.
GUESS THIS MUST MEAN...
AGH!
IT'S HER!
YES?
I DON'T THINK I KNOW YOU.
UM... I'M A NEW HANDMAIDEN.
THE HAND-MAIDEN!
...SHE WAS HERE ALL ALONG.
SHE WAS?
SO SHE CAME HERE RIGHT AFTER I LEFT?
BUT WHY?
UZUME IS ONE THING, BUT NEYA...?

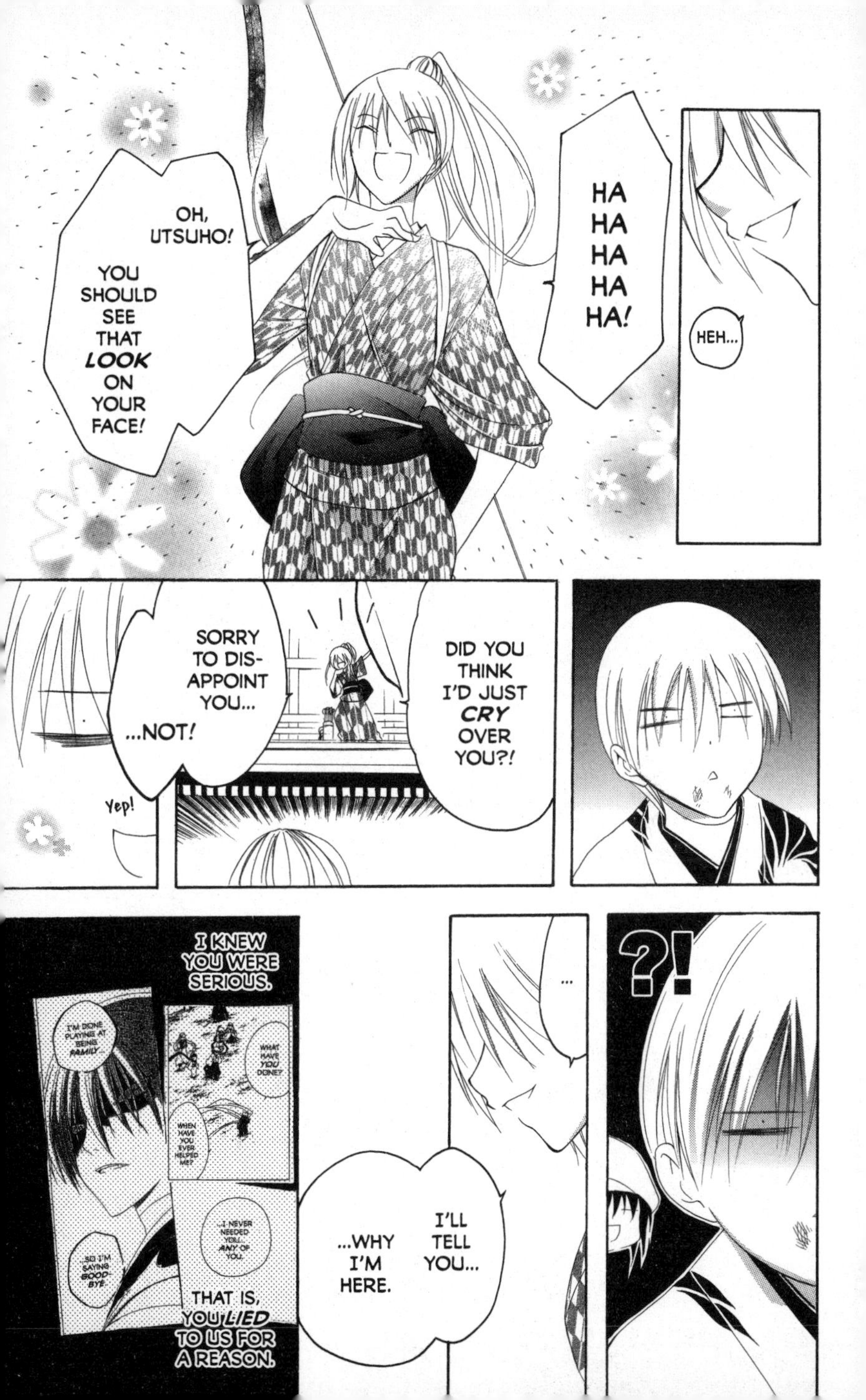

HEH...
HA HA HA HA HA!
OH, UTSUHO!
YOU SHOULD SEE THAT **LOOK** ON YOUR FACE!
DID YOU THINK I'D JUST **CRY** OVER YOU?!
SORRY TO DIS-APPOINT YOU...
...NOT!
Yep!
?!
...
I'LL TELL YOU...
...WHY I'M HERE.
I KNEW YOU WERE SERIOUS.
WHAT HAVE **YOU** DONE?
I'M DONE PLAYING AT BEING **FAMILY**...
WHEN HAVE YOU EVER HELPED ME?
...I NEVER NEEDED YOU... **ANY** OF YOU.
...SO I'M SAYING **GOOD-BYE**.
THAT IS, YOU **LIED** TO US FOR A REASON.

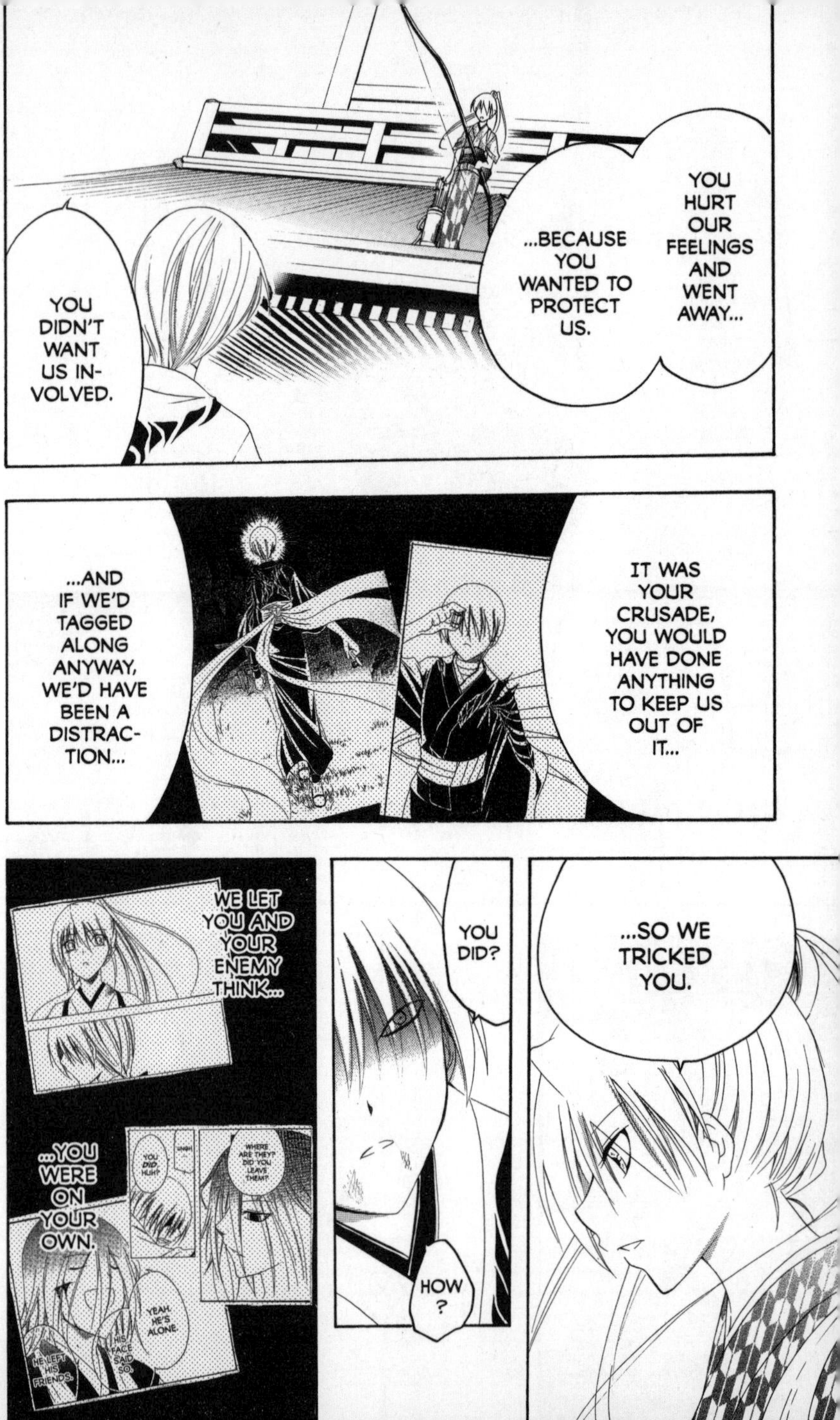
YOU HURT OUR FEELINGS AND WENT AWAY...
...BECAUSE YOU WANTED TO PROTECT US.
YOU DIDN'T WANT US IN-VOLVED.
IT WAS YOUR CRUSADE, YOU WOULD HAVE DONE ANYTHING TO KEEP US OUT OF IT...
...AND IF WE'D TAGGED ALONG ANYWAY, WE'D HAVE BEEN A DISTRAC-TION...
...SO WE TRICKED YOU.
YOU DID?
HOW?
WE LET YOU AND YOUR ENEMY THINK...
WHERE ARE THEY? DID YOU LEAVE THEM?
UNGH...
YOU DID, HUH?
YEAH. HE'S ALONE.
HIS FACE SAID SO.
HE LEFT HIS FRIENDS.
...YOU WERE ON YOUR OWN.

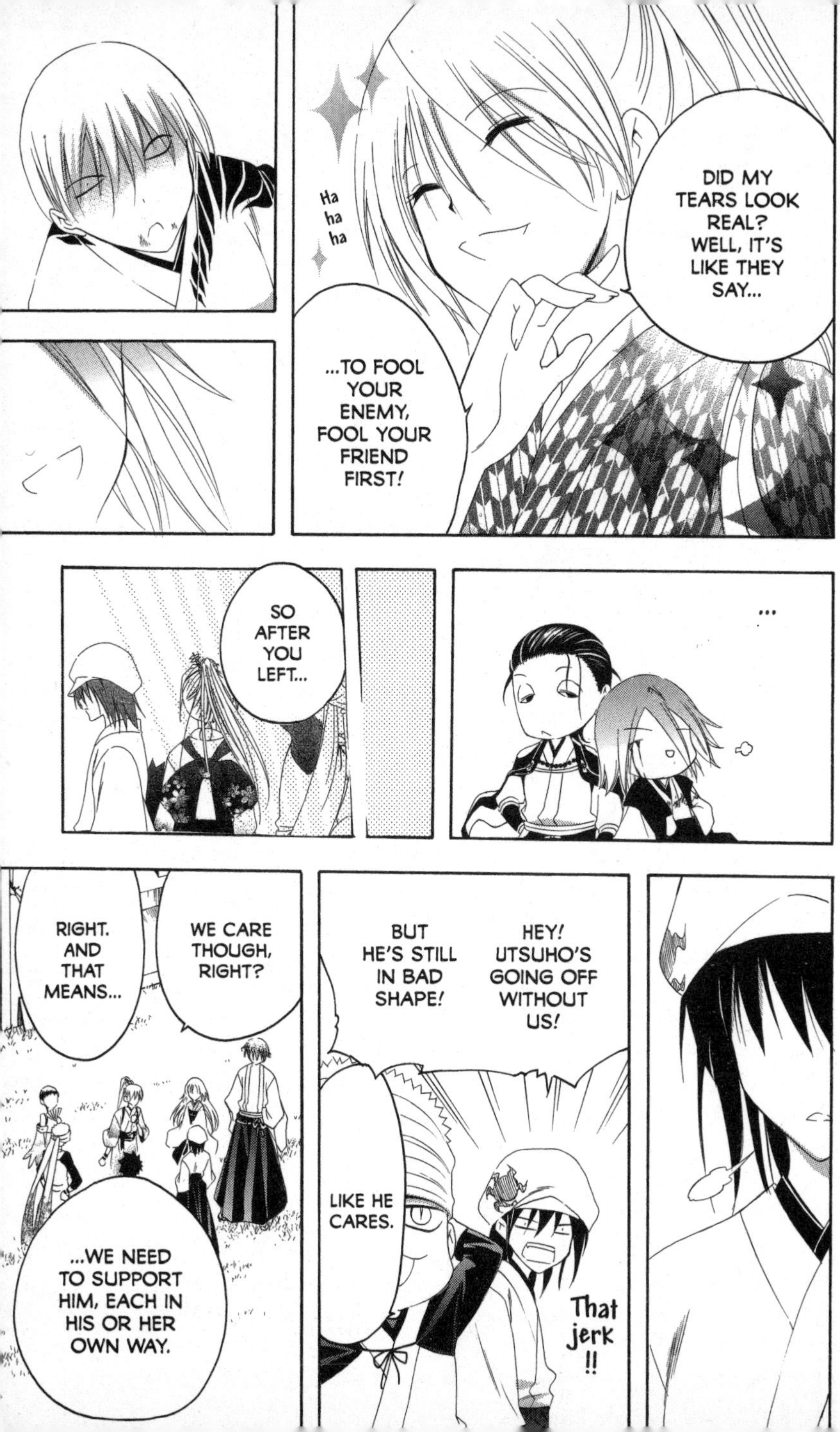
DID MY TEARS LOOK REAL? WELL, IT'S LIKE THEY SAY...
Ha ha ha
...TO FOOL YOUR ENEMY, FOOL YOUR FRIEND FIRST!
...
SO AFTER YOU LEFT...
HEY! UTSUHO'S GOING OFF WITHOUT US!
BUT HE'S STILL IN BAD SHAPE!
LIKE HE CARES.
That jerk!!
WE CARE THOUGH, RIGHT?
RIGHT. AND THAT MEANS...
...WE NEED TO SUPPORT HIM, EACH IN HIS OR HER OWN WAY.

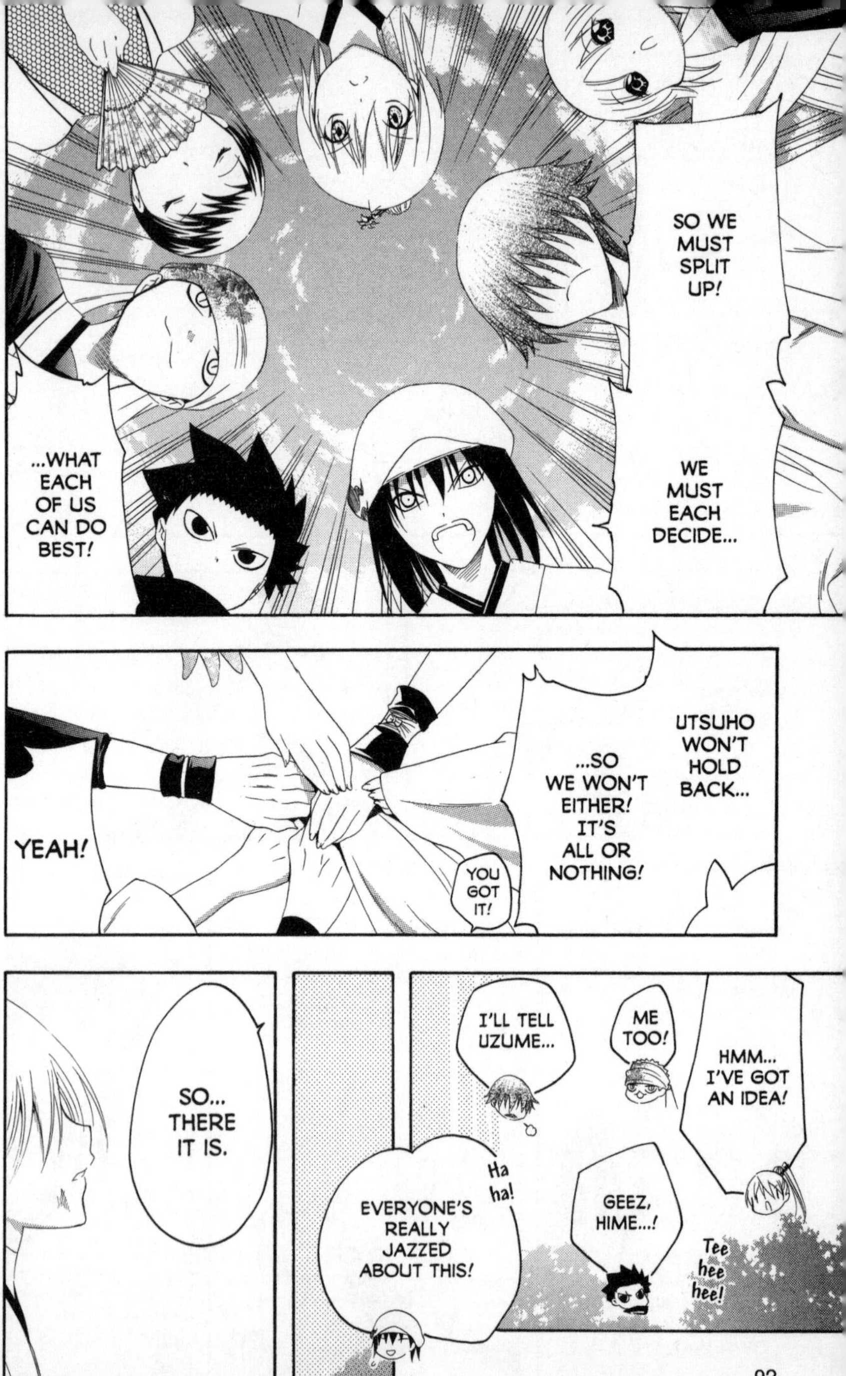
SO WE MUST SPLIT UP!
WE MUST EACH DECIDE...
...WHAT EACH OF US CAN DO BEST!
UTSUHO WON'T HOLD BACK...
...SO WE WON'T EITHER! IT'S ALL OR NOTHING!
YOU GOT IT!
YEAH!
HMM... I'VE GOT AN IDEA!
ME TOO!
I'LL TELL UZUME...
Tee hee hee!
GEEZ, HIME...!
Ha ha!
EVERYONE'S REALLY JAZZED ABOUT THIS!
SO... THERE IT IS.

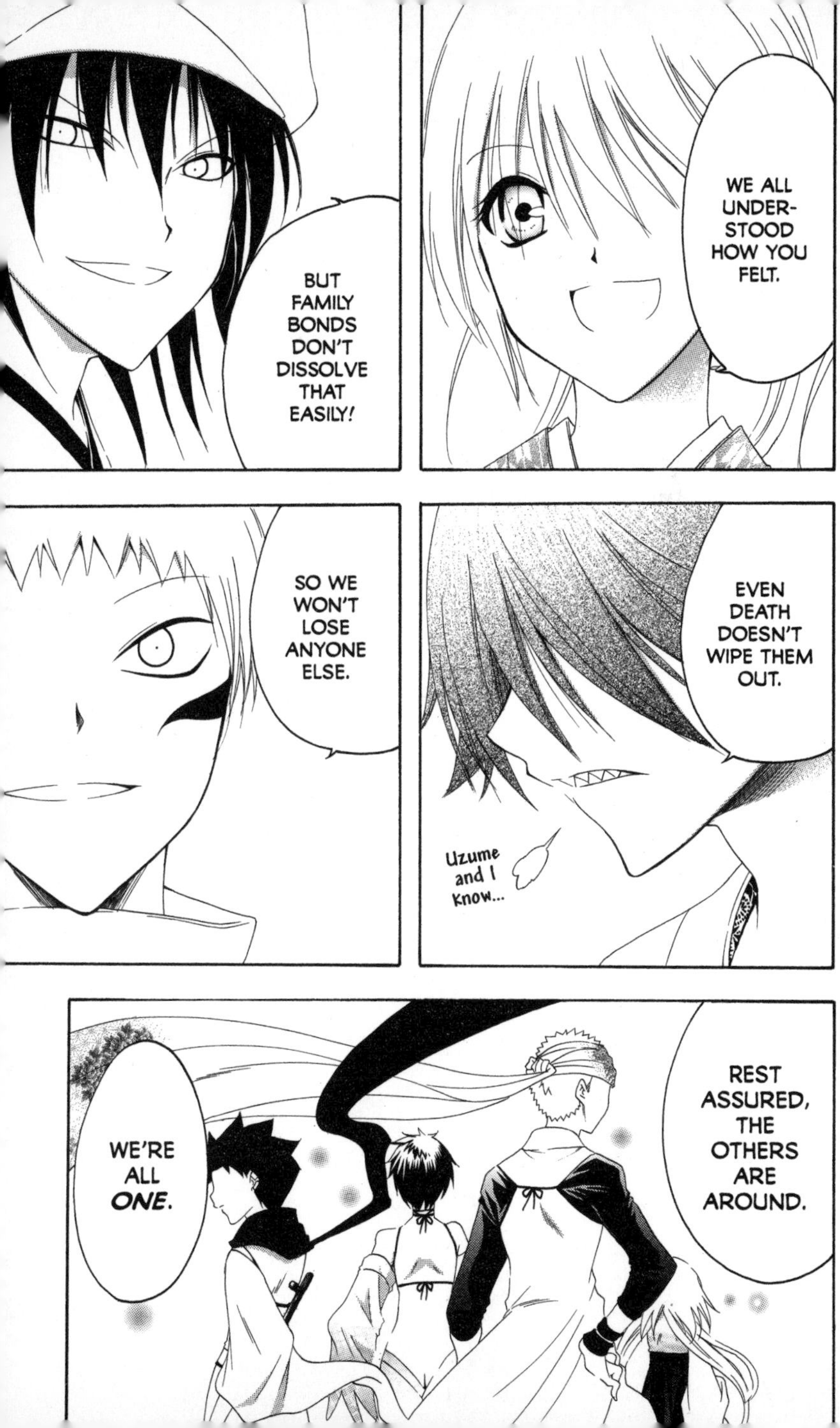
WE ALL UNDERSTOOD HOW YOU FELT.
BUT FAMILY BONDS DON'T DISSOLVE THAT EASILY!
EVEN DEATH DOESN'T WIPE THEM OUT.
Uzume and I know...
SO WE WON'T LOSE ANYONE ELSE.
REST ASSURED, THE OTHERS ARE AROUND.
WE'RE ALL *ONE*.

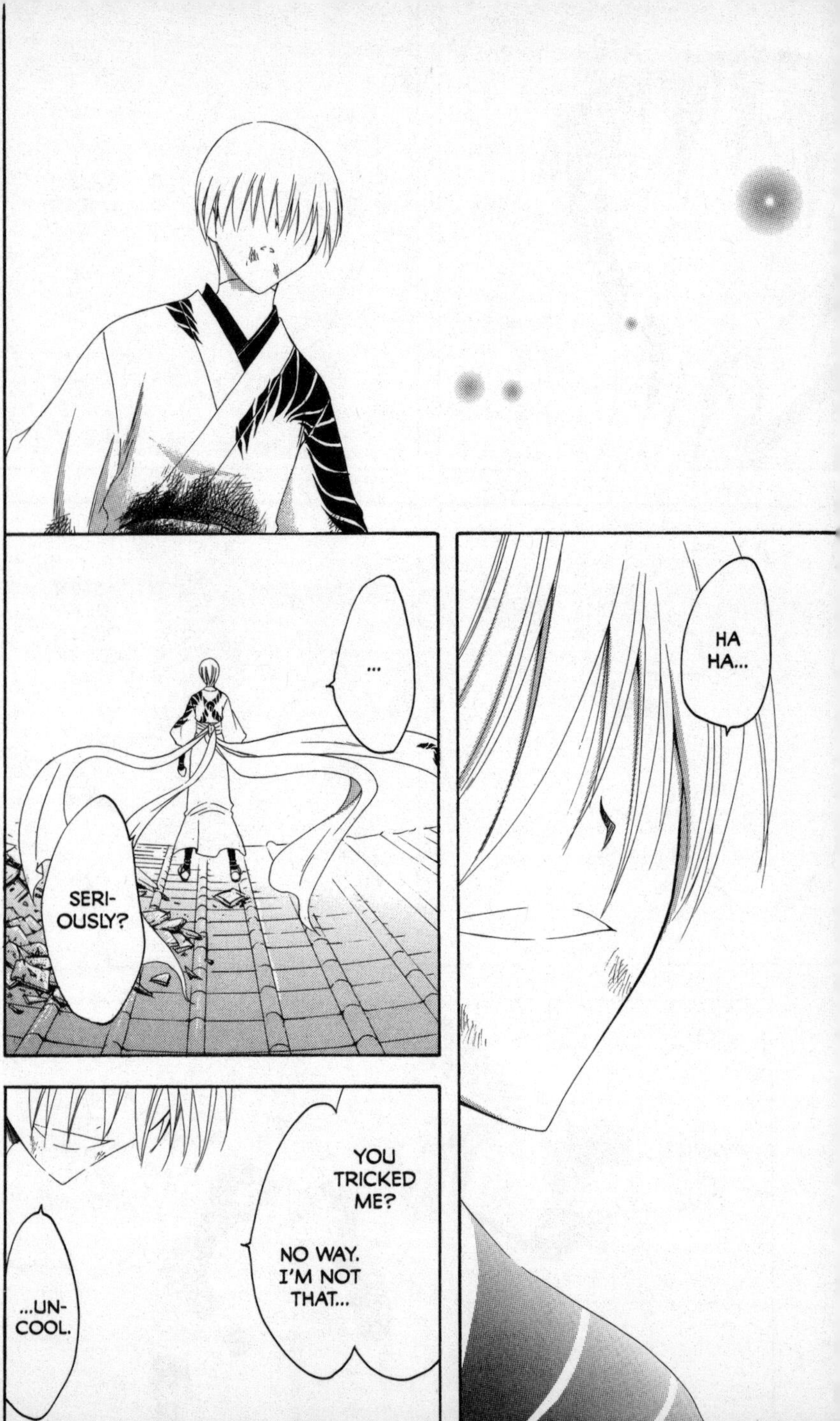
HA HA...
...
SERI-OUSLY?
YOU TRICKED ME?
NO WAY. I'M NOT THAT...
...UN-COOL.

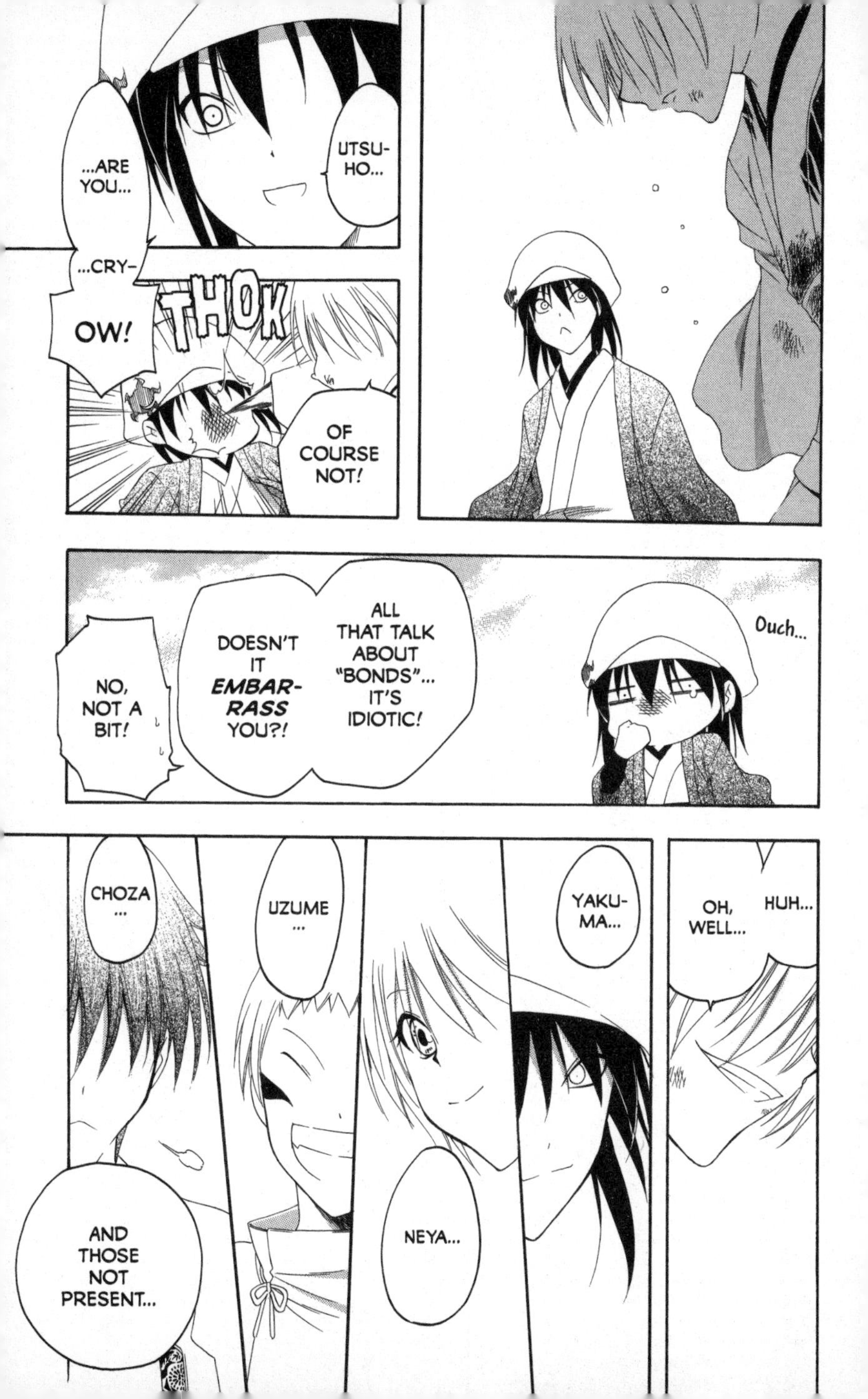
UTSU-HO...
...ARE YOU... ...CRY-
THOK
OW!
OF COURSE NOT!
Ouch...
ALL THAT TALK ABOUT "BONDS"... IT'S IDIOTIC!
DOESN'T IT *EMBARRASS* YOU?!
NO, NOT A BIT!
HUH...
OH, WELL...
YAKUMA...
NEYA...
UZUME...
CHOZA...
AND THOSE NOT PRESENT...

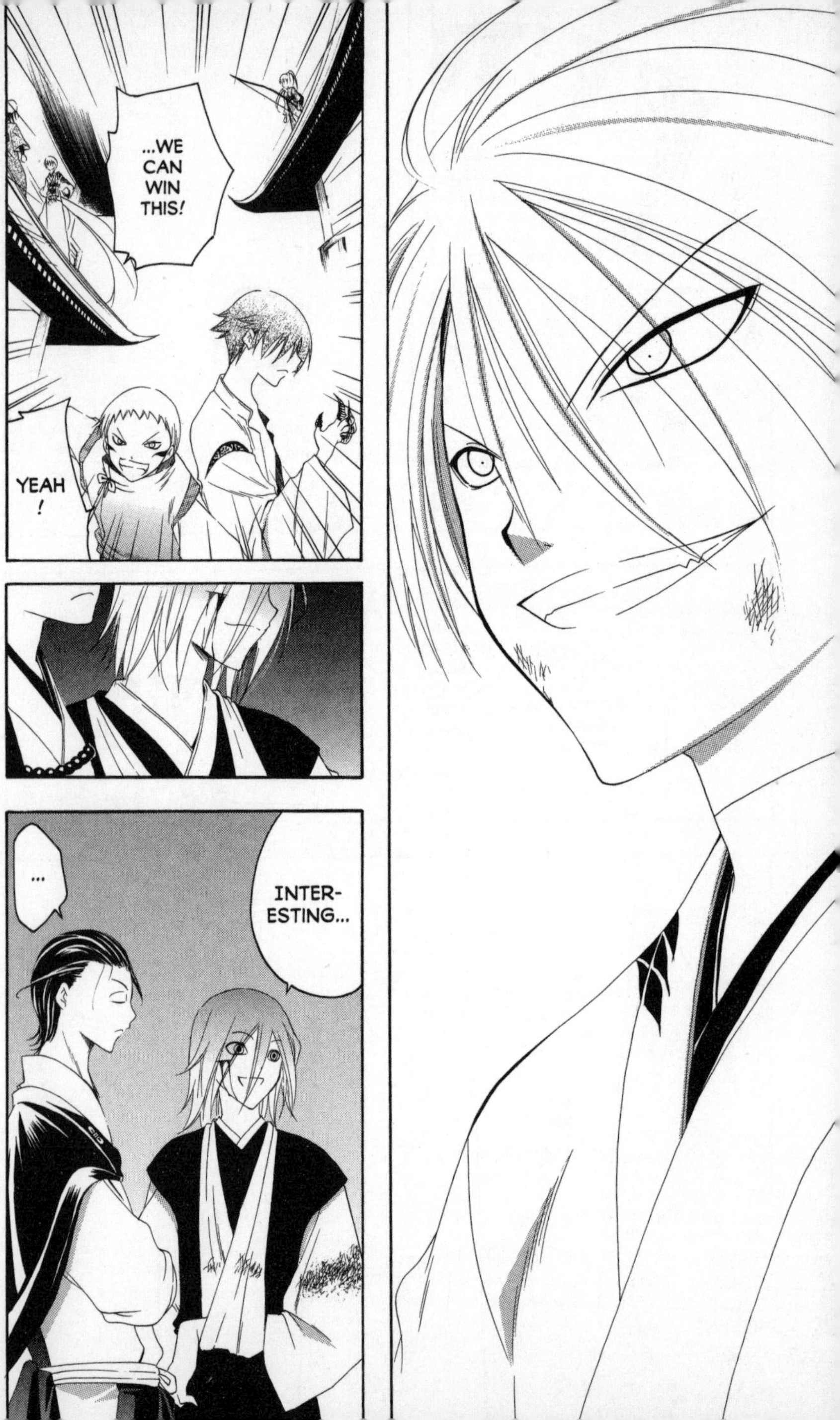
...WE CAN WIN THIS!
YEAH!
INTER-ESTING...
...

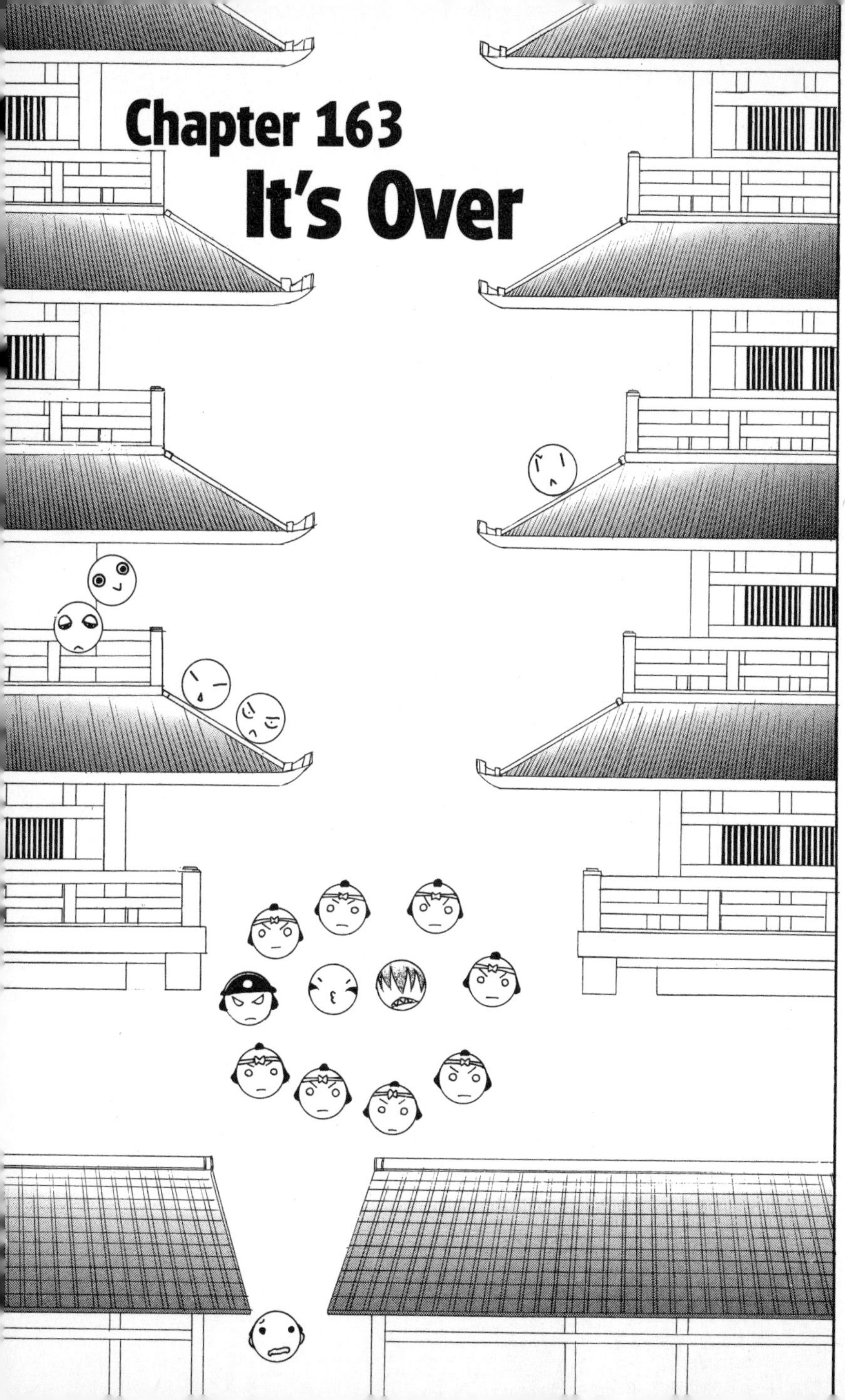
Chapter 163
It's Over

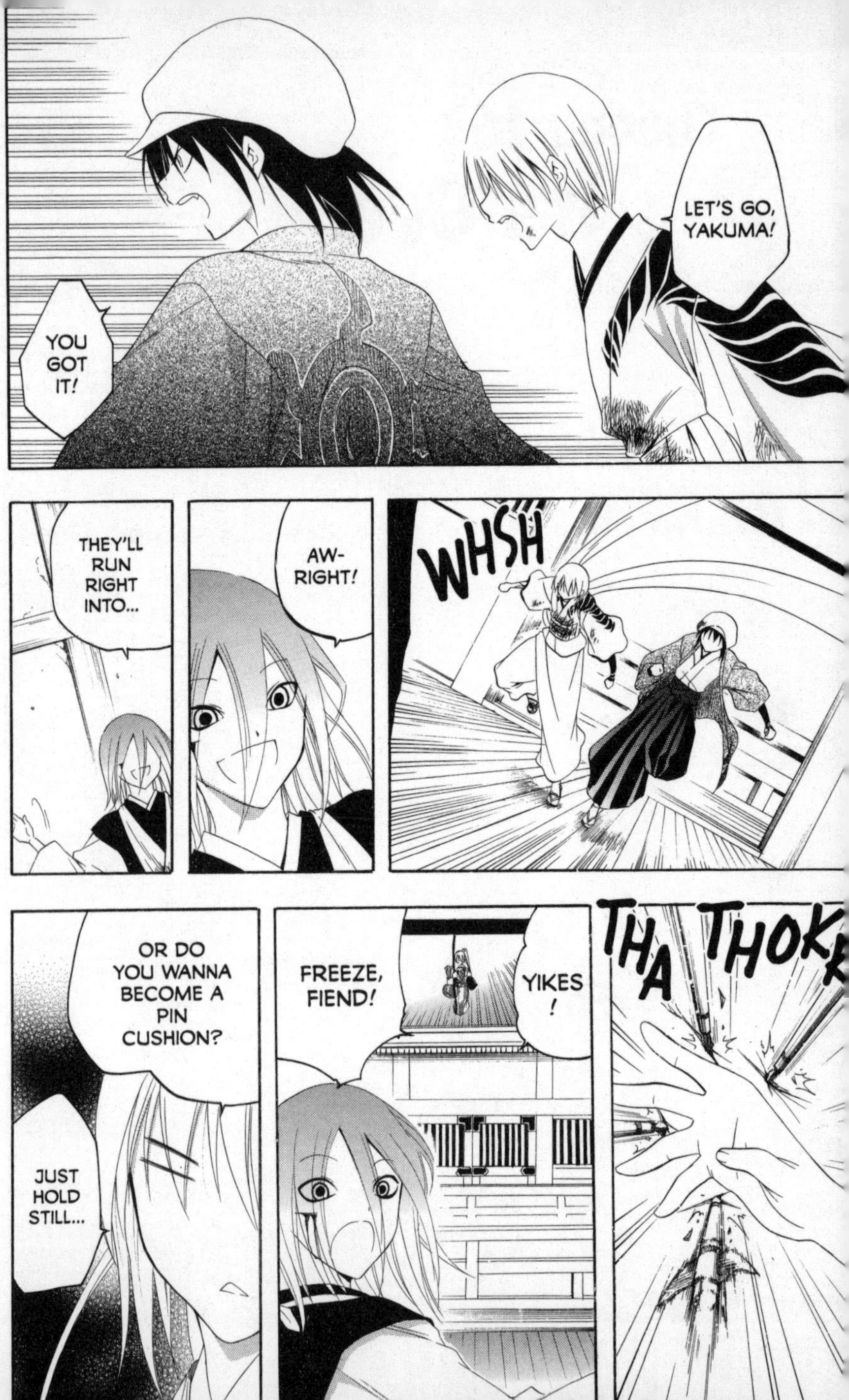
LET'S GO, YAKUMA!
YOU GOT IT!
WHSH
AW-RIGHT!
THEY'LL RUN RIGHT INTO...
THA THOK
YIKES!
FREEZE, FIEND!
OR DO YOU WANNA BECOME A PIN CUSHION?
JUST HOLD STILL...

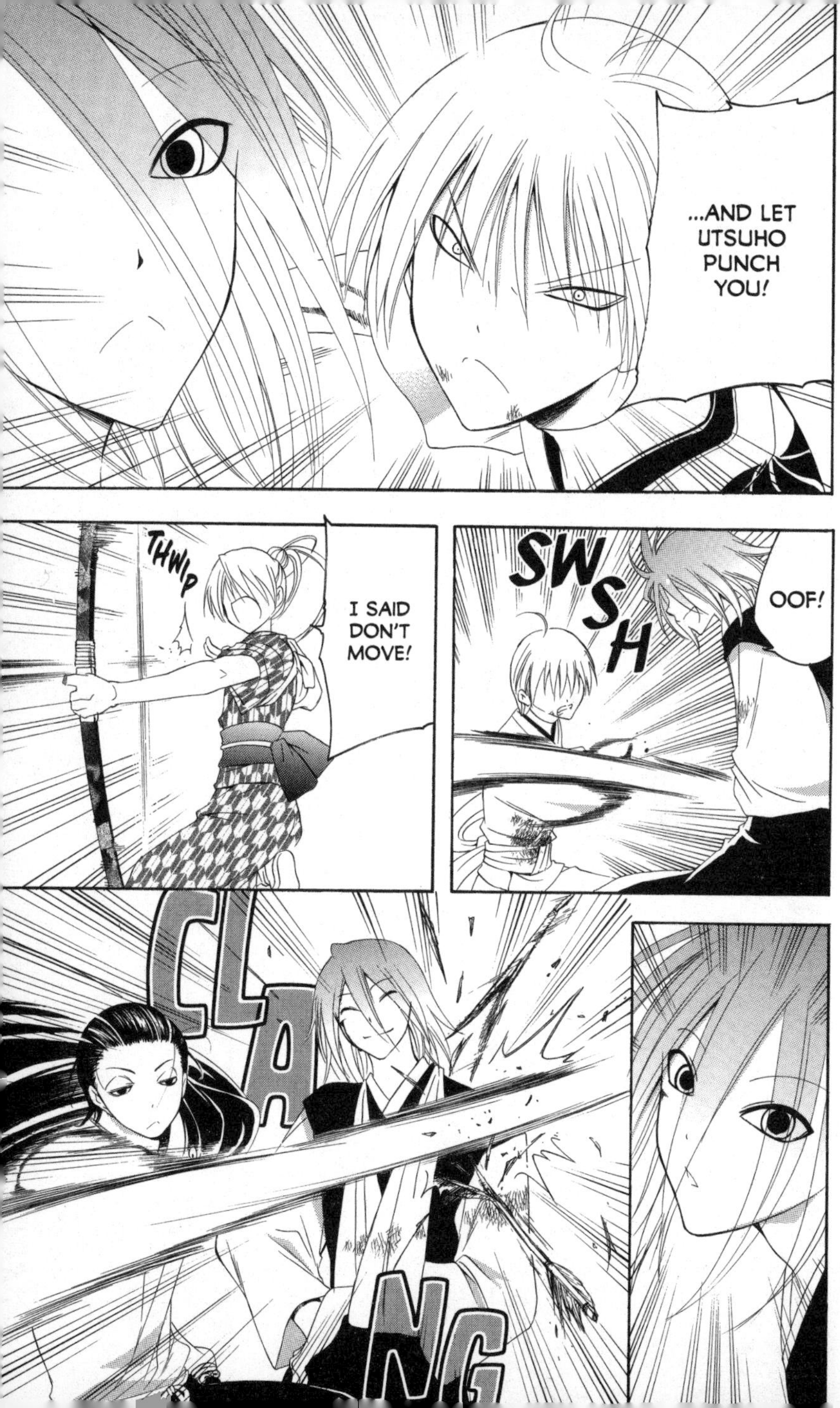
...AND LET UTSUHO PUNCH YOU!
SWSH
OOF!
THWIP
I SAID DON'T MOVE!
CLANG

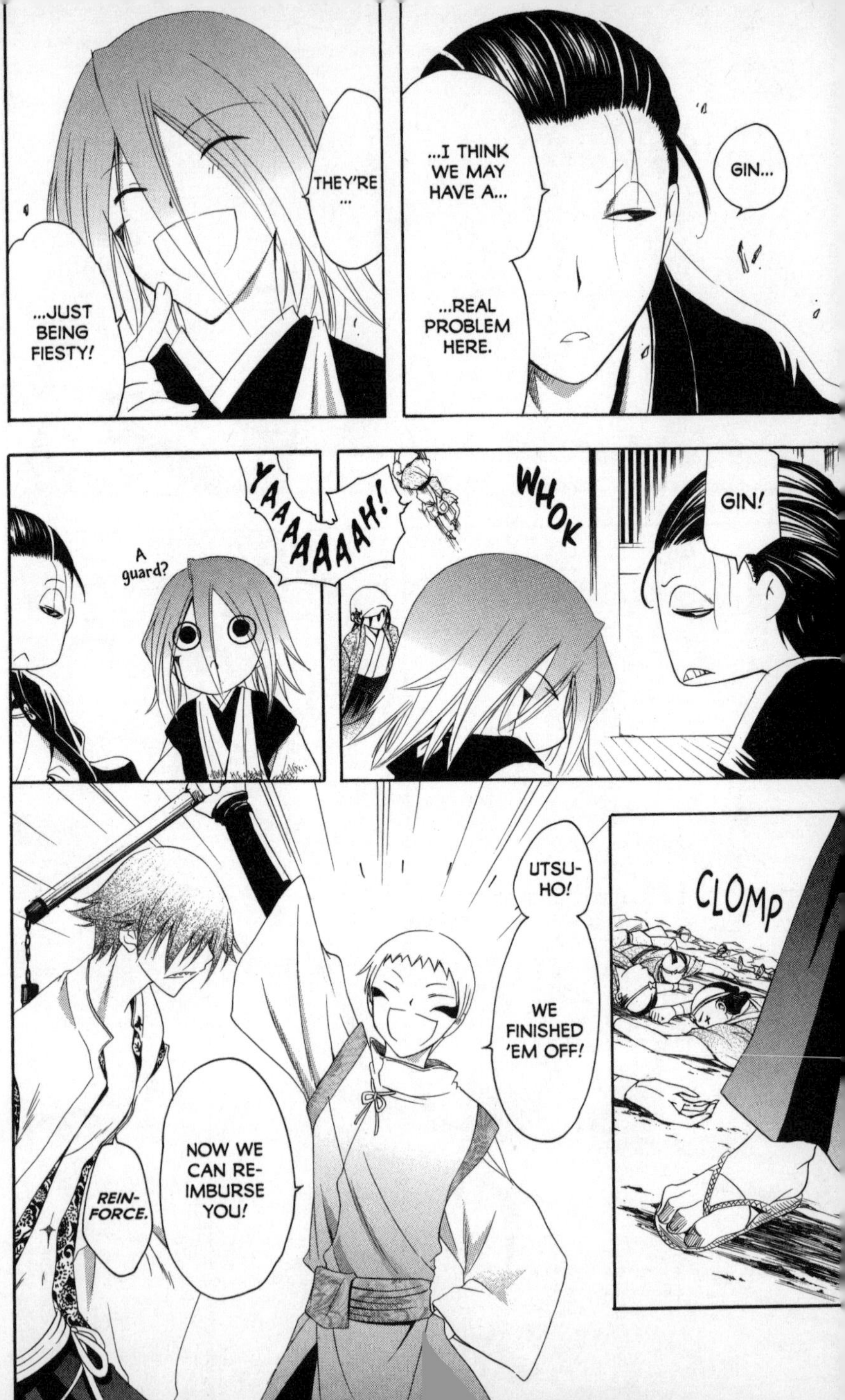
GIN...
...I THINK WE MAY HAVE A...
...REAL PROBLEM HERE.
THEY'RE ...
...JUST BEING FIESTY!
GIN!
WHOK
YAAAAAAAAH!
A guard?
CLOMP
UTSU-HO!
WE FINISHED 'EM OFF!
NOW WE CAN RE-IMBURSE YOU!
REIN-FORCE.

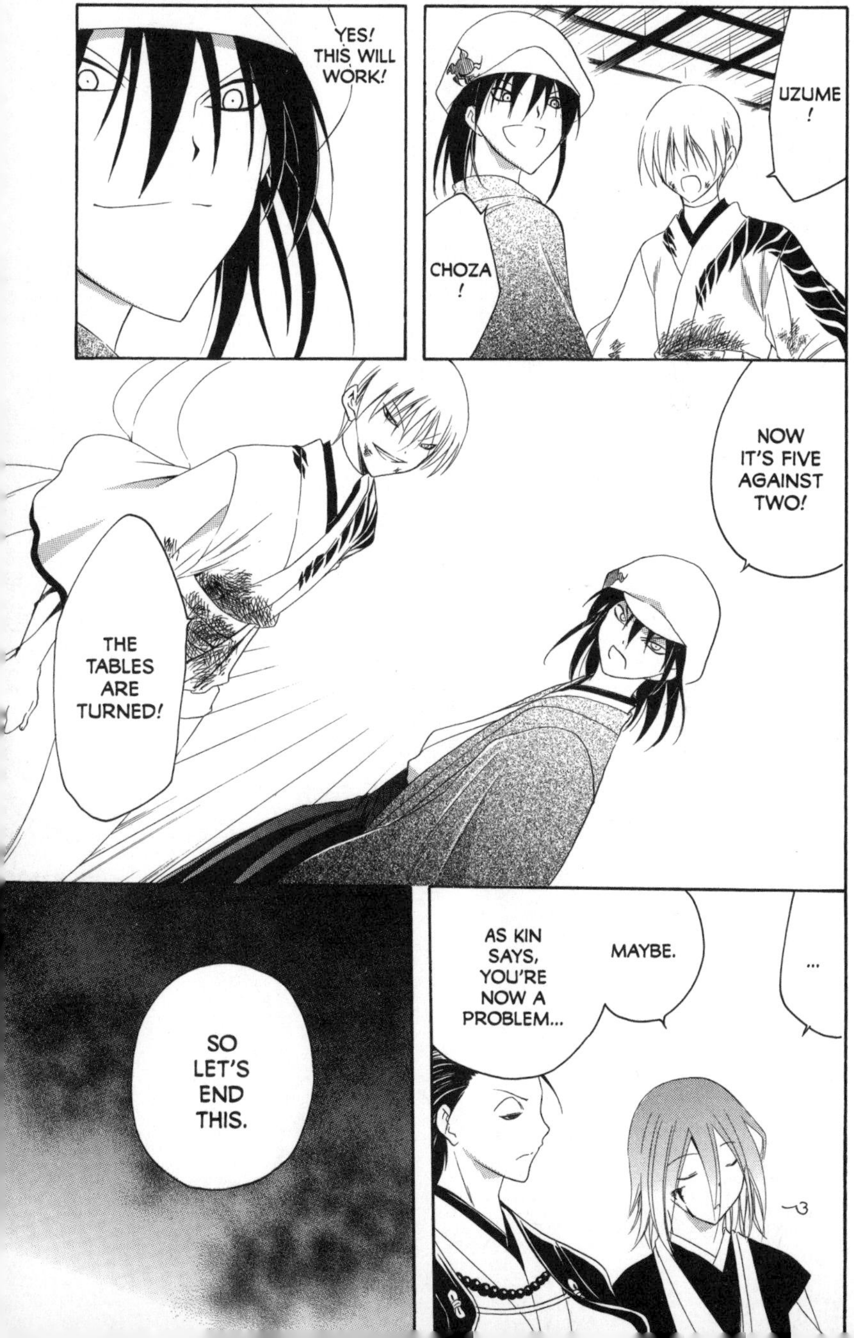
UZUME!
CHOZA!
YES! THIS WILL WORK!
NOW IT'S FIVE AGAINST TWO!
THE TABLES ARE TURNED!
...
MAYBE.
AS KIN SAYS, YOU'RE NOW A PROBLEM...
SO LET'S END THIS.

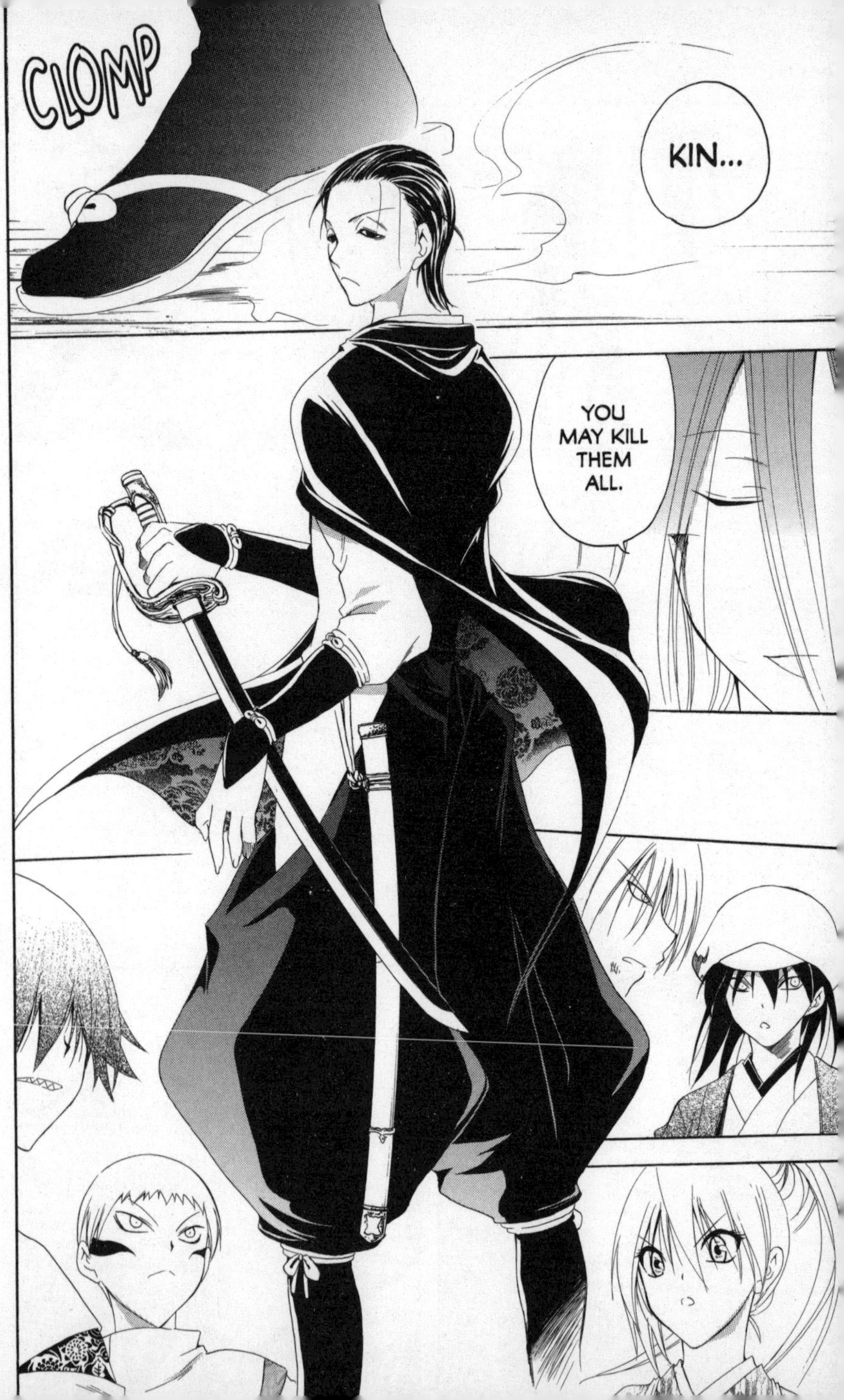
KIN...
CLOMP
YOU MAY KILL THEM ALL.

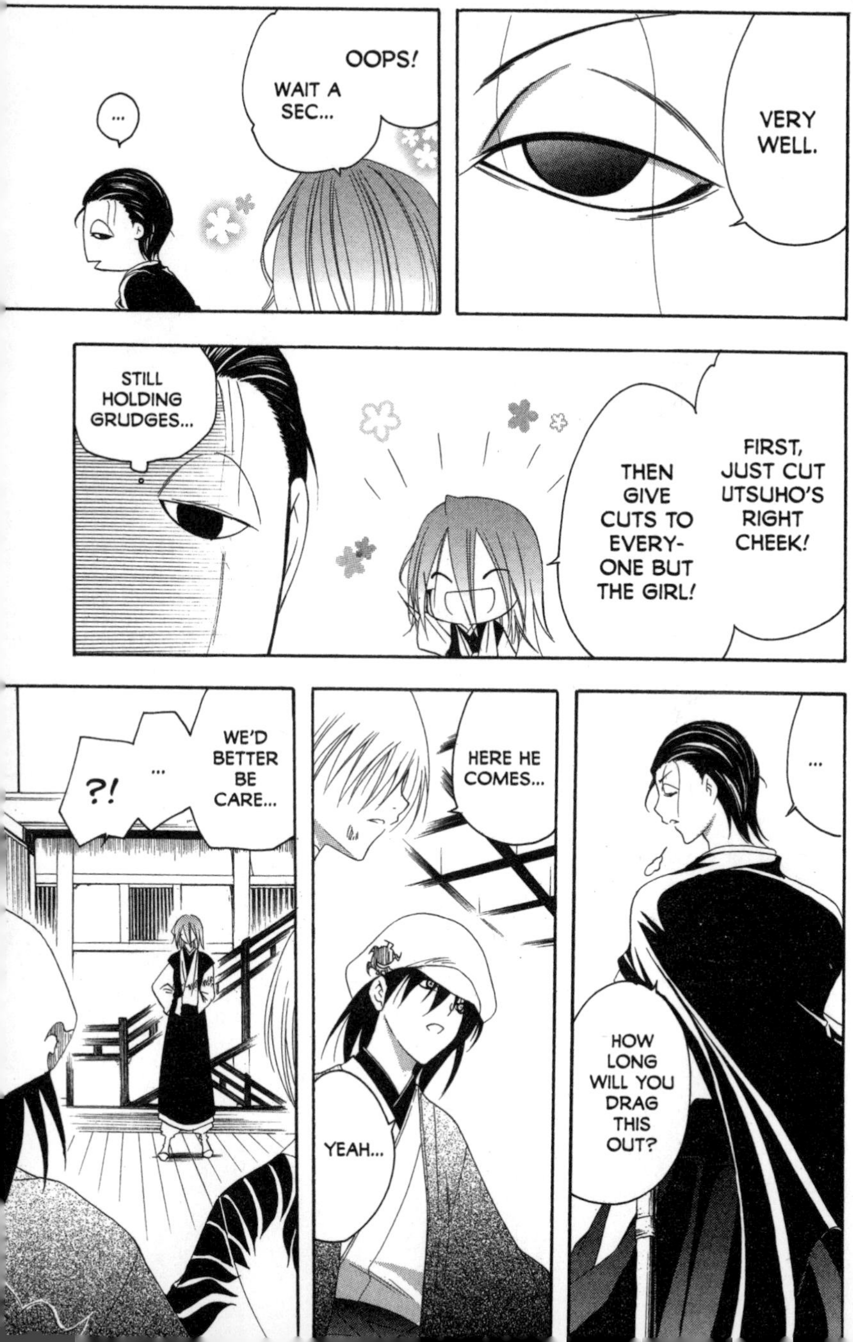
VERY WELL.
OOPS!
WAIT A SEC...
...
FIRST, JUST CUT UTSUHO'S RIGHT CHEEK!
THEN GIVE CUTS TO EVERY-ONE BUT THE GIRL!
STILL HOLDING GRUDGES...
...
HOW LONG WILL YOU DRAG THIS OUT?
HERE HE COMES...
YEAH...
WE'D BETTER BE CARE...
...
?!

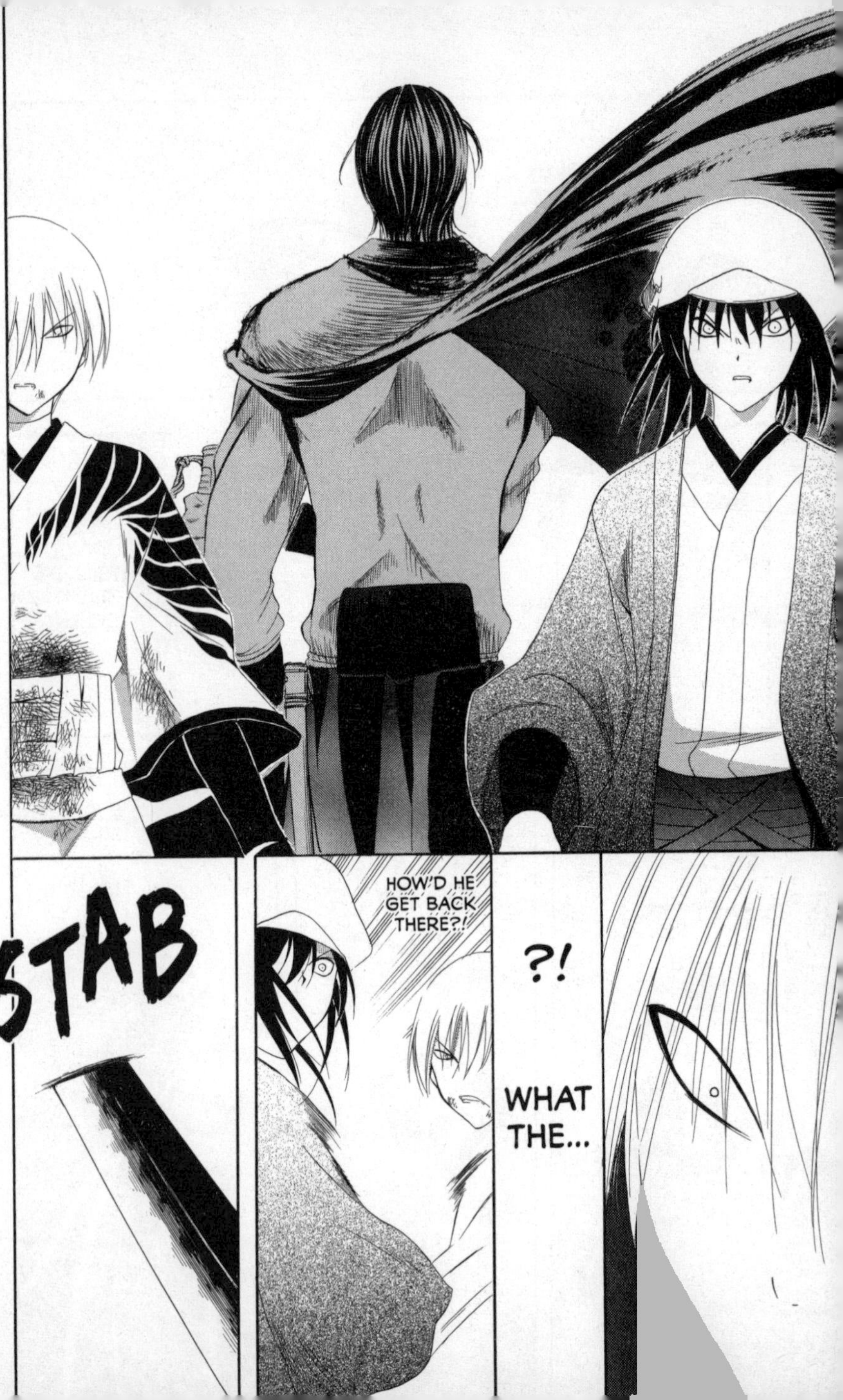
?!
WHAT THE...
HOW'D HE GET BACK THERE?!
STAB

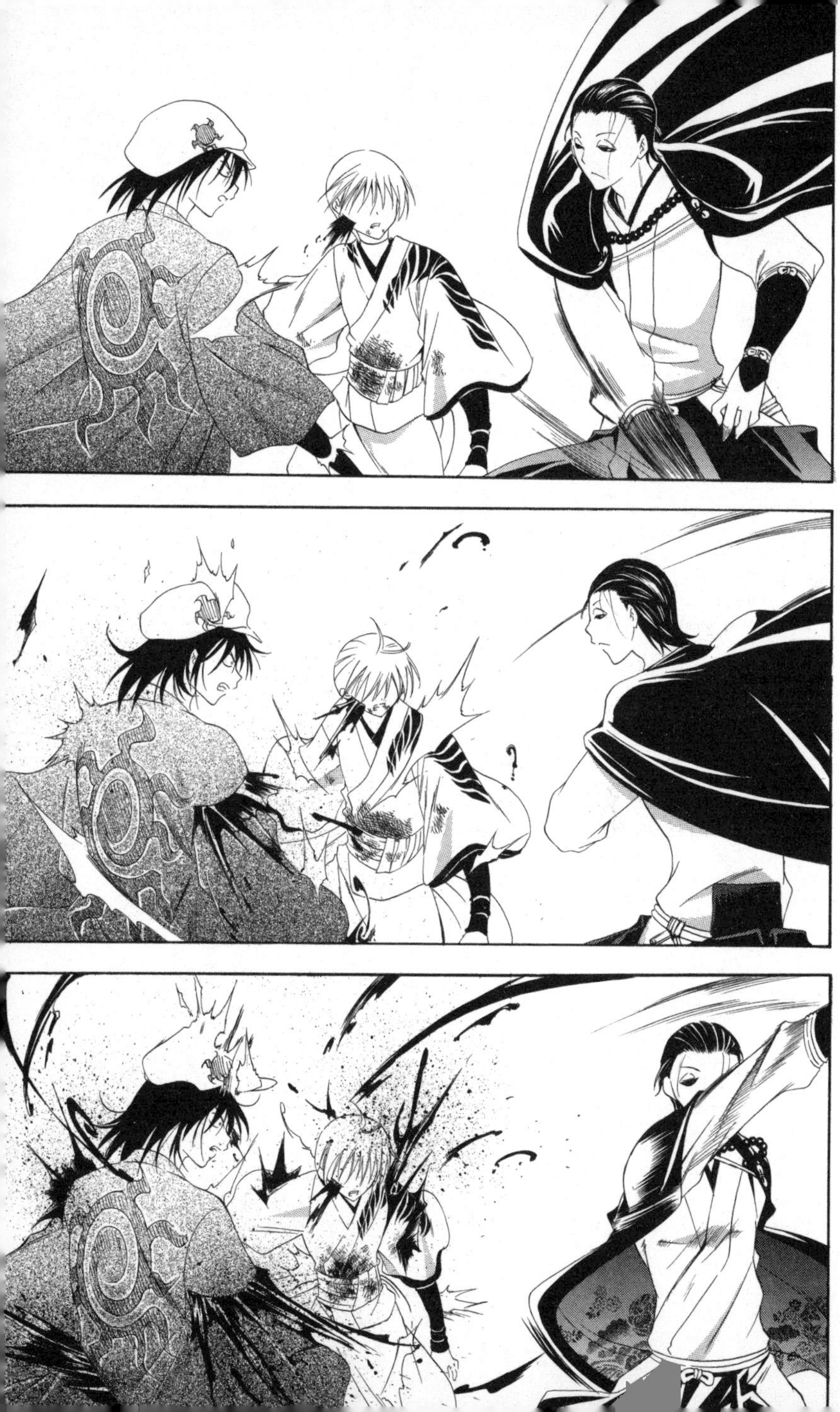

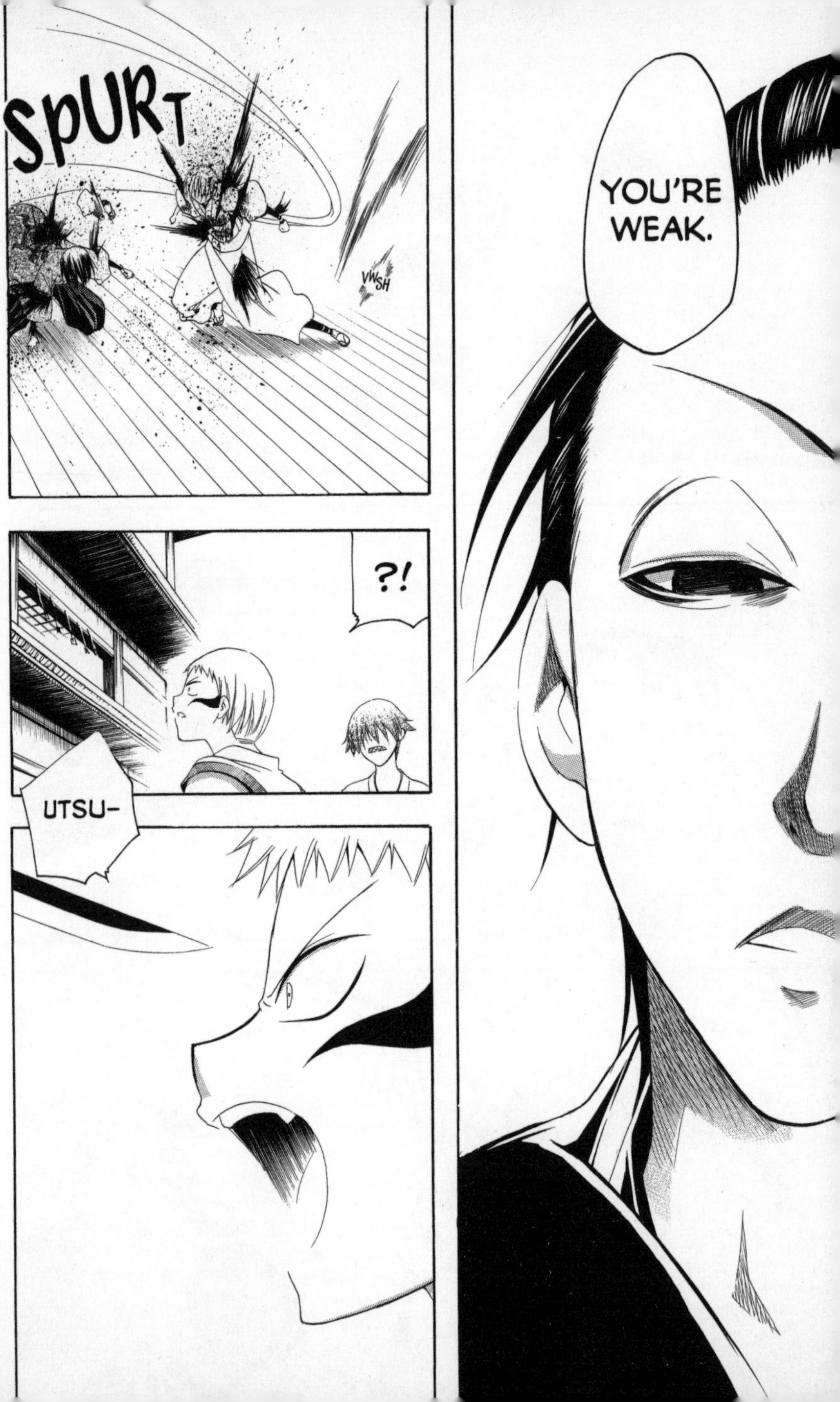
YOU'RE WEAK.
SPURT
VWSH
?!
UTSU-

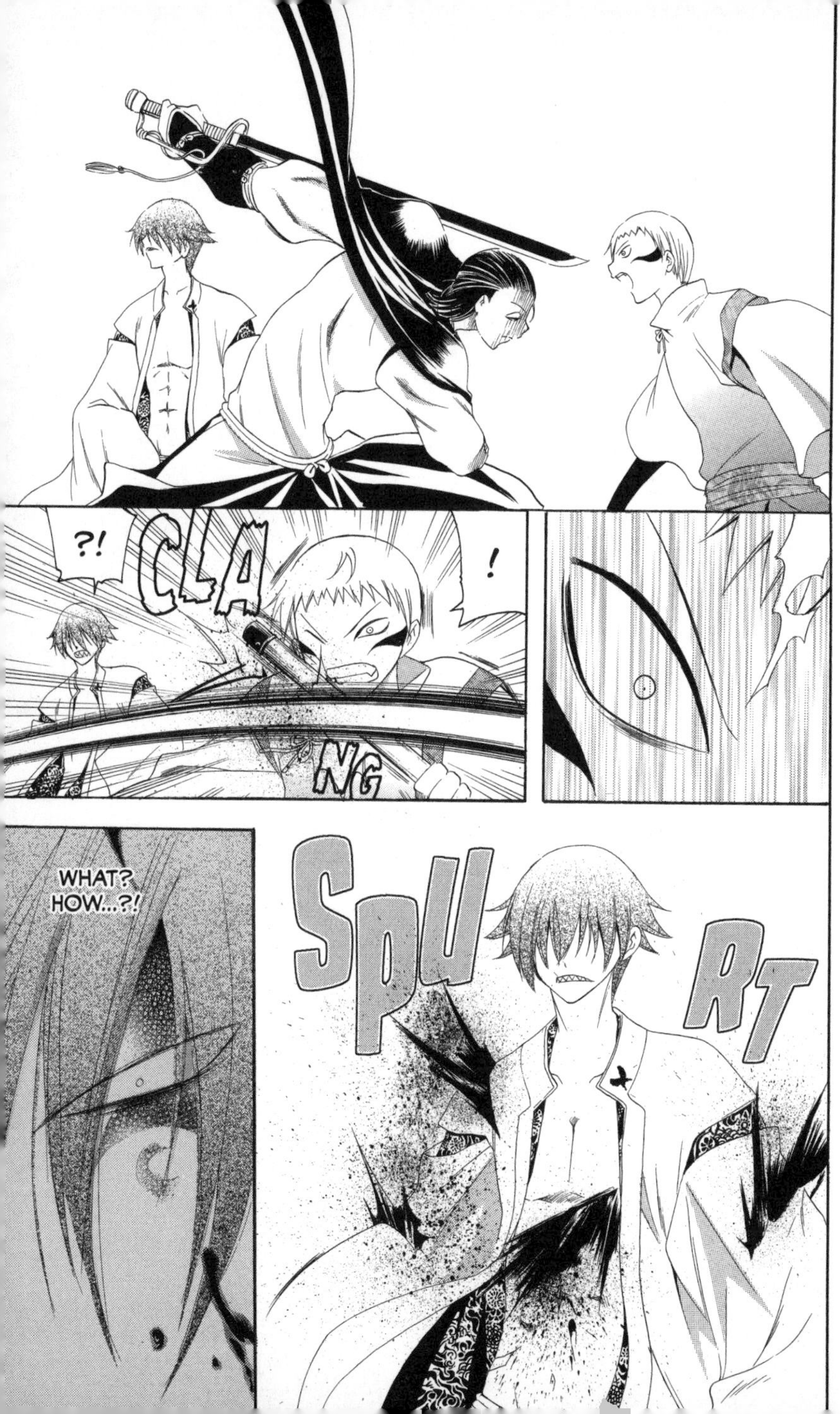
!
CLANG
?!
WHAT? HOW...?!
SPURT

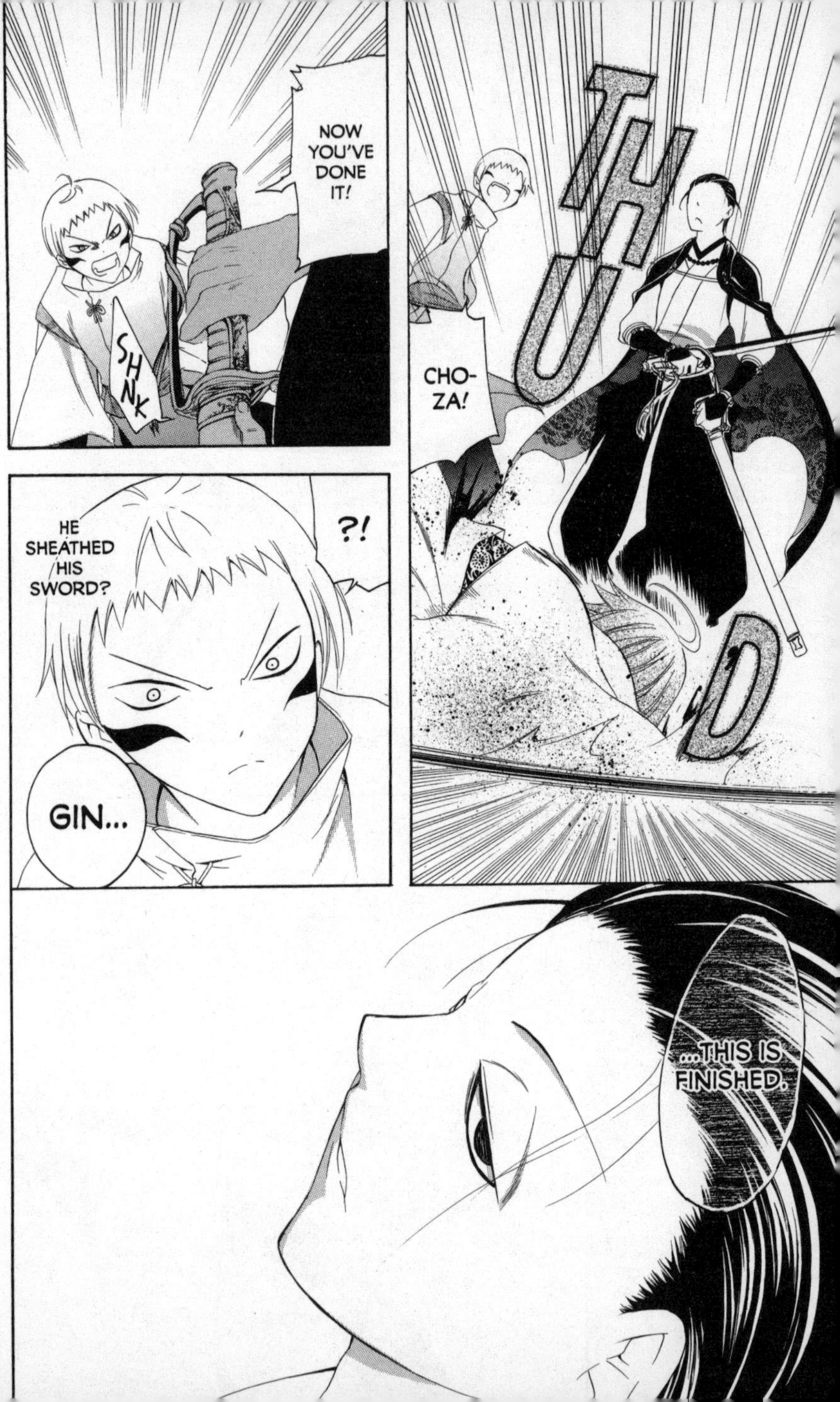
THUD
CHO-ZA!
NOW YOU'VE DONE IT!
SHNK
?!
HE SHEATHED HIS SWORD?
GIN...
...THIS IS FINISHED.

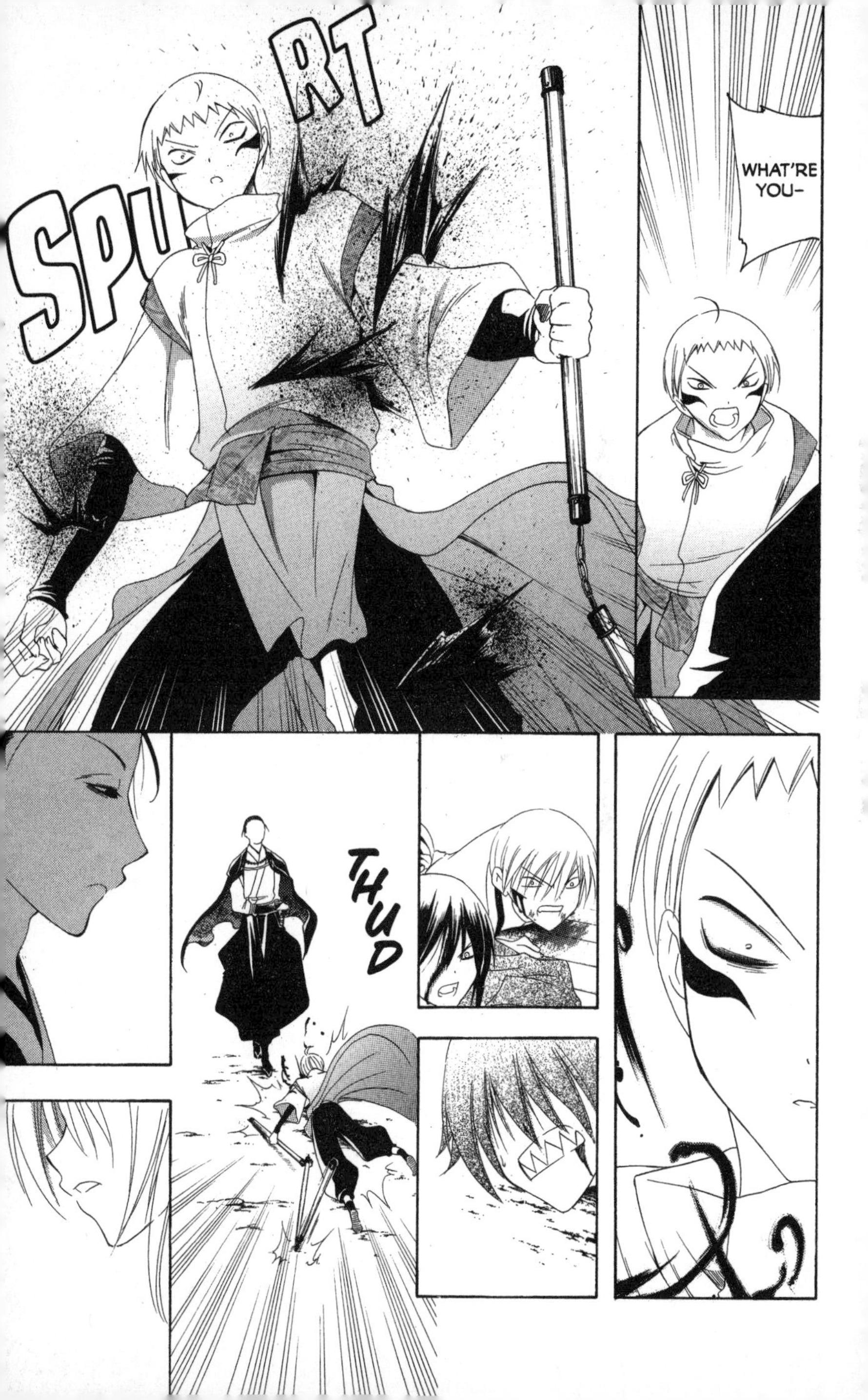
WHAT'RE YOU-
SPURT
THUD

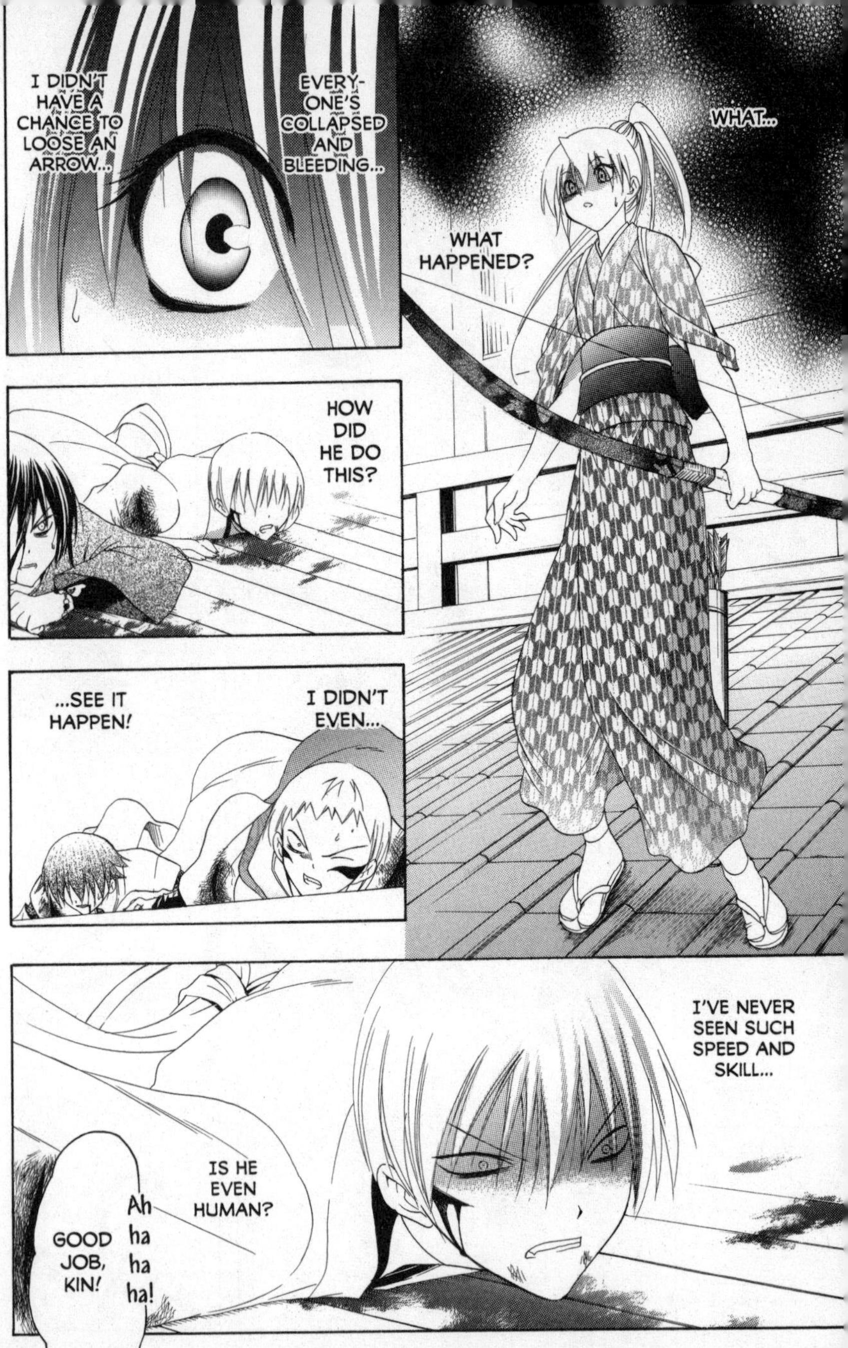
WHAT...
WHAT HAPPENED?
EVERY-ONE'S COLLAPSED AND BLEEDING...
I DIDN'T HAVE A CHANCE TO LOOSE AN ARROW...
HOW DID HE DO THIS?
I DIDN'T EVEN...
...SEE IT HAPPEN!
I'VE NEVER SEEN SUCH SPEED AND SKILL...
IS HE EVEN HUMAN?
Ah ha ha ha!
GOOD JOB, KIN!

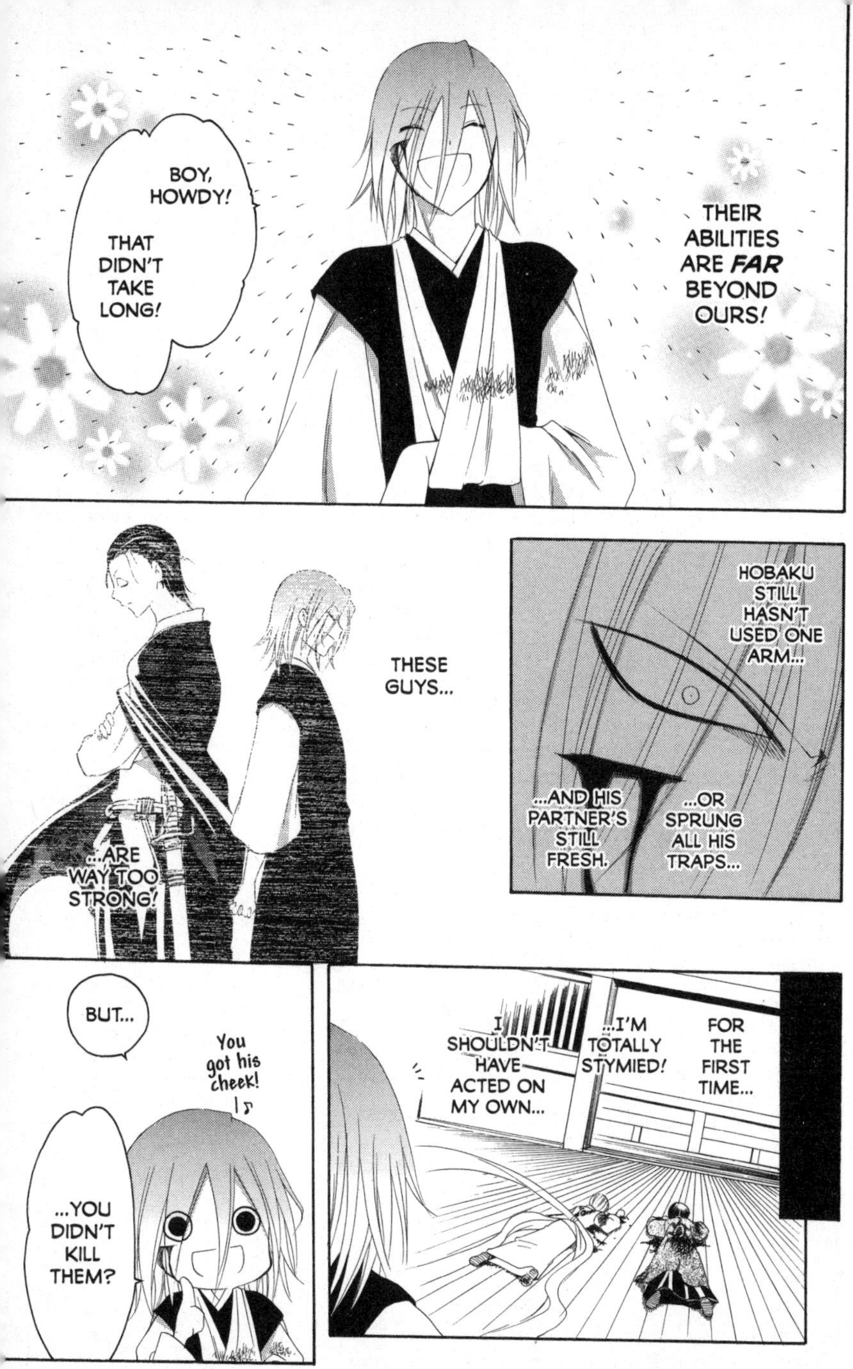
THEIR ABILITIES ARE FAR BEYOND OURS!
BOY, HOWDY!
THAT DIDN'T TAKE LONG!
HOBAKU STILL HASN'T USED ONE ARM...
...OR SPRUNG ALL HIS TRAPS...
...AND HIS PARTNER'S STILL FRESH.
THESE GUYS...
...ARE WAY TOO STRONG!
FOR THE FIRST TIME...
...I'M TOTALLY STYMIED!
I SHOULDN'T HAVE ACTED ON MY OWN...
BUT...
You got his cheek! ♪
...YOU DIDN'T KILL THEM?

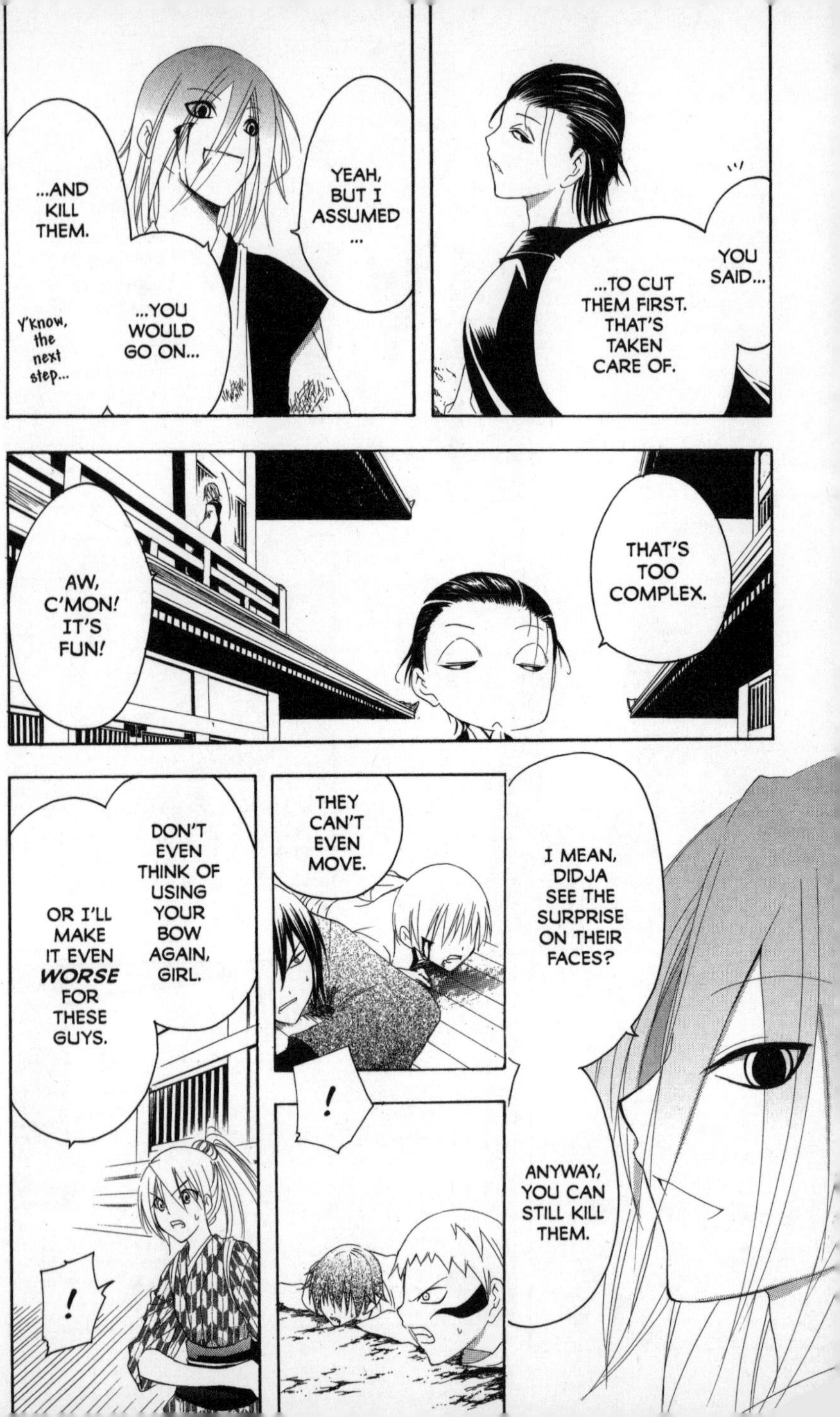
YOU SAID...
...TO CUT THEM FIRST. THAT'S TAKEN CARE OF.
YEAH, BUT I ASSUMED ...
...YOU WOULD GO ON...
...AND KILL THEM.
Y'know, the next step...
THAT'S TOO COMPLEX.
AW, C'MON! IT'S FUN!
I MEAN, DIDJA SEE THE SURPRISE ON THEIR FACES?
ANYWAY, YOU CAN STILL KILL THEM.
THEY CAN'T EVEN MOVE.
!
DON'T EVEN THINK OF USING YOUR BOW AGAIN, GIRL.
OR I'LL MAKE IT EVEN *WORSE* FOR THESE GUYS.
!

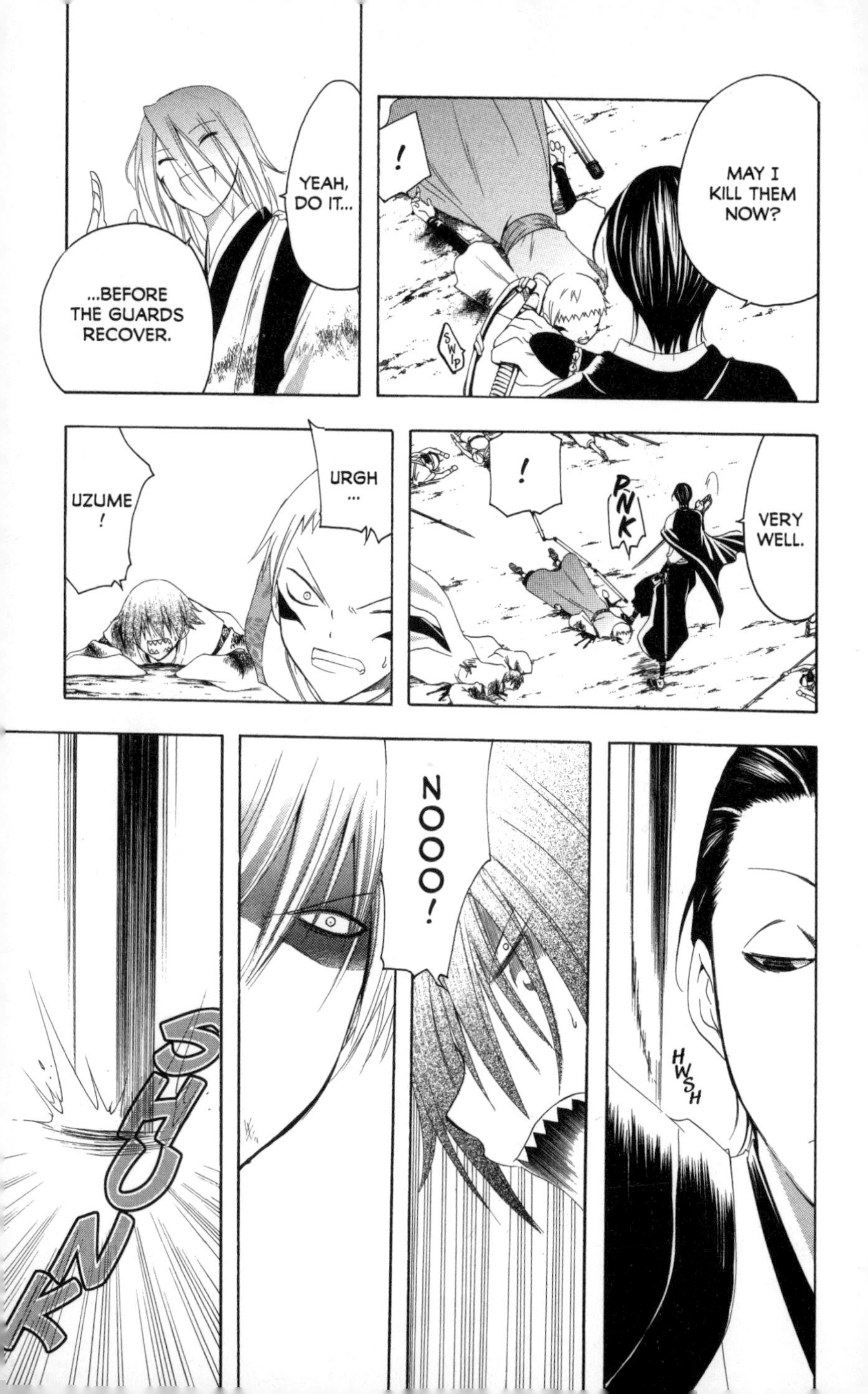
MAY I KILL THEM NOW?
!
SWIP
YEAH, DO IT...
...BEFORE THE GUARDS RECOVER.
VERY WELL.
PNK
!
URGH ...
UZUME !
HWSH
NOOOO!
SHUNK

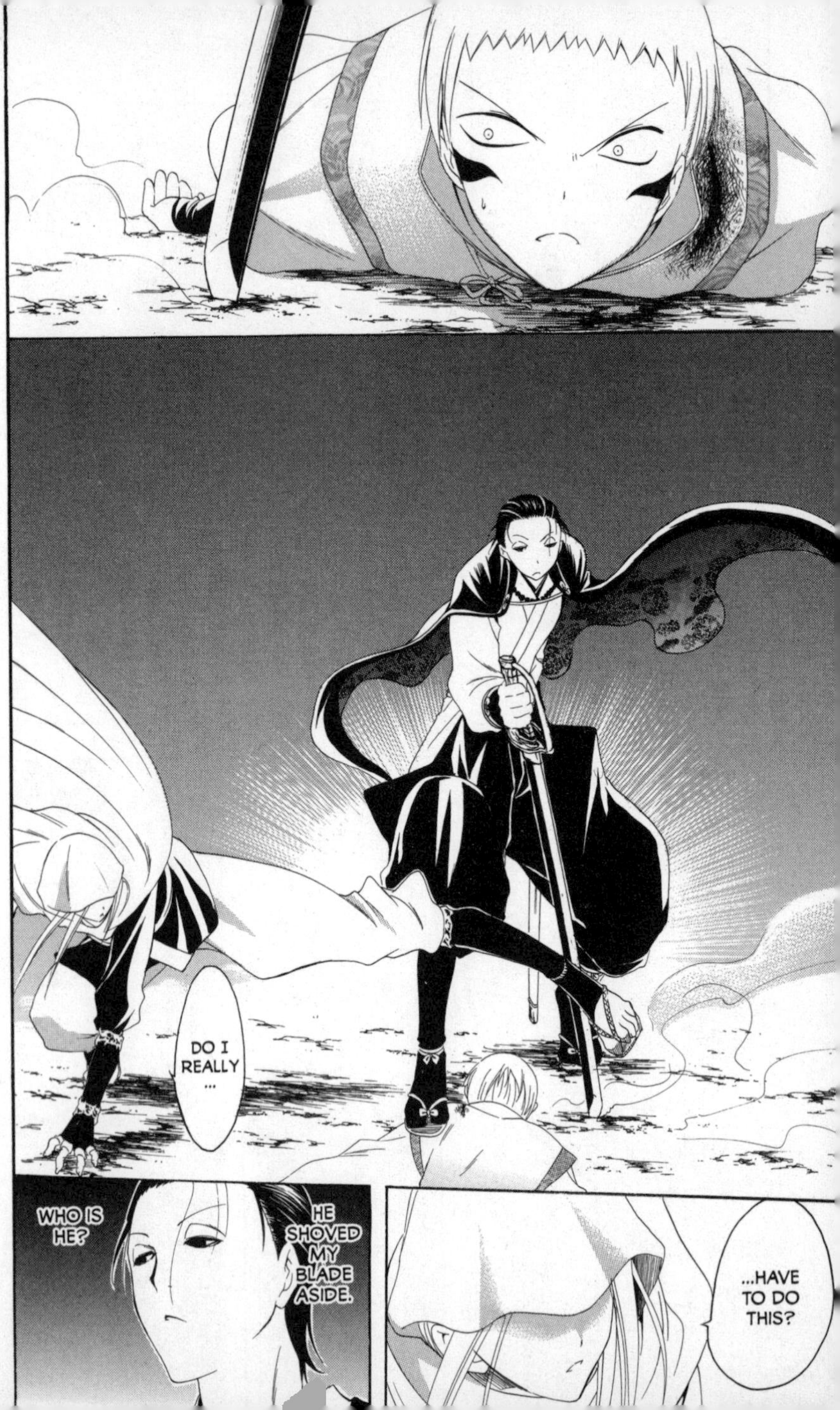
DO I REALLY ...
...HAVE TO DO THIS?
WHO IS HE?
HE SHOVED MY BLADE ASIDE.

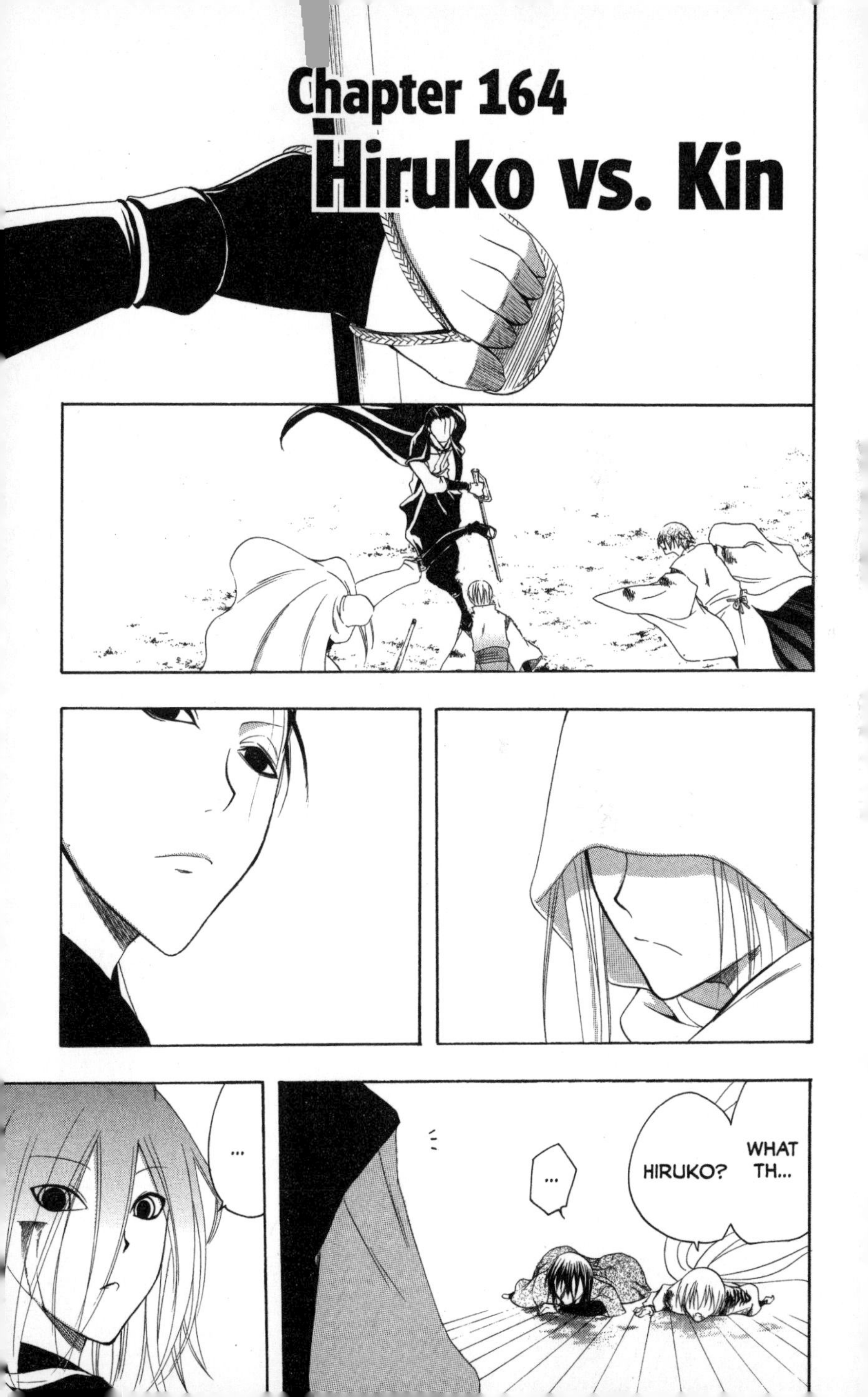
Chapter 164
Hiruko vs. Kin
WHAT TH... HIRUKO?
...
...

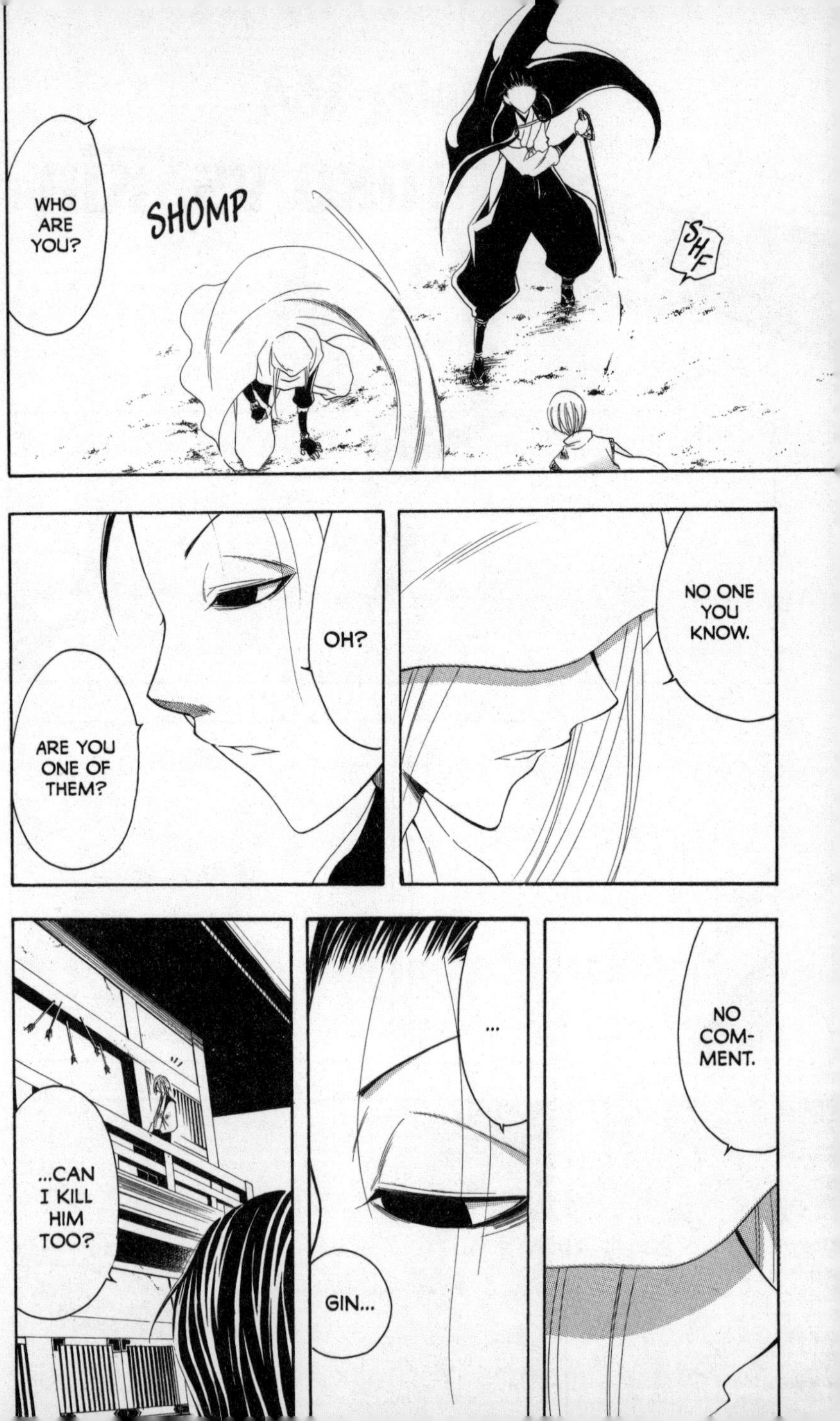
SHF
SHOMP
WHO ARE YOU?
NO ONE YOU KNOW.
OH?
ARE YOU ONE OF THEM?
NO COM-MENT.
...
GIN...
...CAN I KILL HIM TOO?

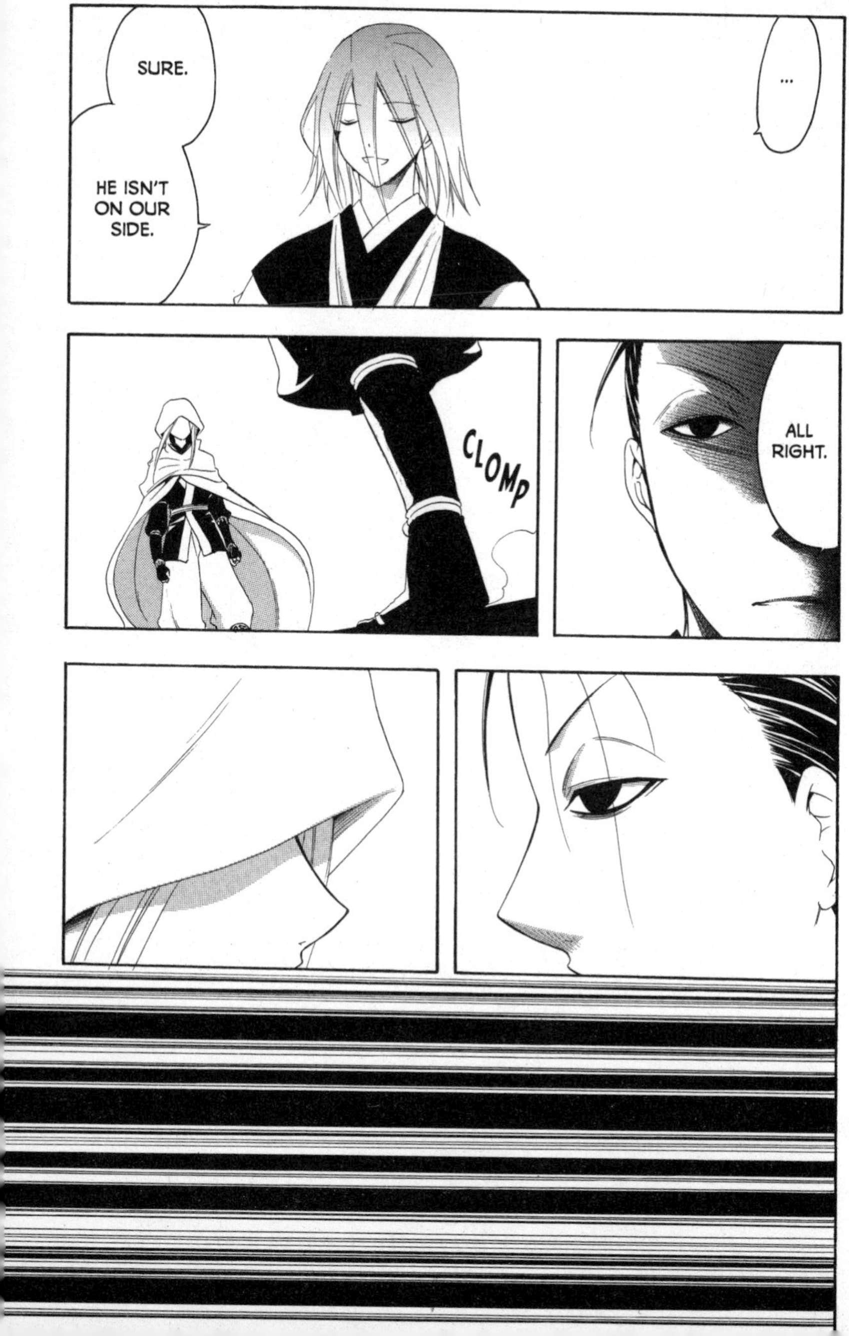
...
SURE.
HE ISN'T ON OUR SIDE.
ALL RIGHT.
CLOMP

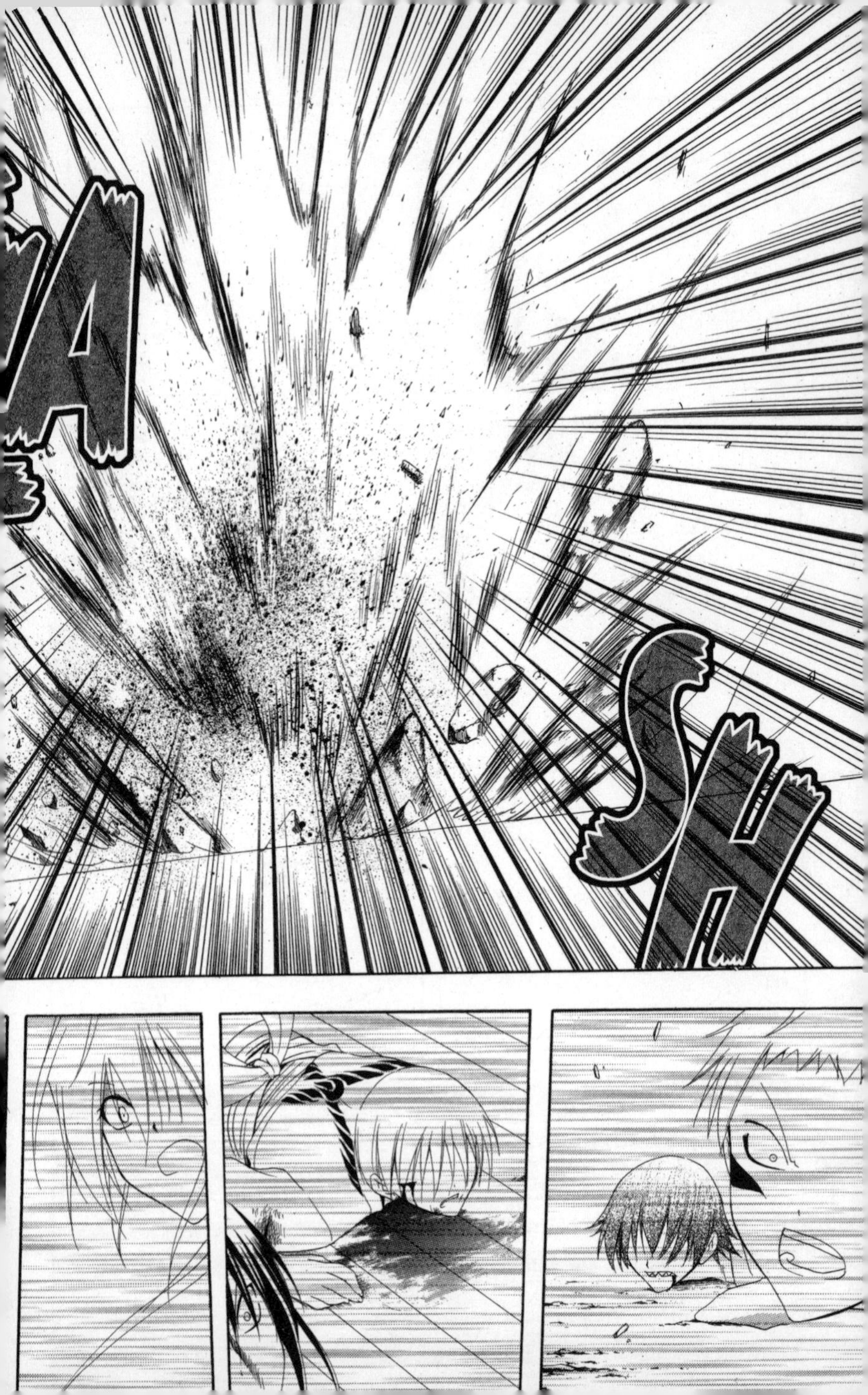
A
SH

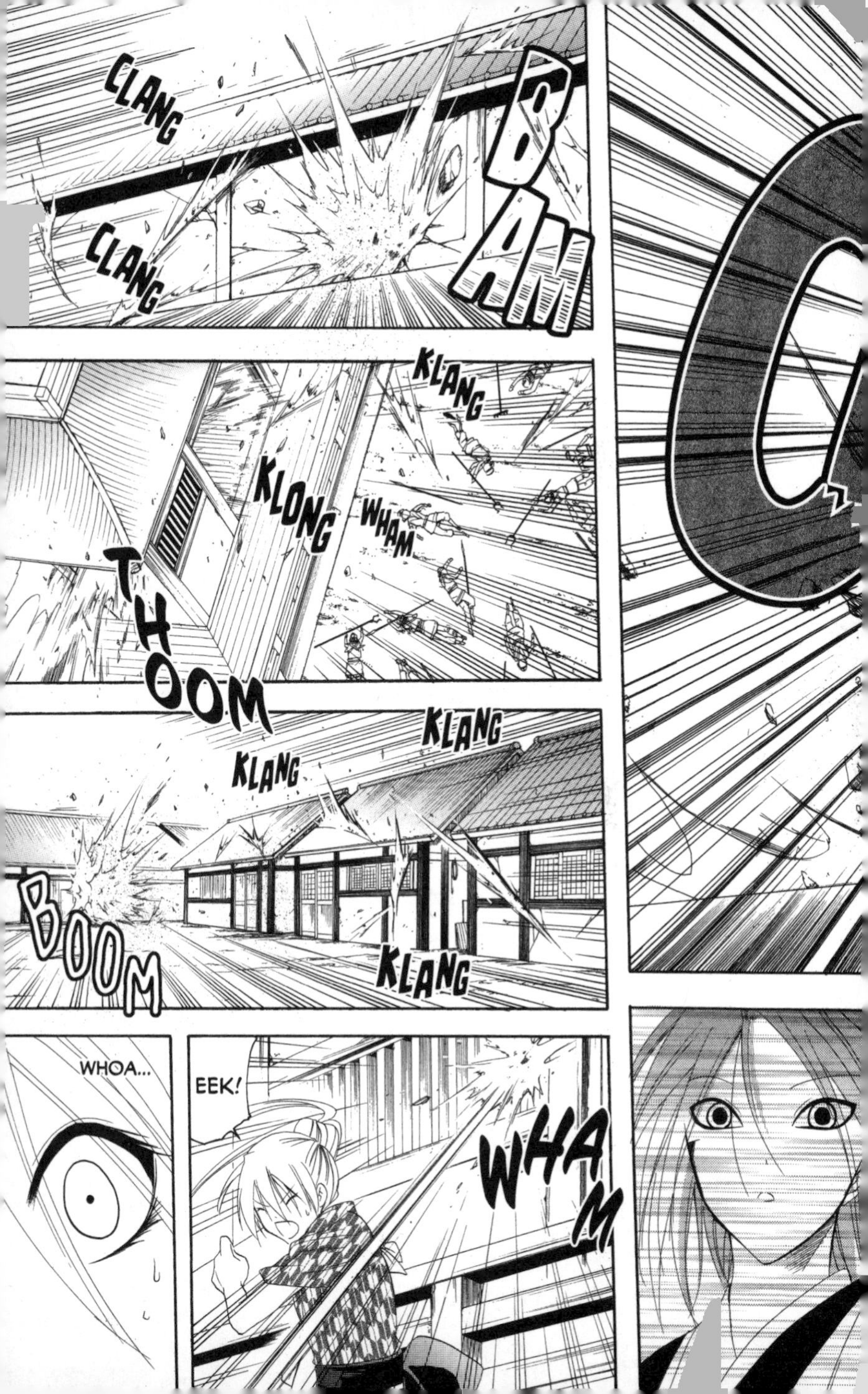
BAM
CLANG
CLANG
KLANG
WHAM
KLONG
THOOM
KLANG
KLANG
KLANG
BOOM
WHAM
EEK!
WHOA...

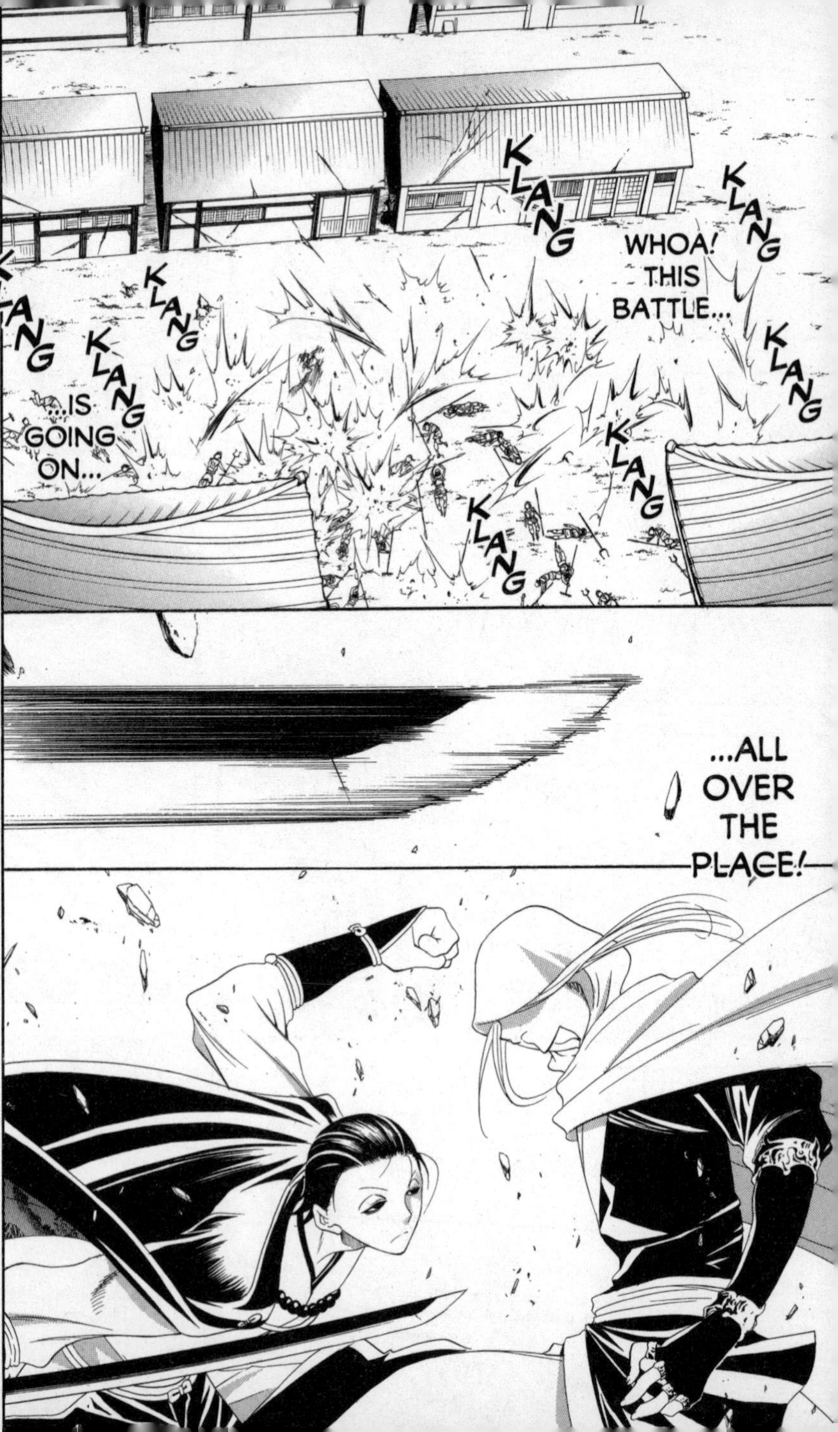
KLANG
KLANG
WHOA! THIS BATTLE...
KLANG
KLANG
KLANG
KLANG
KLANG
KLANG
...IS GOING ON...
...ALL OVER THE PLACE!

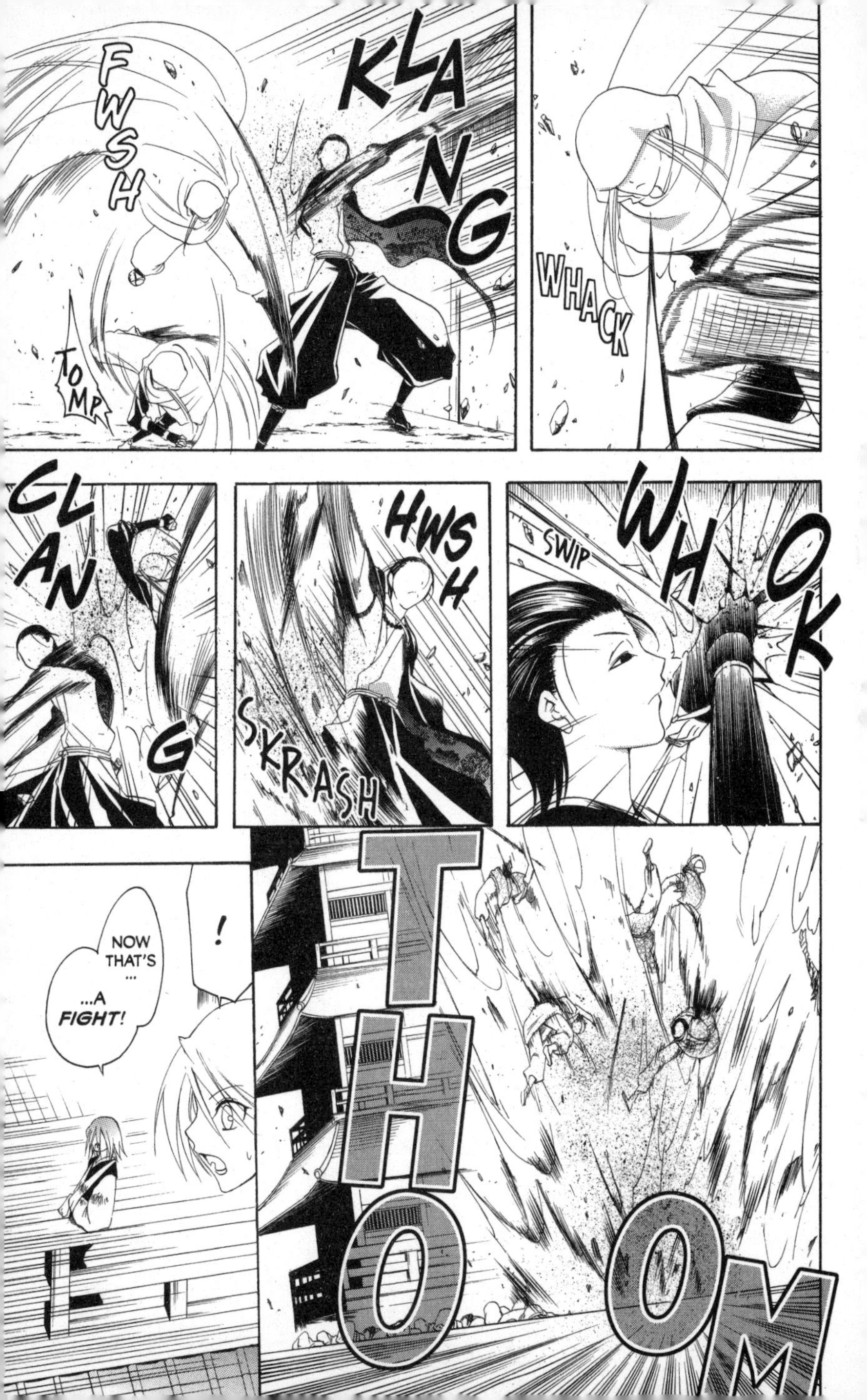
WHACK
KLANG
FWSH
TOMP
WHOOK
SWIP
HWSH
SKRASH
CLANG
THOOM
!
NOW THAT'S... ...A FIGHT!

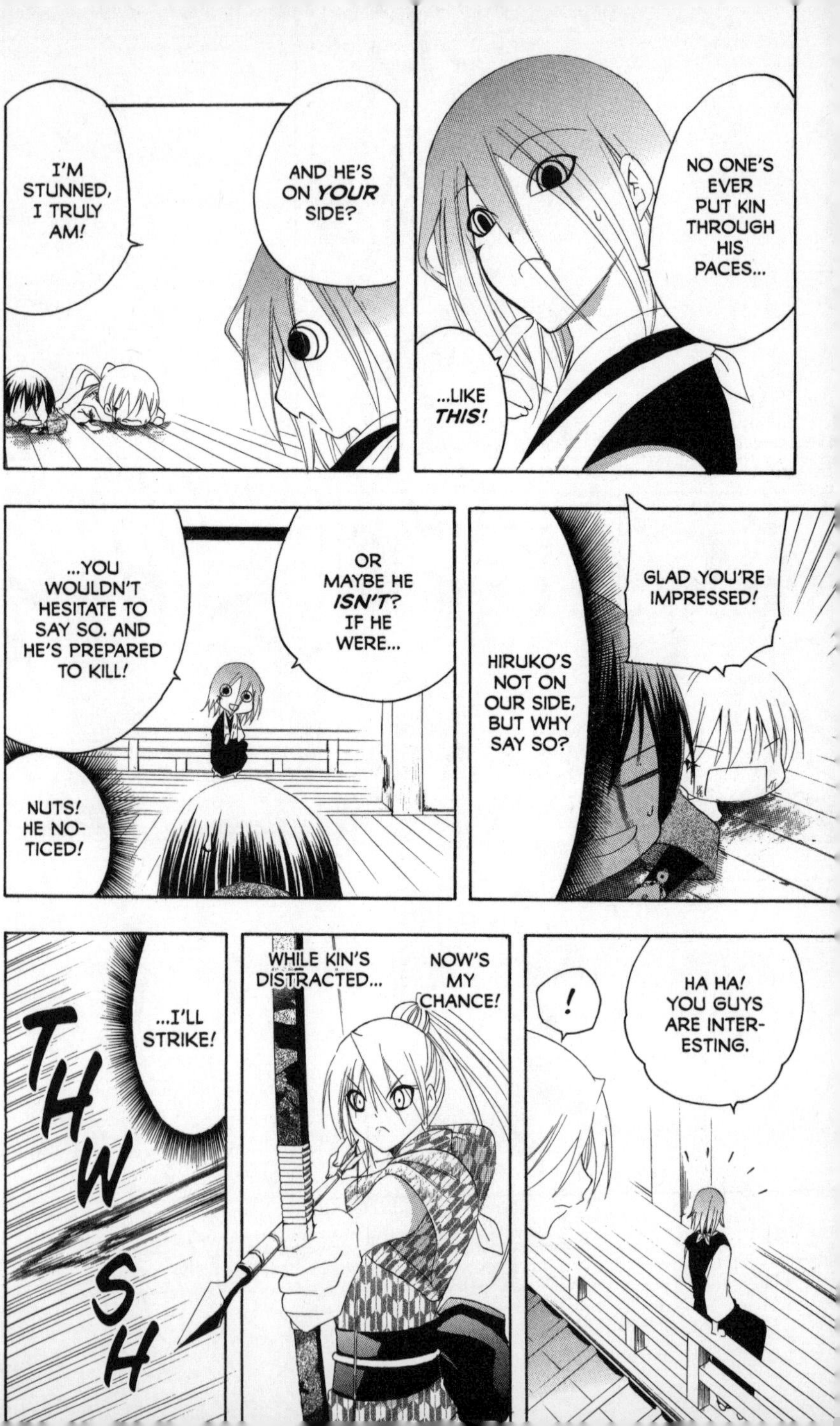
NO ONE'S EVER PUT KIN THROUGH HIS PACES...
...LIKE *THIS!*
AND HE'S ON *YOUR* SIDE?
I'M STUNNED, I TRULY AM!
GLAD YOU'RE IMPRESSED!
HIRUKO'S NOT ON OUR SIDE, BUT WHY SAY SO?
OR MAYBE HE *ISN'T*? IF HE WERE...
...YOU WOULDN'T HESITATE TO SAY SO. AND HE'S PREPARED TO KILL!
NUTS! HE NOTICED!
HA HA! YOU GUYS ARE INTERESTING.
!
NOW'S MY CHANCE!
WHILE KIN'S DISTRACTED...
...I'LL STRIKE!
THWSH

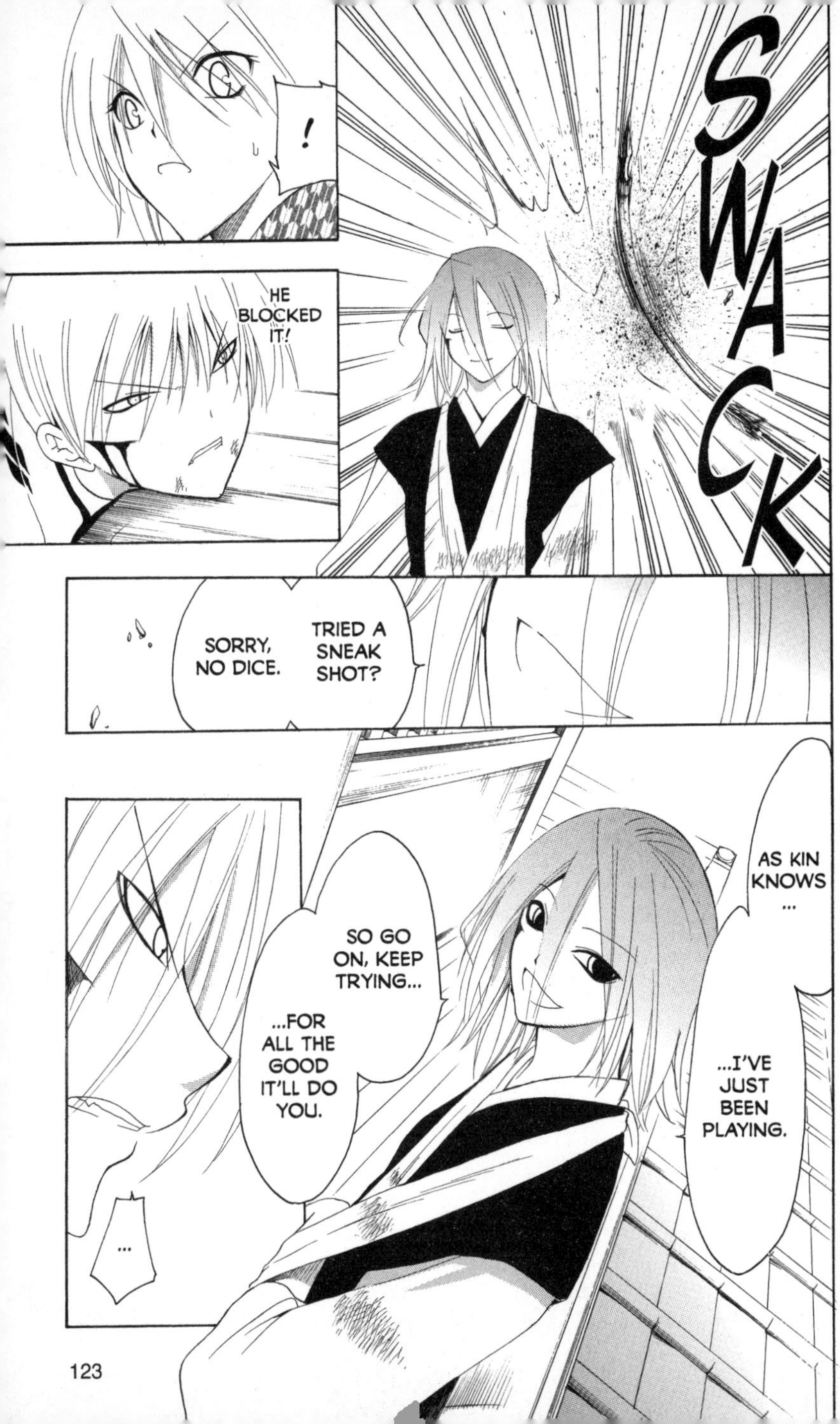
SWACK
!
HE BLOCKED IT!
TRIED A SNEAK SHOT?
SORRY, NO DICE.
AS KIN KNOWS ...
...I'VE JUST BEEN PLAYING.
SO GO ON, KEEP TRYING...
...FOR ALL THE GOOD IT'LL DO YOU.
...

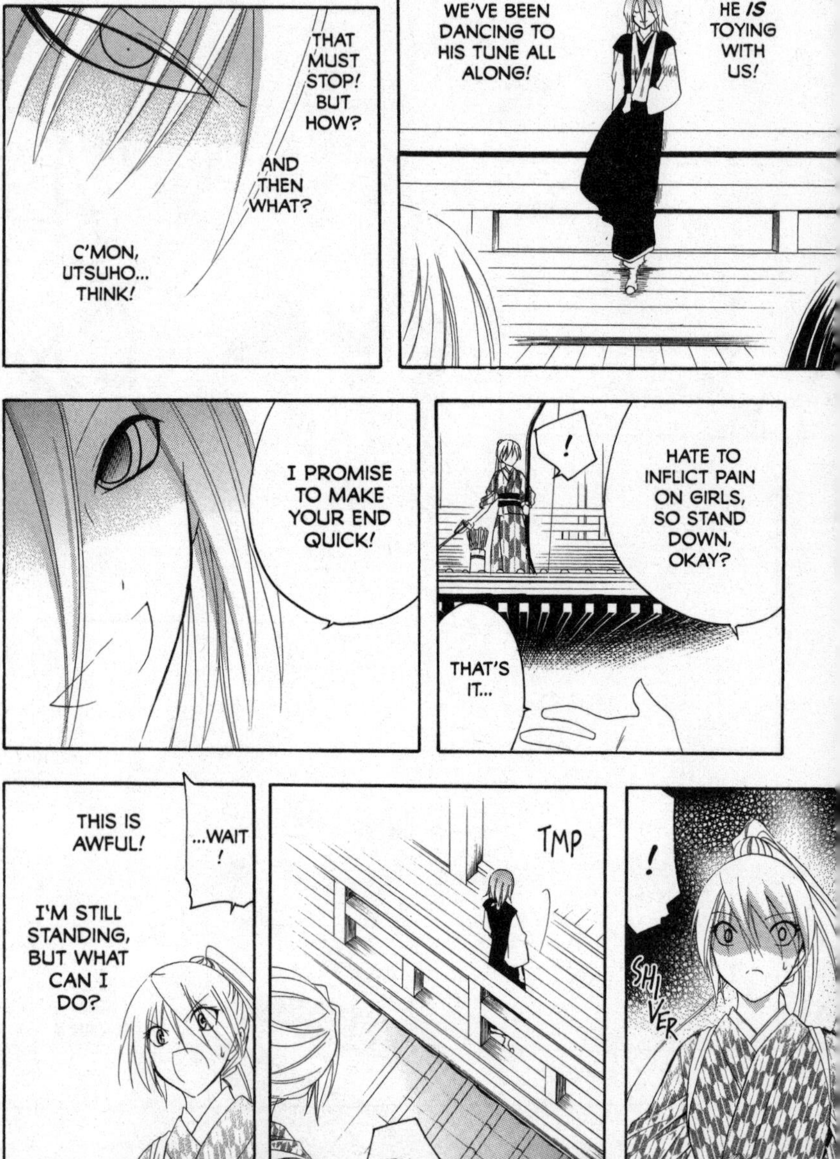
HE *IS* TOYING WITH US!
WE'VE BEEN DANCING TO HIS TUNE ALL ALONG!
THAT MUST STOP! BUT HOW?
AND THEN WHAT?
C'MON, UTSUHO... THINK!
!
HATE TO INFLICT PAIN ON GIRLS, SO STAND DOWN, OKAY?
THAT'S IT...
I PROMISE TO MAKE YOUR END QUICK!
!
SHIVER
TMP
HEY...
...WAIT!
THIS IS AWFUL!
I'M STILL STANDING, BUT WHAT CAN I DO?

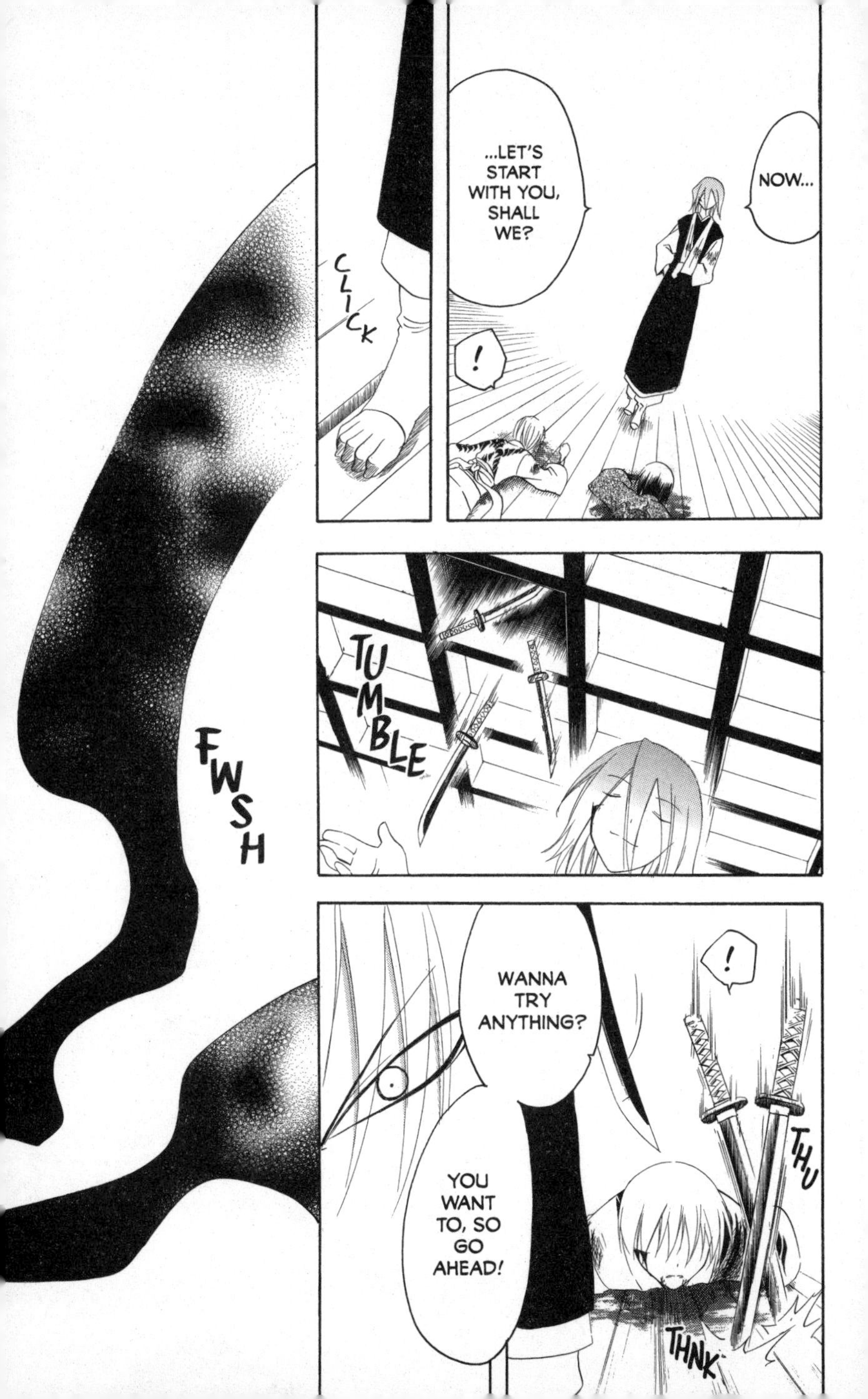

NOW...
...LET'S START WITH YOU, SHALL WE?
!
CLICK
TUMBLE
!
WANNA TRY ANYTHING?
YOU WANT TO, SO GO AHEAD!
THU
THNK
FWSH

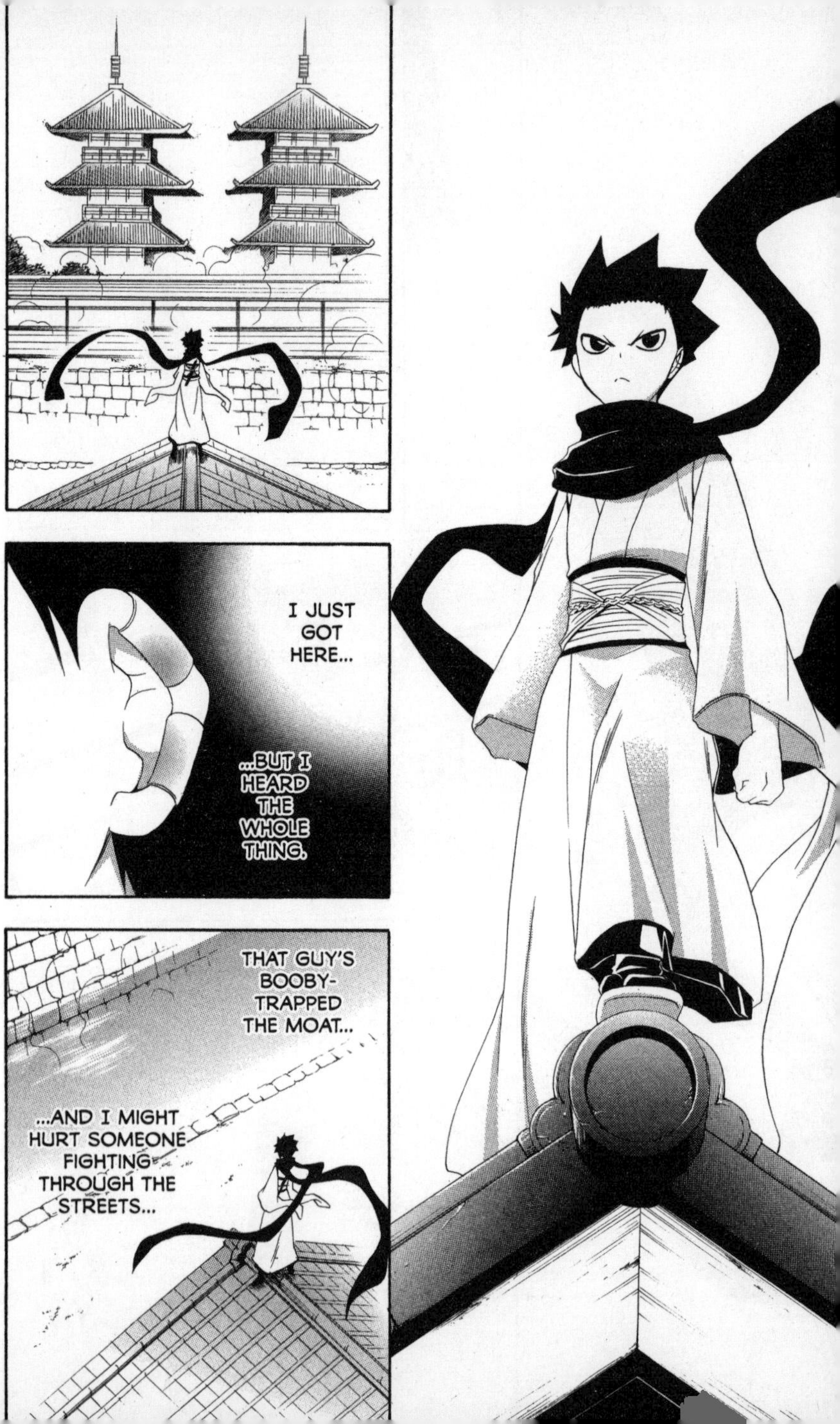
I JUST GOT HERE...
...BUT I HEARD THE WHOLE THING.
THAT GUY'S BOOBY-TRAPPED THE MOAT...
...AND I MIGHT HURT SOMEONE FIGHTING THROUGH THE STREETS...

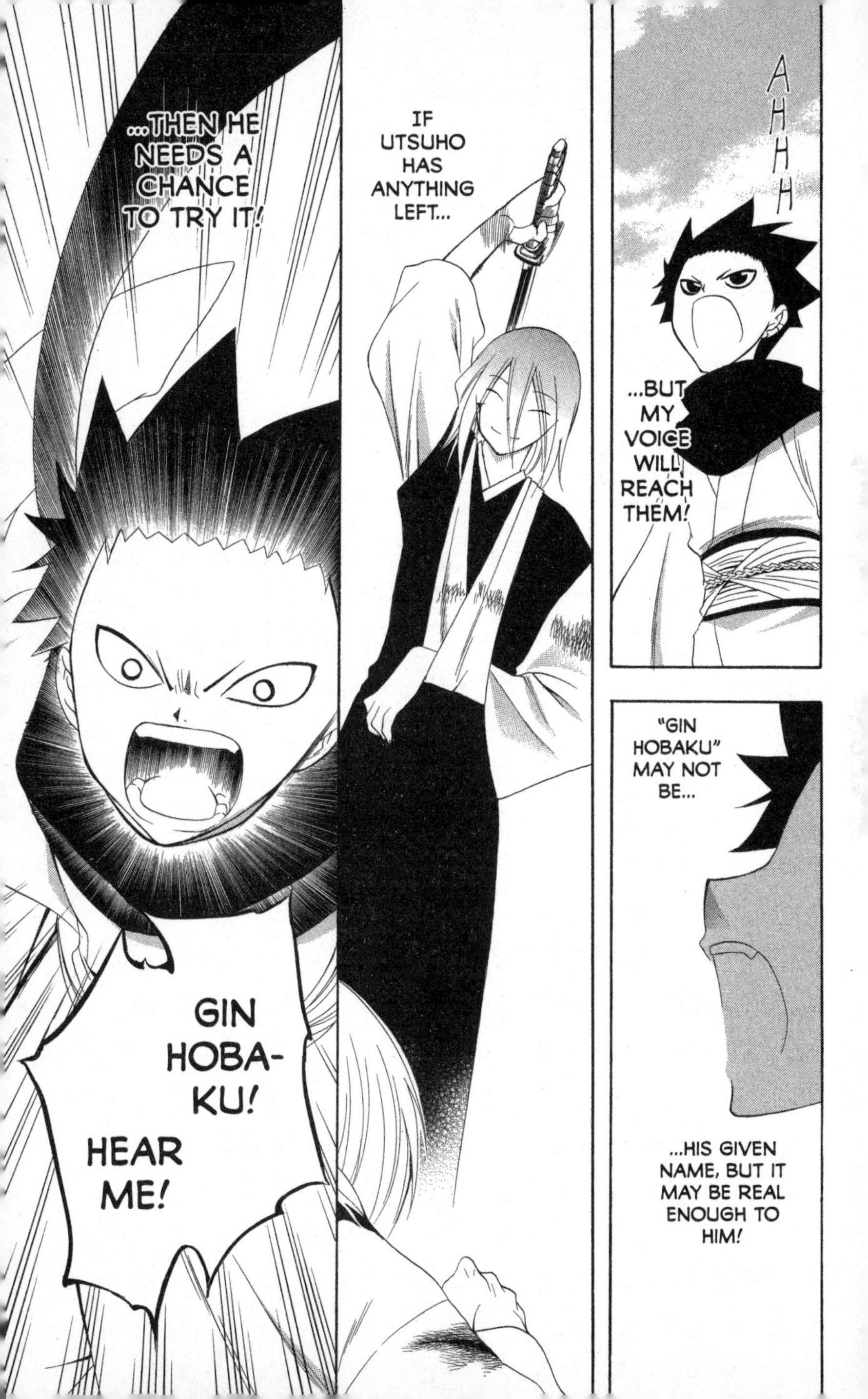
AHHH
...BUT MY VOICE WILL REACH THEM!
"GIN HOBAKU" MAY NOT BE...
...HIS GIVEN NAME, BUT IT MAY BE REAL ENOUGH TO HIM!
IF UTSUHO HAS ANYTHING LEFT...
...THEN HE NEEDS A CHANCE TO TRY IT!
GIN HOBA-KU!
HEAR ME!

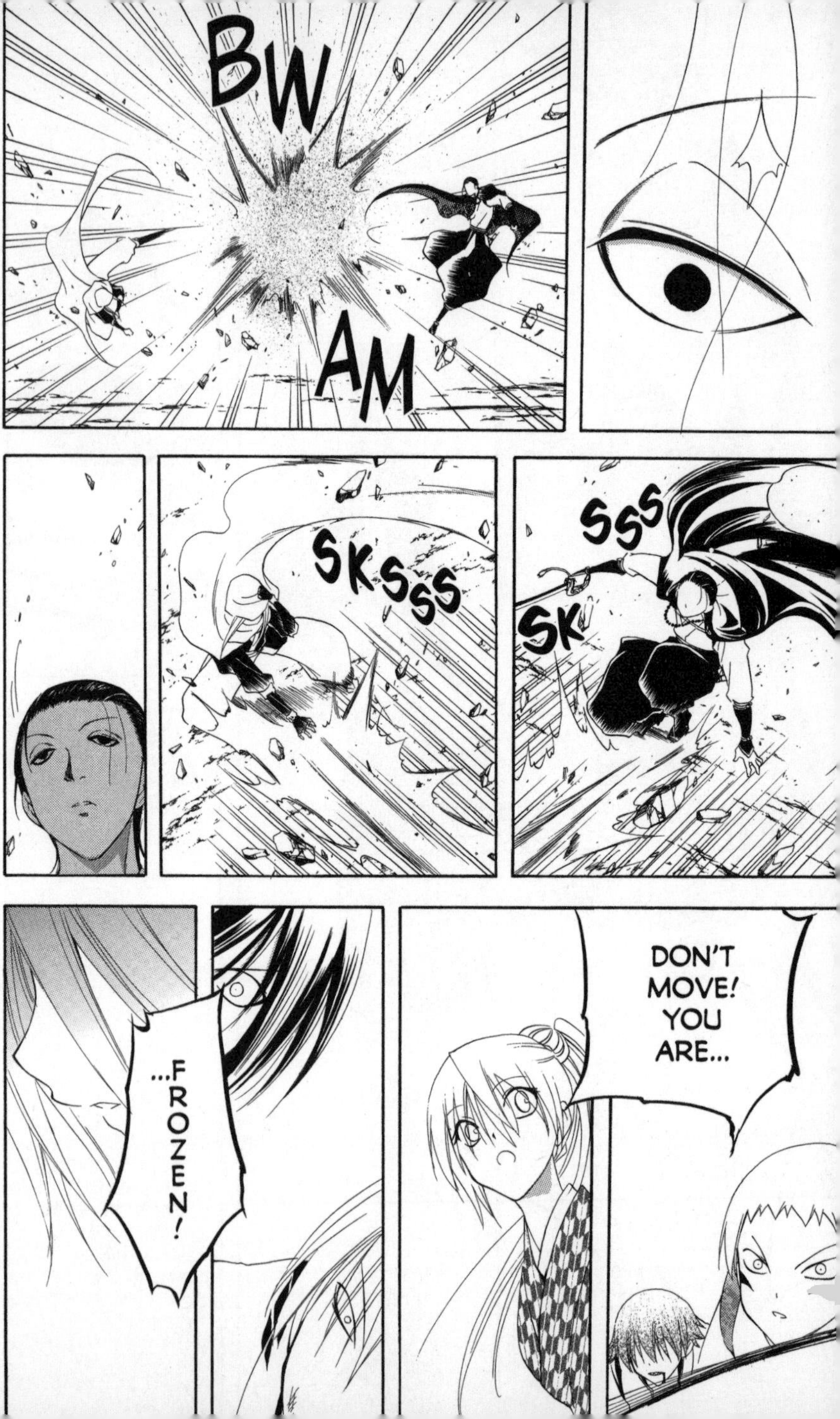
BW
AM
SSS
SK
SKSSSS
DON'T MOVE! YOU ARE...
...FROZEN!

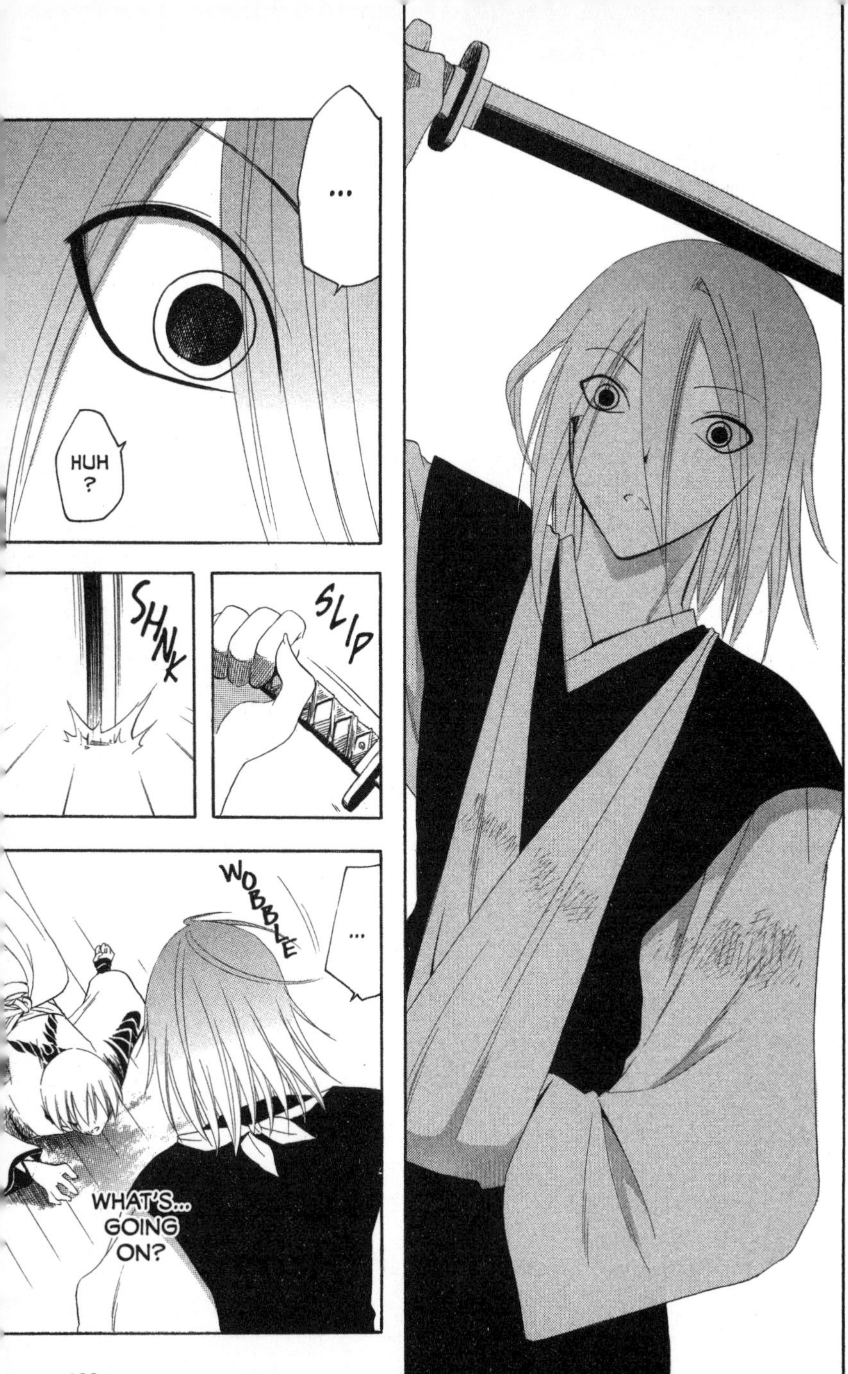
...
HUH ?
SLIP
SHNK
WOBBLE
...
WHAT'S... GOING ON?

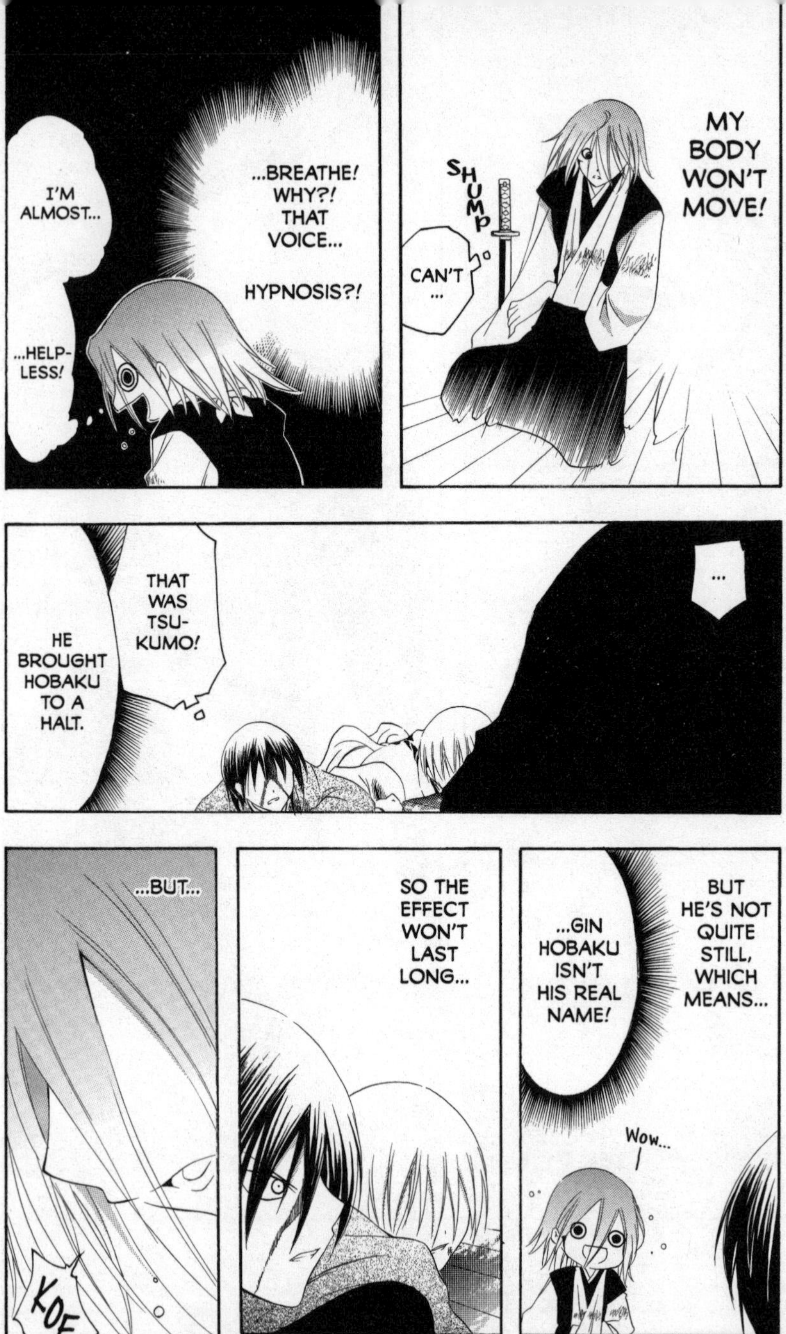
MY BODY WON'T MOVE!
SHUMP
CAN'T ...
...BREATHE! WHY?! THAT VOICE...
HYPNOSIS?!
I'M ALMOST...
...HELP-LESS!
...
THAT WAS TSU-KUMO!
HE BROUGHT HOBAKU TO A HALT.
BUT HE'S NOT QUITE STILL, WHICH MEANS...
...GIN HOBAKU ISN'T HIS REAL NAME!
WOW...!
SO THE EFFECT WON'T LAST LONG...
...BUT...
KOFF

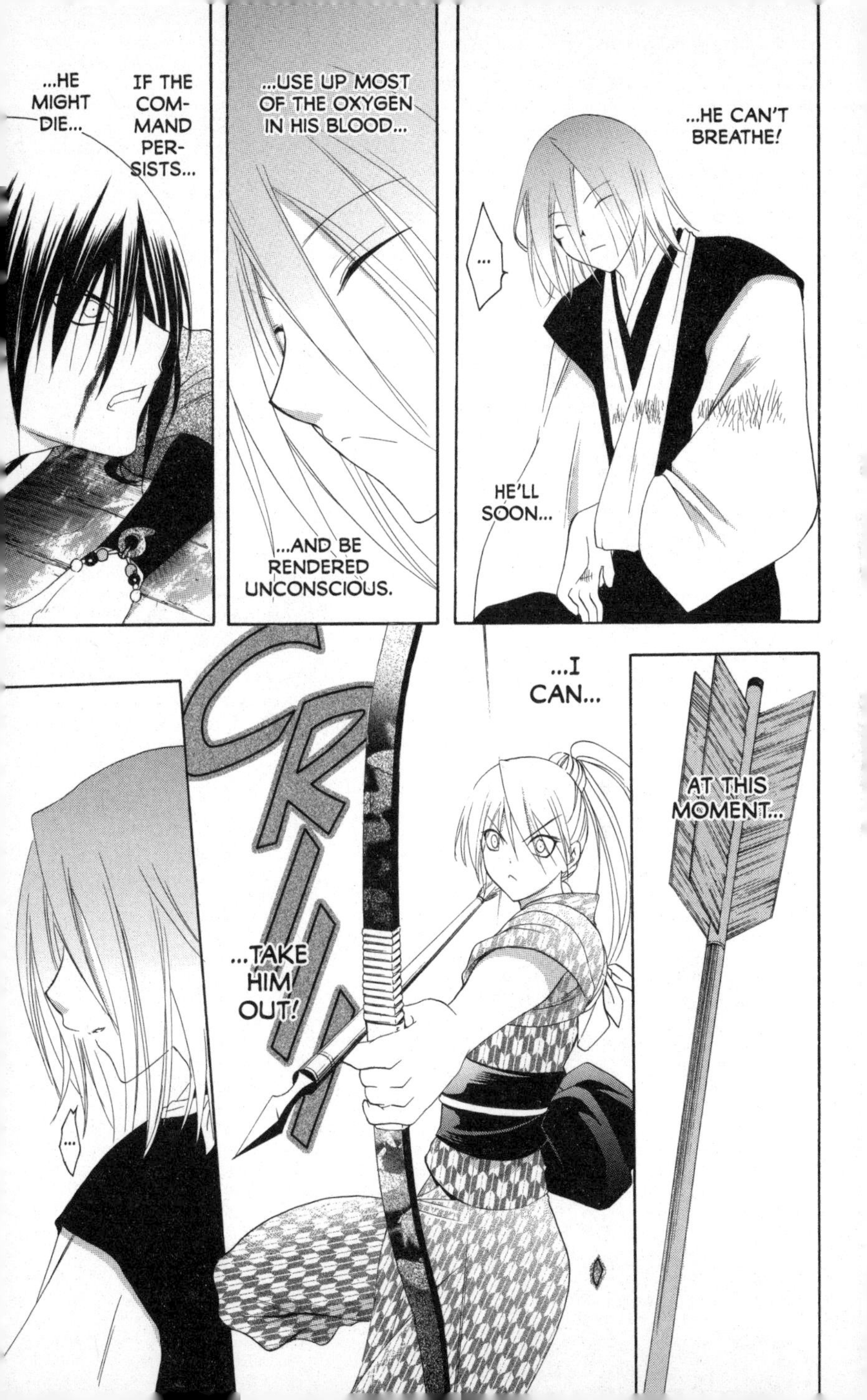
...HE CAN'T BREATHE!
...
HE'LL SOON...
...USE UP MOST OF THE OXYGEN IN HIS BLOOD...
...AND BE RENDERED UNCONSCIOUS.
IF THE COM-MAND PER-SISTS...
...HE MIGHT DIE...
AT THIS MOMENT...
...I CAN...
...TAKE HIM OUT!
...

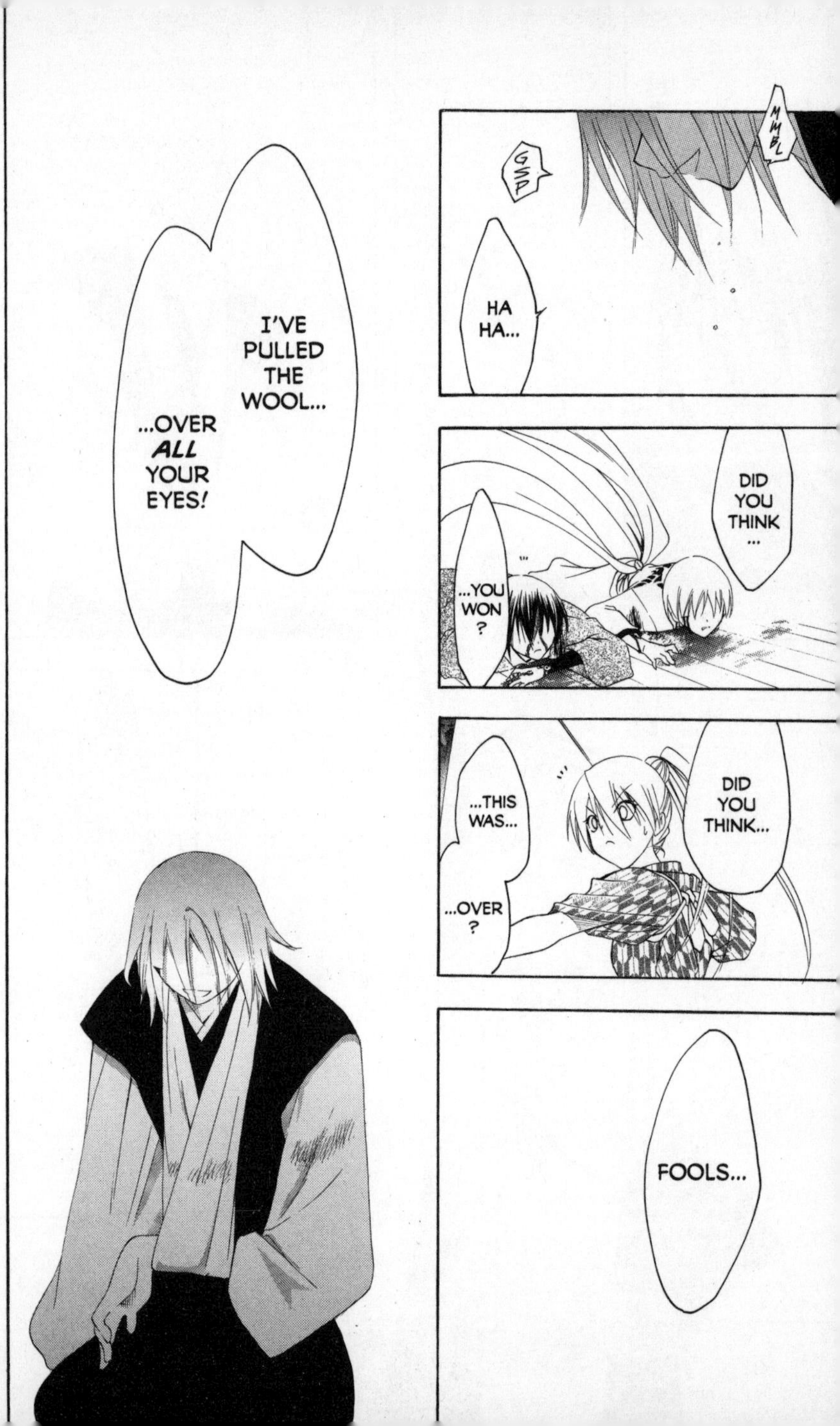
MMBL
GSP
HA HA...
DID YOU THINK...
...YOU WON?
DID YOU THINK...
...THIS WAS...
...OVER?
FOOLS...
I'VE PULLED THE WOOL...
...OVER ALL YOUR EYES!

...STILL PLAYING!

WHEEZ...

I'M...

Chapter 165
Mahoroba

HOW CAN HE BE?

IS THAT TRUE?

HE'S LYING!

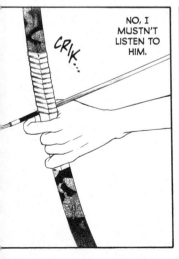

CRIK...

NO, I MUSTN'T LISTEN TO HIM.

...

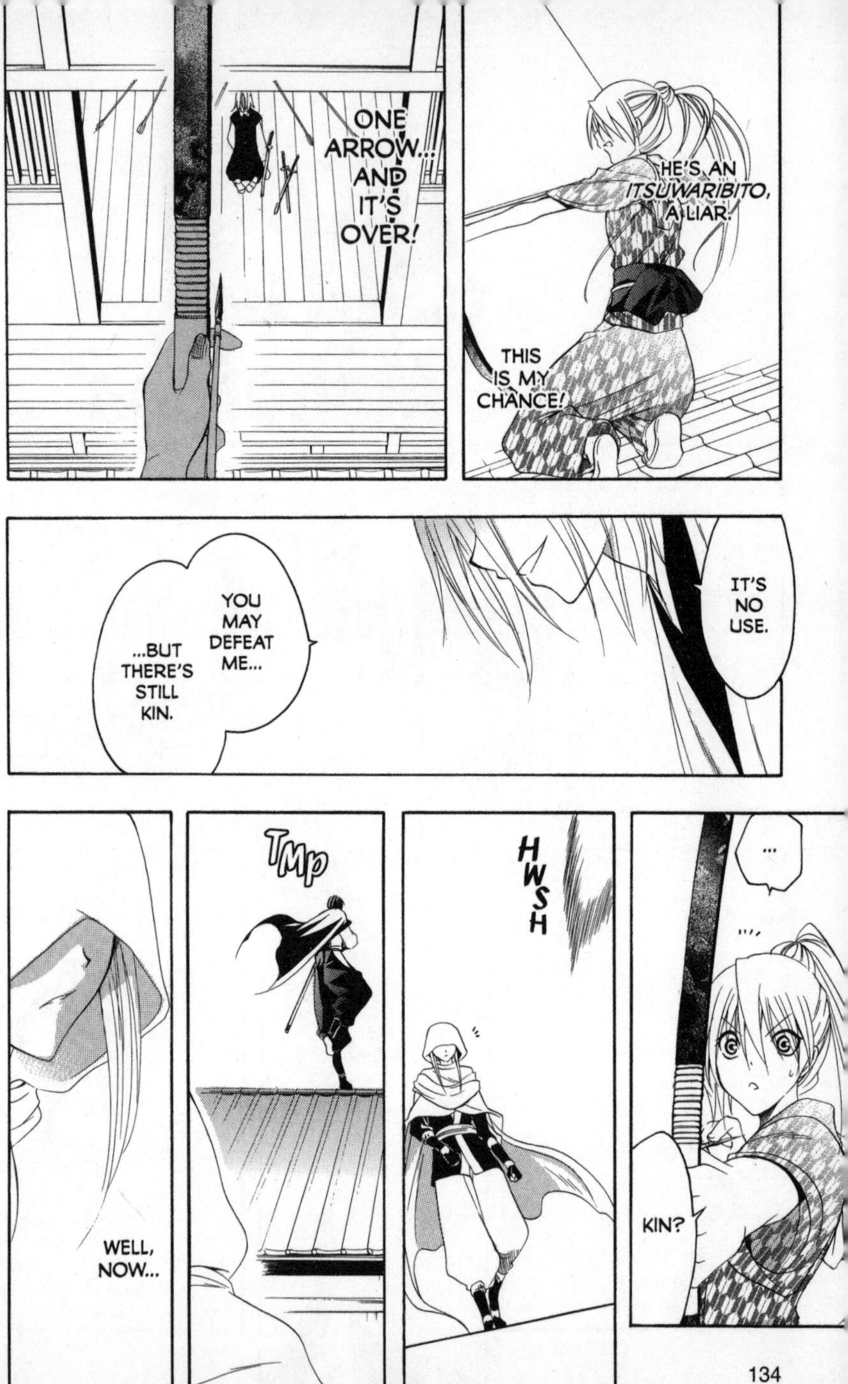
HE'S AN ITSUWARIBITO, A LIAR.
THIS IS MY CHANCE!
ONE ARROW... AND IT'S OVER!
IT'S NO USE.
YOU MAY DEFEAT ME...
...BUT THERE'S STILL KIN.
...
KIN?
HWSH
TMP
WELL, NOW...

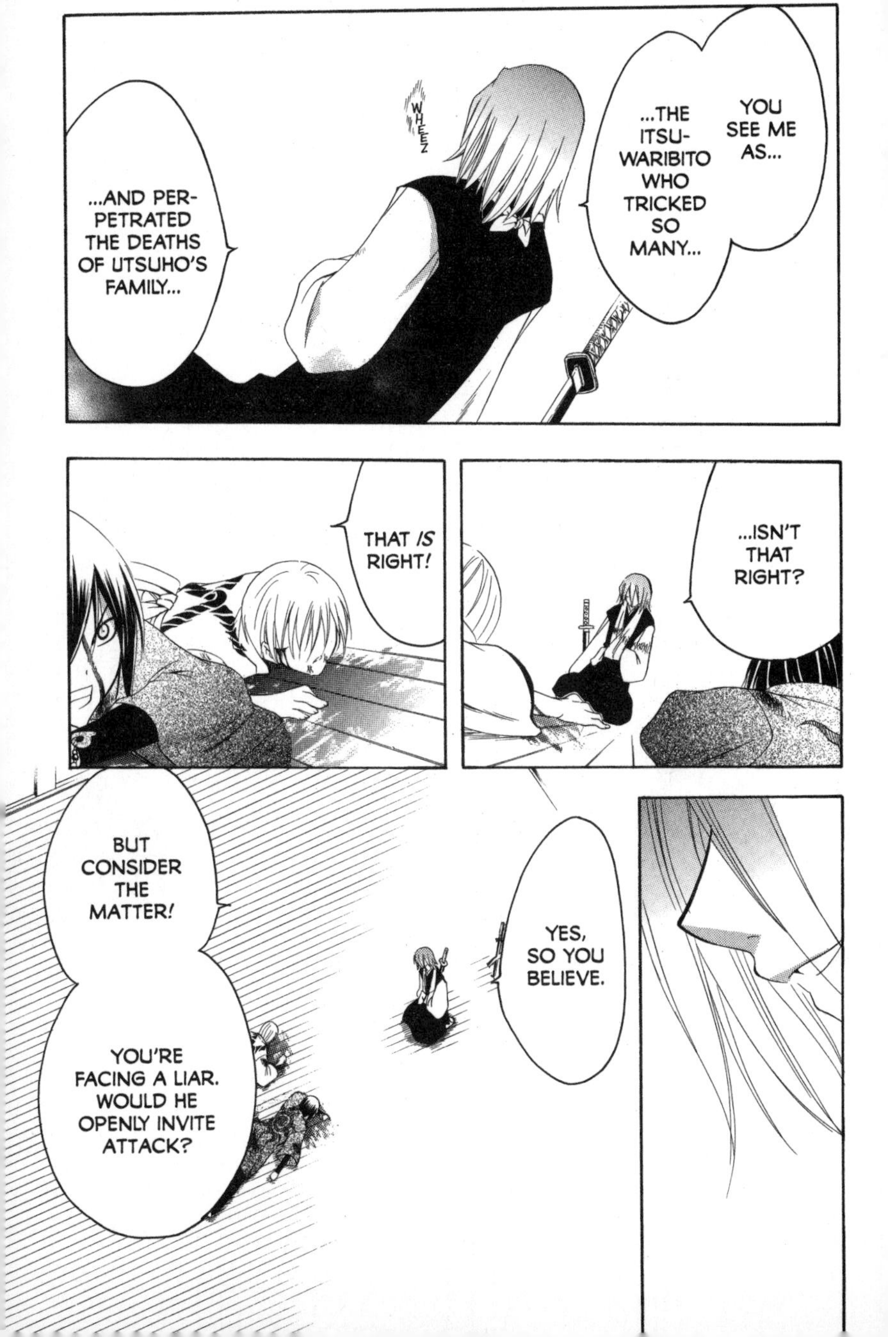
YOU SEE ME AS...
...THE ITSU-WARIBITO WHO TRICKED SO MANY...
WHEEZ
...AND PERPETRATED THE DEATHS OF UTSUHO'S FAMILY...
...ISN'T THAT RIGHT?
THAT *IS* RIGHT!
YES, SO YOU BELIEVE.
BUT CONSIDER THE MATTER!
YOU'RE FACING A LIAR. WOULD HE OPENLY INVITE ATTACK?

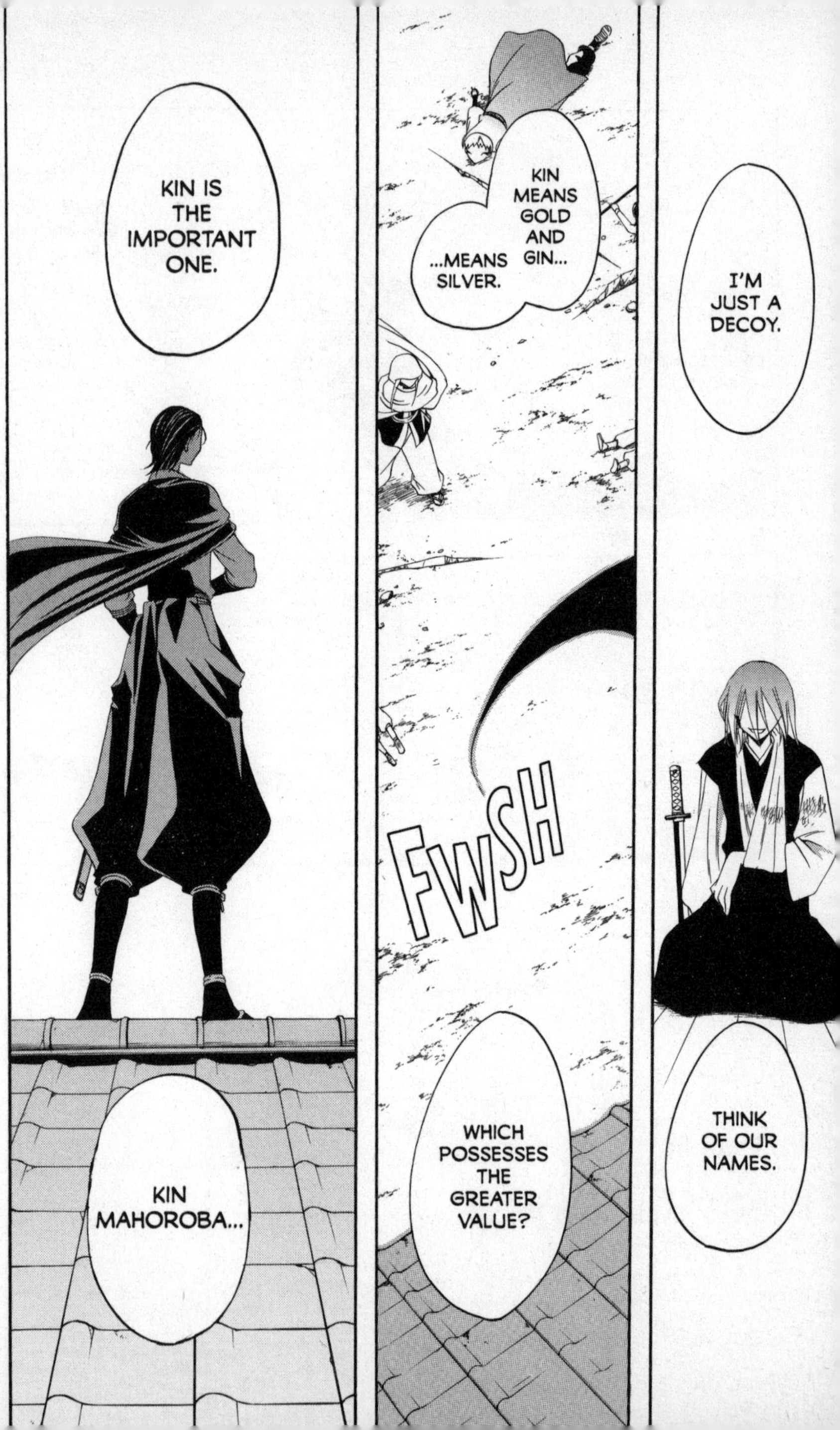
I'M JUST A DECOY.
THINK OF OUR NAMES.
KIN MEANS GOLD AND GIN...
...MEANS SILVER.
FWSH
WHICH POSSESSES THE GREATER VALUE?
KIN IS THE IMPORTANT ONE.
KIN MAHOROBA...

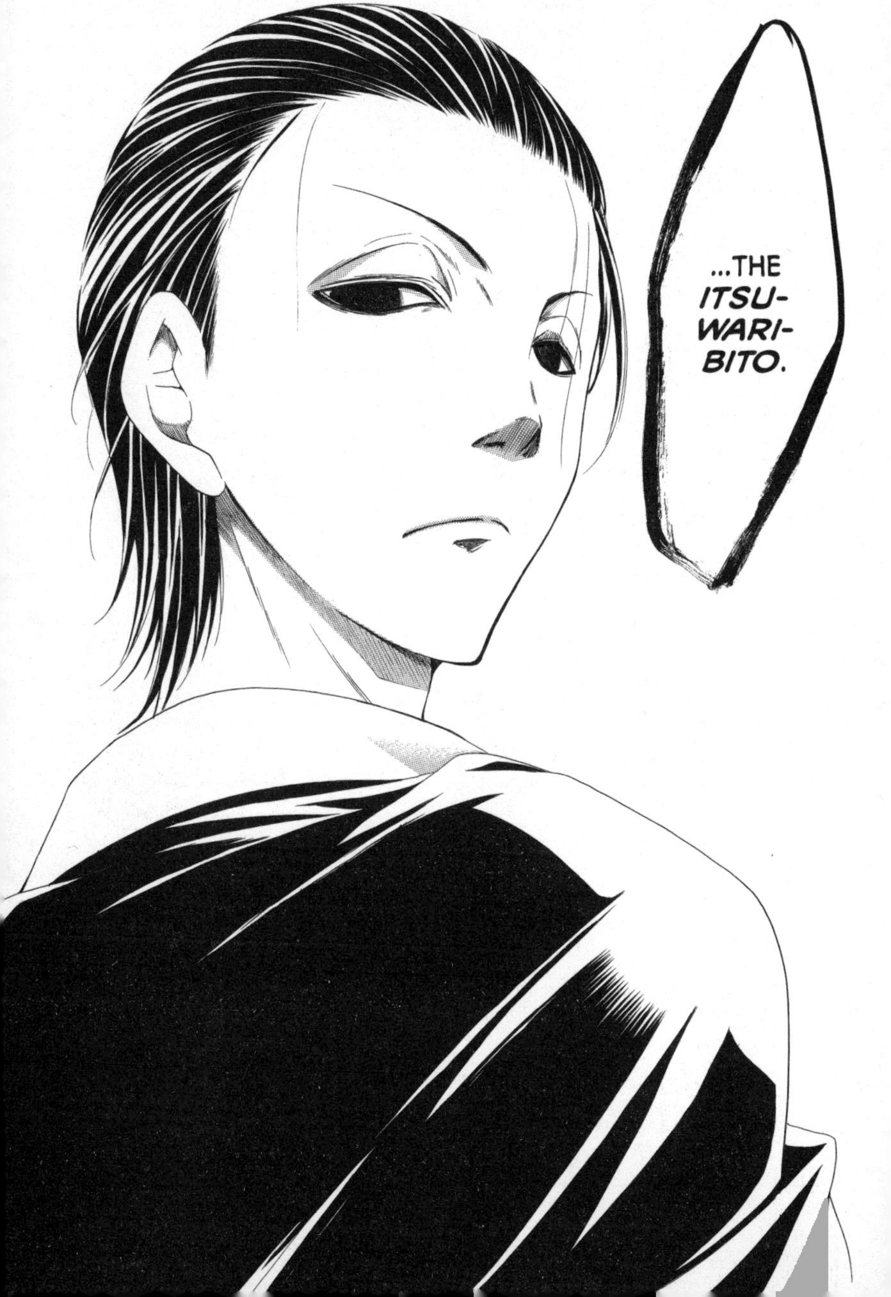
...THE *ITSU-WARI-BITO*.

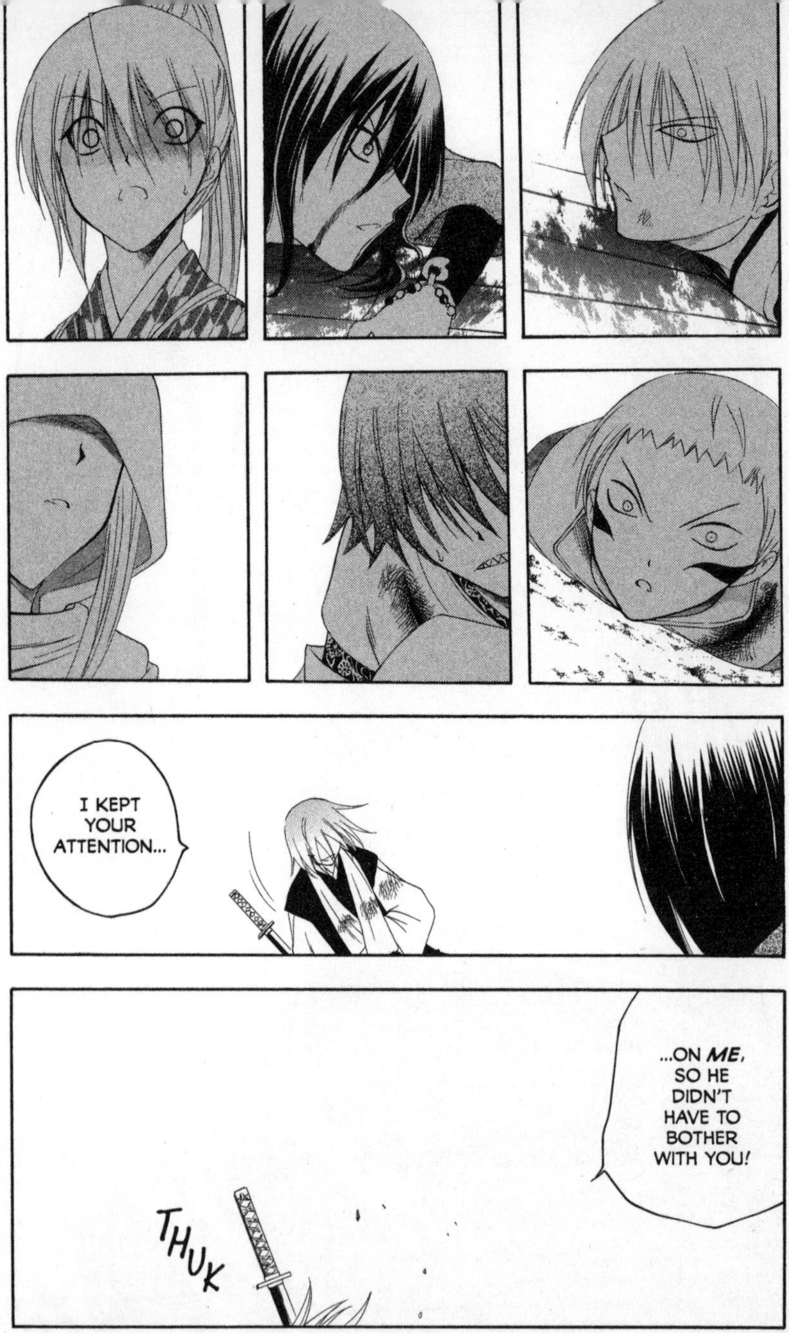
I KEPT YOUR ATTENTION...
...ON ME, SO HE DIDN'T HAVE TO BOTHER WITH YOU!
THUK

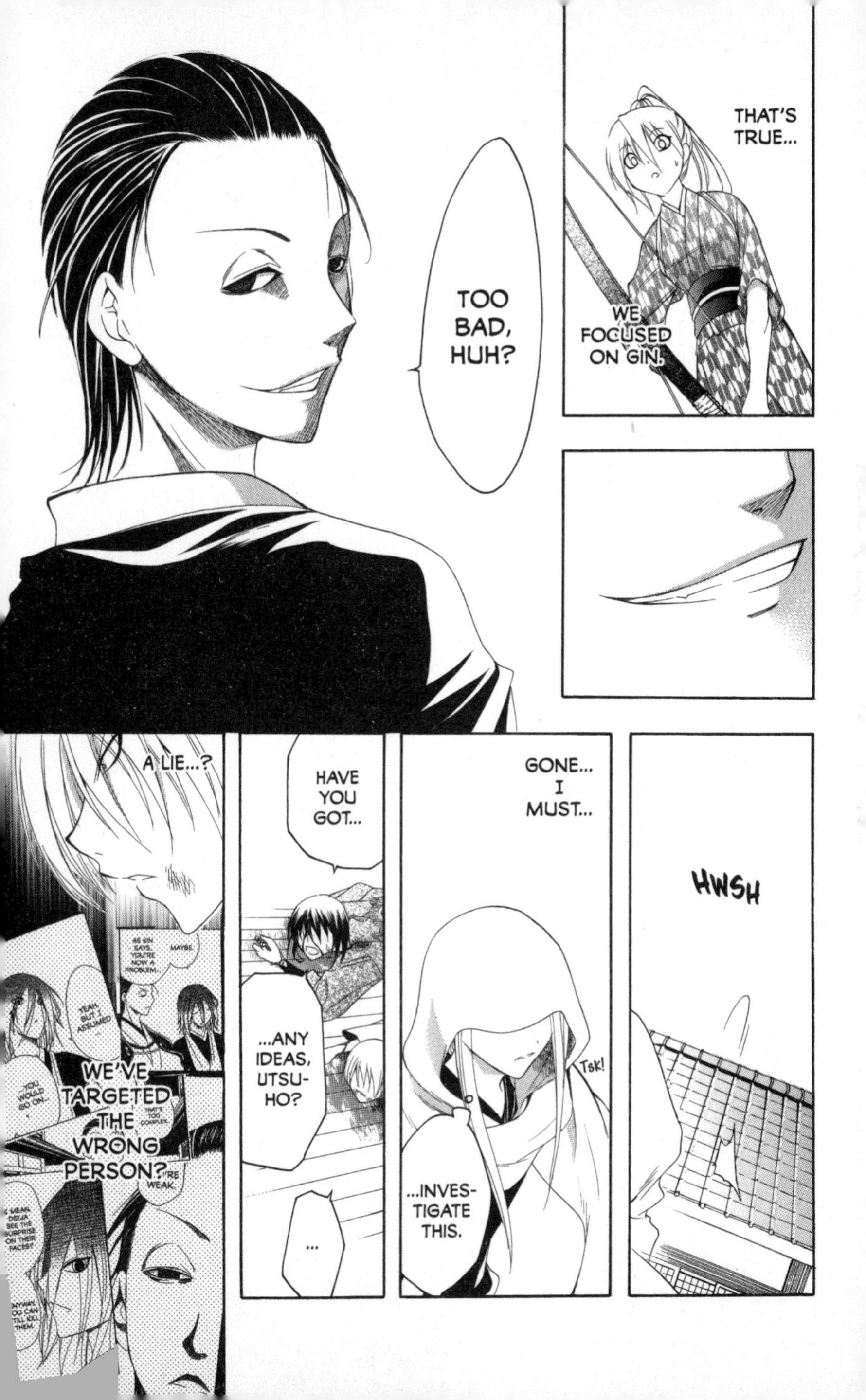
THAT'S TRUE...
WE FOCUSED ON GIN.
TOO BAD, HUH?
HWSH
GONE... I MUST...
Tsk!
...INVESTIGATE THIS.
HAVE YOU GOT...
...ANY IDEAS, UTSU-HO?
...
A LIE...?
AS GIN SAYS, YOU'RE NOW A PROBLEM...
MAYBE.
YEAH, BUT I ASSUMED...
YOU WOULD GO ON...
THAT'S TOO COMPLEX.
WE'VE TARGETED THE WRONG PERSON?
I MEAN, DIDJA SEE THE SURPRISE ON THEIR FACES?
ANYWAY, YOU CAN STILL KILL THEM.

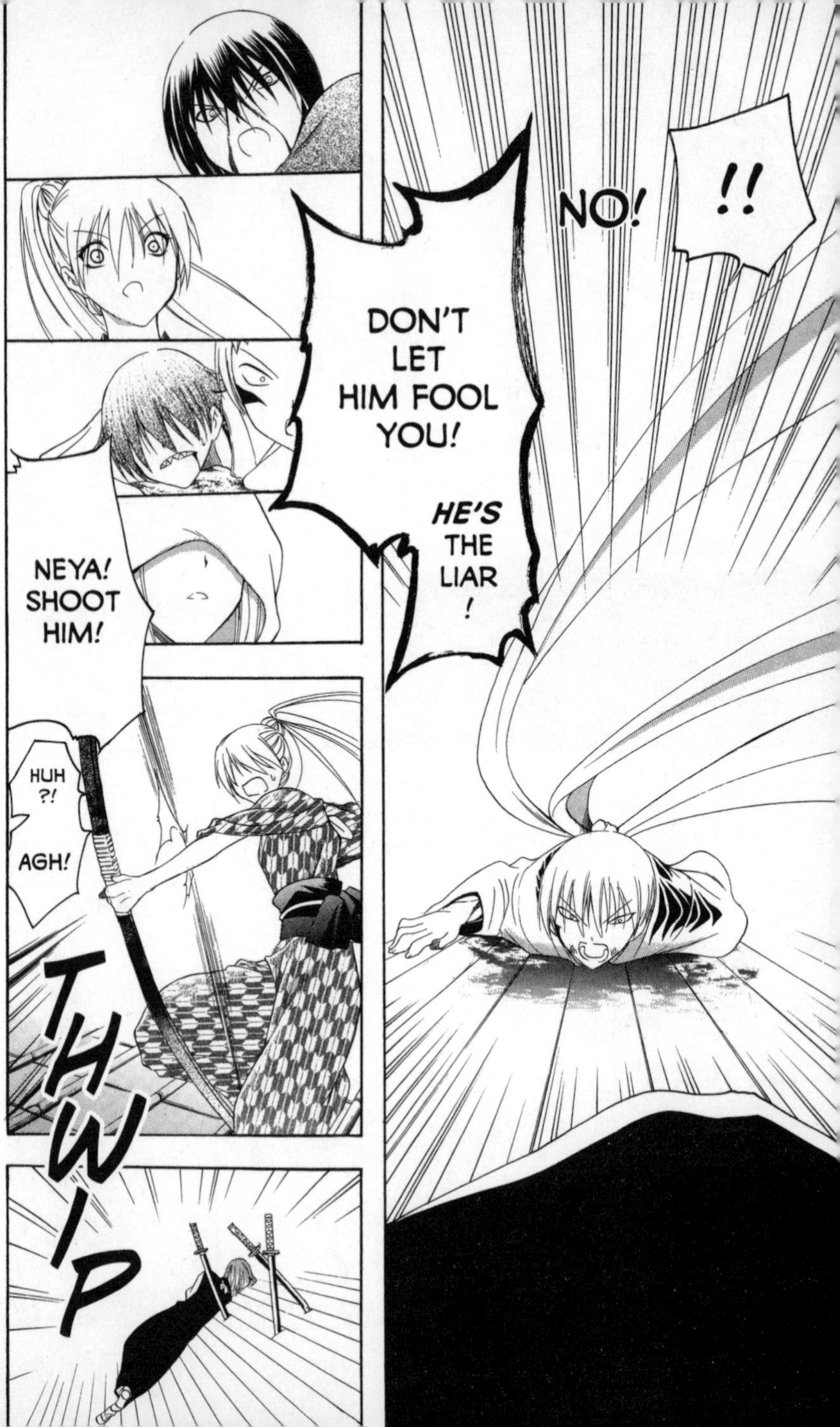
!!
NO!
DON'T LET HIM FOOL YOU!
HE'S THE LIAR!
NEYA! SHOOT HIM!
HUH?!
AGH!
THWIP

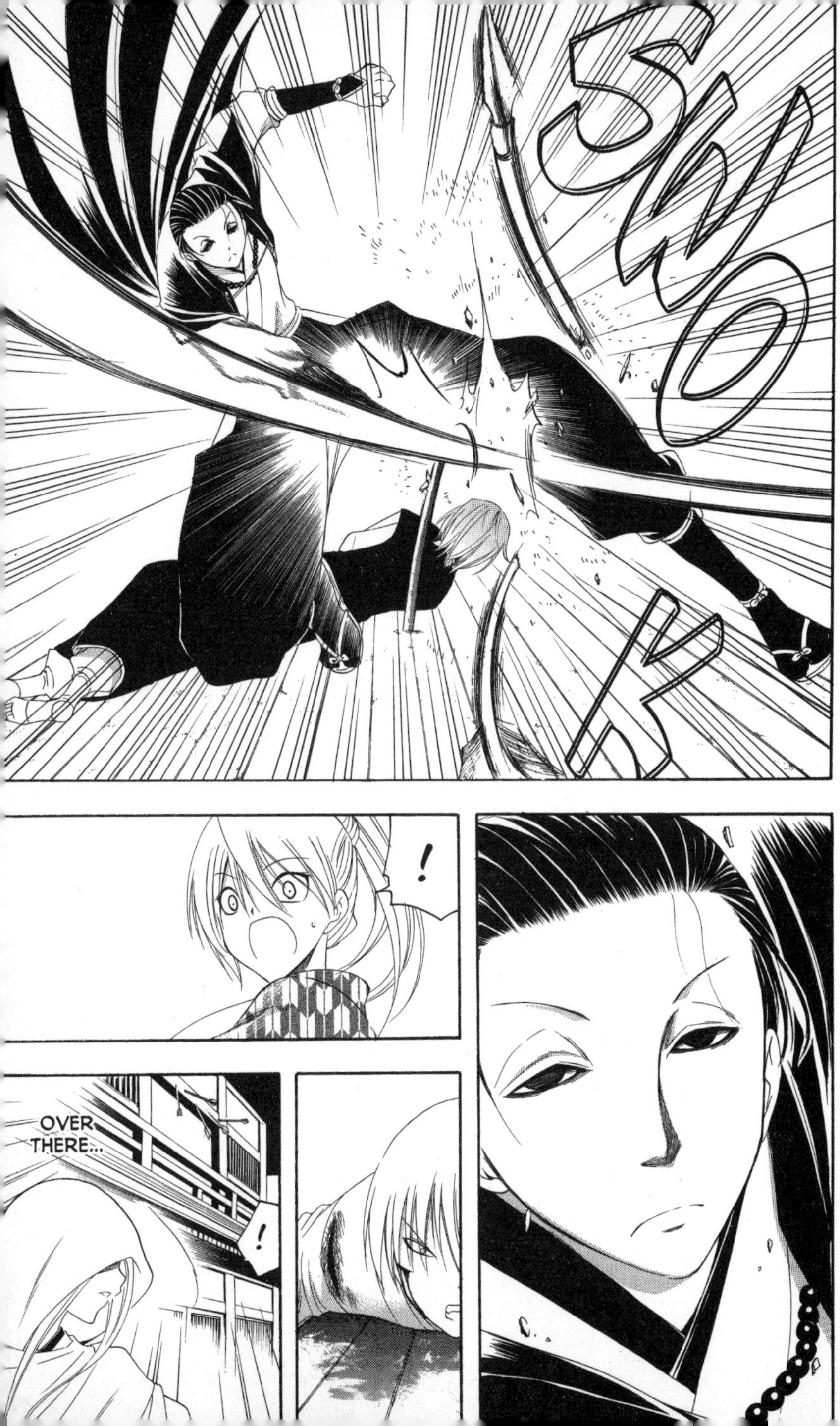
SHWOK
!
!
OVER THERE...

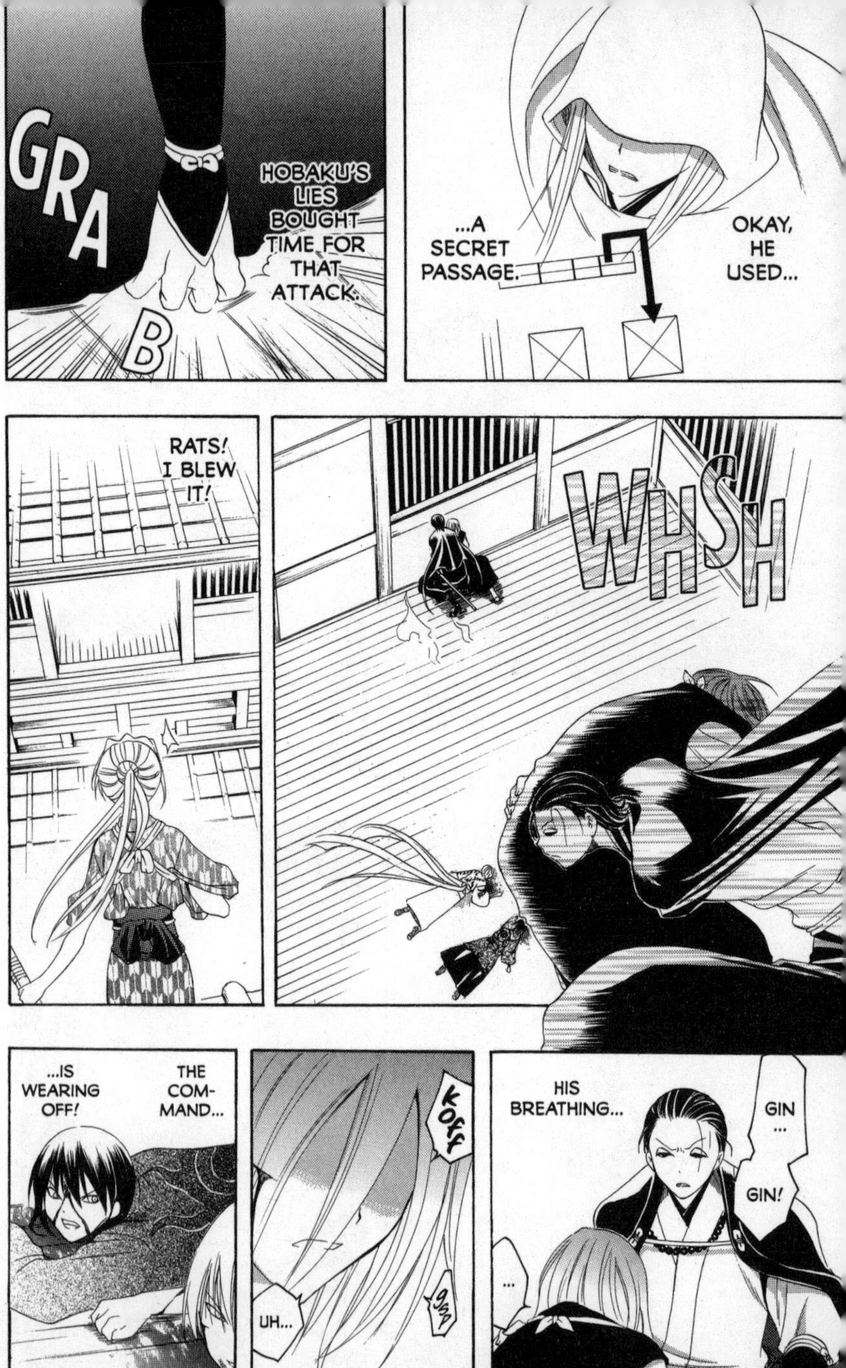
OKAY, HE USED...
...A SECRET PASSAGE.
GRAB
HOBAKU'S LIES BOUGHT TIME FOR THAT ATTACK.
WHSH
RATS! I BLEW IT!
GIN...
GIN!
HIS BREATHING...
...
KOFF
GSP
UH...
THE COM-MAND...
...IS WEARING OFF!

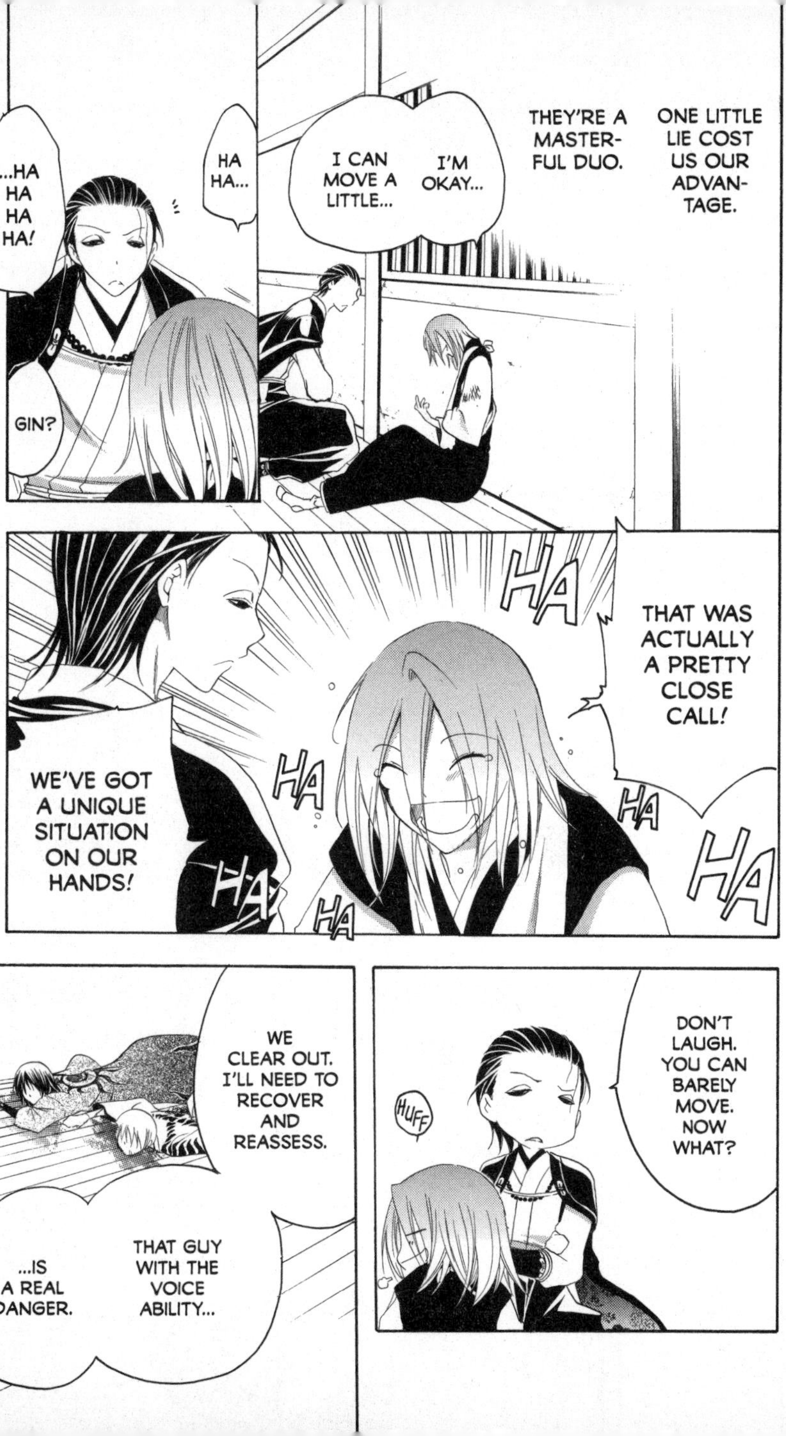
ONE LITTLE LIE COST US OUR ADVANTAGE.
THEY'RE A MASTERFUL DUO.
I'M OKAY...
I CAN MOVE A LITTLE...
HA HA...
...HA HA HA HA!
GIN?
HA
THAT WAS ACTUALLY A PRETTY CLOSE CALL!
HA
HA
HA
HA
HA
WE'VE GOT A UNIQUE SITUATION ON OUR HANDS!
DON'T LAUGH. YOU CAN BARELY MOVE. NOW WHAT?
HUFF
WE CLEAR OUT. I'LL NEED TO RECOVER AND REASSESS.
THAT GUY WITH THE VOICE ABILITY...
...IS A REAL DANGER.

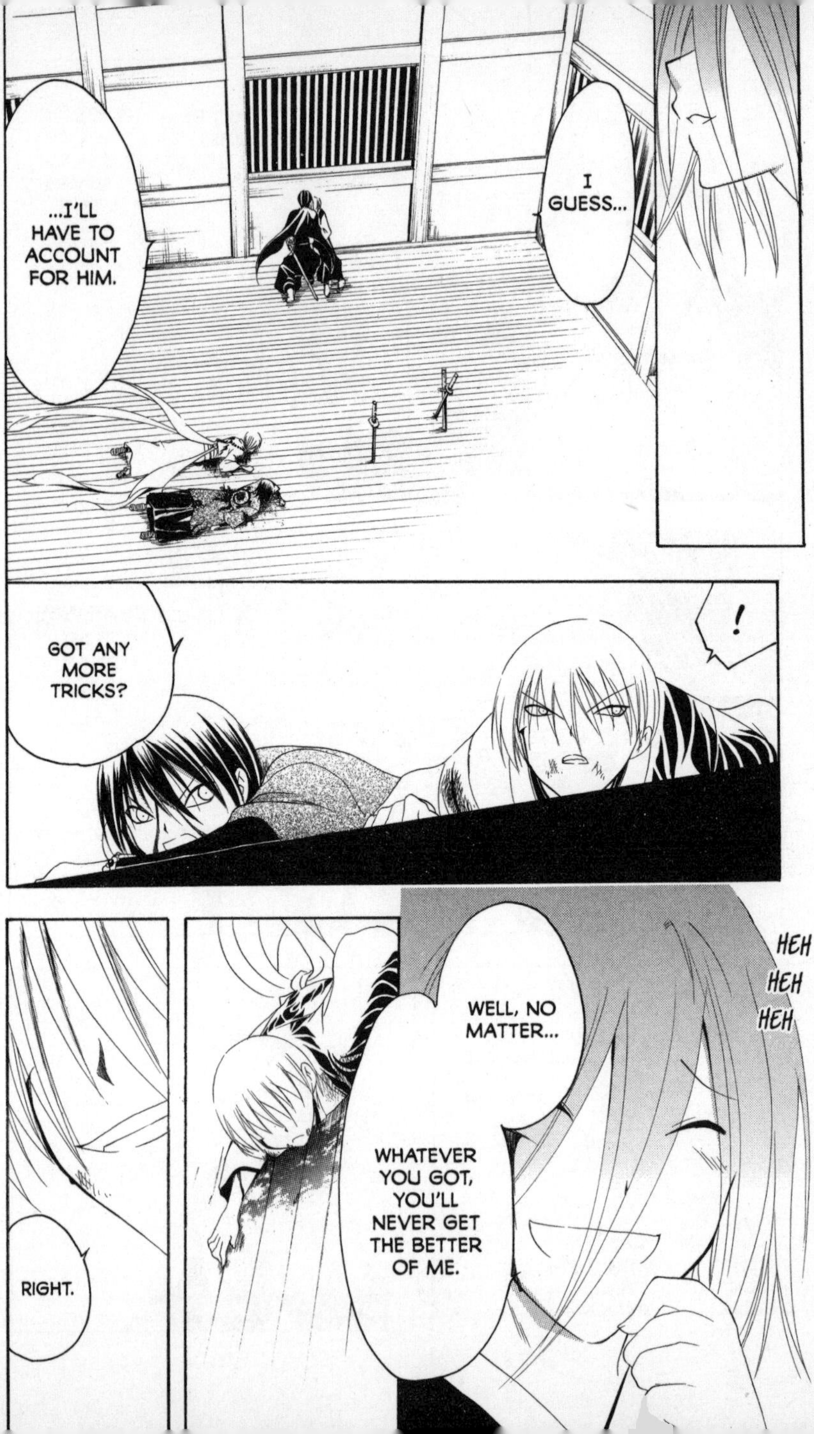
I GUESS...
...I'LL HAVE TO ACCOUNT FOR HIM.
!
GOT ANY MORE TRICKS?
HEH HEH HEH
WELL, NO MATTER...
WHATEVER YOU GOT, YOU'LL NEVER GET THE BETTER OF ME.
RIGHT.

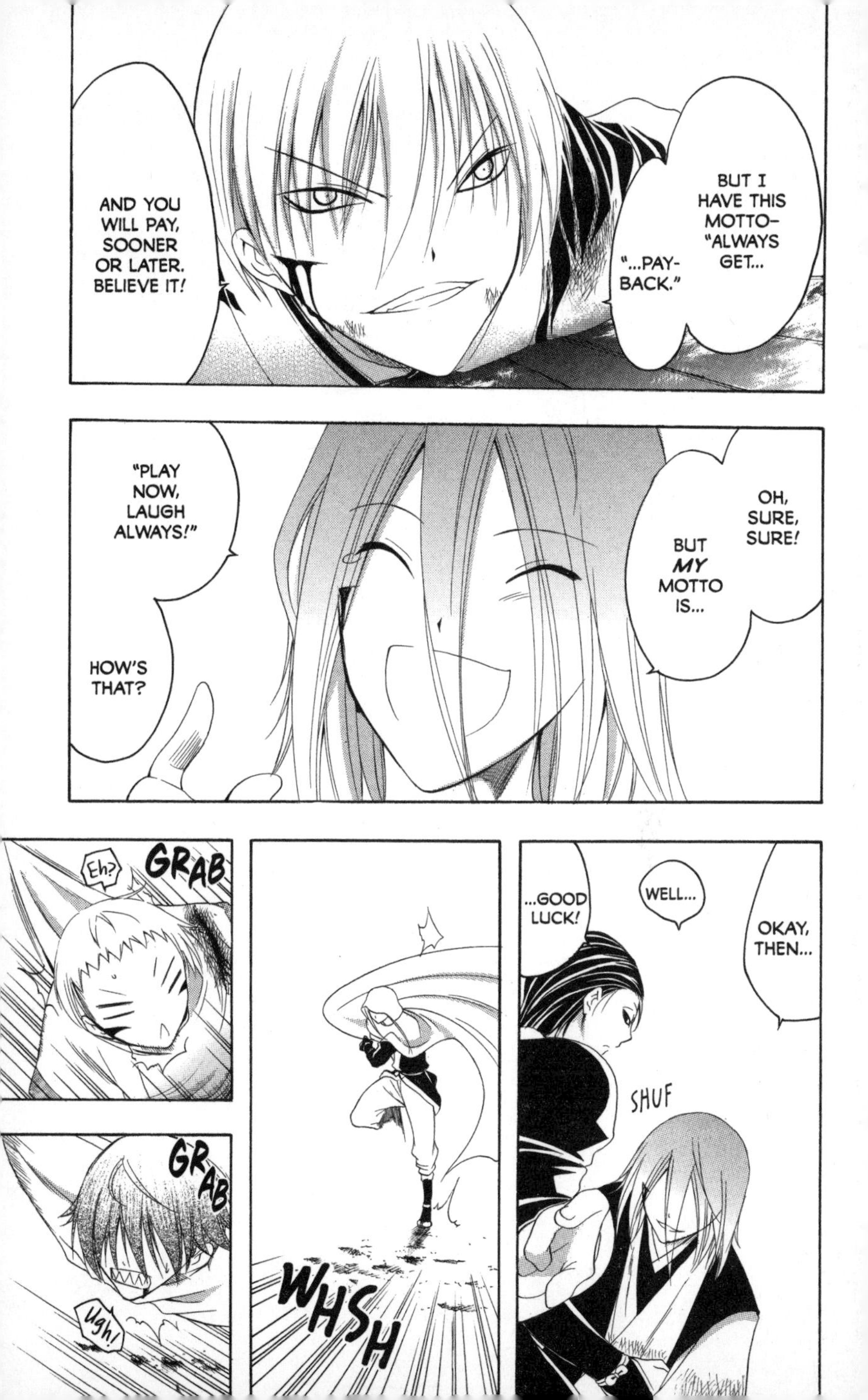
BUT I HAVE THIS MOTTO— "ALWAYS GET...
"...PAY-BACK."
AND YOU WILL PAY, SOONER OR LATER. BELIEVE IT!
OH, SURE, SURE!
BUT MY MOTTO IS...
"PLAY NOW, LAUGH ALWAYS!"
HOW'S THAT?
OKAY, THEN...
WELL...
...GOOD LUCK!
SHUF
WHSH
Eh?
GRAB
GRAB
Ugh!

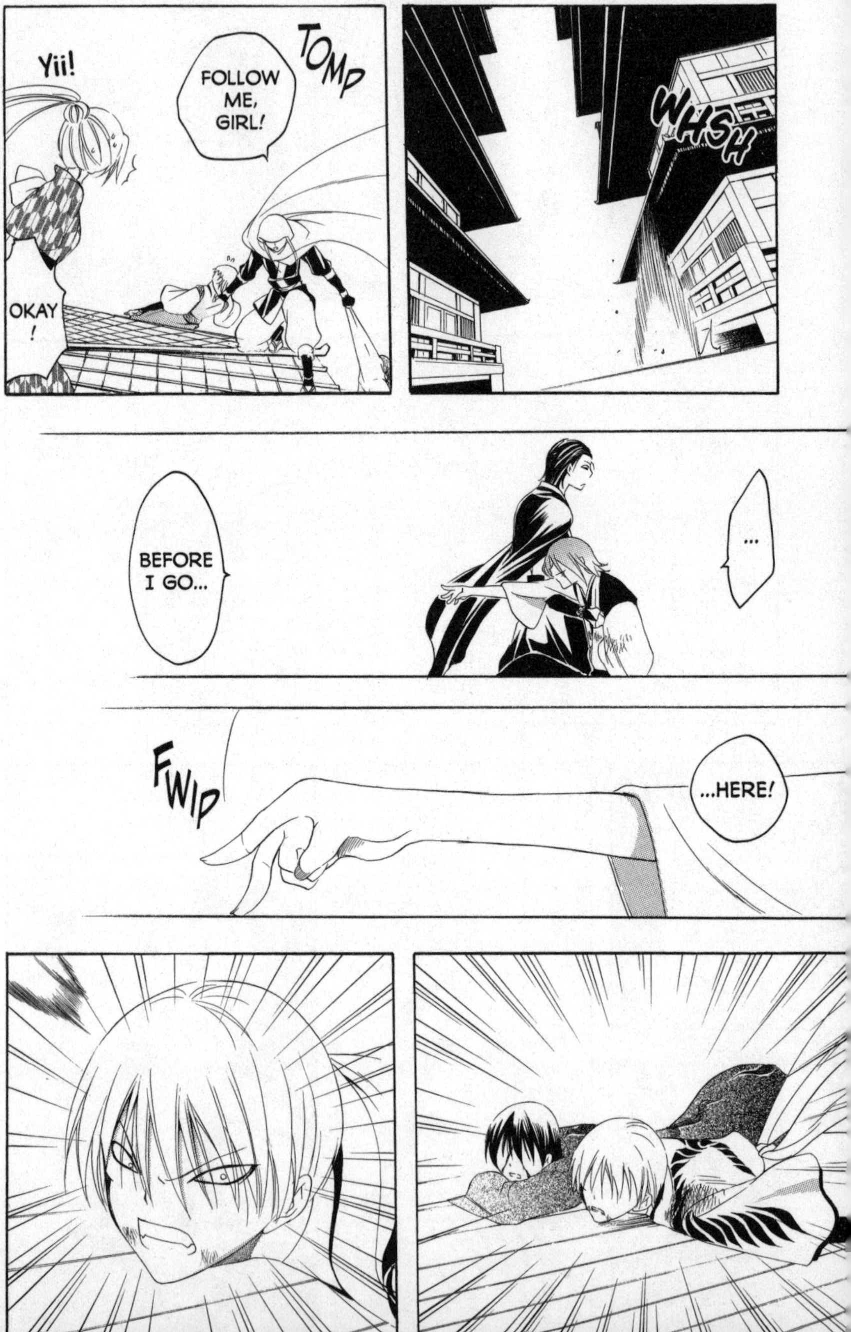
WHSH
TOMP
FOLLOW ME, GIRL!
Yii!
OKAY!
...
BEFORE I GO...
...HERE!
FWIP

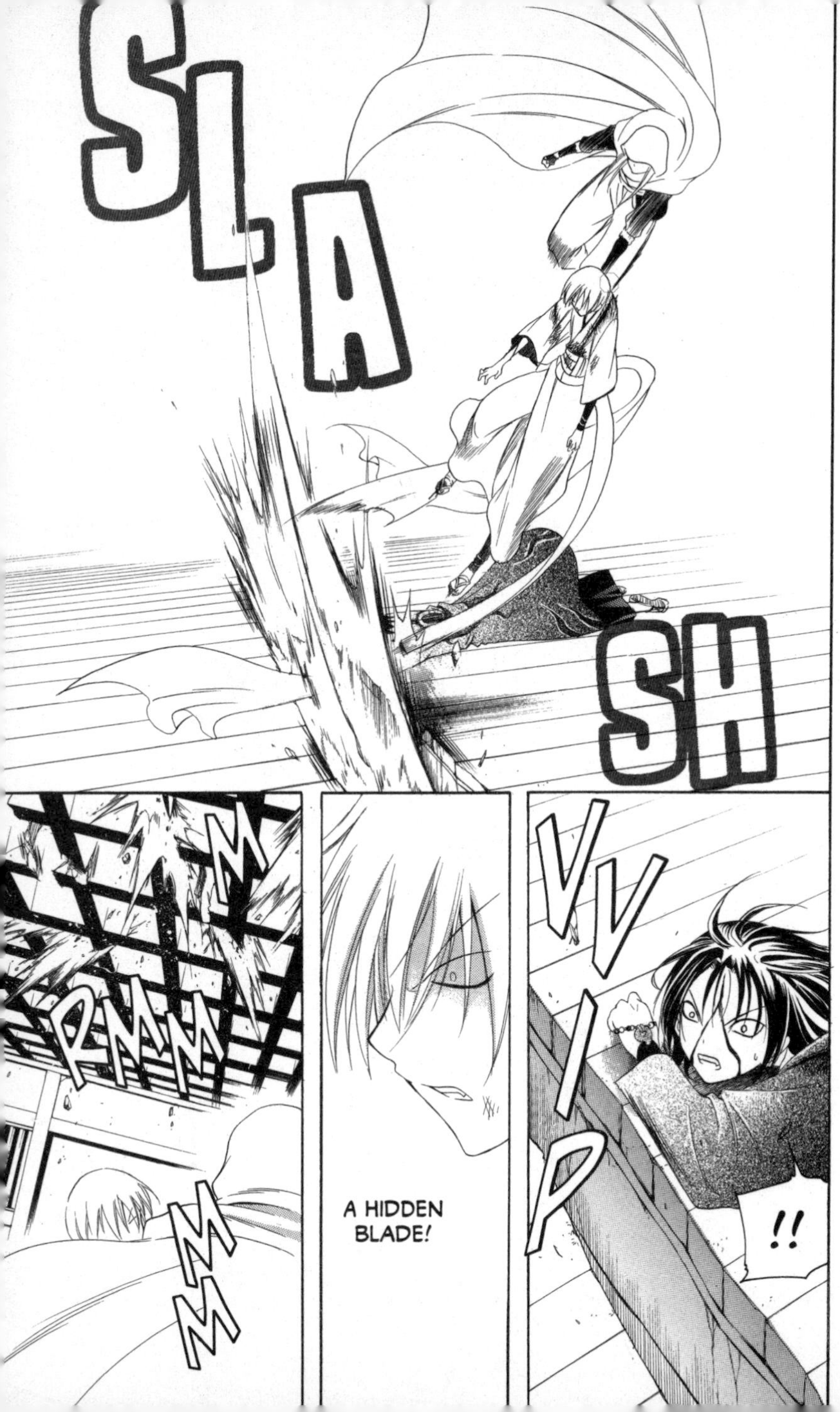
SLASH
VVIP
!!
A HIDDEN BLADE!
M
RMMM
MMM

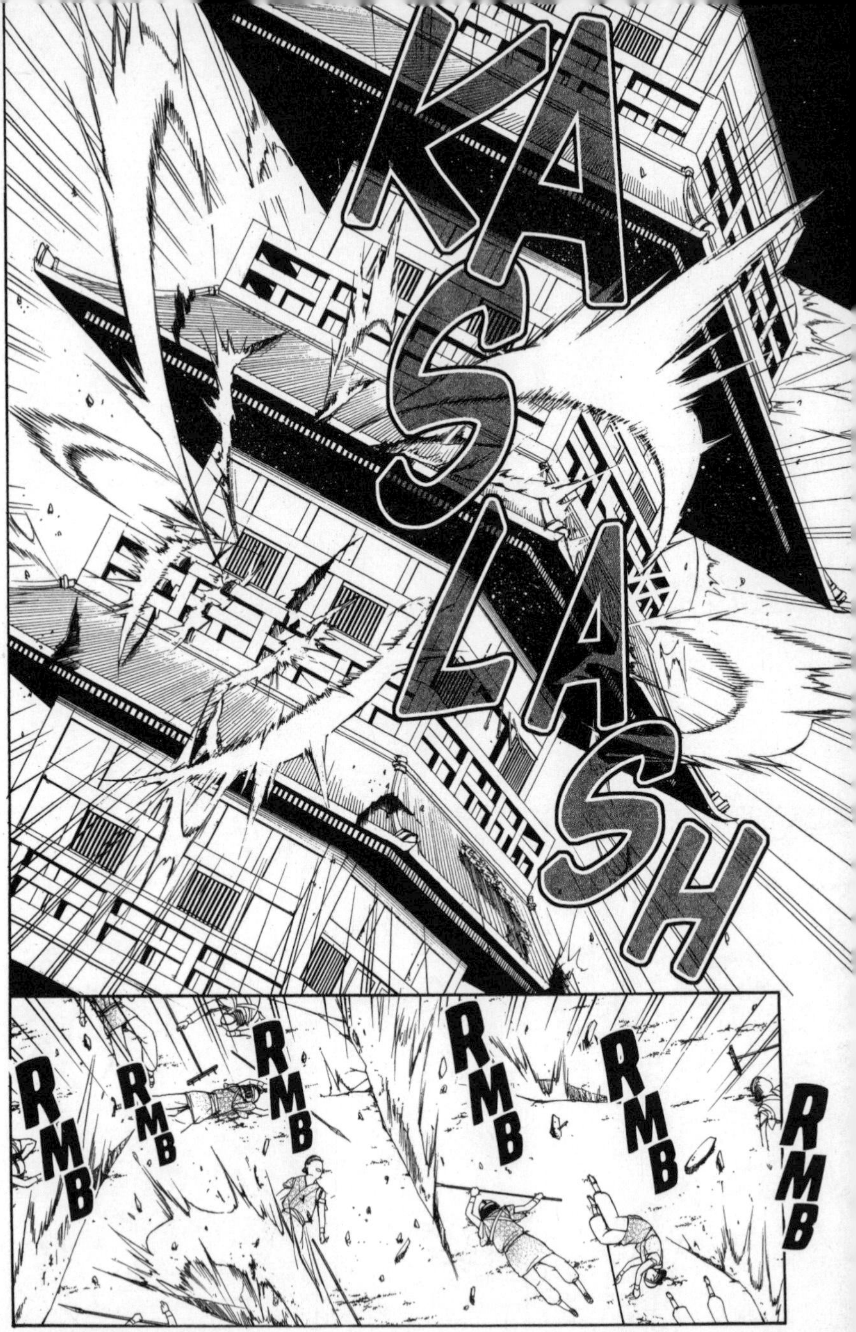
KASLASH
RMB
RMB
RMB
RMB
RMB
RMB

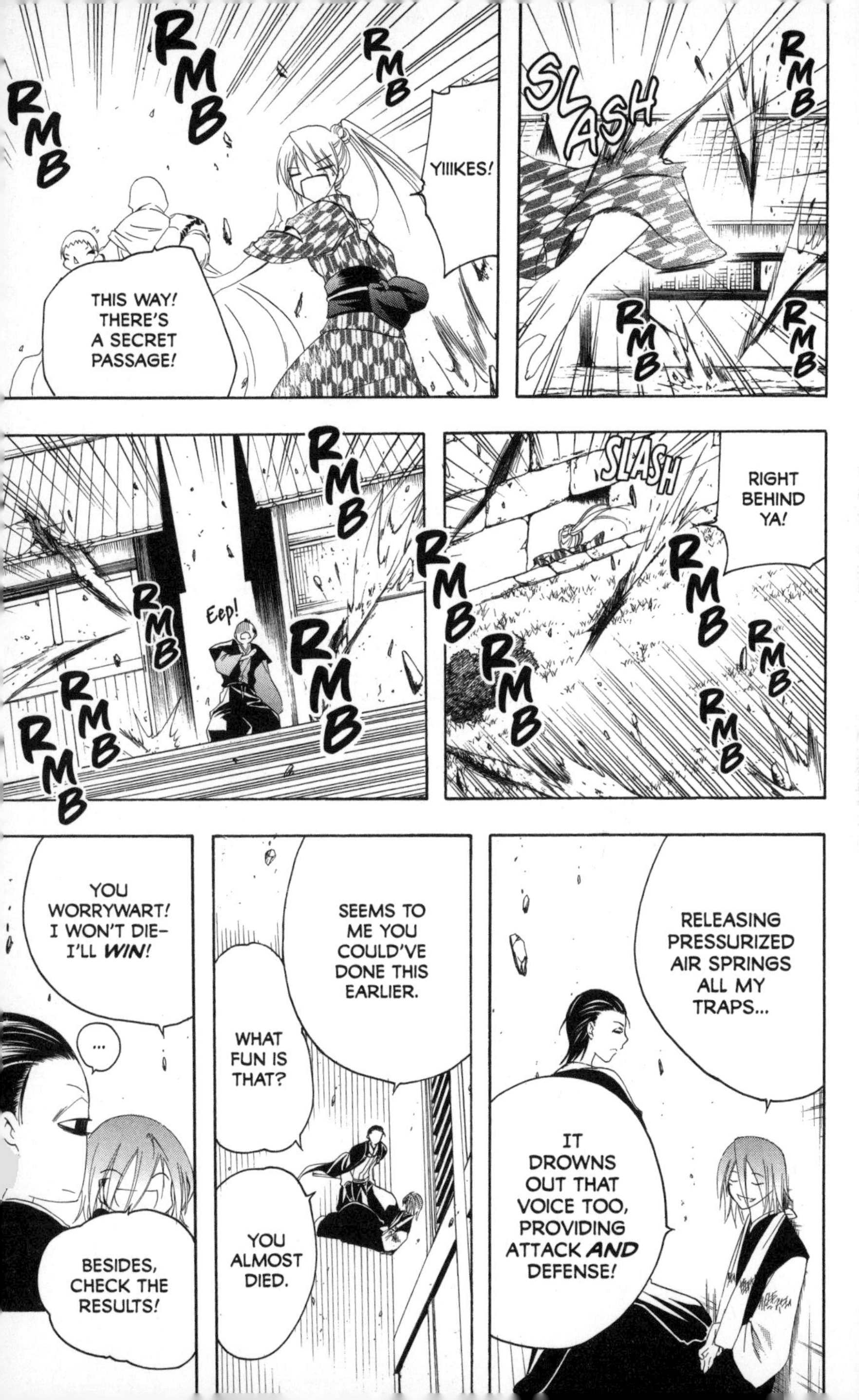
RMB
SLASH
RMB
RMB
RMB
YIIIKES!
RMB
RMB
THIS WAY! THERE'S A SECRET PASSAGE!
RIGHT BEHIND YA!
SLASH
RMB
RMB
RMB
RMB
RMB
RMB
Eep!
RMB
RMB
RMB
RMB
RELEASING PRESSURIZED AIR SPRINGS ALL MY TRAPS...
IT DROWNS OUT THAT VOICE TOO, PROVIDING ATTACK *AND* DEFENSE!
SEEMS TO ME YOU COULD'VE DONE THIS EARLIER.
WHAT FUN IS THAT?
YOU ALMOST DIED.
YOU WORRYWART! I WON'T DIE– I'LL *WIN*!
...
BESIDES, CHECK THE RESULTS!

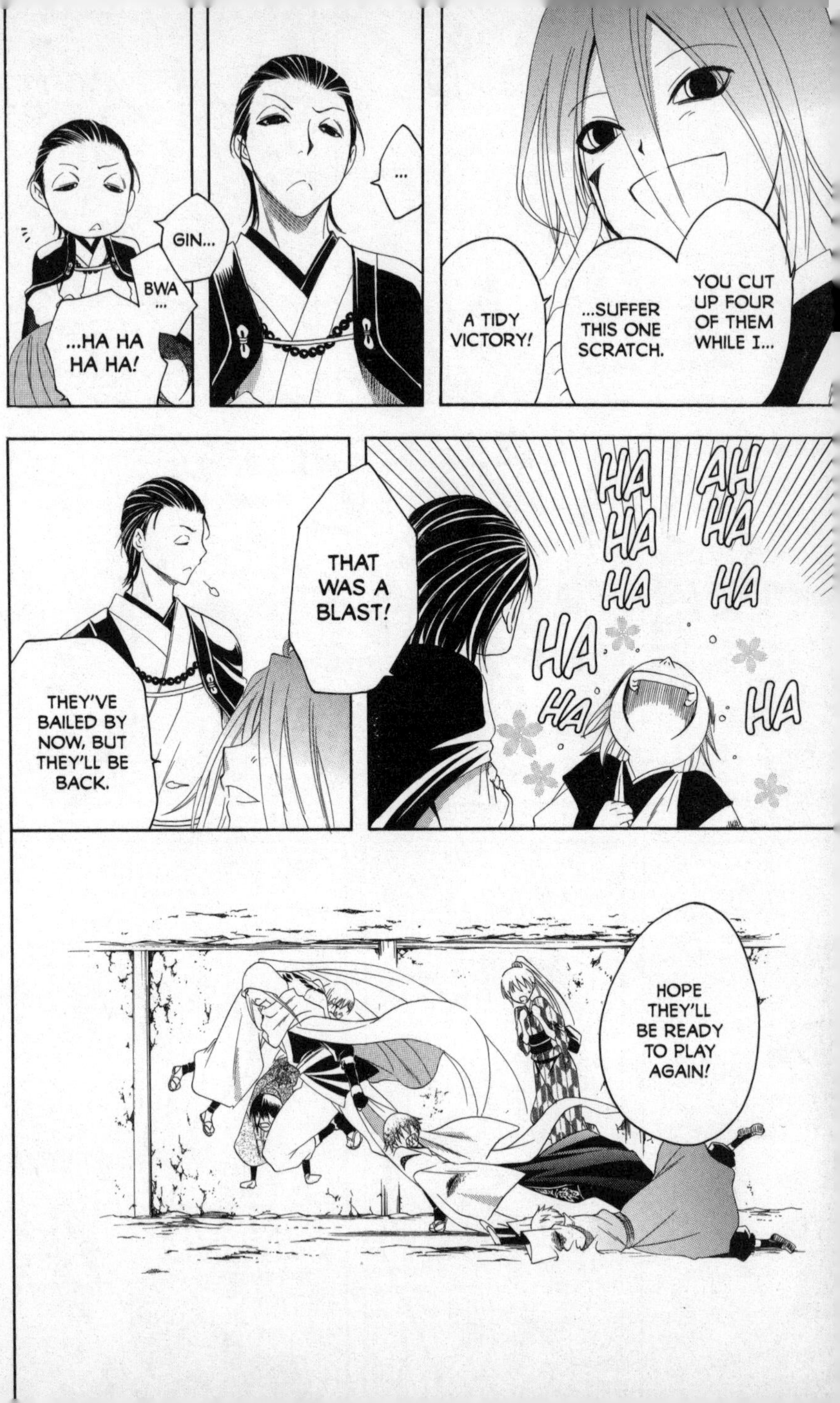
YOU CUT UP FOUR OF THEM WHILE I...
...SUFFER THIS ONE SCRATCH.
A TIDY VICTORY!
...
GIN...
BWA ...
...HA HA HA HA!
AH HA HA HA
HA HA HA
HA HA
HA
THAT WAS A BLAST!
THEY'VE BAILED BY NOW, BUT THEY'LL BE BACK.
HOPE THEY'LL BE READY TO PLAY AGAIN!

Chapter 166 Back Home

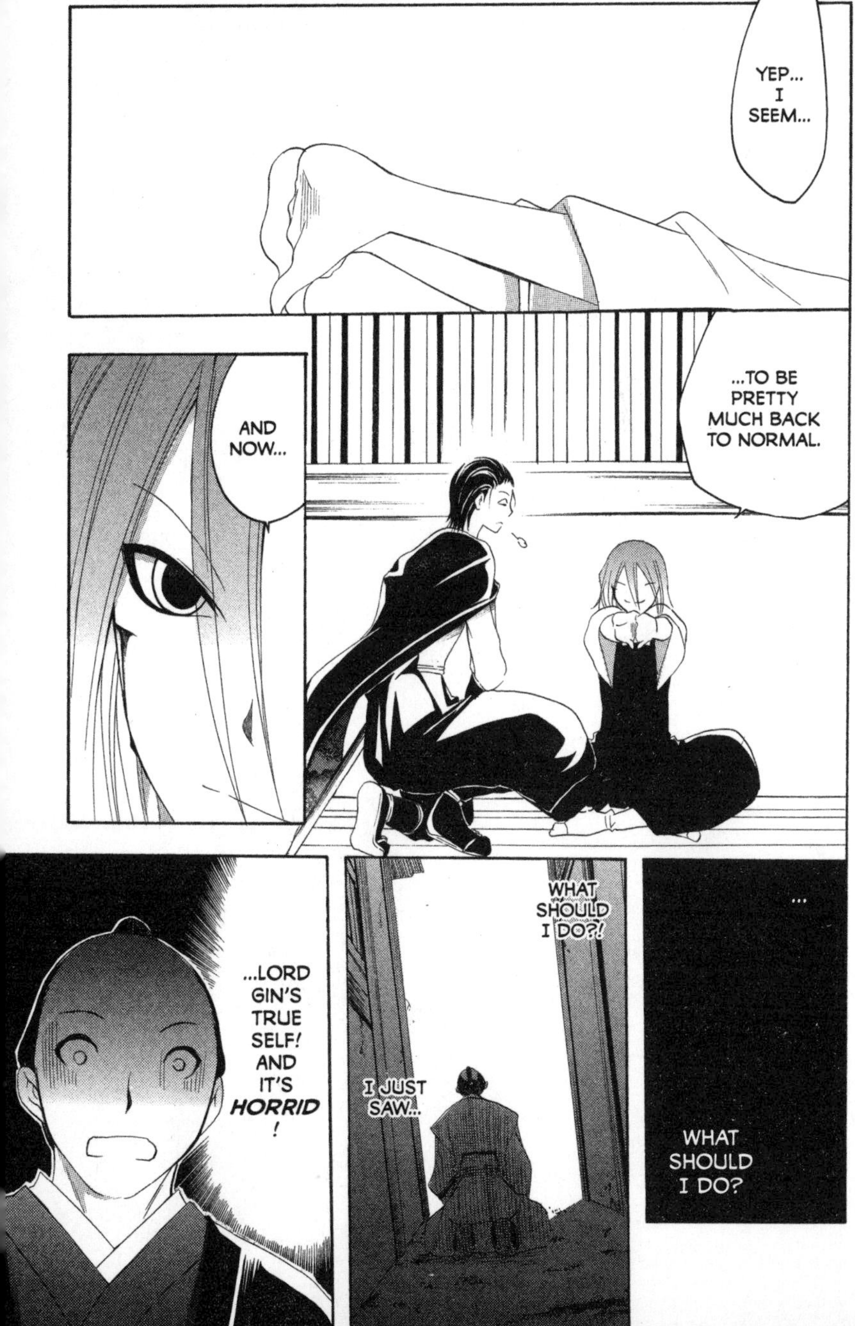
YEP... I SEEM...
...TO BE PRETTY MUCH BACK TO NORMAL.
AND NOW...
...
WHAT SHOULD I DO?
WHAT SHOULD I DO?!
I JUST SAW...
...LORD GIN'S TRUE SELF! AND IT'S HORRID!

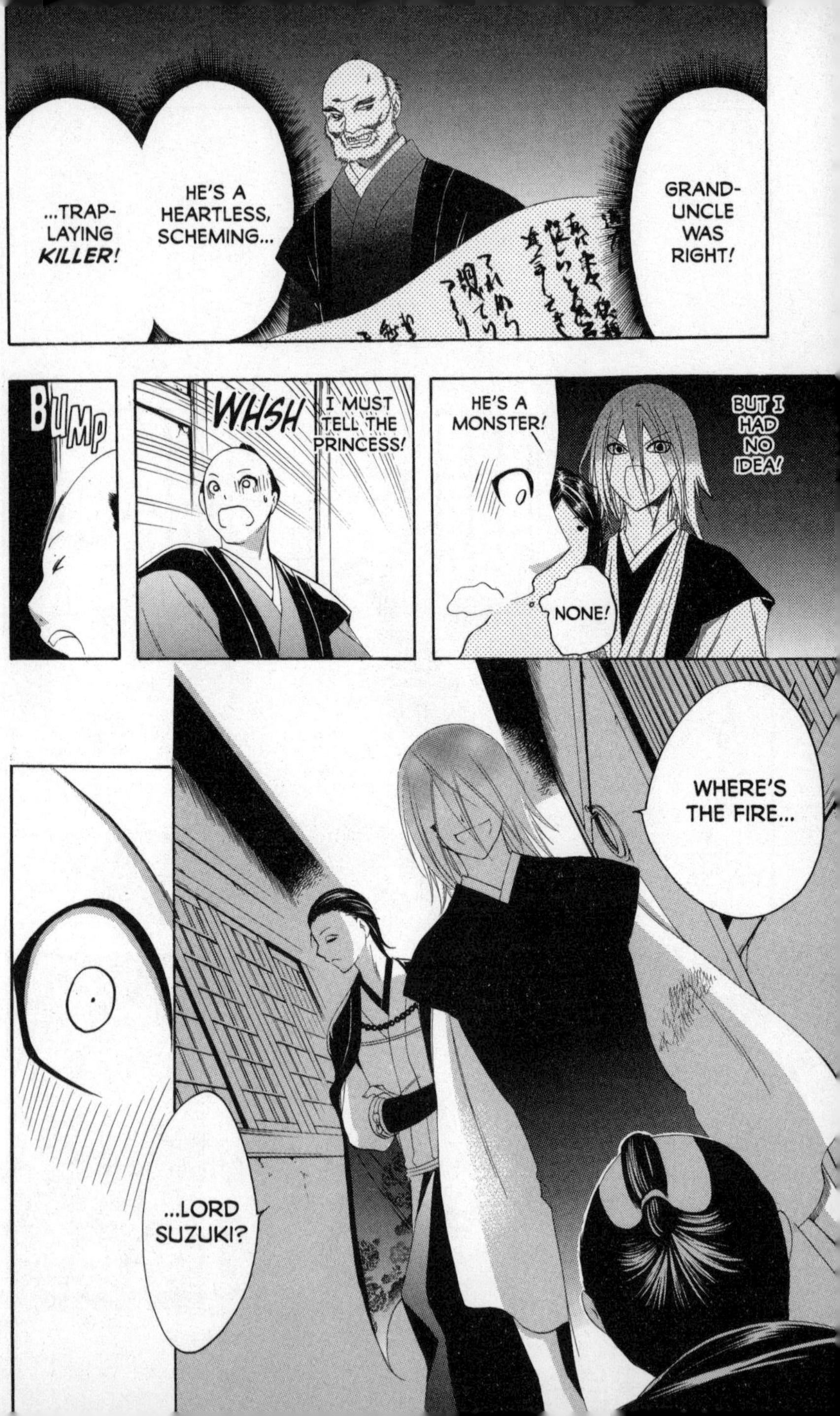
GRAND-UNCLE WAS RIGHT!
HE'S A HEARTLESS, SCHEMING...
...TRAP-LAYING KILLER!
BUT I HAD NO IDEA!
HE'S A MONSTER!
NONE!
I MUST TELL THE PRINCESS!
WHSH
BUMP
WHERE'S THE FIRE...
...LORD SUZUKI?

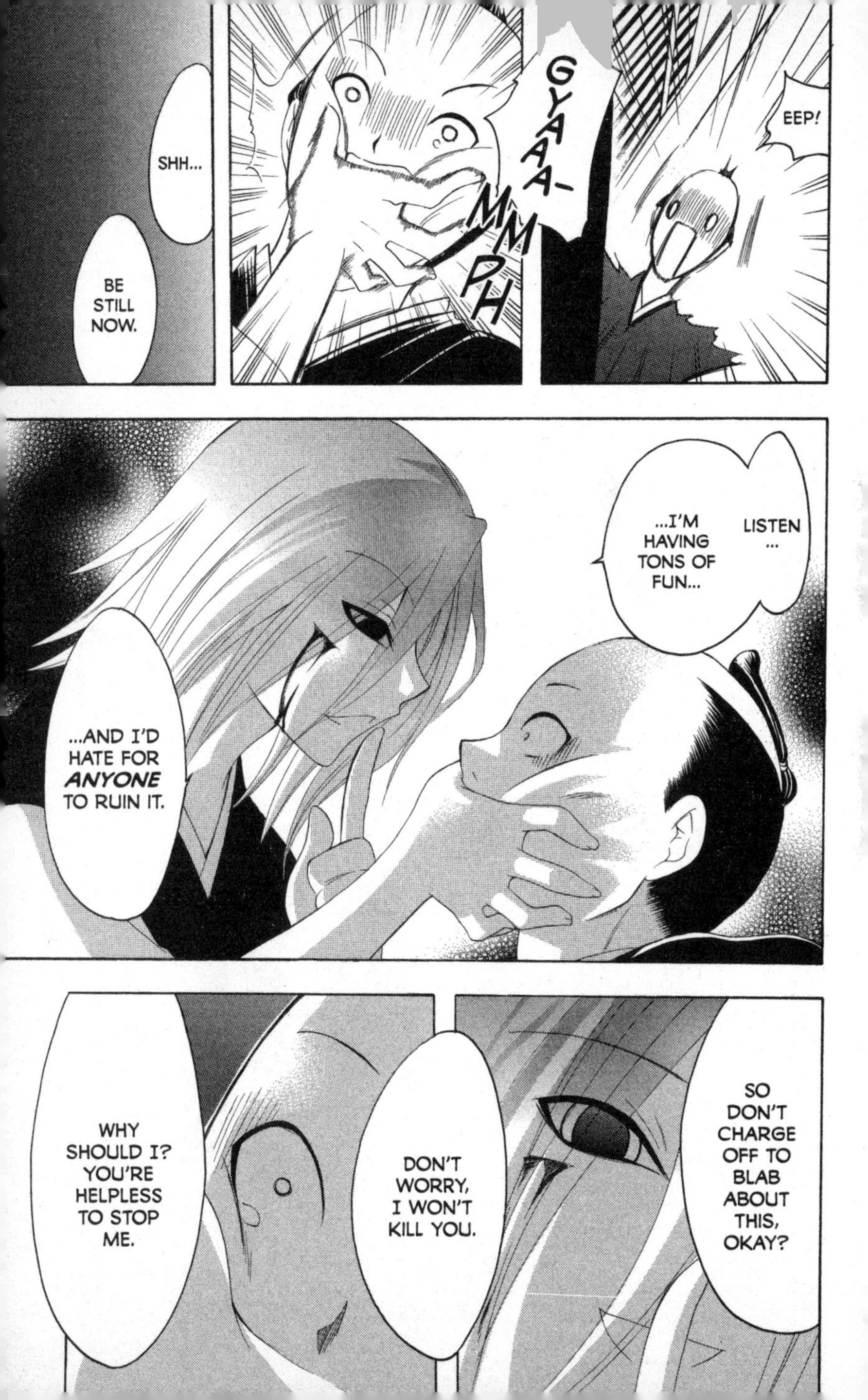
EEP!
GYAAA-MMMPH
SHH...
BE STILL NOW.
LISTEN ...
...I'M HAVING TONS OF FUN...
...AND I'D HATE FOR ***ANYONE*** TO RUIN IT.
SO DON'T CHARGE OFF TO BLAB ABOUT THIS, OKAY?
DON'T WORRY, I WON'T KILL YOU.
WHY SHOULD I? YOU'RE HELPLESS TO STOP ME.

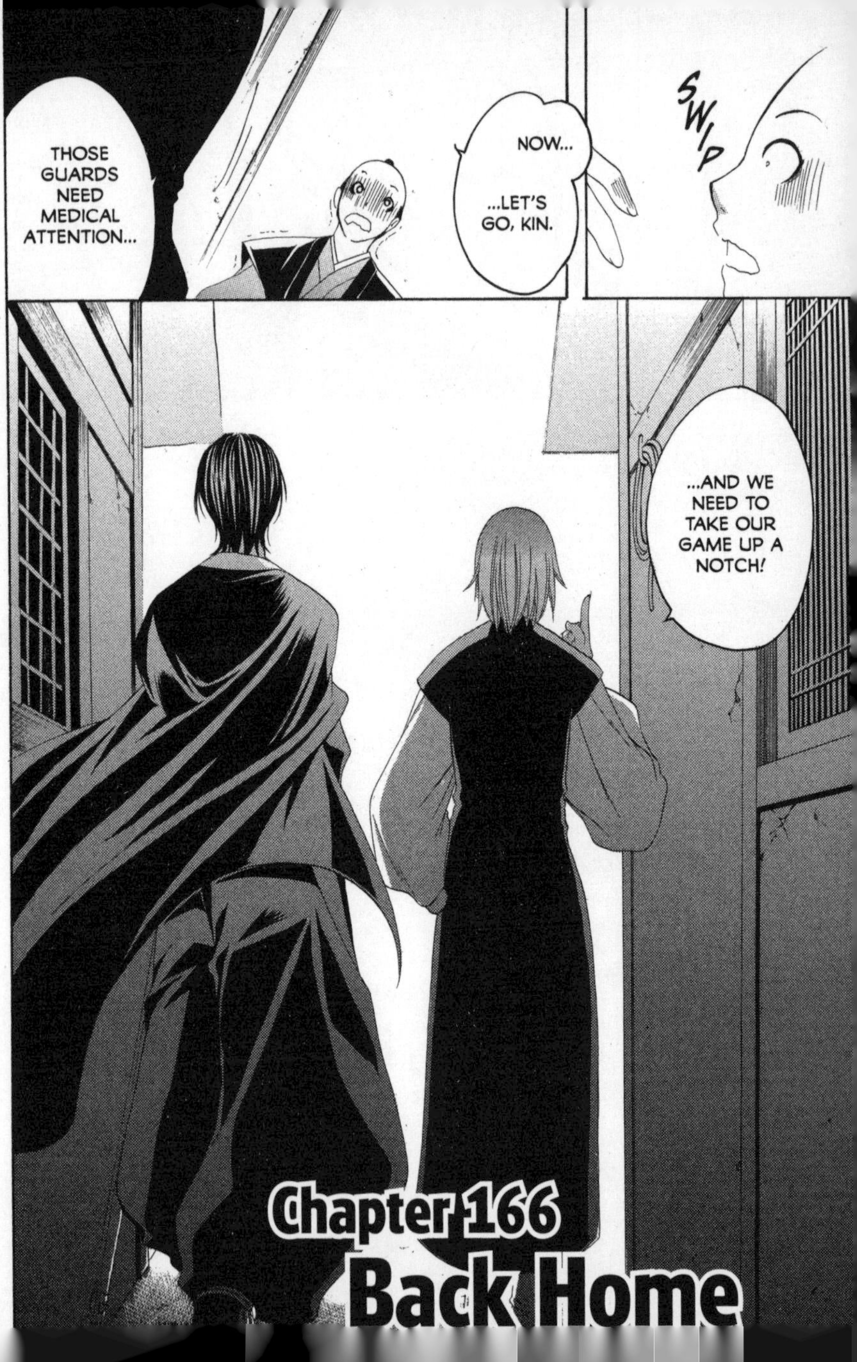
SWIP
NOW... ...LET'S GO, KIN.
THOSE GUARDS NEED MEDICAL ATTENTION...
...AND WE NEED TO TAKE OUR GAME UP A NOTCH!
Chapter 166
Back Home

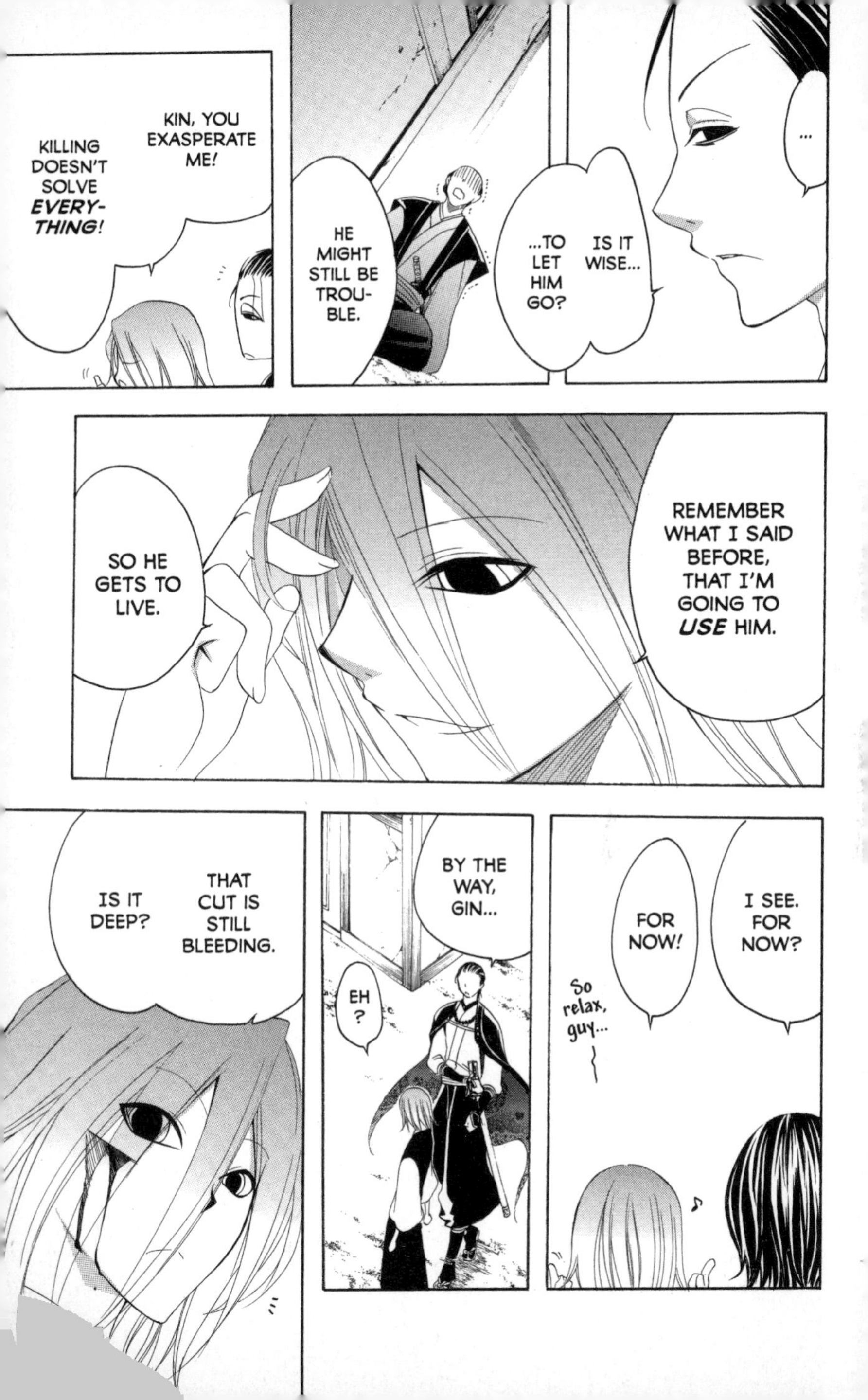
...
IS IT WISE... ...TO LET HIM GO?
HE MIGHT STILL BE TROU-BLE.
KIN, YOU EXASPERATE ME!
KILLING DOESN'T SOLVE *EVERY-THING*!
REMEMBER WHAT I SAID BEFORE, THAT I'M GOING TO *USE* HIM.
SO HE GETS TO LIVE.
I SEE. FOR NOW?
FOR NOW!
So relax, guy...
BY THE WAY, GIN...
EH?
THAT CUT IS STILL BLEEDING.
IS IT DEEP?

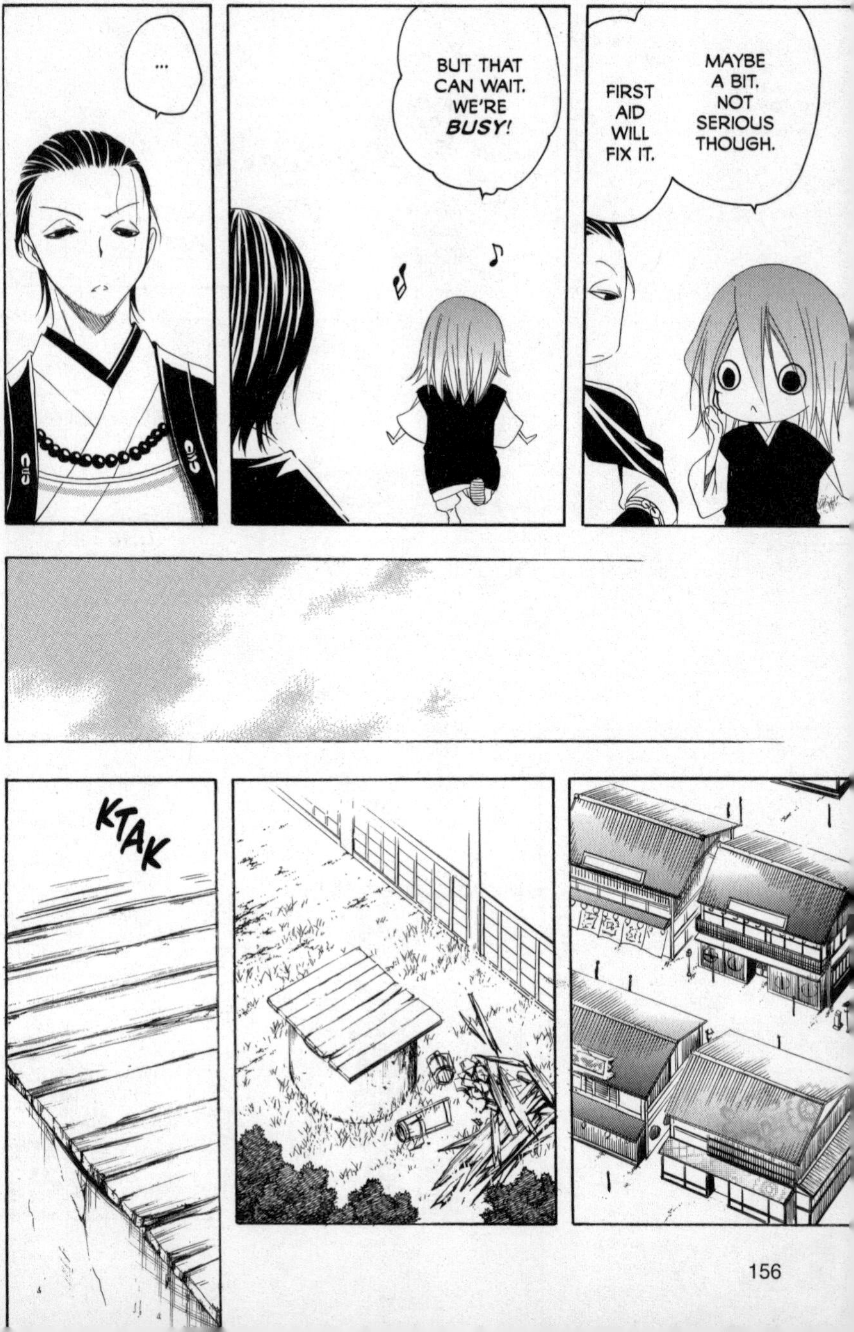
MAYBE A BIT. NOT SERIOUS THOUGH.
FIRST AID WILL FIX IT.
BUT THAT CAN WAIT. WE'RE *BUSY*!
...
KTAK

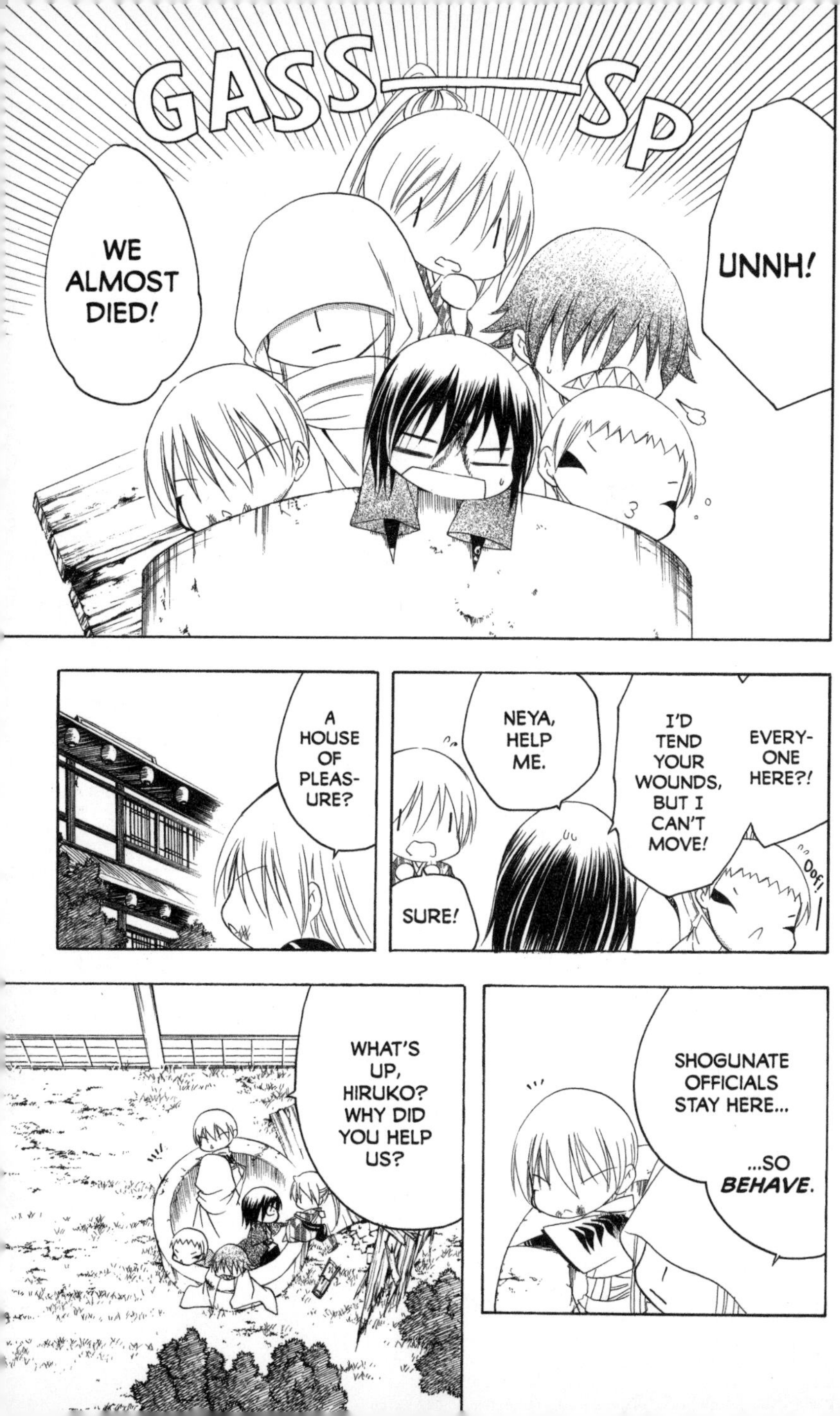
GASS——SP
UNNH!
WE ALMOST DIED!
EVERY-ONE HERE?!
I'D TEND YOUR WOUNDS, BUT I CAN'T MOVE!
NEYA, HELP ME.
Oof!
SURE!
A HOUSE OF PLEAS-URE?
SHOGUNATE OFFICIALS STAY HERE...
...SO *BEHAVE*.
WHAT'S UP, HIRUKO? WHY DID YOU HELP US?

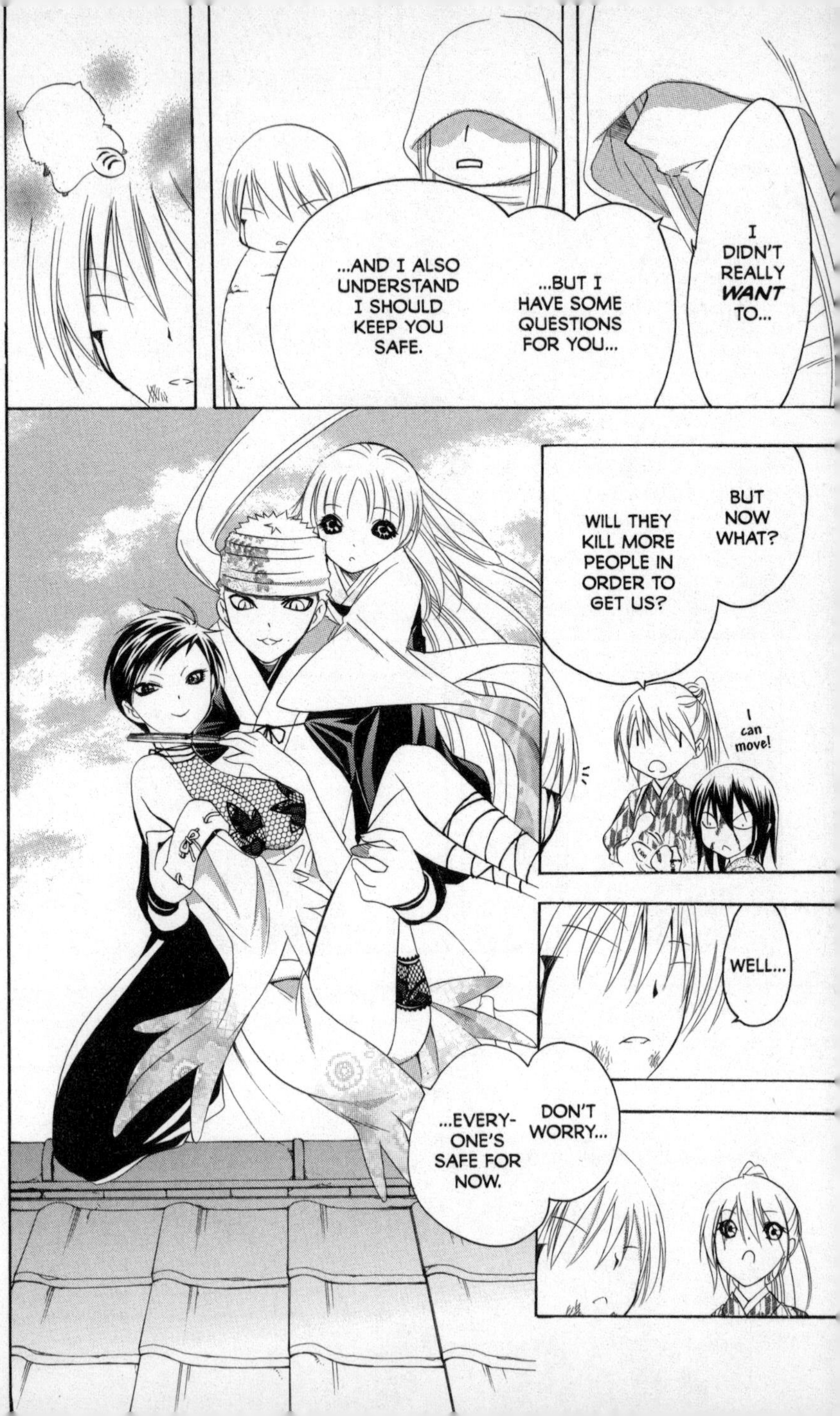
I DIDN'T REALLY *WANT* TO...
...BUT I HAVE SOME QUESTIONS FOR YOU...
...AND I ALSO UNDERSTAND I SHOULD KEEP YOU SAFE.
BUT NOW WHAT?
WILL THEY KILL MORE PEOPLE IN ORDER TO GET US?
I can move!
WELL...
DON'T WORRY...
...EVERY-ONE'S SAFE FOR NOW.

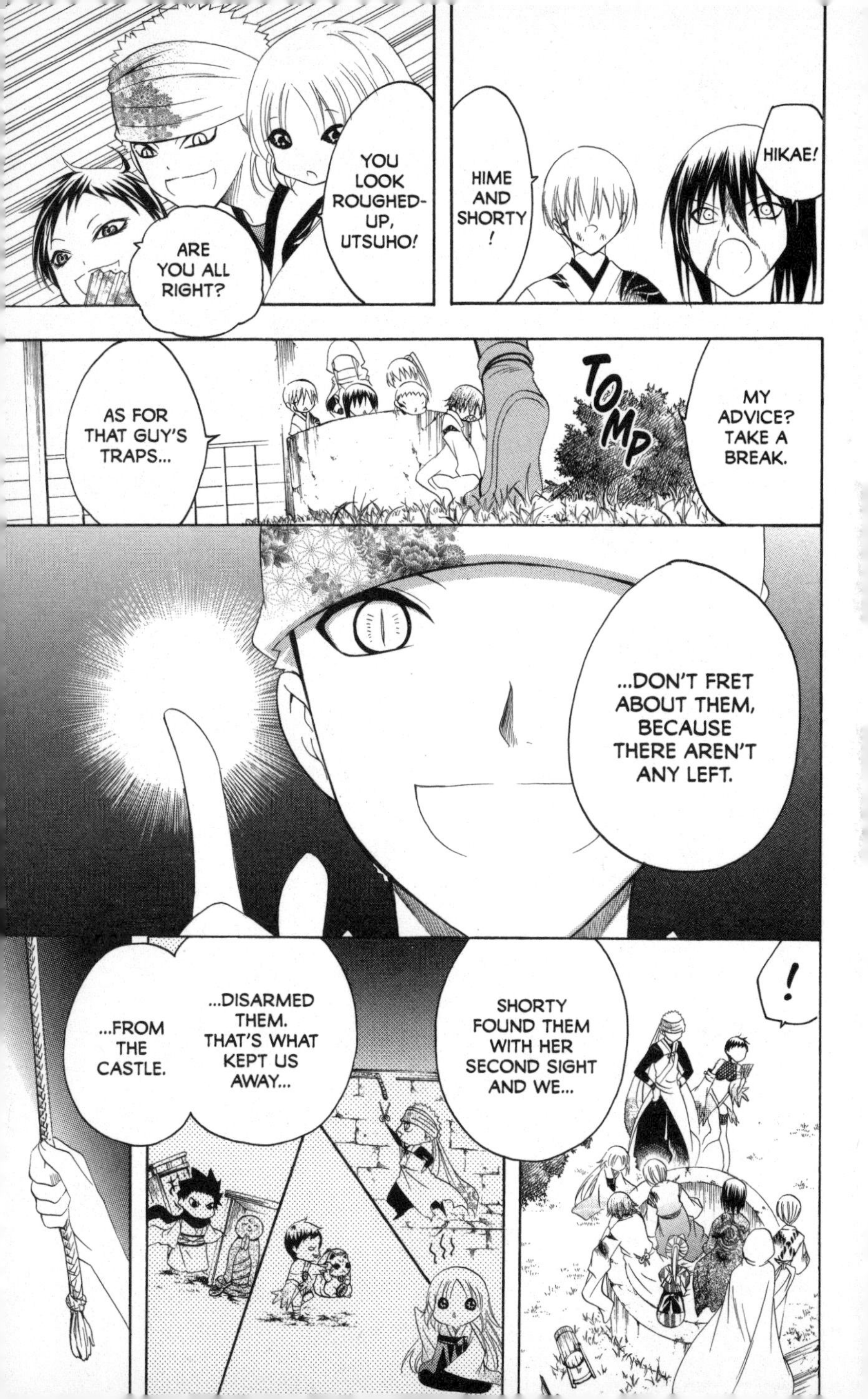
HIKAE!
HIME AND SHORTY!
YOU LOOK ROUGHED-UP, UTSUHO!
ARE YOU ALL RIGHT?
MY ADVICE? TAKE A BREAK.
TOMP
AS FOR THAT GUY'S TRAPS...
...DON'T FRET ABOUT THEM, BECAUSE THERE AREN'T ANY LEFT.
!
SHORTY FOUND THEM WITH HER SECOND SIGHT AND WE...
...DISARMED THEM. THAT'S WHAT KEPT US AWAY...
...FROM THE CASTLE.

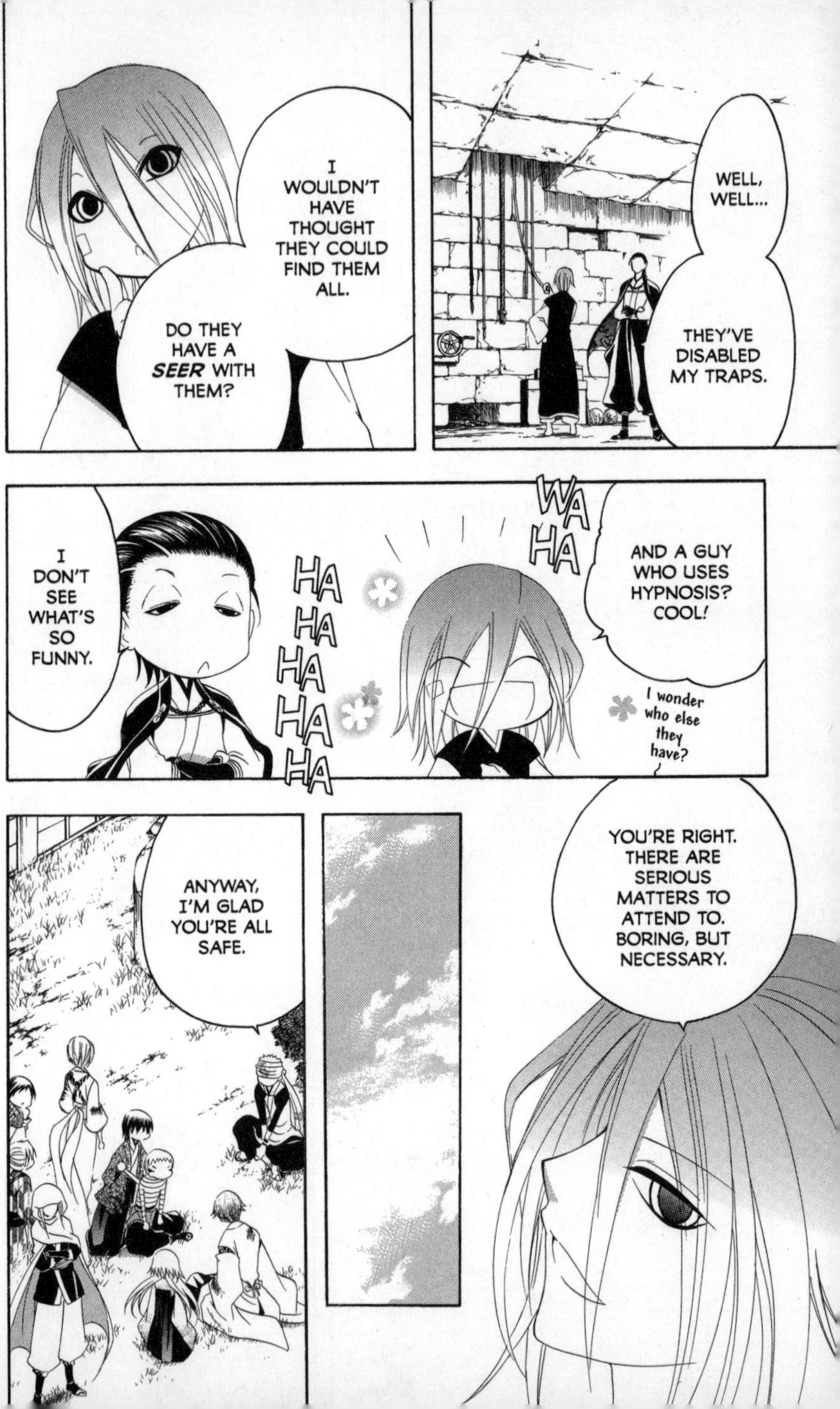
WELL, WELL...
THEY'VE DISABLED MY TRAPS.
I WOULDN'T HAVE THOUGHT THEY COULD FIND THEM ALL.
DO THEY HAVE A *SEER* WITH THEM?
AND A GUY WHO USES HYPNOSIS? COOL!
WA HA
I wonder who else they have?
HA HA HA HA HA HA
I DON'T SEE WHAT'S SO FUNNY.
YOU'RE RIGHT. THERE ARE SERIOUS MATTERS TO ATTEND TO. BORING, BUT NECESSARY.
ANYWAY, I'M GLAD YOU'RE ALL SAFE.

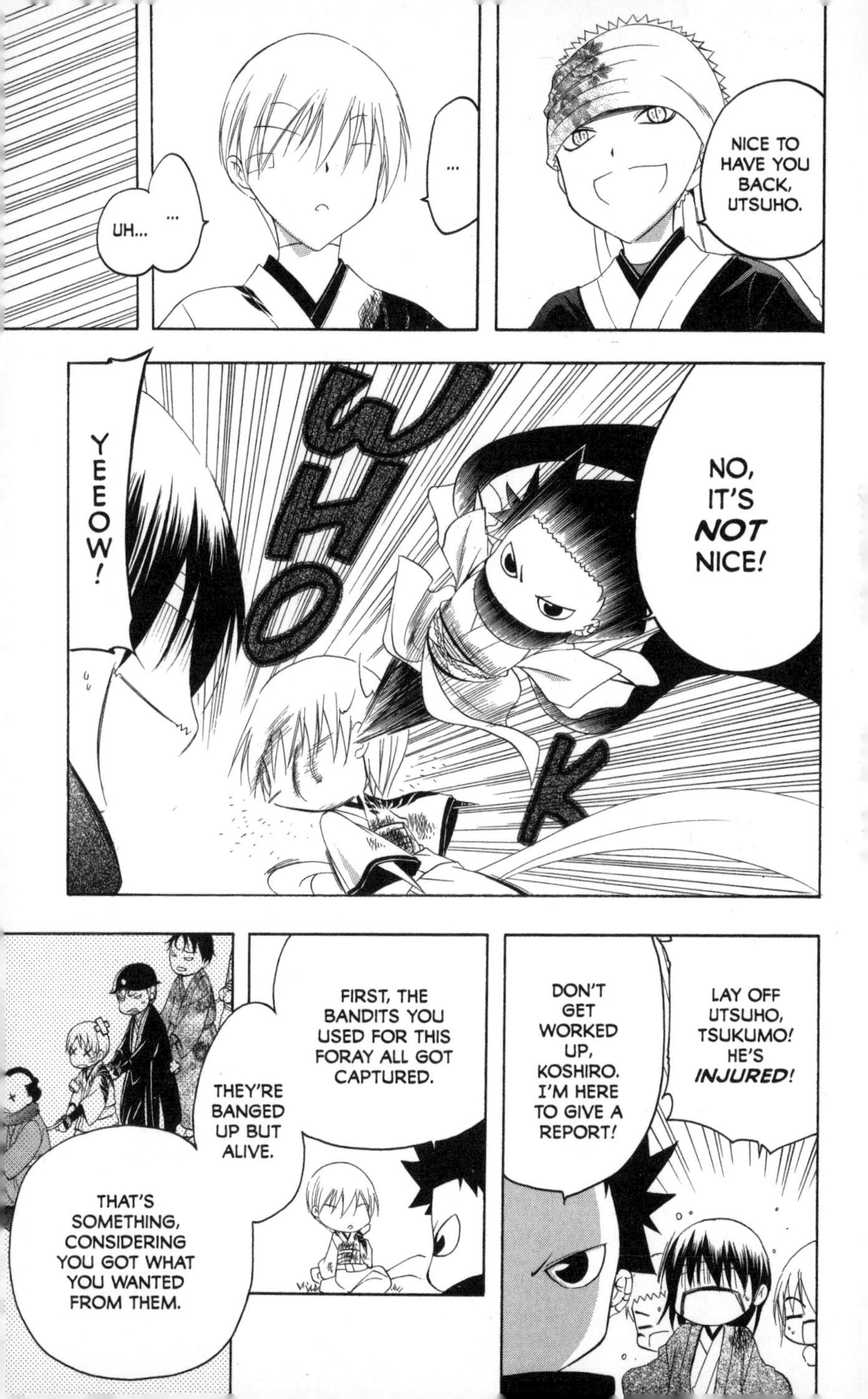
NICE TO HAVE YOU BACK, UTSUHO.
...
UH... ...
NO, IT'S **NOT** NICE!
WHOK
YEEOW!
LAY OFF UTSUHO, TSUKUMO! HE'S **INJURED**!
DON'T GET WORKED UP, KOSHIRO. I'M HERE TO GIVE A REPORT!
FIRST, THE BANDITS YOU USED FOR THIS FORAY ALL GOT CAPTURED.
THEY'RE BANGED UP BUT ALIVE.
THAT'S SOMETHING, CONSIDERING YOU GOT WHAT YOU WANTED FROM THEM.

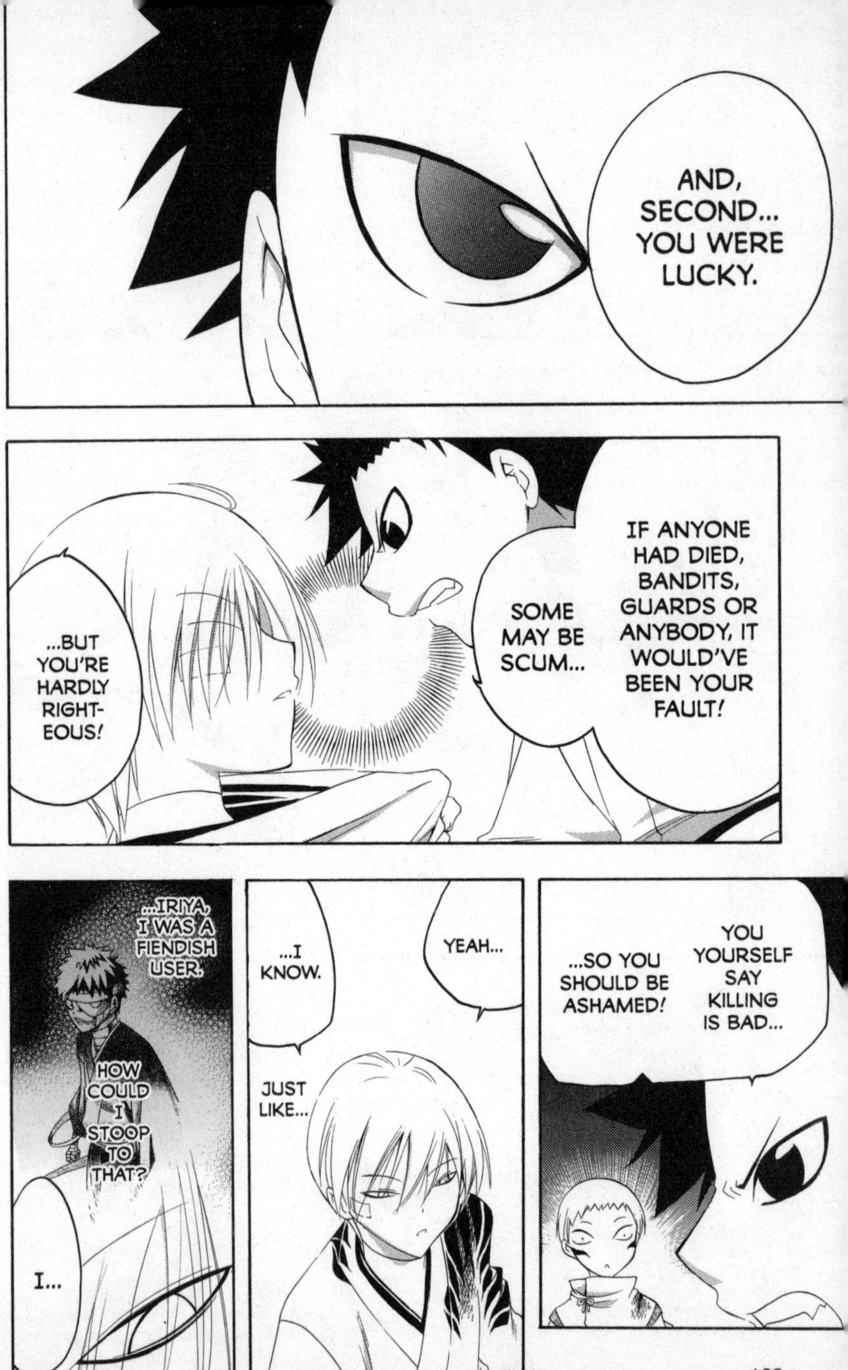
AND, SECOND... YOU WERE LUCKY.
IF ANYONE HAD DIED, BANDITS, GUARDS OR ANYBODY, IT WOULD'VE BEEN YOUR FAULT!
SOME MAY BE SCUM...
...BUT YOU'RE HARDLY RIGHTEOUS!
YOU YOURSELF SAY KILLING IS BAD...
...SO YOU SHOULD BE ASHAMED!
YEAH...
...I KNOW.
JUST LIKE...
...IRIYA, I WAS A FIENDISH USER.
HOW COULD I STOOP TO THAT?
I...

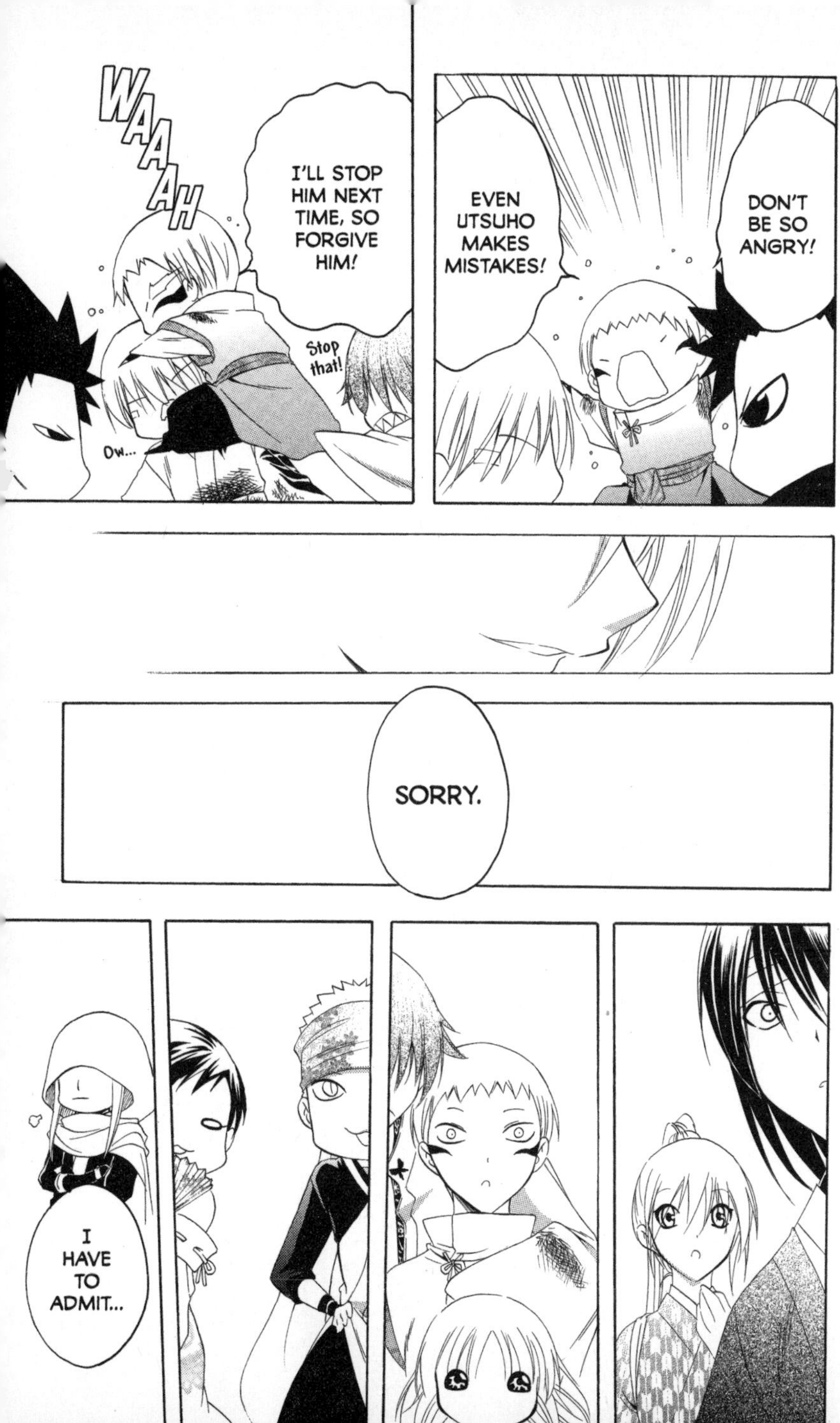
DON'T BE SO ANGRY!
EVEN UTSUHO MAKES MISTAKES!
I'LL STOP HIM NEXT TIME, SO FORGIVE HIM!
WAAAAH
Stop that!
Ow...
SORRY.
I HAVE TO ADMIT...

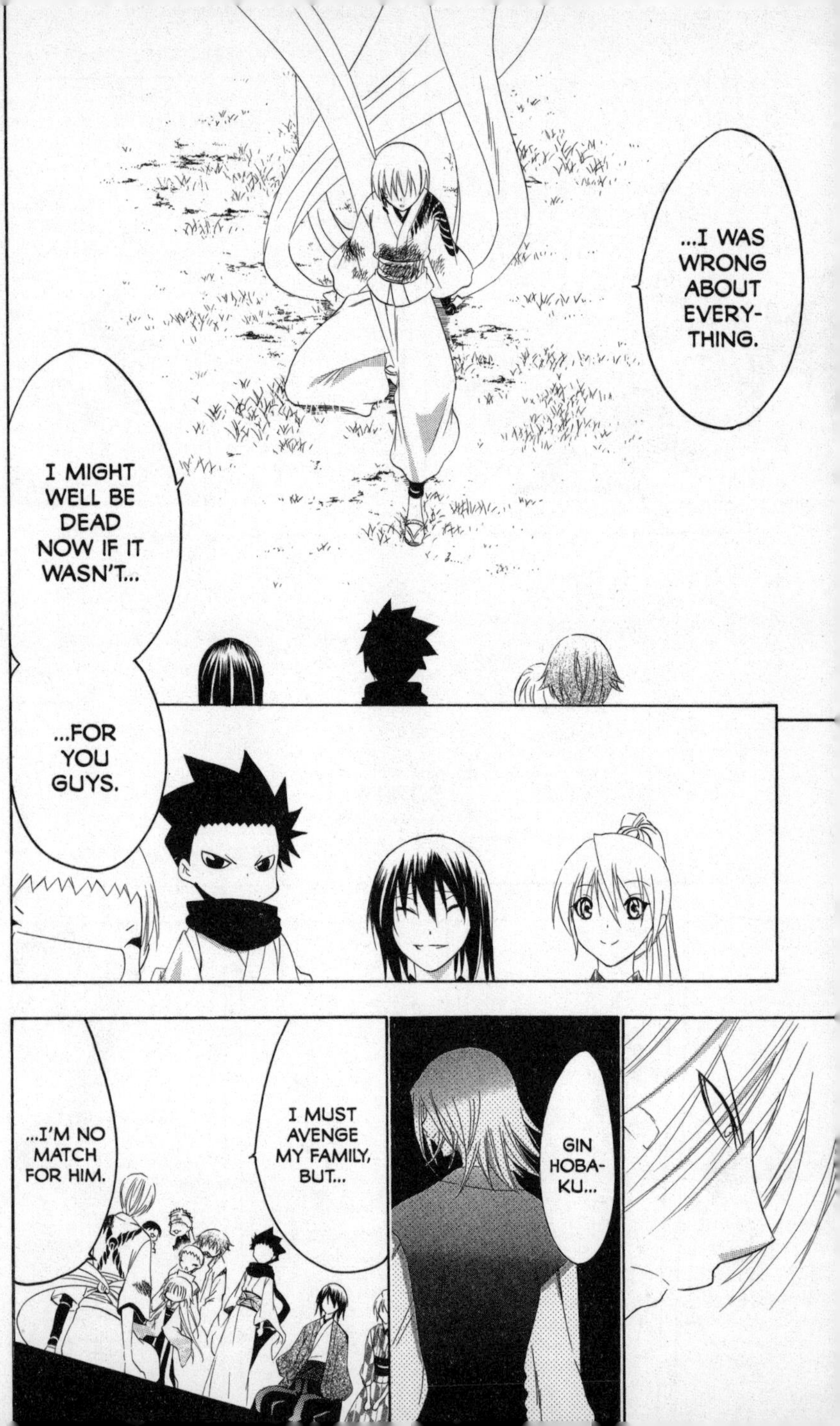
...I WAS WRONG ABOUT EVERY-THING.
I MIGHT WELL BE DEAD NOW IF IT WASN'T...
...FOR YOU GUYS.
GIN HOBA-KU...
I MUST AVENGE MY FAMILY, BUT...
...I'M NO MATCH FOR HIM.

PLEASE, HELP ME.

YOU GOT IT!

...

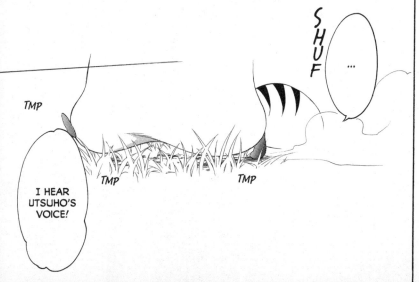

SHUF

...

TMP

TMP

TMP

I HEAR UTSUHO'S VOICE!

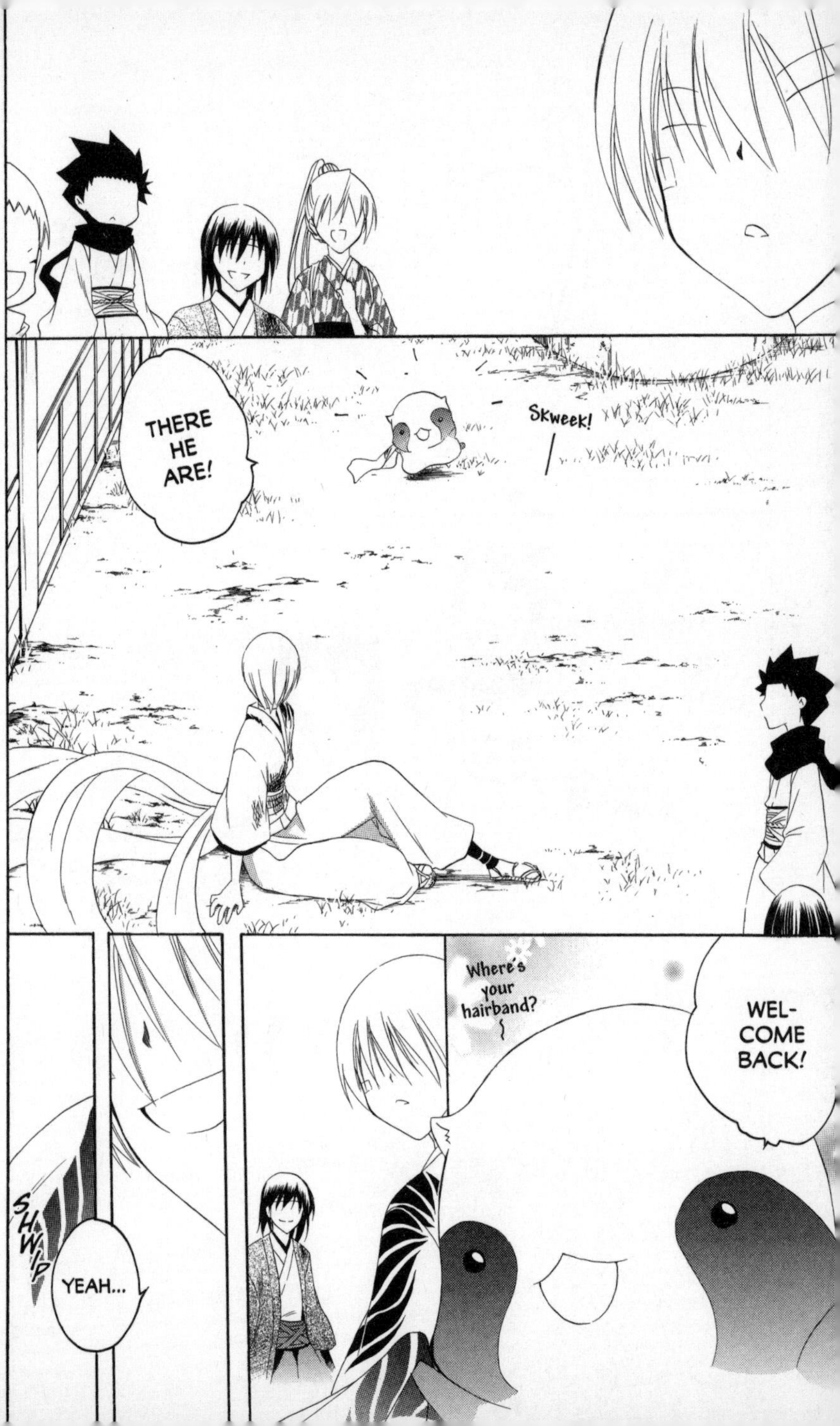
THERE HE ARE!
Skweek!
WEL-COME BACK!
Where's your hairband?
SHWIP
YEAH...

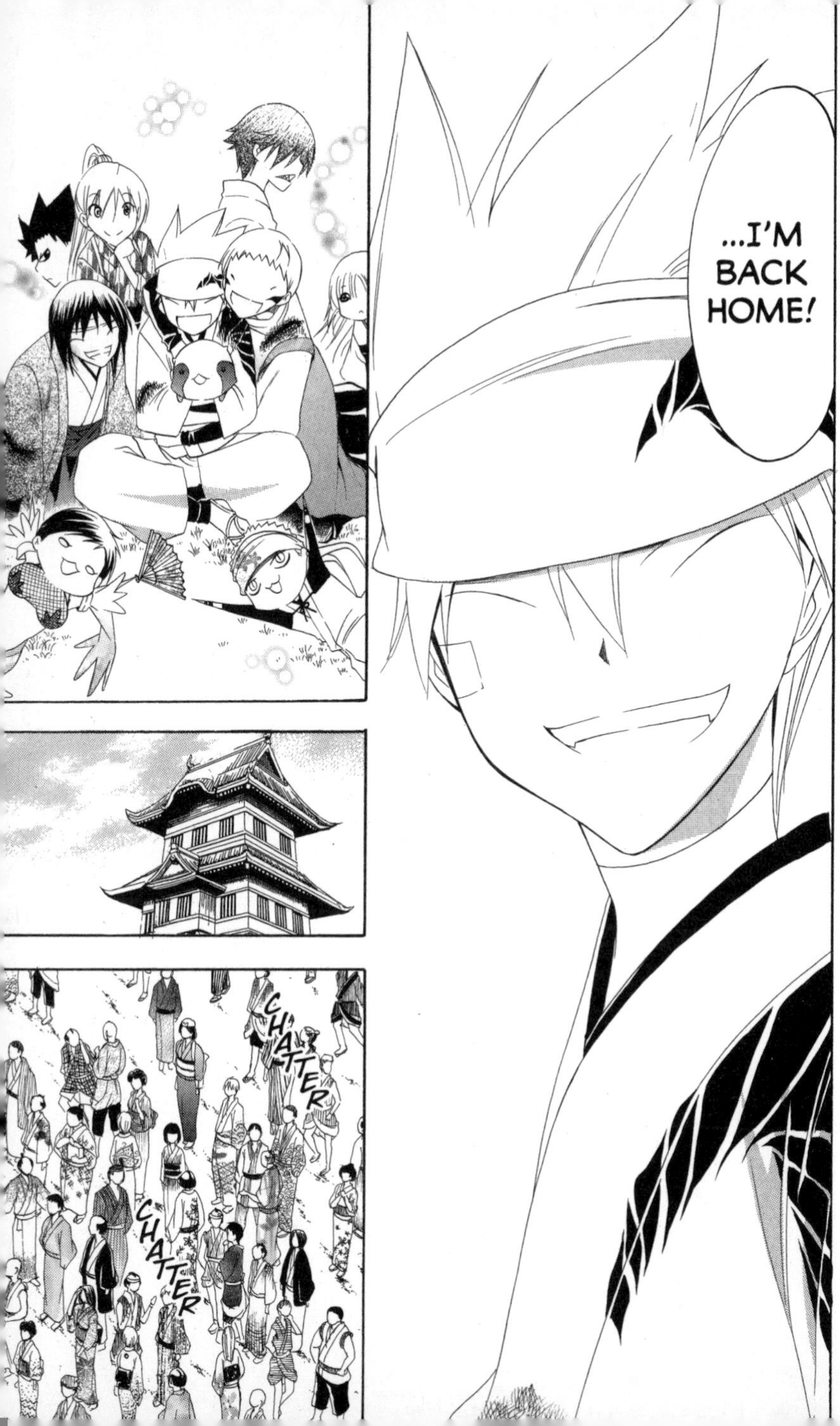
...I'M BACK HOME!
CHATTER
CHATTER

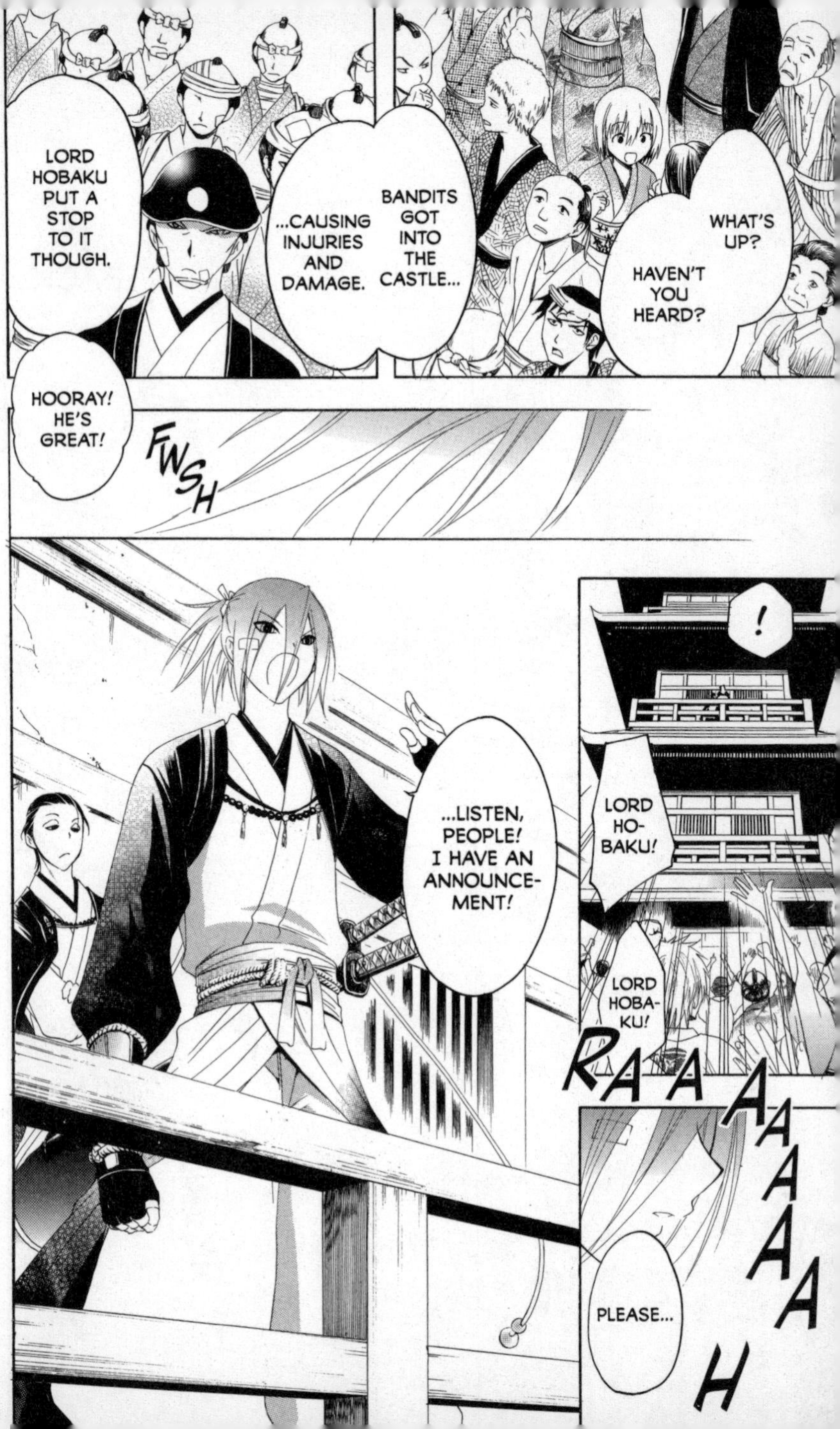
WHAT'S UP?
HAVEN'T YOU HEARD?
BANDITS GOT INTO THE CASTLE...
...CAUSING INJURIES AND DAMAGE.
LORD HOBAKU PUT A STOP TO IT THOUGH.
HOORAY! HE'S GREAT!
FWSH
!
LORD HO-BAKU!
LORD HOBA-KU!
RAAAAAAAAAH
PLEASE...
...LISTEN, PEOPLE! I HAVE AN ANNOUNCEMENT!

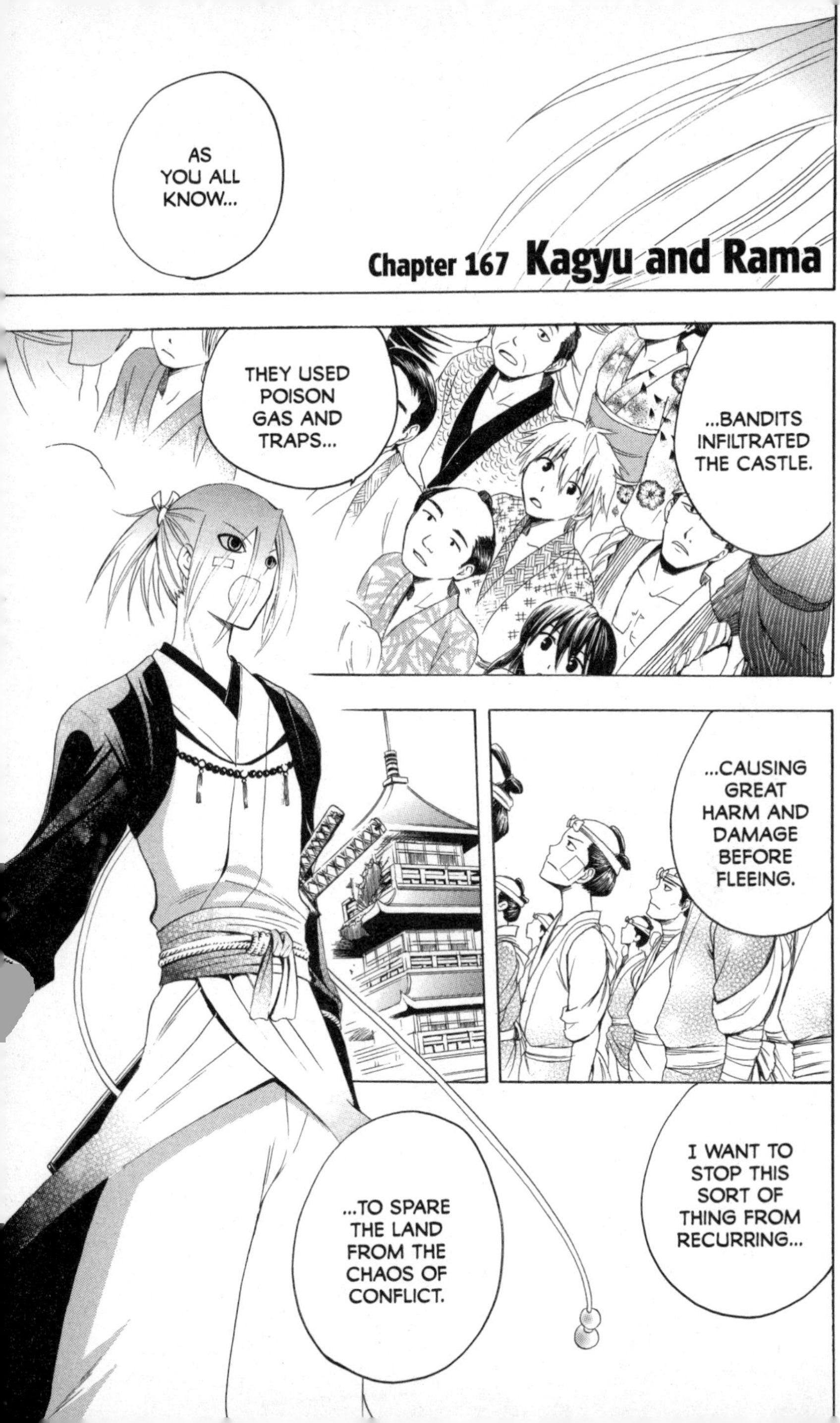
Chapter 167 Kagyu and Rama
AS YOU ALL KNOW...
...BANDITS INFILTRATED THE CASTLE.
THEY USED POISON GAS AND TRAPS...
...CAUSING GREAT HARM AND DAMAGE BEFORE FLEEING.
I WANT TO STOP THIS SORT OF THING FROM RECURRING...
...TO SPARE THE LAND FROM THE CHAOS OF CONFLICT.

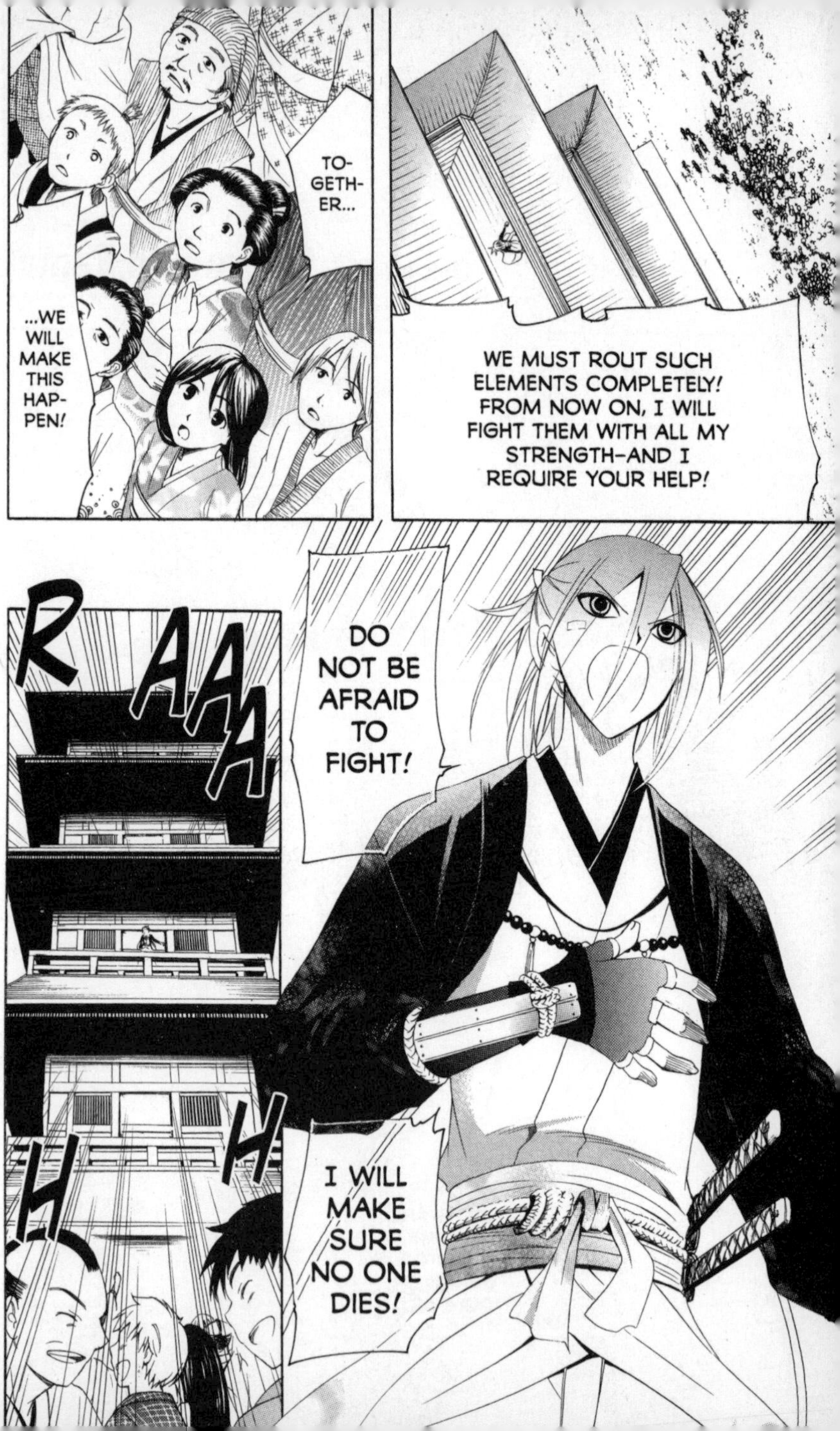
WE MUST ROUT SUCH ELEMENTS COMPLETELY! FROM NOW ON, I WILL FIGHT THEM WITH ALL MY STRENGTH–AND I REQUIRE YOUR HELP!
TO-GETH-ER...
...WE WILL MAKE THIS HAP-PEN!
DO NOT BE AFRAID TO FIGHT!
I WILL MAKE SURE NO ONE DIES!
RAAAHH

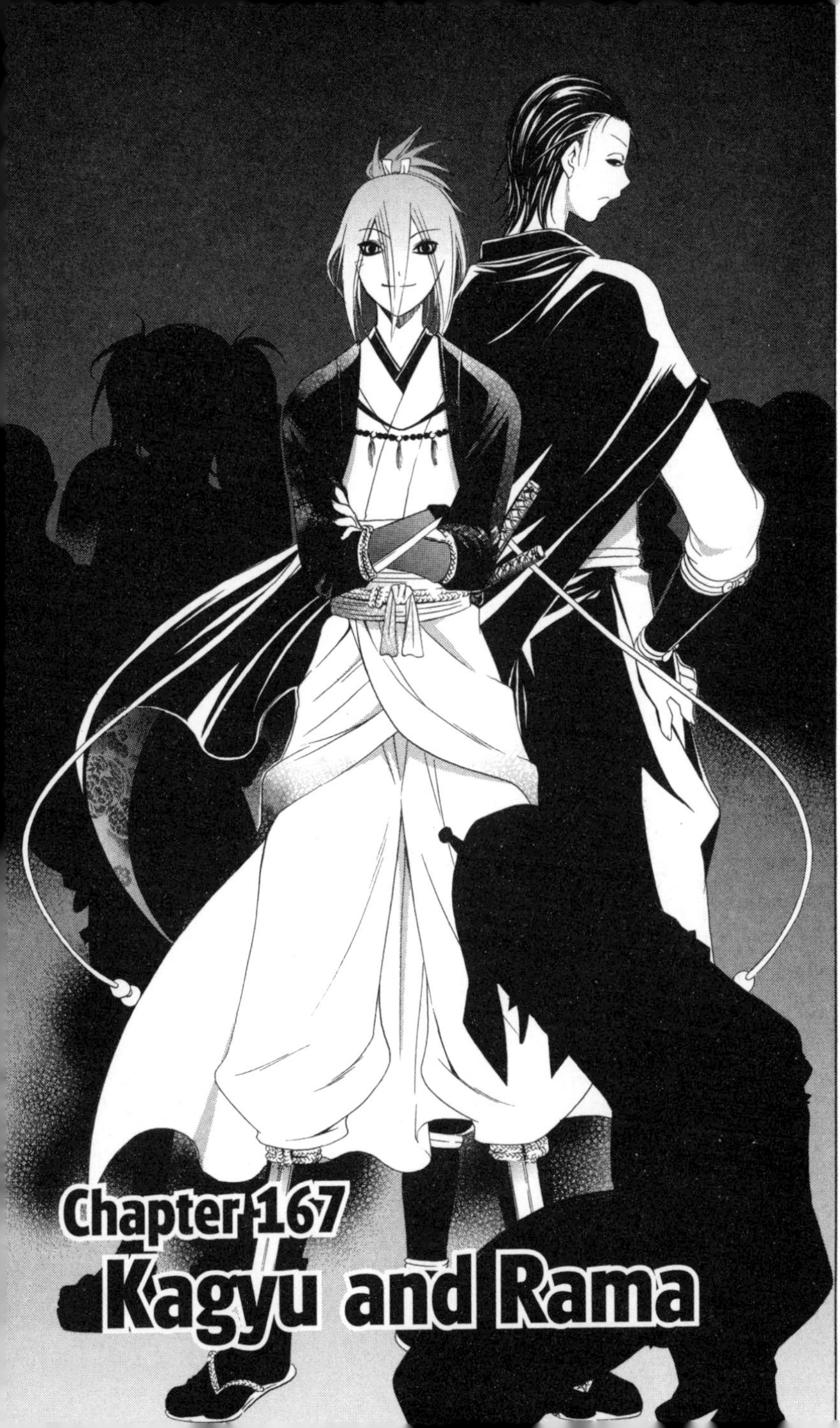
Chapter 167
Kagyu and Rama

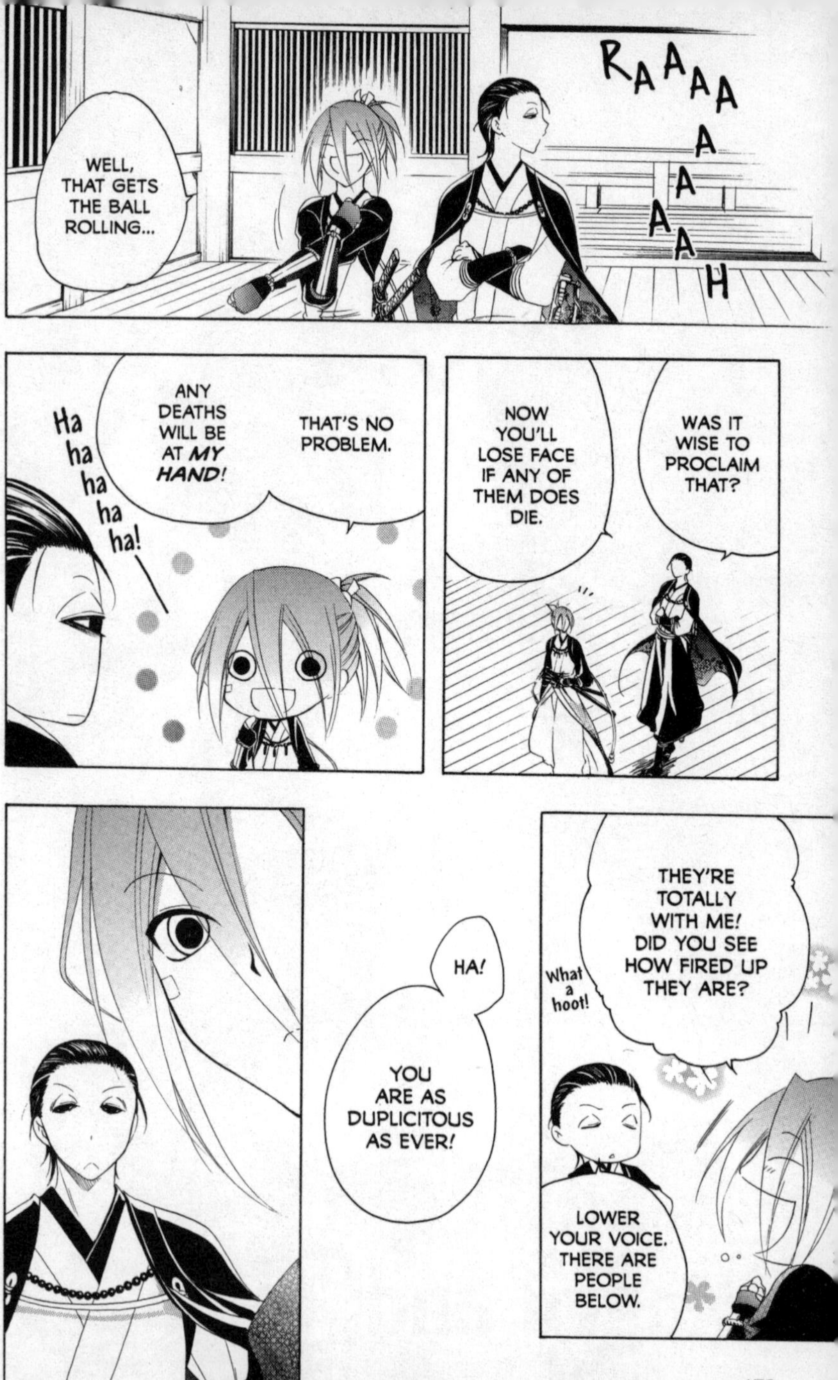
RAAAAAAAAH
WELL, THAT GETS THE BALL ROLLING...
WAS IT WISE TO PROCLAIM THAT?
NOW YOU'LL LOSE FACE IF ANY OF THEM DOES DIE.
THAT'S NO PROBLEM.
ANY DEATHS WILL BE AT *MY HAND*!
Ha ha ha ha ha!
THEY'RE TOTALLY WITH ME! DID YOU SEE HOW FIRED UP THEY ARE?
What a hoot!
LOWER YOUR VOICE. THERE ARE PEOPLE BELOW.
HA!
YOU ARE AS DUPLICITOUS AS EVER!

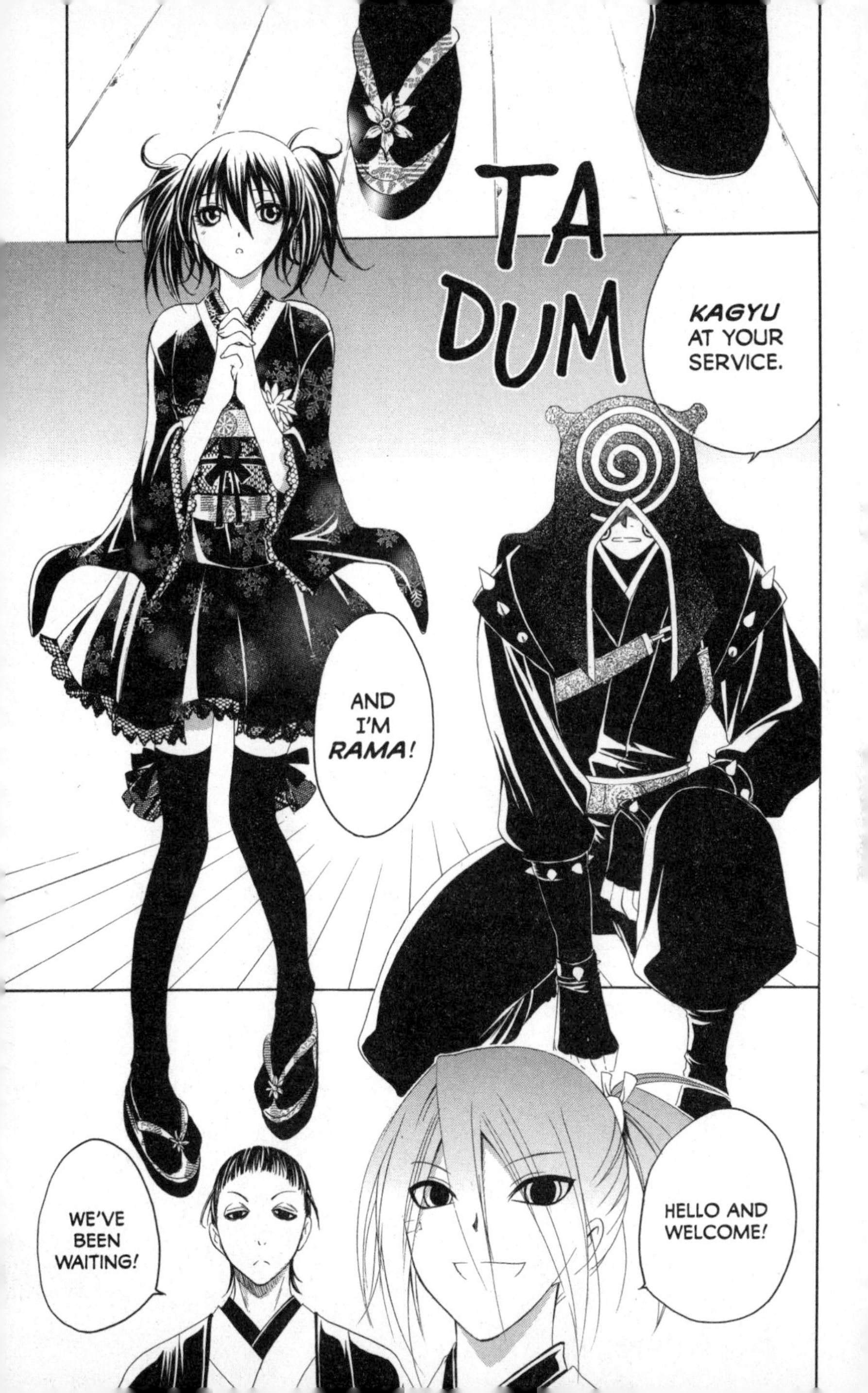
TA DUM
KAGYU AT YOUR SERVICE.
AND I'M RAMA!
HELLO AND WELCOME!
WE'VE BEEN WAITING!

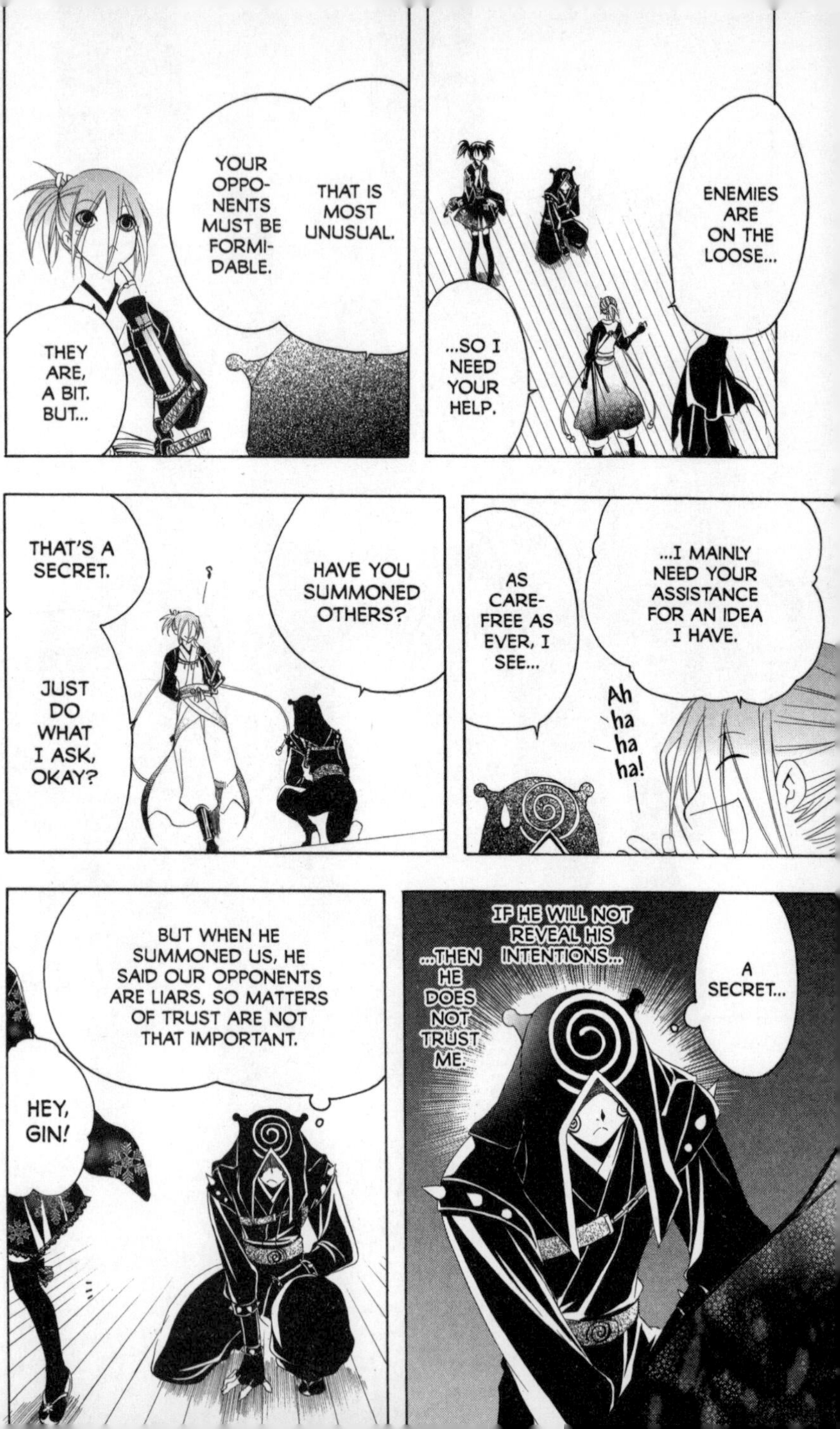
ENEMIES ARE ON THE LOOSE...
...SO I NEED YOUR HELP.
THAT IS MOST UNUSUAL.
YOUR OPPONENTS MUST BE FORMIDABLE.
THEY ARE, A BIT. BUT...
...I MAINLY NEED YOUR ASSISTANCE FOR AN IDEA I HAVE.
Ah ha ha ha!
AS CAREFREE AS EVER, I SEE...
HAVE YOU SUMMONED OTHERS?
THAT'S A SECRET.
JUST DO WHAT I ASK, OKAY?
A SECRET...
IF HE WILL NOT REVEAL HIS INTENTIONS...
...THEN HE DOES NOT TRUST ME.
BUT WHEN HE SUMMONED US, HE SAID OUR OPPONENTS ARE LIARS, SO MATTERS OF TRUST ARE NOT THAT IMPORTANT.
HEY, GIN!

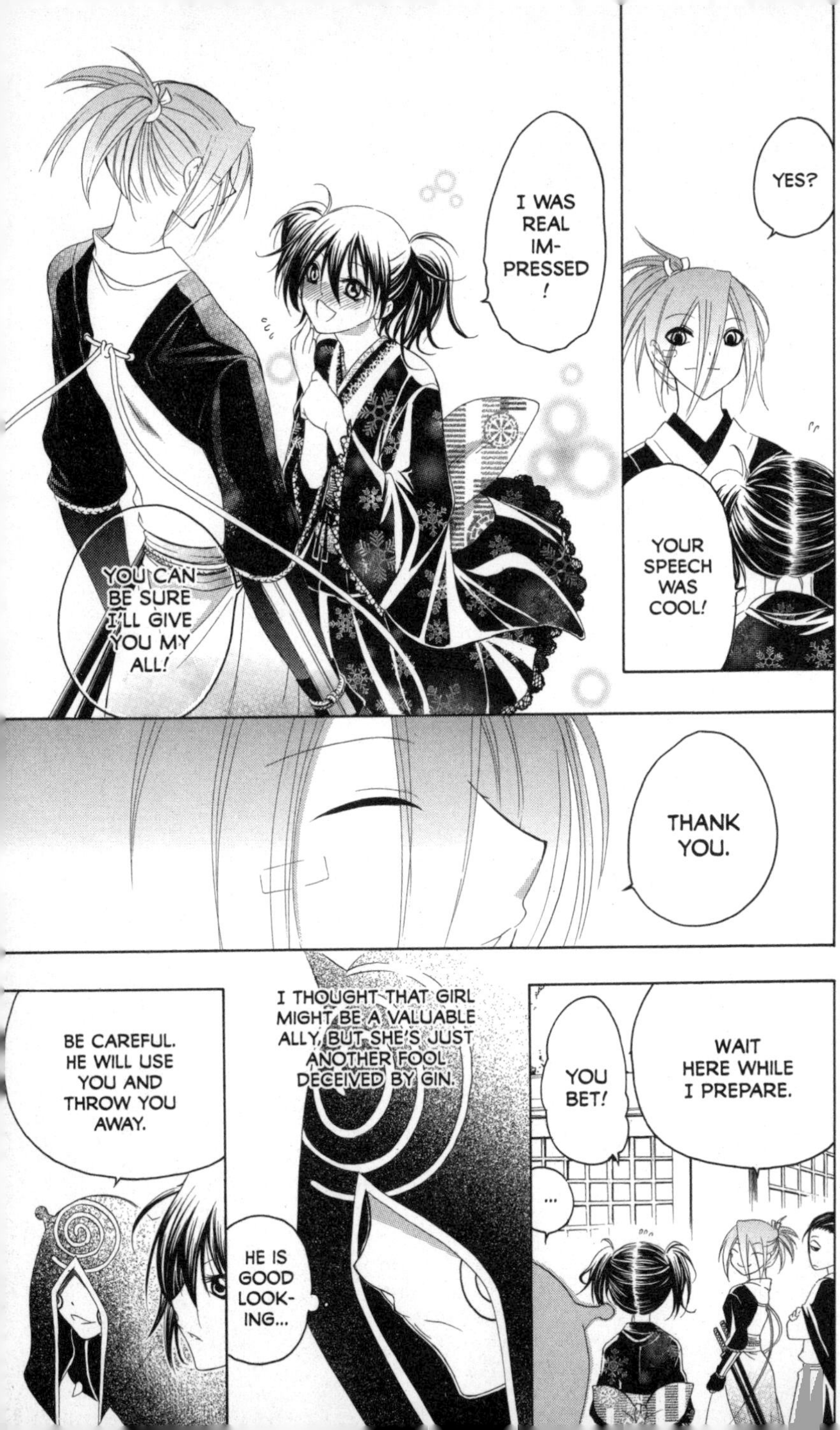
YES?
YOUR SPEECH WAS COOL!
I WAS REAL IM-PRESSED!
YOU CAN BE SURE I'LL GIVE YOU MY ALL!
THANK YOU.
WAIT HERE WHILE I PREPARE.
YOU BET!
...
I THOUGHT THAT GIRL MIGHT BE A VALUABLE ALLY, BUT SHE'S JUST ANOTHER FOOL DECEIVED BY GIN.
HE IS GOOD LOOKING...
BE CAREFUL. HE WILL USE YOU AND THROW YOU AWAY.

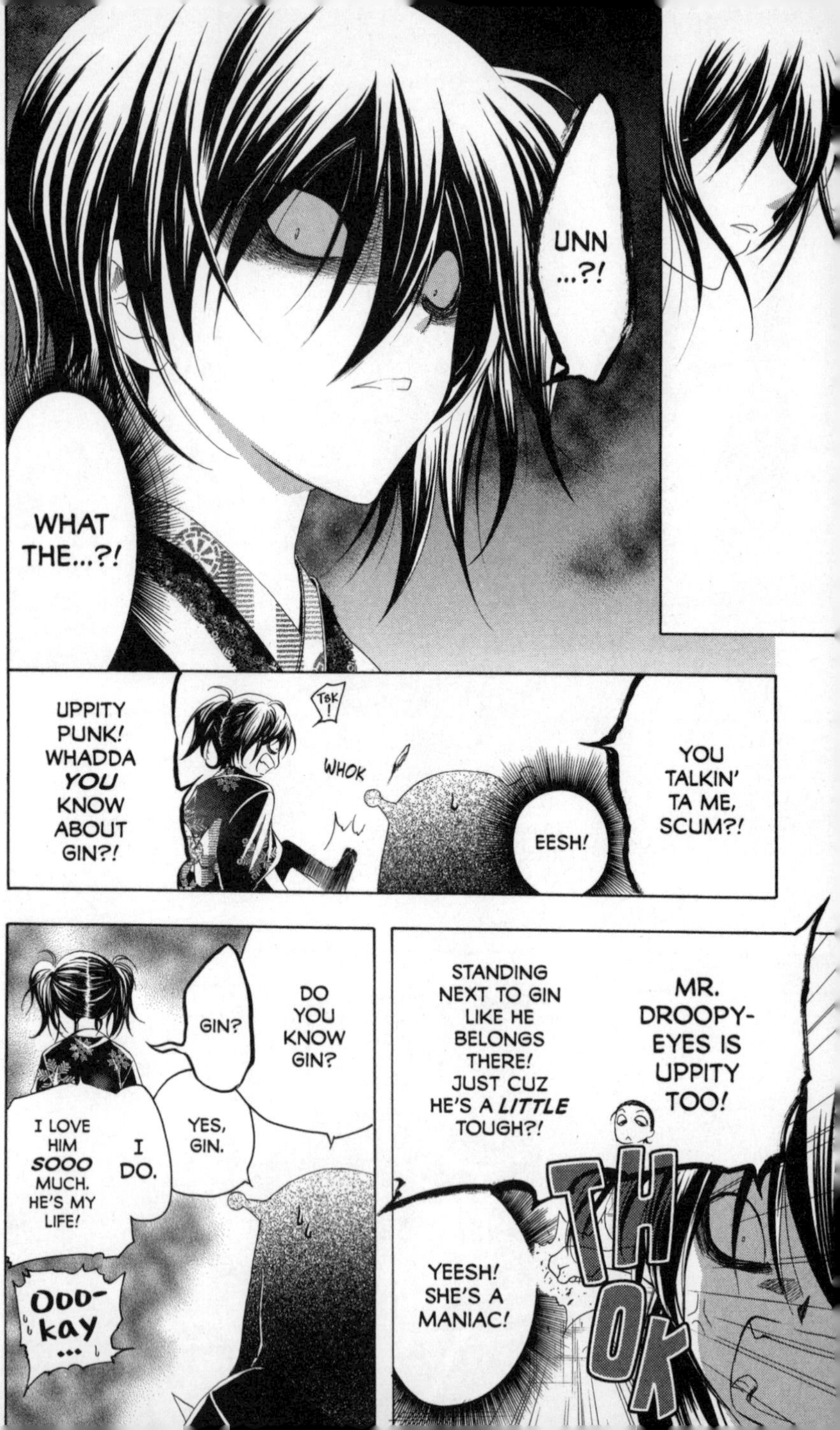
UNN ...?!
WHAT THE...?!
YOU TALKIN' TA ME, SCUM?!
EESH!
WHOK
TSK!
UPPITY PUNK! WHADDA *YOU* KNOW ABOUT GIN?!
MR. DROOPY-EYES IS UPPITY TOO!
STANDING NEXT TO GIN LIKE HE BELONGS THERE! JUST CUZ HE'S A *LITTLE* TOUGH?!
THOK
YEESH! SHE'S A MANIAC!
DO YOU KNOW GIN?
GIN?
YES, GIN.
I DO.
I LOVE HIM *SOOO* MUCH. HE'S MY LIFE!
Ooo-kay...

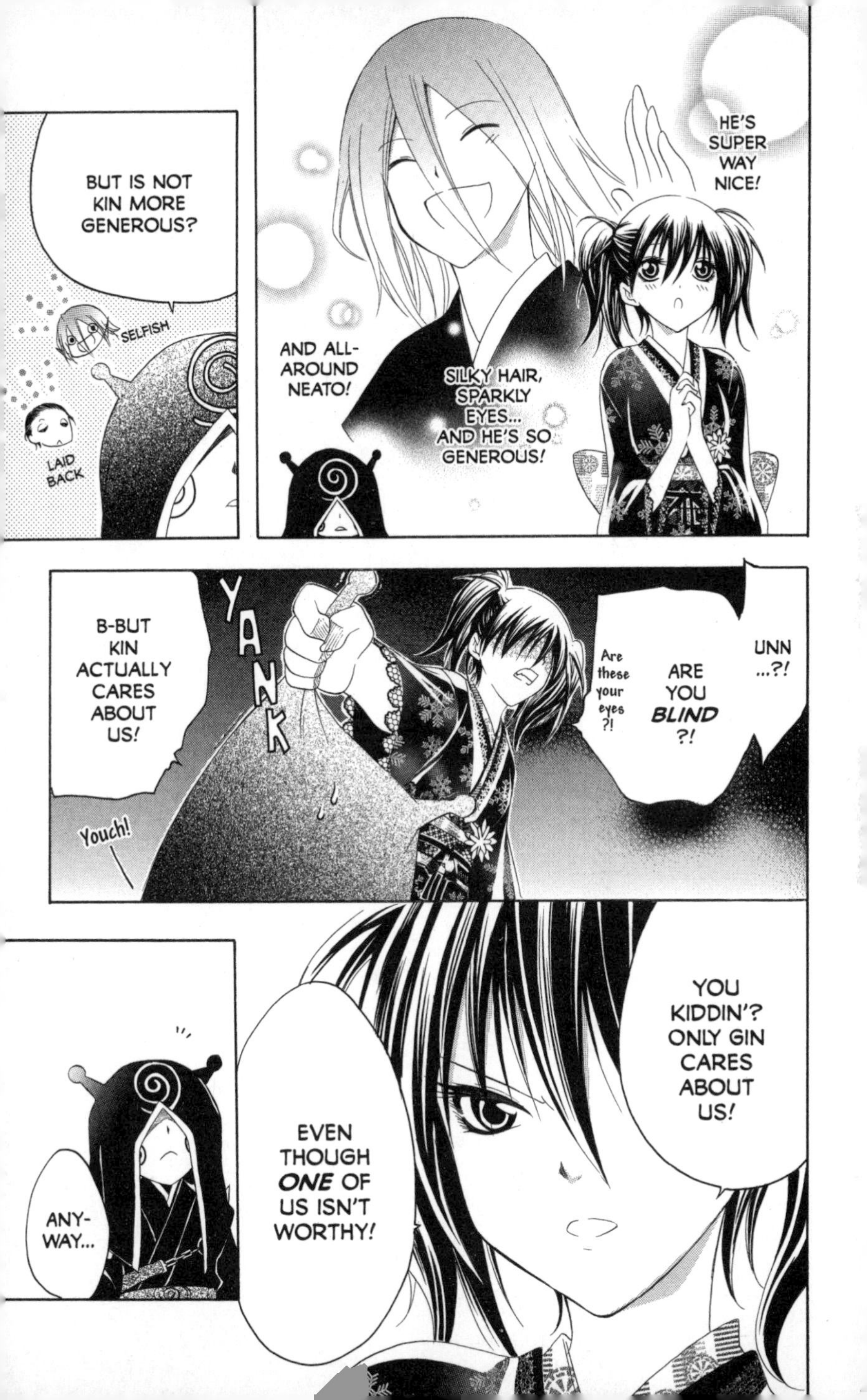
HE'S SUPER WAY NICE!
SILKY HAIR, SPARKLY EYES... AND HE'S SO GENEROUS!
AND ALL-AROUND NEATO!
BUT IS NOT KIN MORE GENEROUS?
SELFISH
LAID BACK
UNN ...?!
ARE YOU BLIND ?!
Are these your eyes ?!
YANK
B-BUT KIN ACTUALLY CARES ABOUT US!
Youch!
YOU KIDDIN'? ONLY GIN CARES ABOUT US!
EVEN THOUGH ONE OF US ISN'T WORTHY!
ANY-WAY...

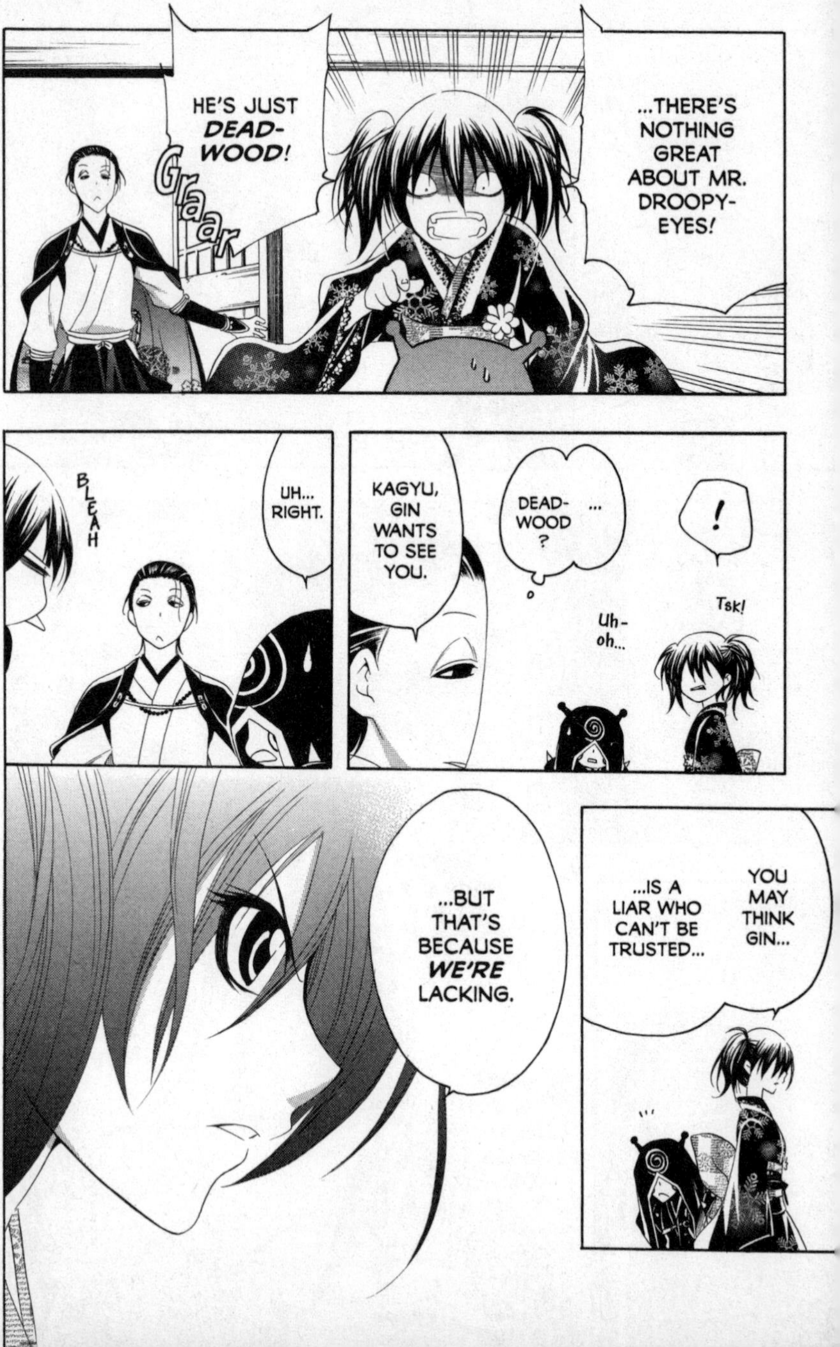
...THERE'S NOTHING GREAT ABOUT MR. DROOPY-EYES!
HE'S JUST DEAD-WOOD!
Graaar
!
Tsk!
DEAD-WOOD? ...
Uh-oh...
KAGYU, GIN WANTS TO SEE YOU.
UH... RIGHT.
BLEAH
YOU MAY THINK GIN...
...IS A LIAR WHO CAN'T BE TRUSTED...
...BUT THAT'S BECAUSE WE'RE LACKING.

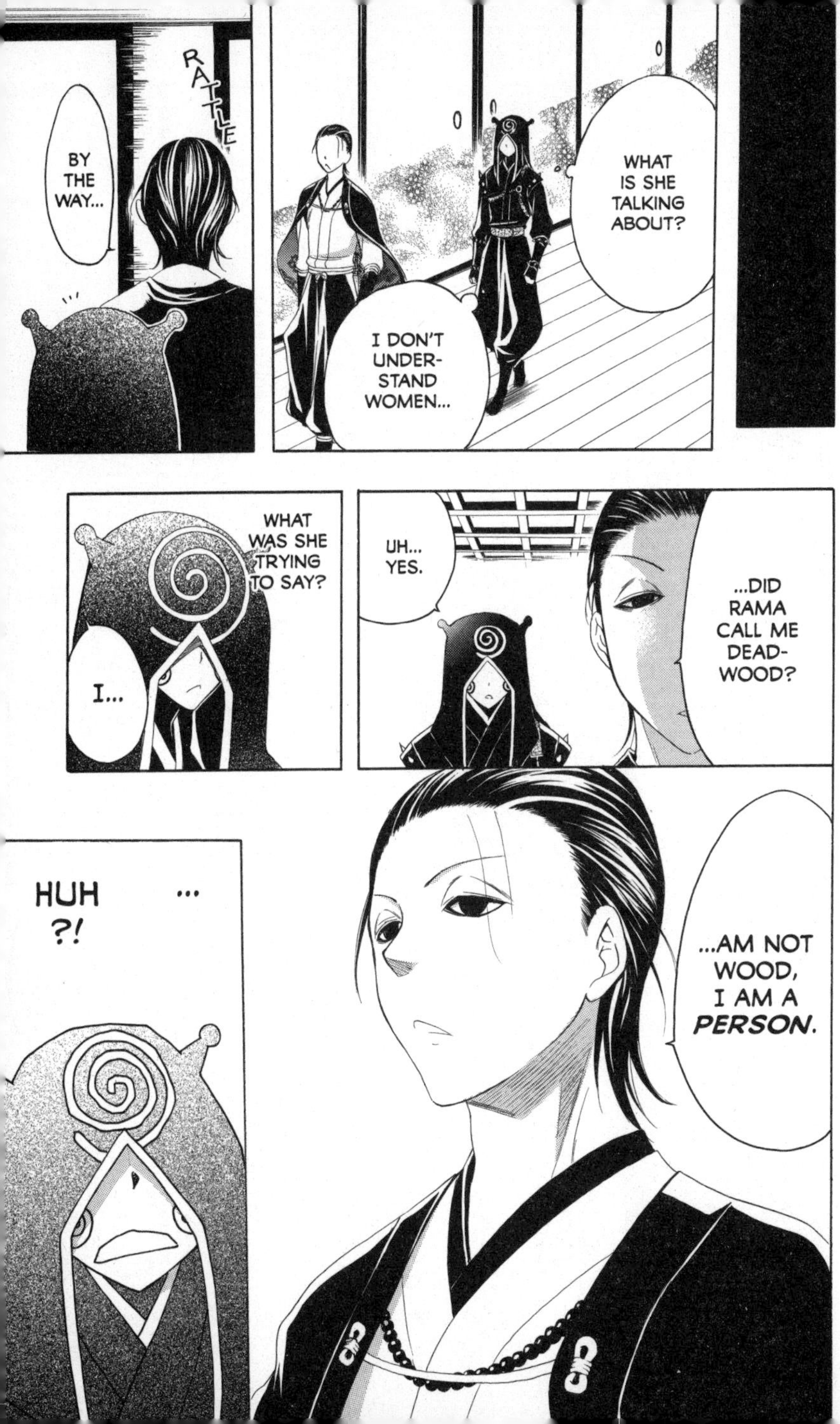
WHAT IS SHE TALKING ABOUT?
I DON'T UNDER-STAND WOMEN...
RATTLE
BY THE WAY...
...DID RAMA CALL ME DEAD-WOOD?
UH... YES.
WHAT WAS SHE TRYING TO SAY?
I...
...AM NOT WOOD, I AM A *PERSON*.
...
HUH ?!

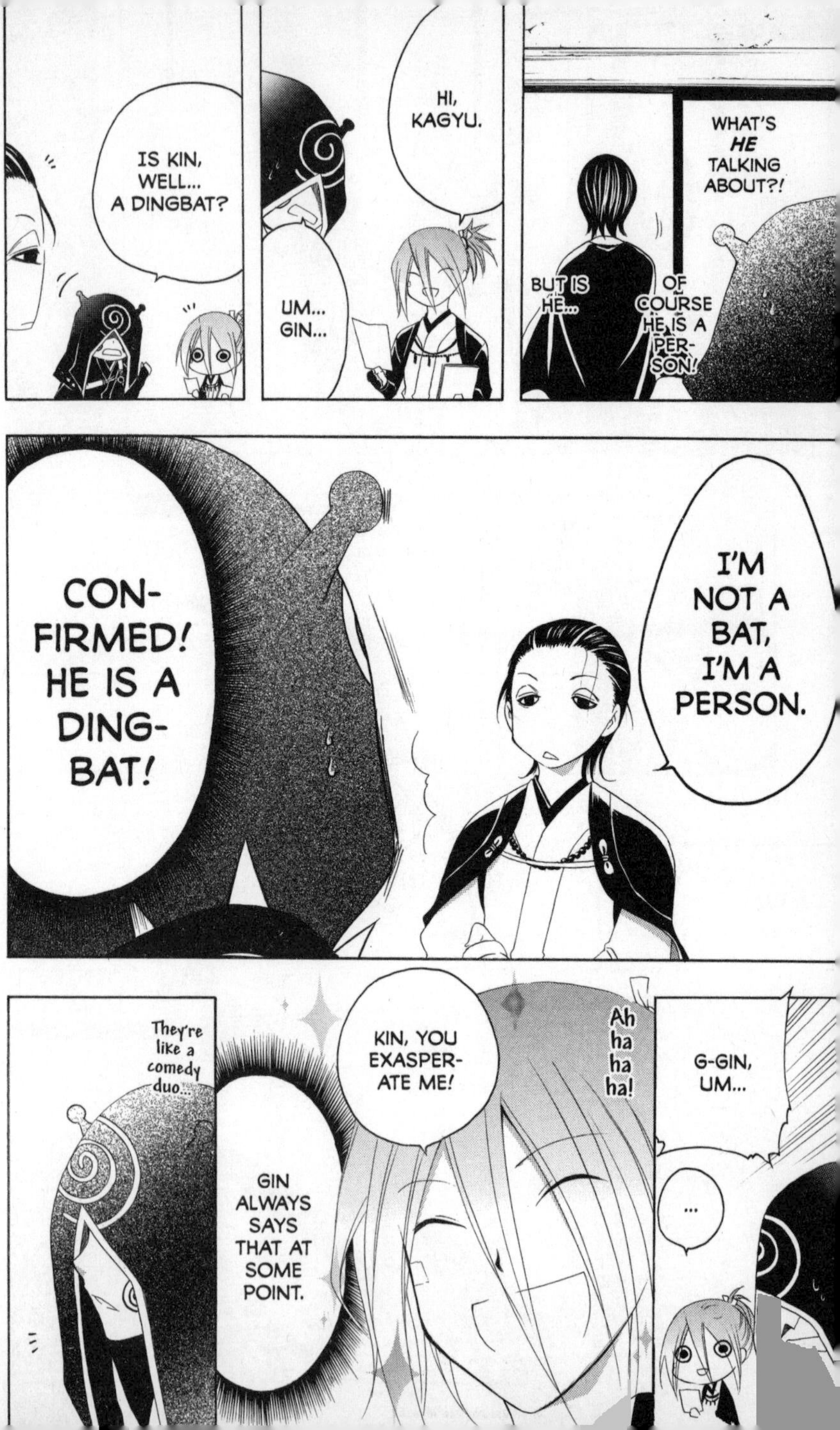
WHAT'S HE TALKING ABOUT?!
OF COURSE HE IS A PER-SON!
BUT IS HE...
HI, KAGYU.
UM... GIN...
IS KIN, WELL... A DINGBAT?
I'M NOT A BAT, I'M A PERSON.
CON-FIRMED! HE IS A DING-BAT!
G-GIN, UM...
...
Ah ha ha ha!
KIN, YOU EXASPER-ATE ME!
They're like a comedy duo...
GIN ALWAYS SAYS THAT AT SOME POINT.

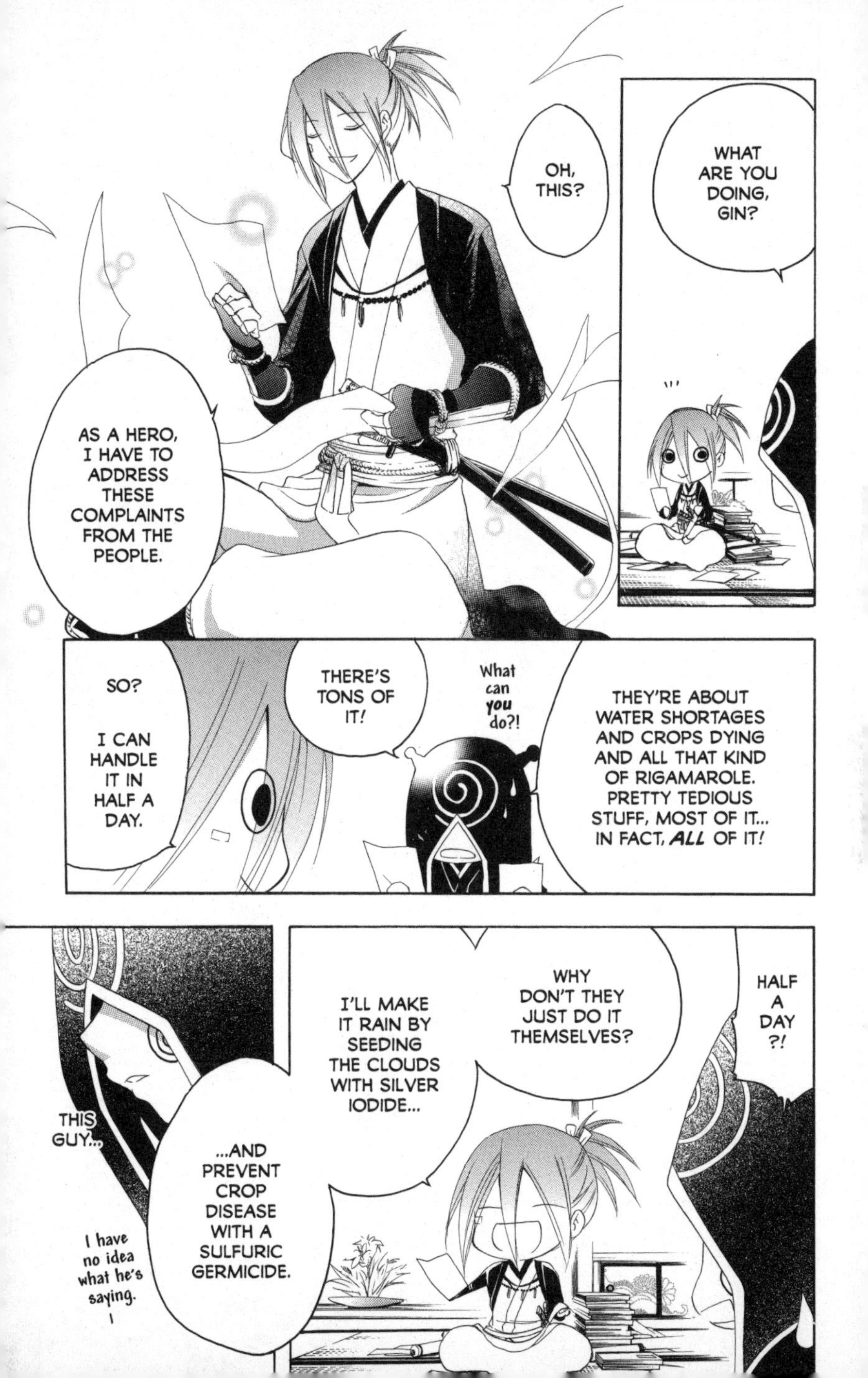
WHAT ARE YOU DOING, GIN?
OH, THIS?
AS A HERO, I HAVE TO ADDRESS THESE COMPLAINTS FROM THE PEOPLE.
THEY'RE ABOUT WATER SHORTAGES AND CROPS DYING AND ALL THAT KIND OF RIGAMAROLE. PRETTY TEDIOUS STUFF, MOST OF IT... IN FACT, ALL OF IT!
What can you do?!
THERE'S TONS OF IT!
SO?
I CAN HANDLE IT IN HALF A DAY.
HALF A DAY?!
WHY DON'T THEY JUST DO IT THEMSELVES?
I'LL MAKE IT RAIN BY SEEDING THE CLOUDS WITH SILVER IODIDE...
...AND PREVENT CROP DISEASE WITH A SULFURIC GERMICIDE.
THIS GUY...
I have no idea what he's saying.

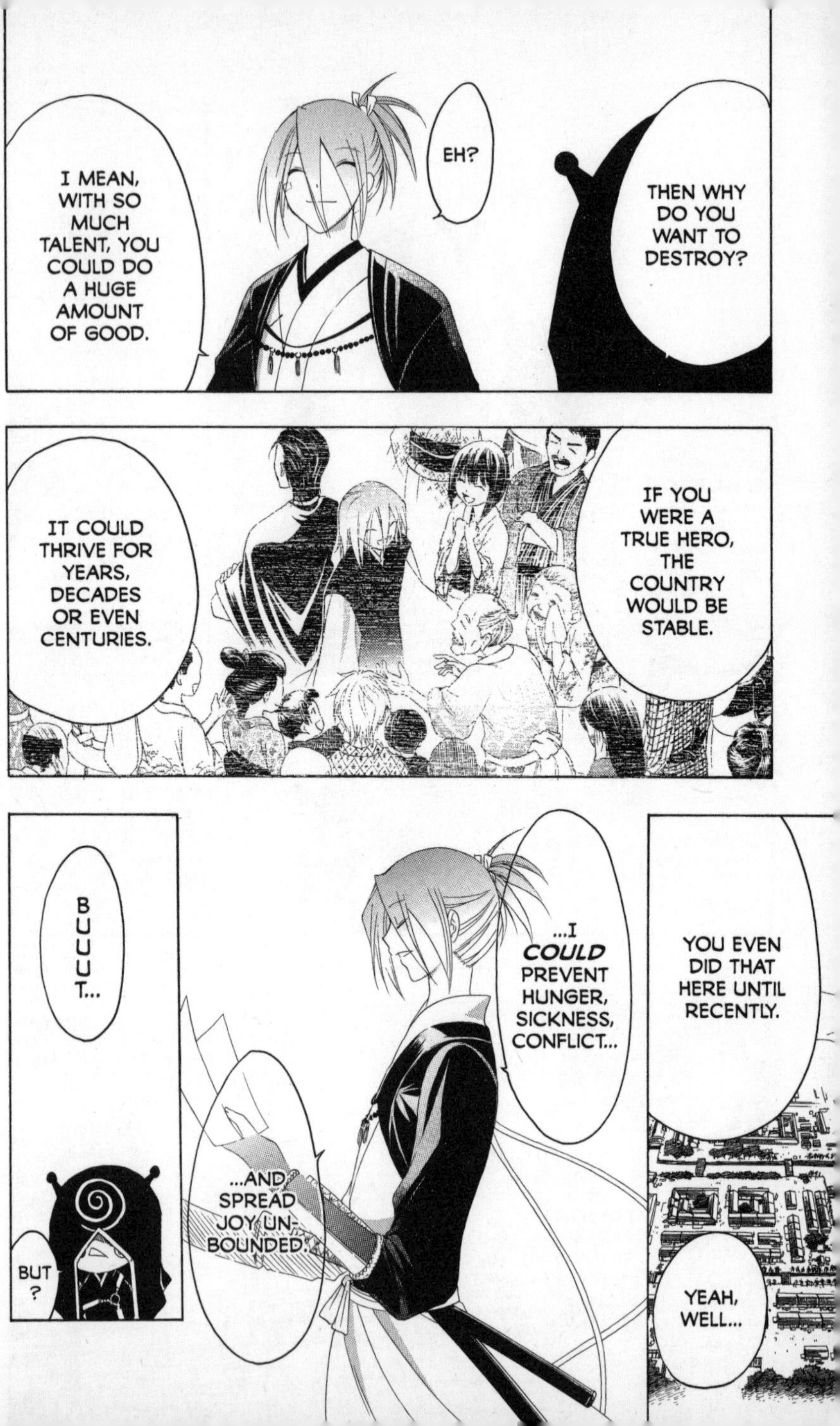
THEN WHY DO YOU WANT TO DESTROY?
EH?
I MEAN, WITH SO MUCH TALENT, YOU COULD DO A HUGE AMOUNT OF GOOD.
IF YOU WERE A TRUE HERO, THE COUNTRY WOULD BE STABLE.
IT COULD THRIVE FOR YEARS, DECADES OR EVEN CENTURIES.
YOU EVEN DID THAT HERE UNTIL RECENTLY.
YEAH, WELL...
...I *COULD* PREVENT HUNGER, SICKNESS, CONFLICT...
...AND SPREAD JOY UN-BOUNDED.
BUUUT...
BUT?

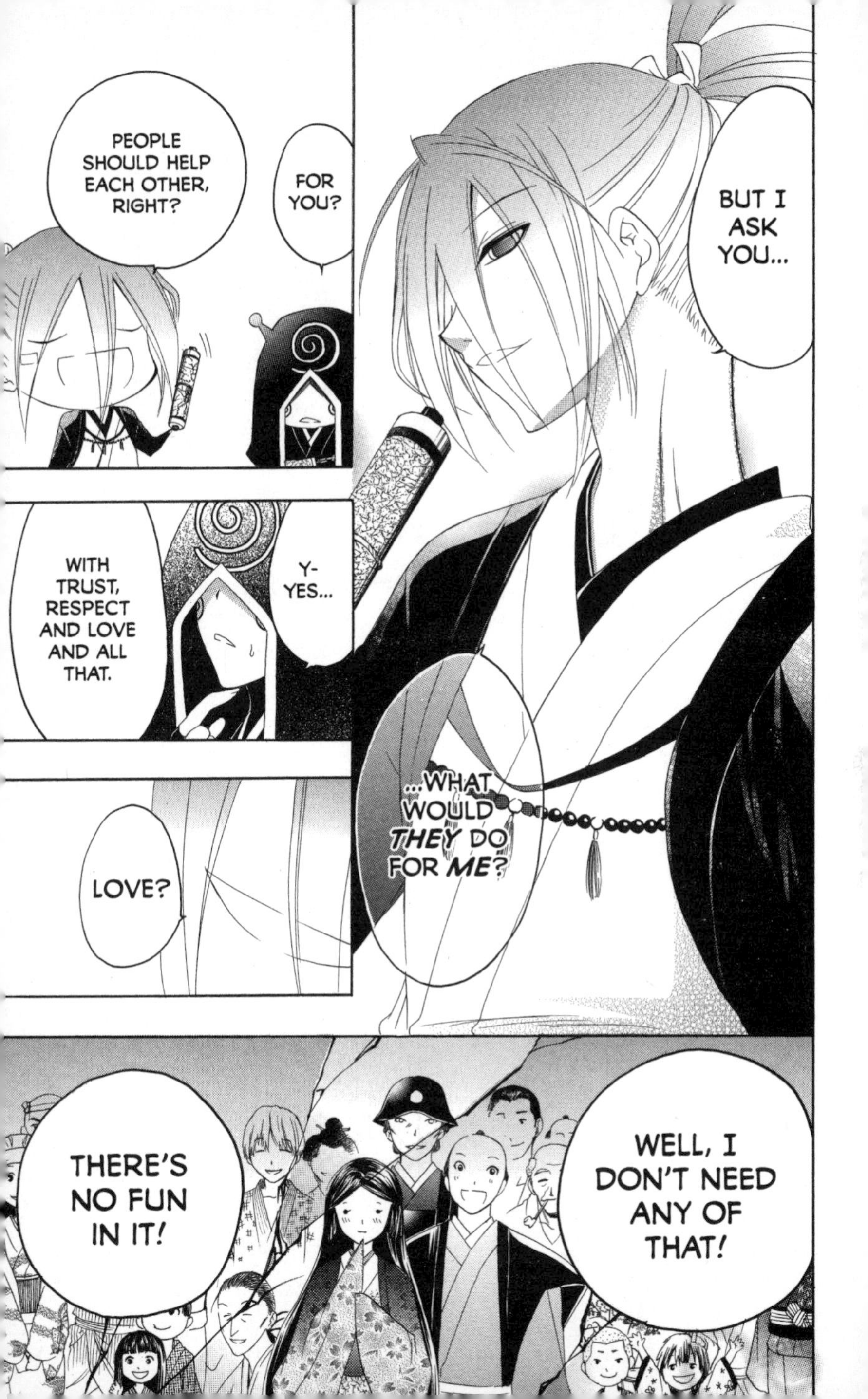
BUT I ASK YOU...
...WHAT WOULD *THEY* DO FOR *ME*?
FOR YOU?
PEOPLE SHOULD HELP EACH OTHER, RIGHT?
Y-YES...
WITH TRUST, RESPECT AND LOVE AND ALL THAT.
LOVE?
WELL, I DON'T NEED ANY OF THAT!
THERE'S NO FUN IN IT!

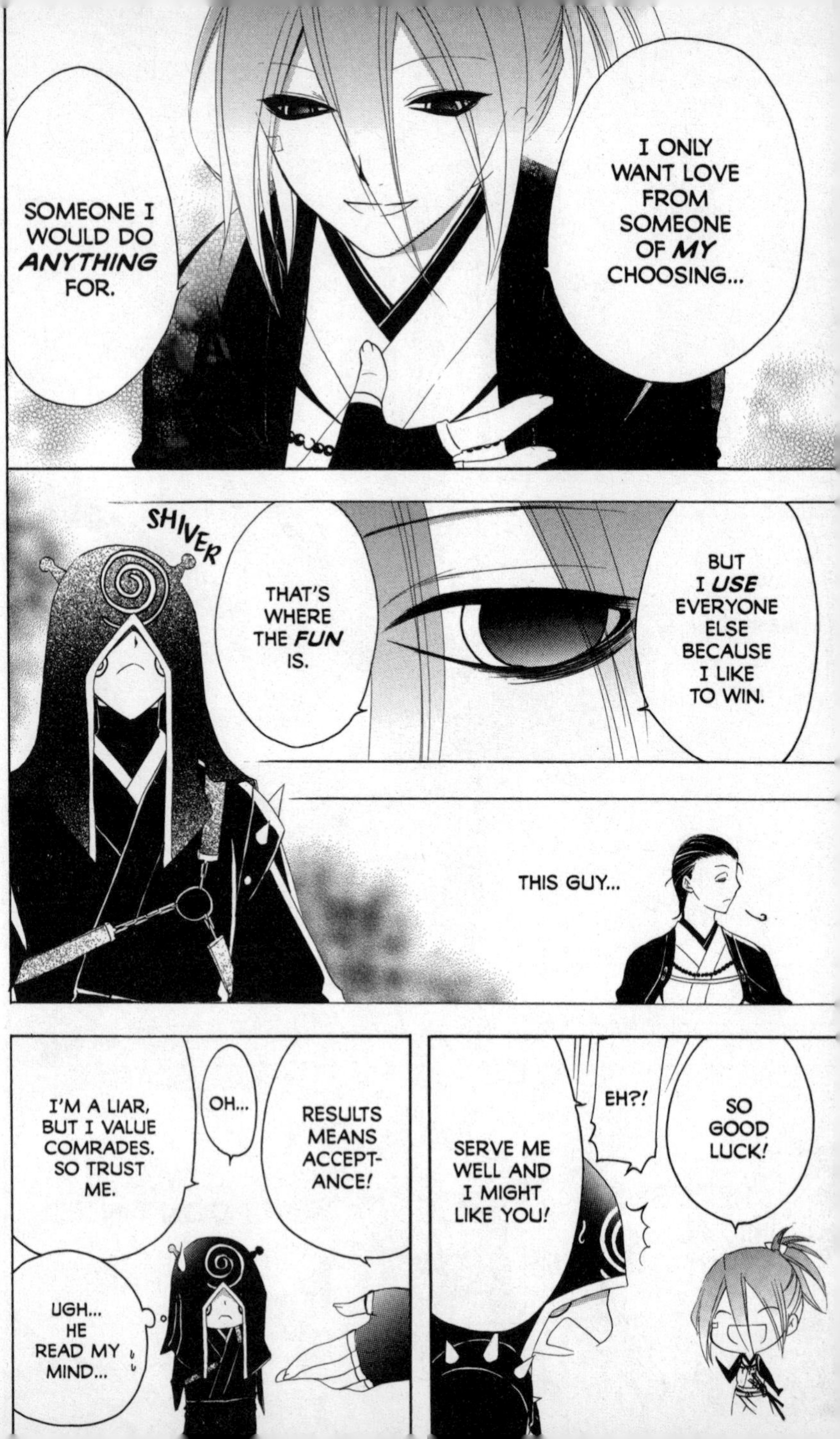
I ONLY WANT LOVE FROM SOMEONE OF *MY* CHOOSING...
SOMEONE I WOULD DO *ANYTHING* FOR.
BUT I *USE* EVERYONE ELSE BECAUSE I LIKE TO WIN.
THAT'S WHERE THE *FUN* IS.
SHIVER
THIS GUY...
SO GOOD LUCK!
EH?!
SERVE ME WELL AND I MIGHT LIKE YOU!
RESULTS MEANS ACCEPT-ANCE!
OH...
I'M A LIAR, BUT I VALUE COMRADES. SO TRUST ME.
UGH... HE READ MY MIND...

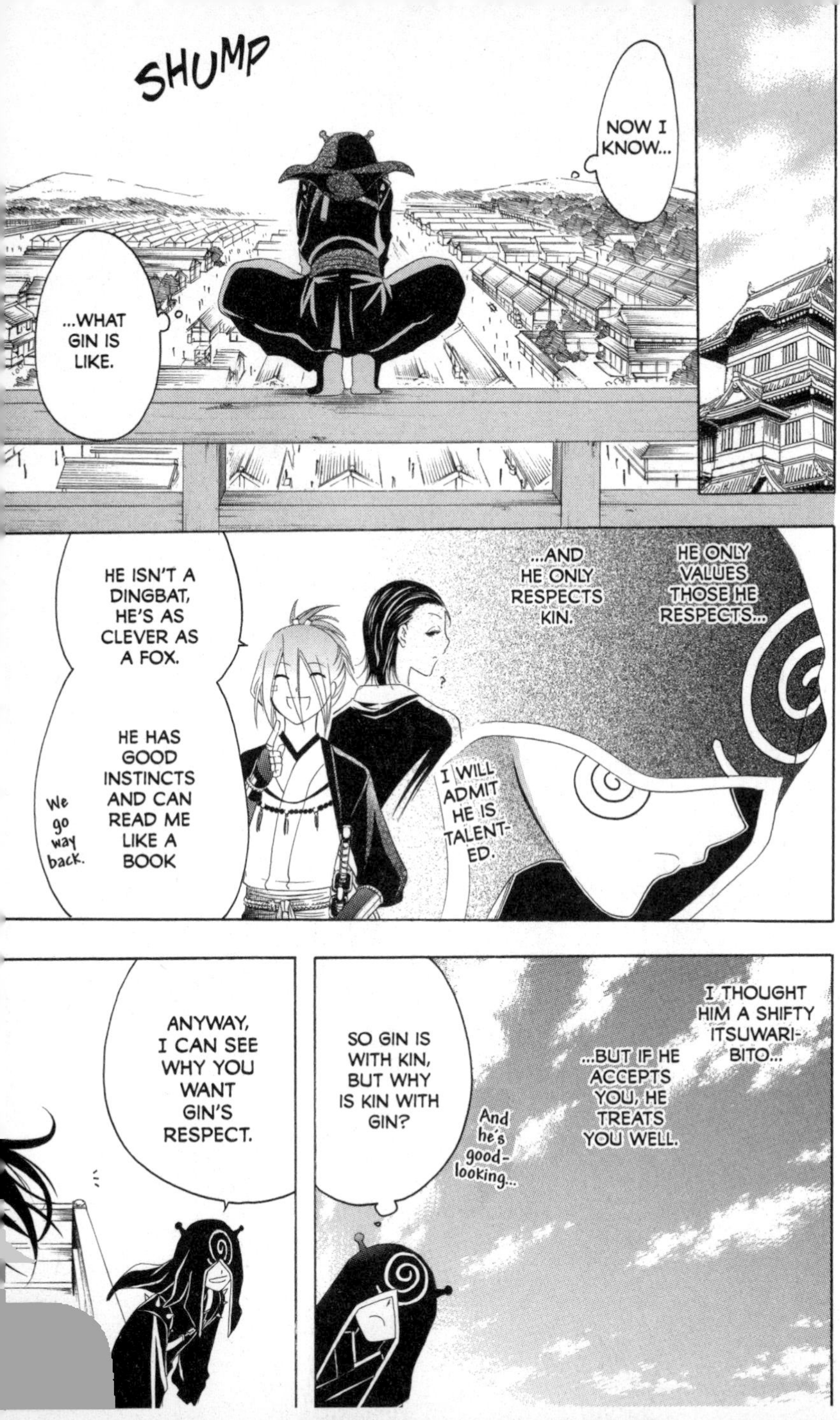
SHUMP
NOW I KNOW...
...WHAT GIN IS LIKE.
HE ONLY VALUES THOSE HE RESPECTS...
...AND HE ONLY RESPECTS KIN.
I WILL ADMIT HE IS TALENTED.
HE ISN'T A DINGBAT, HE'S AS CLEVER AS A FOX.
HE HAS GOOD INSTINCTS AND CAN READ ME LIKE A BOOK
We go way back.
I THOUGHT HIM A SHIFTY ITSUWARIBITO...
...BUT IF HE ACCEPTS YOU, HE TREATS YOU WELL.
And he's good-looking...
SO GIN IS WITH KIN, BUT WHY IS KIN WITH GIN?
ANYWAY, I CAN SEE WHY YOU WANT GIN'S RESPECT.

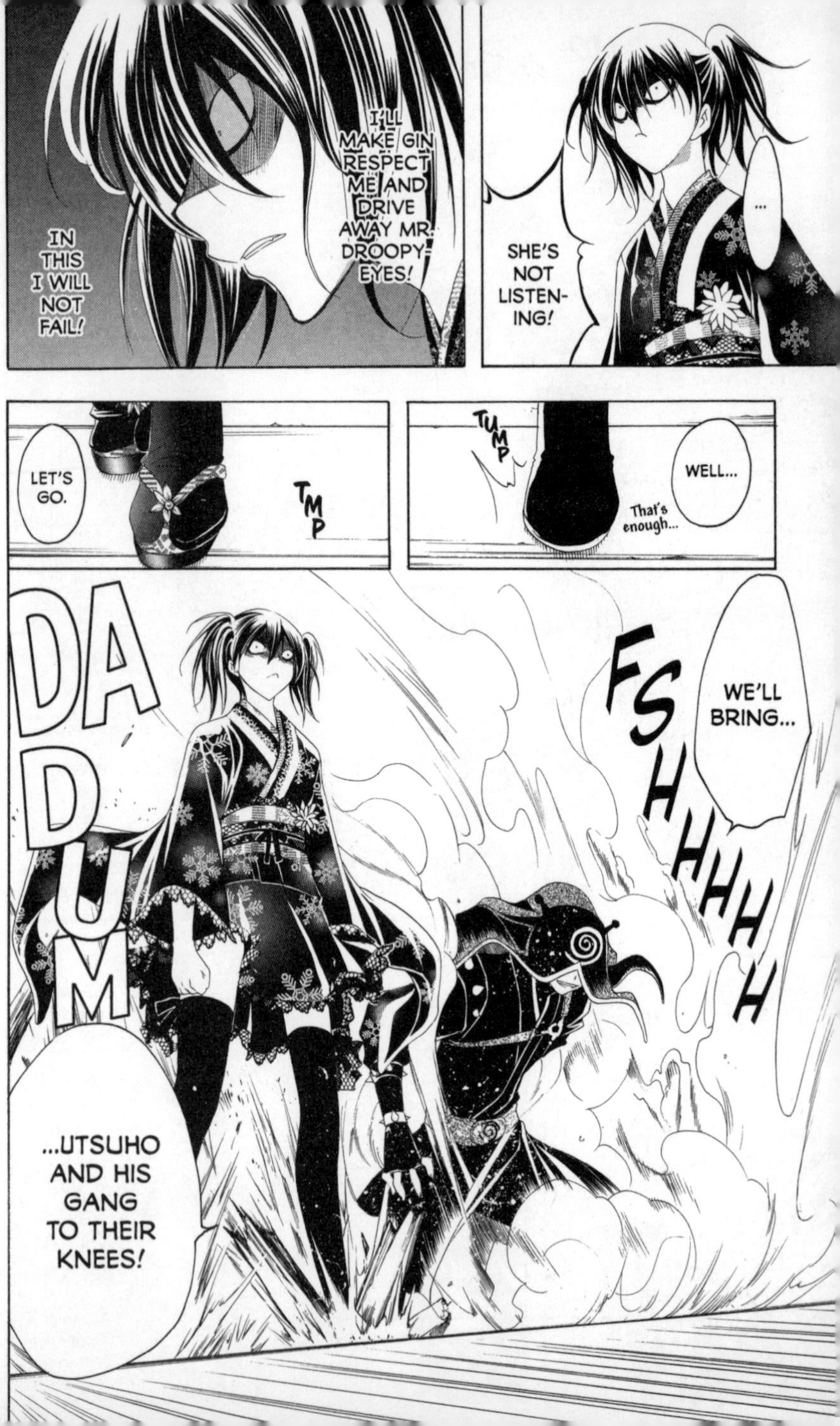
...
SHE'S NOT LISTENING!
I'LL MAKE GIN RESPECT ME AND DRIVE AWAY MR. DROOPY-EYES!
IN THIS I WILL NOT FAIL!
WELL...
That's enough...
TUMP
TMP
LET'S GO.
WE'LL BRING...
FSHHHHHH
DADUM
...UTSUHO AND HIS GANG TO THEIR KNEES!

◆Bonus Manga◆

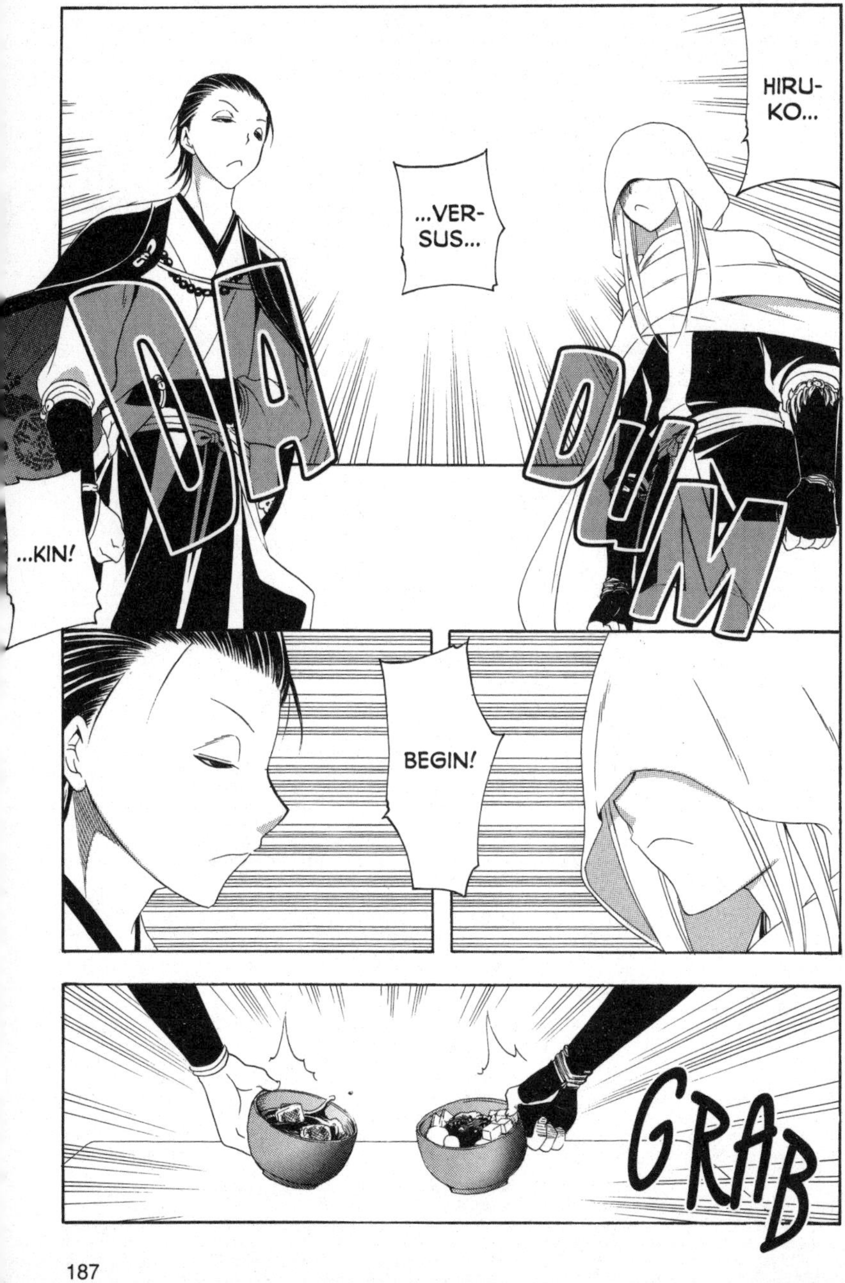

HIRU-
KO...
...VER-
SUS...
DA DUM
...KIN!
BEGIN!
GRAB

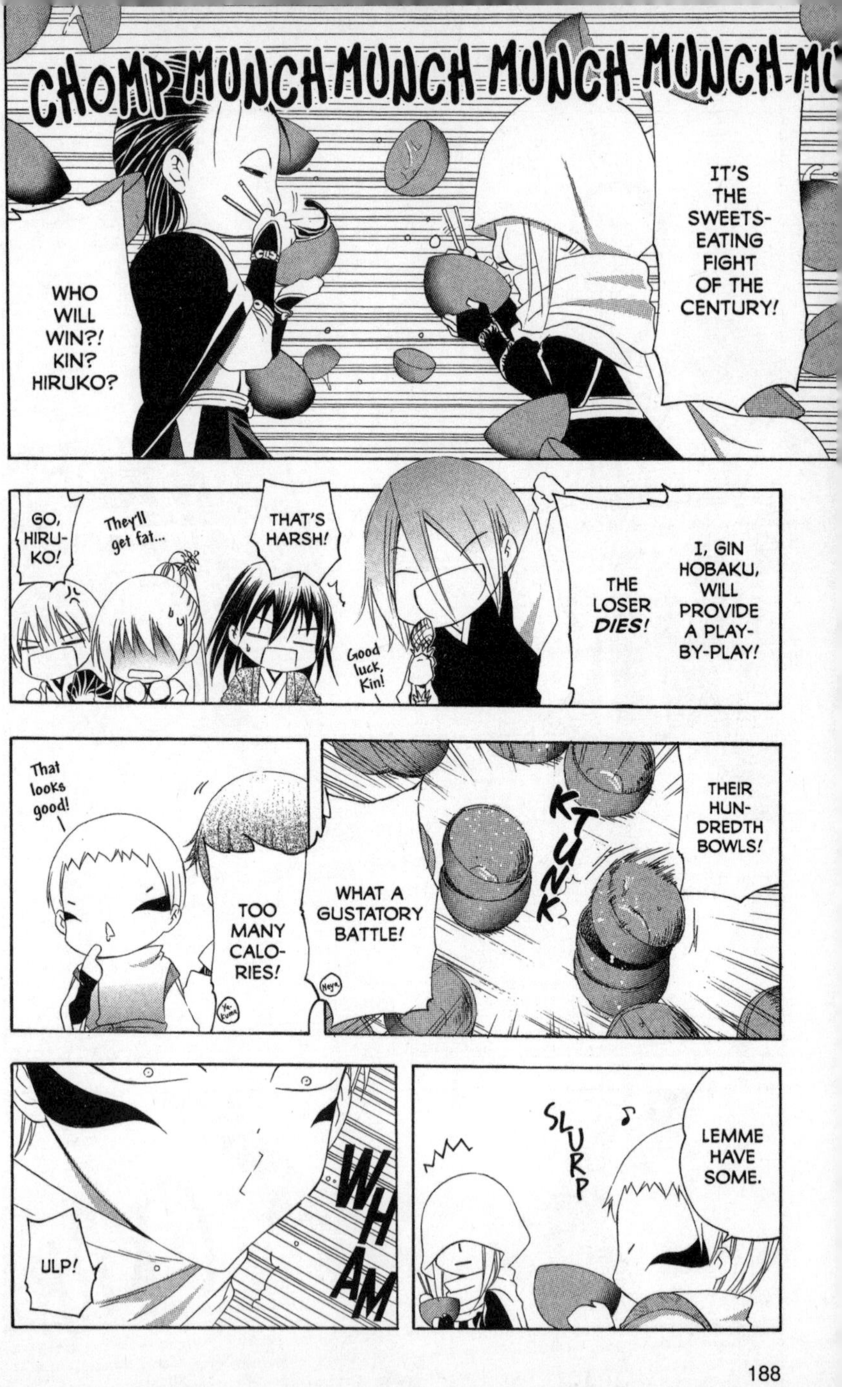
CHOMP MUNCH MUNCH MUNCH MUNCH MU
IT'S THE SWEETS-EATING FIGHT OF THE CENTURY!
WHO WILL WIN?! KIN? HIRUKO?
I, GIN HOBAKU, WILL PROVIDE A PLAY-BY-PLAY!
THE LOSER DIES!
Good luck, Kin!
THAT'S HARSH!
They'll get fat...
GO, HIRUKO!
THEIR HUNDREDTH BOWLS!
KTUNK
WHAT A GUSTATORY BATTLE!
TOO MANY CALORIES!
That looks good!
LEMME HAVE SOME.
SLURP
WHAM
ULP!

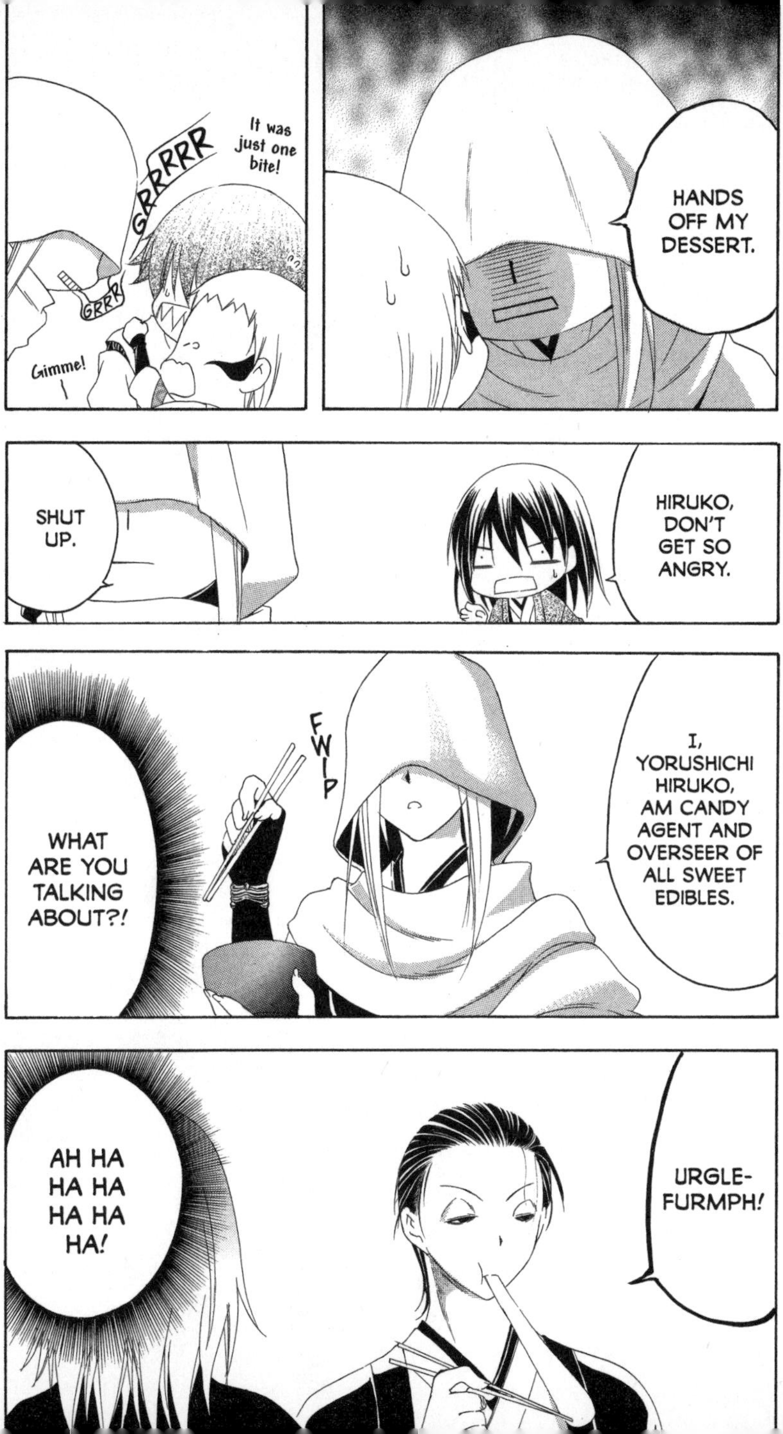
HANDS OFF MY DESSERT.
It was just one bite!
GRRRRR
GRRR
Gimme!
HIRUKO, DON'T GET SO ANGRY.
SHUT UP.
I, YORUSHICHI HIRUKO, AM CANDY AGENT AND OVERSEER OF ALL SWEET EDIBLES.
FWIP
WHAT ARE YOU TALKING ABOUT?!
URGLE-FURMPH!
AH HA HA HA HA HA HA!

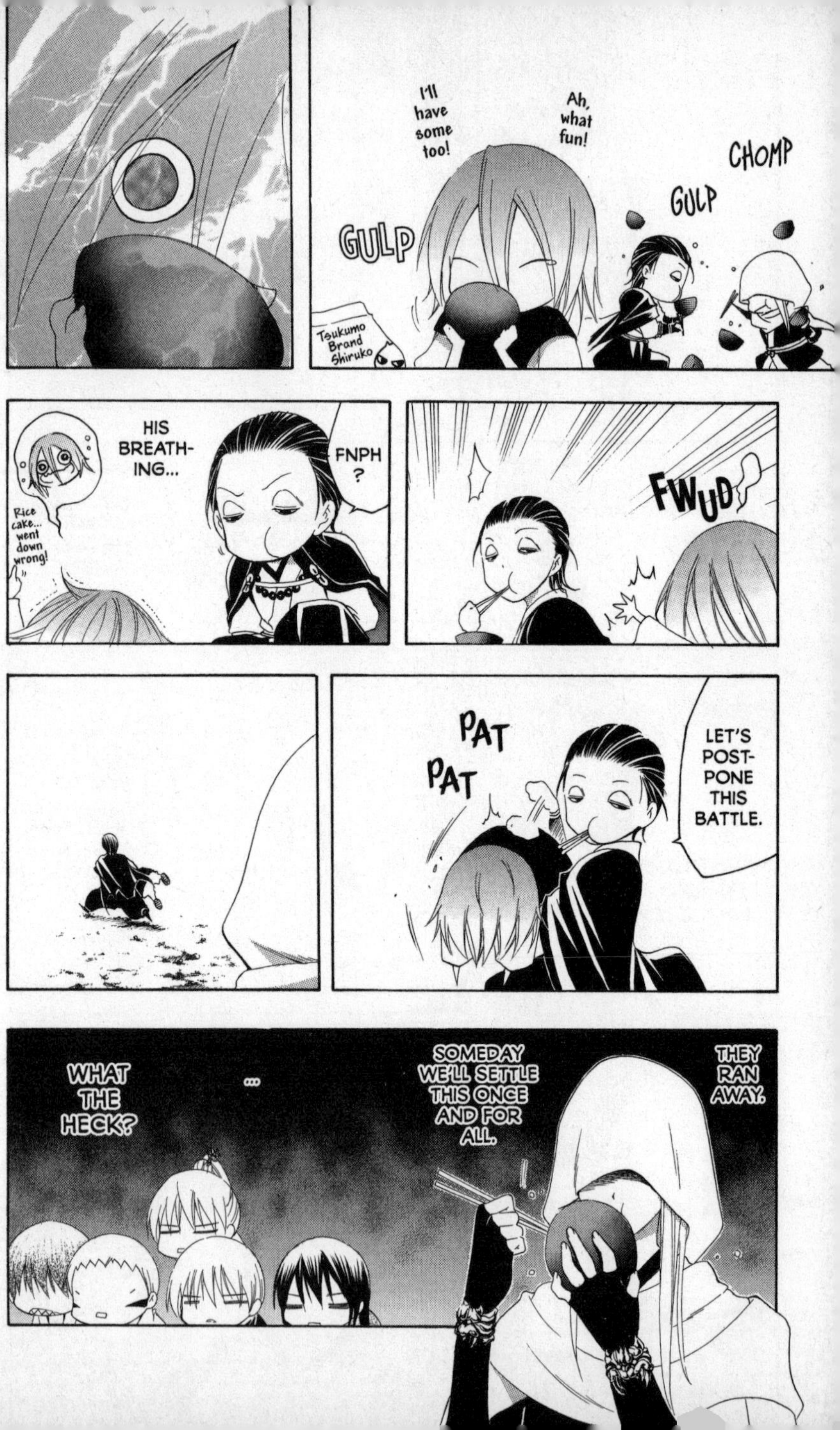
CHOMP
Ah, what fun!
I'll have some too!
GULP
GULP
Tsukumo Brand Shiruko
FWUD
FNPH ?
HIS BREATH- ING...
Rice cake... went down wrong!
LET'S POST- PONE THIS BATTLE.
PAT
PAT
THEY RAN AWAY.
SOMEDAY WE'LL SETTLE THIS ONCE AND FOR ALL.
...
WHAT THE HECK?

ITSUWARIBITO
Volume 17
Shonen Sunday Edition

Story and Art by
YUUKI IINUMA

ITSUWARIBITO ◆ UTSUHO ◆ Vol. 17
by Yuuki IINUMA
© 2009 Yuuki IINUMA
All rights reserved.
Original Japanese edition published by SHOGAKUKAN.
English translation rights in the United States of America and Canada
arranged with SHOGAKUKAN.

Translation/John Werry
Touch-up Art & Lettering/Susan Daigle-Leach
Design/Matt Hinrichs
Editor/Gary Leach

The stories, characters and incidents mentioned
in this publication are entirely fictional.

Printed in the U.S.A.

Published by VIZ Media, LLC
P.O. Box 77010
San Francisco, CA 94107

10 9 8 7 6 5 4 3 2 1
First printing, April 2016

www.viz.com   WWW.SHONENSUNDAY.COM

ANSWER MY QUESTIONS CORRECTLY WITH "YES" OR "NO," AND YOU WIN.
Then I'll do whatever you say!
FINE! ASK AWAY!
WILL YOU ANSWER THIS QUESTION WITH "NO"?